Over 1,000 Practical Teaching Strategies

Super Teaching

Eric Jensen
Third Edition

The Brain Store®, Inc.
San Diego, California

Super Teaching

Editor: Karen Markowitz
Design and layout: Tracy Linares

*Additional copies may be ordered through the publisher listed below. Call, write, or fax for
volume pricing. Checks, purchase orders, and credit cards welcome.*

The Brain Store®, Inc.
4202 Sorrento Valley Blvd. Suite B
San Diego, CA 92121
(858) 546-7555 phone
(858) 546-7560 fax
E-Mail: info@thebrainstore.com
www.thebrainstore.com

ISBN # 1-890460-02-8

First Edition 1995
Second Edition 1996
Third Edition 1998

Preface

George Bernard Shaw once penned a thought that the Kennedy brothers made famous in the 1960s: "Some men [people] see things that are and ask, why while others dream of things that could be and ask, why not?" This book is born of the vision, why not. It's a vision of possibilities—a perspective of how education can be, not how it is—one where students run *to* school instead of *from* school. One where students *ask* for homework rather than *complain* about it. It's a vision where teachers are heard, appreciated, and respected—where they have the power to affect decisions about the curriculum, their classroom, their students, and school policies. It's also a vision of partnership - where teachers learn and work *with* students, not teach *at* them. And it is one where teachers, students, parents, and administrators work as a team, sharing ideas, supporting each other, and enjoying the privilege (not burden) of facilitating quality learning that empowers students.

Sound like a dream? It's not. A dream is a vision without a plan. There is a plan and you are the most important part of it. The plan is almost too simple. Start right now with yourself. Start figuring out where you are in your role as an educator, what is needed, and what you can do next to make teaching work for you and your learners. Where do you begin? With this book and yourself.

Make small changes first. Build your confidence in new areas. Get comfortable with change. Then, begin to network and support others in growing. What will support you as you continue to impact education? You have your hands on it! *Super Teaching* is designed to be a companion, a traveler's aid, and owner's manual for you, the educator with more than just a dream. It is for the educator with the commitment to make it happen. As partners, you and I can break the back of mediocrity in education. Step by step, one by one, we can make it happen. It is inspiring what a single person can do. Are you resigned to the way things are? Or, are you a twenty-first century traveler? If you're a traveler, you're holding the passport. Turn the page, the voyage of discovery is about to begin!

The real voyage of discovery
consists not in seeking new
landscapes, but in having
new eyes.

Marcel Proust
(1871-1922)

Table of Contents

This book is not about the problems facing today's educators. It is about the vision and possibility that can be brought forth to make education work. The problems we face as educators are, to a large degree, merely symptoms. It's time to stand back, take a deep breath and re-think what it means to be a teacher.

Eric Jensen

Chapter 1 —————————————————————————

The Game Has Changed

Chapter Preview:

- ✦ **What's Really Going On?**
- ✦ **Greater Velocity of Change**
- ✦ **The Information Age**
- ✦ **The Electronic Authority**
- ✦ **Changing Relationships**
- ✦ **Shifting Priorities**
- ✦ **Leadership Drain**
- ✦ **Increased Market-Driven Consumerism**
- ✦ **Multi-Culturalism**
- ✦ **Less Predictability**
- ✦ **Job Market Changes**
- ✦ **The Knowledge Revolution**
- ✦ **School as a Social Reformer**
- ✦ **Discoveries in Neuroscience**
- ✦ **So... Now What?**

What's Really Going On?

This book is not about the problems facing today's educators. It is about the vision and possibility that can be brought forth to make education work. After all, the problems we face as educators are, to a large degree, merely symptoms. Addressing the symptoms will not change education. New ones appear faster than we can solve the old ones. We are bailing water out of a boat that we already know has holes in it!

We've spent trillions of dollars in education since landing on the moon, yet many measuring sticks say the quality has remained the same or gotten worse. Teachers experience widespread powerlessness, bitterness and resignation. Teacher strikes have doubled in the last decade. Instead of a conversation about the joys of learning, education has become a conversation about dropouts, low test scores, school security, teenage pregnancy, vandalism, AIDS, drunk driving, violence, drug abuse and suicides. Not that these areas don't deserve attention; they do. But somehow the focus of education has changed.

What has caused this? How can we identify the real source of the frustration? How do we get off the treadmill? And is it possible to win the education game? The questions we raise seem to point to something fundamental. The world has changed in many profound ways. We cannot play by the old rules and succeed. A return to the basics will not work. Another simple "band-aid" will not work. Why? The basic foundation upon which the traditional education system was established is crumbling.

We cannot solve our problems at the same level of thinking that got us into them. Outcome-based education, cooperative learning, inclusion, cultural diversity or any other "quick fix" in education is not the answer. Nearly everything we've hailed as "the answer" has proven inadequate. We simply cannot approach education in a business-as-usual fashion. Life, as we know it, has changed; and our approach to education has yet to catch up. One such change is the pace at which change is occurring.

Greater Velocity of Change

Entire industries start up and stop within a single decade. Schools no longer prepare students for only one job or career focus. The average high-school graduate in 2010 will have three to five careers (not jobs) compared to the one to two jobs his/her parents held. Jobs simply become extinct faster today. Students need to learn *how* to learn, not *what* to learn. Many students believe that their curriculum is outdated and does not provide them with the necessary tools for life. Greater numbers of students are being schooled at home, are attending alternative classes, alternative schools, summer programs or taking "home study." Classroom enthusiasm is at an all-time low. Dropout rates are staggering. High school dropout rates in urban schools average 30 to 50 percent. Nationwide, one out of four students drops out of school!

Many of the ideas and programs offered as solutions to problems in our schools are obsolete by the time they are implemented. Teachers have become tired of having to learn something new only to have it dropped and replaced by something even "newer." This constant "band-aid" approach leaves teachers burned out and cynical about additional teacher training since most programs continue to teach content - the *what* rather than the *how*. Even if a program is useful, it often trains teachers in an area so specific that it exemplifies the saying, "If what you hold is a hammer, you only look for nails."

Quotable

*It is the learners
who will inherit the future;
the "so-called learned,"
who think they "know it all"
will find themselves frustrated
by a world that has
passed them by.*

The Information Age

The gap between what's known and what's implemented in schools is wide. Research findings from the fields of psychology, sociology, neuroscience, biology, physics and education usually experience an enormous lag time before implementation. In fact, the lag time for innovation within the system is usually 5 to 10 years for pilot programs, and 10 to 25 years for widespread implementation!

This lapse creates a sense of hopelessness about staying informed. Teachers stop trying to stay updated. Textbooks are often out of date by print time. When the wheels turn this slow, students begin to believe that what happens at school is reflective of the rest of the world. High frustration levels reduce teacher and student motivation. Many perceive education today as an irrelevant or bankrupt system.

Since the new currency is information systems, how can our students become culturally, socially and economically wealthy if they are still being taught to recite rote history dates and math facts, states and capitals; and excel in spelling drills, home economics and woodshop? We've become a world dependent on calculators, CD-ROM encyclopedias, The Internet, digital communication and carbon-fiber plastics. But students, in many schools are still being taught what students were taught in the 1950s and in the same ways. Since only a limited amount of concrete knowledge can be absorbed by the human brain at a given time, what's the solution? Simply put, we must move our students away from being content-absorbers; and redirect them towards being "information navigators."

Quotable

The new currency of our time is not factory skills, but information and the ability to access information at will. Highly successful people know what's going on and have the knowledge to navigate skillfully.

The Electronic Authority

The sophistication of the information age means that we have created a new entity, "the electronic authority." Students now turn to the Internet, home computers, television, radio, CD-ROM, compact discs, and videotapes as their source of up-to-the-moment information. The degree of learning that happens through alternate sources beyond school has multiplied and expanded dramatically. Trends, values, fashions, manners, customs, and ethics are influenced and transmitted phenomenally fast via such means. Historically, this information was taught through the authority of parents, churches, or schools. Yet today, none of these traditional institutions seem to be the primary source of authoritative information for young people.

Quotable

Where yesterday's teacher used to be the leader and provider, today's teacher is the catalyst and navigator.

Though most of us would not argue the value of advanced technology, we do experience the problems associated with it. In the midst of the information age, nearly any information, regardless of its integrity, can be transmitted quickly and world-wide. Keeping current with the advances poses another layer of challenge; and information overload is real. Relationships established via electronic means are on the rise - many nurtured in the isolation and anonymity of a home office. In such an environment, accountability, personal bonding, and sense of community are impacted. Classroom discipline problems, delinquency and crime continue to escalate. Students don't *have* to seek critical information from their parents, anymore. The menu is greatly expanded.

Standards for communication have been greatly influenced by the power and charisma of the media. The congruency of the actors and impact of multi-media electronic presentations create students who expect to receive information packaged for easy digestion. Two generations ago, the classroom teacher was one of the most visible and powerful role models in a student's life. Now role models come from sports, theater, film and entertainment - celebrities made famous and visible by the media. Teachers just simply can't compete, nor should they. Students who bring the mindset of television to class each day often see teachers as inadequate or boring. As a result, today's students typically have less respect for their teachers, they daydream more, and they participate less in class.

Changing Relationships

In the past, school was designed as a "provider" of information for students who were considered the "users". This created a power structure that maintained the teacher as dispenser of wisdom and knowledge and the student as powerless receiver. In this role, the student was passive, a vessel to be filled.

Quotable

The old model of education instructed the teacher to stand and deliver; that model is dead. Today, you are a learning catalyst; and your students are the stars of your class.

When the teacher controls the information, the student expects the teacher to "provide the learning." Ideally, the student is rather a partner in a responsible learning relationship. The old method keeps students from being accountable for their own learning. The information age has enabled students to become their own "provider." They are no longer at the mercy of teachers to disseminate information. Hence the old "provider-user" relationship is obsolete.

Years ago, teachers had fewer demands placed on them. Today, the demands are extraordinary and the school structure is not set up to handle these changes efficiently and effectively. Our educational system simply does not support and nurture the teacher - teachers need both, especially now. There are insufficient pathways for teachers to express themselves and to be heard. There is a chilling lack of acknowledgment and support for the job teachers do. Even in this day of reform, too many schools are still designed to bypass the teacher on some of the most important decisions teachers must live with: teacher-student ratio, class hours, curriculum and classroom design. To add to the insult, teachers' salaries have lagged behind other comparable professions.

As a result of these and other changes, teachers have been left with less prestige and respect in the community. The resulting sense of powerlessness, lack of respect, support and nurturing, have left most teachers in a state of resignation. To survive, they have simply adapted to the problems and circumstances. This is evidenced in both conversation and action. While the prevailing conversation in education is about problems and circumstances, it ought to be about possibilities and resources.

Shifting Priorities

In industrialized countries another shift has been occurring. The voting tax base during the 1950s through 1970s was largely comprised of a husband and wife with one to three children. These taxpayers voted in their own and children's best interests. If a community needed to raise bond money for schools, parents voted for it. But times have changed.

Today, the educated populace votes more than the uneducated. The middle class and upper class vote more than the lower class. But these blocks of voters are now voting for tax cuts, not educational bond issues. The traditional two parent family with school children, now makes up less than 30 percent of the total population. The remainder is composed of seniors, parents with grown children, childless couples and singles. Those who would vote in favor of educational issues are now the minority. Today, the traditional or single parent family, who may truly want better schools for their children, may not be able to afford it. The tax rebellion has voters thinking of today's paycheck, not tomorrow's generation. Without a tax supported system of education, the future is being mortgaged.

In California's tax-supported university system, annual tuition was under $500 in 1965. By 1995, it was over $4,000. This is not inflation; it's a runaway anti-tax populist movement gone awry. The impact of this is simple. In a society where education is the passkey to opportunity, fewer and fewer students can afford to go to college. It's now up to those who can afford it, not those who deserve it.

In 1960, 95 percent of all unwed mothers put their babies up for adoption. In 1994, however, 92 percent of all unwed mothers kept their babies. Unfortunately, these mothers generally don't vote, and older parents and childless couples do vote, changing the dynamics of the electorate dramatically. More mothers than ever work outside the home. More children live with just one parent. And parents spend less time with their children. In addi-

Quotable

Although education used to be considered a right, it's now becoming more of a privilege. Expect learners to become more self-taught; and anticipate more pay-as-you-go students.

tion, Jerald Bachman of the Survey Research Center in Michigan says that two-thirds of all high-school students are working part-time. He adds that one-quarter of them work over 20 hours a week! The impact of this is staggering. We have "latch-key kids" who come home to an empty house in the afternoon, child care centers bulging at the seams, kids without a sense of belonging, and teens spending increased time on the job. Who is left to provide the emotional nurturing, support, sharing of values, and discipline necessary to raise healthy and productive children. Most parents leave the job up to the schools.

Teenagers report experiences of alienation, feelings of separateness, and painful loneliness. Suicide, drop-out, crime and drug abuse rates are at an all-time high. Runaway rates are increasing and so is teenage pregnancy. Working teenagers are frequently exhausted and unable to stay awake in class.

Leadership Drain

Years ago, some of the best and brightest people in the United States provided vision and leadership for our schools. Now, greater economic opportunities elsewhere have attracted many of our visionary leaders to business. Today, schools most often hire administrators for their ability to solve problems, reduce vandalism, raise test scores, and manage disenchanted staffs. The role of school principal today is often compared to that of a police chief or fire-fighter. As a result, such positions don't naturally attract your visionary leaders anymore. Thus, the current school environment consists of conversations about problems, rather than vision. What most schools need, however, is a visionary leader who can empower school faculty to create the kind of nurturing learning environment they know is possible.

Increasing Consumerism

The power of the media has grown so much that nearly anything or anyone can be the next hot item. There's a constant push for being rich, famous, healthy, happy, attractive, and successful. Sports and entertainment salaries have become public record; and making an annual income of one-million dollars seems commonplace. We've all become numb to megabucks, especially with athletes who command 100-million-dollar per-year contracts.

> **Quotable**
>
> *You cannot assume that your learners will come from homes where they get adequate food, nurturing, and life skills.*

> **Quotable**
>
> *Some kids act as if getting the latest pair of athletic shoes is more important than getting an education. In a way, they can't help it; they have been brainwashed.*

Unrealistic expectations are demoralizing our nation's youth. The emphasis on being rich or beautiful places tremendous pressure on them. In this "go for it" world of glitz and glamour, it is just too difficult for them to keep an even keel. Kids don't see any way they can make it in the system so they simply give up. Instead, they escape the stress in ways not conducive to good health or growing brains.

Multi-Culturalism

In many cities, majority and minority populations have reversed. For example, in New York and Los Angeles, more non-whites than whites reside there. This shift in ethnic constituencies means that school staffs must be more sensitive to a wider range of needs.

In the Southwest, there's an increasingly greater Mexican-American and Asian population, while many other areas are seeing an increase in Black and African-American populations. In addition, many more refugees attend American schools today. The old concept of "WASP-based" schools is obsolete.

There is a danger in believing that throwing an annual multi-cultural awareness day at your school will solve the motivation and learning challenges of an ever growing diverse student body. The issues are often much deeper than we want to admit or are able to respond to effectively in a superficial way. The degree to which assimilation should be encouraged in school is highly controversial. Yet, expecting learning communities to adapt to expectations that don't reflect their needs is ethnocentric and non-productive. The complexity of the situation increases as we consider the sometimes vastly different needs and values of the groups we are serving. Culturally, Asians and Eastern Europeans are more likely to assimilate than Hispanics, Native Americans and African-Americans. How do we preserve the richness of different cultures and yet, provide a setting that gives everyone an opportunity to learn? The problems caused by cultural differences will not go away with time alone. It will take an honest concerted effort on the part of everyone to make our education system work for more learners. What's at stake is the future of our civilization.

> *Quotable*
>
> **All motivation and learning is culturally driven. A multi-cultural school requires a re-thinking of the learning process and environment, as well as the curriculum.**

In districts around the country, changes are happening far too slowly. Teachers need to learn how to be a learning catalyst in cultures other than their own. In cities like San Diego, there's an innovative Race and Human Relations Department to assist teachers who are wholly unprepared to deal with student populations of three to five ethnic backgrounds and for whom English is a second language. In some classes, teachers have reported 10 to 15 separate languages spoken at the same time - and remember, each language brings with it its own culture.

Should teachers be asked to teach in other languages? Bilingual and trilingual education has had support for many years. But a backlash has formed. Now, many are saying, where has all this gotten us? Are we better off today, as a country, than 30 years ago? From an educational perspective, this is not a difficult question to answer. No, we are not.

> *Quotable*
>
> **We all are facing a critical decision:
> Do we provide a fragmented, culture-specific education that pleases the people who have the political power to request it that way? Or do we embrace multi-cultural learning communities that serve the many faces making up American schools today?**

Inclusion and honoring diversity are, of course, the ethical answers to the multi-cultural dilemma. But they have created significant challenges for both faculty and staff. Teachers experience consistent communication failures, increased student tension, and more misdiagnosed learners. Many educators predict that with the present immigration policies, our education problems will continue to escalate. Many teachers no longer feel empowered in their own classrooms.

Less Predictability

The difficulty that education faces is compounded by a supremely complex society that constantly gives mixed messages. While 10 trends are increasing, 5 others are decreasing. We have so many indicators and statistics available that even the simplest of issues are clouded. For example, we are nearly paralyzed by the process of creating a responsible and authentic budget. The problem is not that we don't have enough money for education; we do. The problem is not that we don't have enough information; we do. The problem is that we are often unable to sort out the information in a way that tells us what we really need to know in order to spend the money responsibly.

Quotable

Countless research studies have suggested that there is enough money available in education for a quality learning experience. The problem is, however, that few schools or districts allocate the money in a way that makes this happen.

Cost overruns, thoughtless resource allocations and competing budget priorities translate into wasted money while deserving programs suffer. We have larger budgets than ever before, yet there's constant conversation about scarcity of money. It's no wonder that teachers experience feelings of resignation about their jobs.

Job Market Changes

The information age is dramatically impacting the job market. As we near entry into the twenty-first century, there are four dominant occupational groups that have emerged: 1) manual-industrial workers; 2) technology workers or technologists; 3) service providers; and 4) knowledge workers. As teachers, we need to know which of these careers we're preparing our students for.

In the 1950s, industrial workers made up the largest single labor group in the United States. This gave "under-educated" workers a tremendous opportunity to join the middle class through decent wages. But today, such assembly-line manufacturing jobs are increasingly scarce. In fact, in 1990, they accounted for only one fifth of the labor force. By 2010, it is predicted, industrial workers will account for just 12 percent of workers.

The fastest growing occupation is that of the technologist. This group is made up of X-ray technicians, computer programmers, physical therapists, lab technicians, print production houses, nurses, technology repair workers, etc. These workers require some education and they still use their hands. They are the twenty-first century version of the factory or farm worker. They are both a service provider and an industrial worker. These occupations often require a college education, though vocational colleges can sometimes provide the necessary training.

The second largest occupation is that of the service provider. This group includes doctors, lawyers, sales people, designers, teachers, managers, public relations, travel, retail, and airline personnel. Of these jobs, most require a college education. This field has remained somewhat stable since the job market boom of the 1980s.

The Knowledge Revolution

The biggest boom is what social theorist Peter Drucker (1994) calls the "knowledge worker." This person is like an upscale technologist. To succeed, the knowledge worker will require a strong formal education and a sharp ability to apply theory in the practical world. This area of the job market includes producers, inventors, writers, publishers, marketers, executives, neurosurgeons and scientists. While the knowledge worker will not become the majority in the near future, they will redefine what it means to be educated. To knowledge workers, education will mean continually updating their knowledge, upgrading their skills, positioning themselves for a changing global marketplace, and being committed to lifelong learning. They will achieve this through various means including, CD-ROM, cable television, audiotapes, books, and seminars. Their ability to learn will be their greatest asset.

School as a Social Reformer

In the 1950s, the traditional family structure and/or religious institutions were the primary influencers of social policy. For better or worse, it was the family and the church that determined and reinforced our values. In the mid-1960s, however, schools began to see a gradual shift towards this function. How did this transformation happen? As a need to disseminate information arose - in a way that everyone was assured of receiving it - the school system, by default, became the great conduit of our changing culture. Programs like the ones highlighted in the box, eventually fell into the laps of our clearly overburdened schools.

These programs may have great merit, but only a finite amount of time exists in each school day. For every program that is included in the curriculum, something has to give. When school becomes a seemingly "second home" for students, traditional barometers of quality waver tremendously. The feeling of needing to be "all things to all students" is overwhelming, at least, and unrealistic, at best.

Though test-makers deny it, 1995 versions of national and state achievement tests are clearly weaker or more "watered down" than 1965, 1975 or 1985 versions. In spite of this, reading scores, overall achievement levels, and SAT scores are consistently dropping. Should we be lowering our standards in education? *No!* However, in view of the increased responsibility with which schools have been laden, and the increased diversity in our public school system, perhaps, we ought to be more realistic about what we can achieve in a typical academic year. For example, rather than offering 25 separate programs for secondary schools, we might do a better job offering half as many. The old adage, quality versus quantity, may serve us well here.

The Changing Face of School Curriculums

- ✦ *Multiculturalism*
- ✦ *Drug awareness and prevention*
- ✦ *AIDS awareness*
- ✦ *Safety programs*
- ✦ *Inclusion policies*
- ✦ *Drivers education*
- ✦ *Gender awareness*
- ✦ *Life skills*

Regardless of the fact that many students aren't learning what students used to learn, and perhaps aren't learning what they're being tested on, many of them, on close examination, are achieving in comparable ways. There is no doubt that our schools have experienced a dramatic identity crisis in the past few decades; and the challenge that the information age has presented is profound. This same time period though, has also provided educators with a great deal of innovation, research and applied theory that impacts greatly on how teaching and learning in the twenty-first century will look. This new look represents much more than just another superficial facelift; rather, it reflects a way of being and thinking in the classroom that gets at the heart of our school system's health.

Discoveries in Neuroscience

An explosion in brain research is threatening the existing paradigms in education. Dramatic new findings are forcing all of us to look closer at what we are doing. Some of us may even have to stop altogether and redesign what we do and how we do it. This new model is called brain-based or brain-compatible learning; and it is emerging with spellbinding implications. Based on how current research in neuroscience suggests our brain naturally learns best, brain-compatible learning is inclusive of many powerful learning concepts. It includes the role of emotions, patterns, survival, environments, rhythms, positive thinking, assessment, music, gender differences and enrichment in teaching and learning.

Top scientists assert that when we learn something, we may only be discovering something that has already been genetically built-in or "pre-programmed" into our brains. In addition, our brains may not at all be designed for formal instruction, but rather for learning that which is necessary for survival. All learning, we now know, involves our body, emotions and attitudes. New systems theories tell us how to successfully restructure our schools as a complete learning organization. If these postulates hold true, many of our conventional educational models will be shattered like glass. Some would say, it's about time. These insightful discoveries will be explored in chapter two.

So... Now What?

With all this change occurring, where are we? What do we, as educators, need to do to make some sense out of this world in flux? There are no simple answers. Answers wouldn't help anyway. Answers don't empower people. Answers are dead-ends and typically, the quick end of much needed introspection. What, perhaps, is needed is continual inquiry. Who are we as educators? And what do we bring to the party? As knowledge workers in the era of the information age, these are the kinds of questions we need to continually ask ourselves.

Reflections:

What is the rightful role of schools today and how are the roles of teachers changing?

Where Is My Own Level of Commitment in This Job?

Certainly many individuals ponder such questions; but as a profession, do we teachers ask these questions enough? The education of our children is a critical job of staggering importance. Success will require that we be more than "who we are" right now. It is not enough to just "try" our best. We have to do what is really needed. This will require skills, knowledge, vision and a new spirit of empowerment. The next chapter will introduce you to the principles of brain-compatible learning - a model by which learning occurs the way the brain does it best, the way it is biologically designed for the task.

Reactions:

What are your feelings about the topics presented in this chapter?

What are some practical applications for what you're learning?

What do you want to remember about this chapter?

No problem can be solved from the same consciousness that created it. We must learn to see the world anew.

Albert Einstein

Chapter 2

Learning and the Human Brain

Chapter Preview:

- ✦ It All Starts Between the Ears
- ✦ Areas of Our Brain
- ✦ Where Learning Begins
- ✦ How We Learn
- ✦ The Stimulus
- ✦ The Formation of Lasting Learning
- ✦ When Have We Really Learned Something?
- ✦ How We Get Smarter
- ✦ Guidelines for Better Learning
- ✦ Key Brain-Based Learning Concepts
- ✦ Our Unique Brain
- ✦ Our Biological Imperative
- ✦ Our Unlimited Potential

- ✦ A Biochemical Factory
- ✦ Enriching the Brain
- ✦ Feeding the Brain
- ✦ Left and Right Brain Revisited
- ✦ Hormonal Influences
- ✦ Resting the Brain
- ✦ Stress and Threat Impair Learning
- ✦ Emotions and the Brain
- ✦ Multi-modal, Multi-path Learning
- ✦ Our Brain and Rote Learning
- ✦ Maximizing Natural Memory
- ✦ All Learning Is Mind-Body Linked
- ✦ Our Cycles and Rhythms
- ✦ Assessment
- ✦ Relax-to-Energize

It All Starts Between the Ears

Are you curious about how your students learn? You're not alone. Ninety percent of the books written about the human brain and learning (cognitive science) have been written in the past 10 years. There are literally thousands of them! But, what do you realistically need to know about how the brain works to be a great teacher? Generated from recent discoveries in neuroscience and related disciplines, this chapter summarizes the most important brain concepts impacting classroom learning today. These findings, though insightful, are not revolutionary on their own. However, when integrated as a whole into your curriculum, brain-compatible learning will revolutionize your approach to teaching. First, let's review the physical aspects of the brain. Then we'll see how current research has impacted our knowledge about how the brain learns best.

Areas of Our Brain

Scientists divide the brain into four areas called lobes. These areas are identified as the occipital, frontal, parietal, and temporal lobes (figure 2.1). The occipital lobe is located in the middle back of the brain; and it is primarily responsible for vision. The frontal lobe is the area around your forehead; it is involved with purposeful acts like judgment, creativity, problem-solving, and planning. The parietal lobe is located at the top back of the brain; its duties include processing higher sensory and language functions. The temporal lobes (left and right side) are above and around the ears, and are primarily responsible for hearing, memory, meaning and language. There is, of course, some overlap in the functions of the lobes.

There is talk of a fifth lobe, the limbic or mid-brain lobe. It's territory would include the cingulate gyrus, hippocampus, septum, thalamus, fornix and amygdala (figure 2.2). This area - 20 percent of the brain by volume - is responsible for emotions, sleep, attention, body regulation, hormones, sexuality, smell, and the production of most of the brain's chemicals. However, others say there is no "limbic" system, only specific structures that process emotion, like the amygdala.

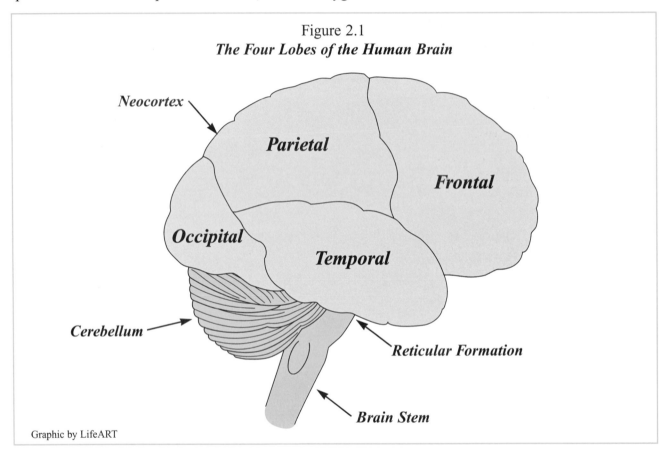

Figure 2.1
The Four Lobes of the Human Brain

Graphic by LifeART

The location of the brain area that allows you to know that you are "you" (consciousness) is disputed. It might be dispersed throughout the cerebral cortex (figure 2.2) or may be located near the reticular formation atop the brain stem (figure 2.1). Much of the cerebral cortex which takes up 75 percent of total brain volume, has no known single task and is often referred to as the "association cortex." Gray neurons or cell bodies form the cerebral cortex and other smaller matter. The white in the brain is either the fibers that connect different regions of the brain or the myelin, a fatty substance that coats the axons.

The sensory cortex (monitoring your skin receptors) and the motor cortex (needed for movement) are narrow bands across the top middle of the brain. In the back lower area of the brain is the cerebellum (Latin for "little brain") which is primarily responsible for balance, posture, motor movement, and some areas of cognition (figure 2.1). Recent experiments strongly support the conclusion that essential long-term memory traces for motor learning are located in the cerebellum. It's the first conclusive evidence that *any* memory actually has an exact location outside of the amygdala (figure 2.2).

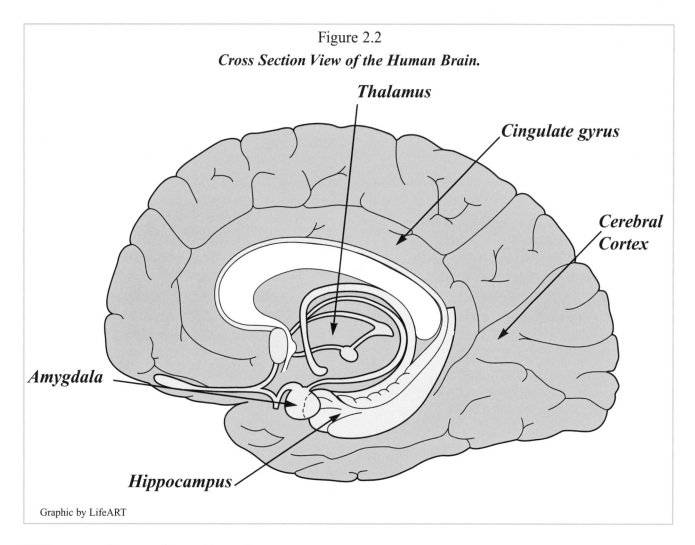

Figure 2.2
Cross Section View of the Human Brain.

Thalamus

Cingulate gyrus

Cerebral Cortex

Amygdala

Hippocampus

Graphic by LifeART

Where Learning Begins

Learning begins on a microscopic cellular level. The brain has several kinds of cells that are involved in learning. The most studied ones are neurons (Greek for bowstring). For the sake of comparison, a fruit fly has one hundred thousand neurons, a mouse has five million, and a monkey has ten billion. You have about one hundred billion neurons. A single cubic millimeter (1/16,000th of an inch) of brain tissue contains over one million neurons. You lose brain cells every day though scientist aren't sure exactly how many. Estimates of brain cell loss through attrition, decay, and disuse vary from 10,000 to 100,000 per day (Howard, 1993). However, there is no doubt that you have enough brain cells for your lifetime since even if you lost one-half-million cells per day, it would still take centuries for you to lose your mind.

The most numerous of your brain's cells are called interneurons or glial (Greek for glue). Outnumbering neurons ten to one, glial cells do not have a cell body. Serving as a nutrient, repair and support function, up to 150 billion glial cells may be contained within your brain. Though, an autopsy revealed that Einstein's brain was of average size, it also revealed far more glial cells than normal. It has been speculated that glial cells may also be responsible for forming the blood-brain barrier and regulating the immune system. And additional speculation assigns them even loftier roles.

Two things are unique about a neuron as opposed to glial cells. First, the brain does not grow new neurons. When they die off, they're not replaced. Second, a normal functioning neuron is continuously firing, integrating and generating information; it's a virtual hotbed of activity. No neuron is an end point or termination point for information - it only serves to pass data on. A single neuron may connect with 1,000 to 10,000 other cells. That's a good sign; the more the connections your cells make the better. Although the cell body has the capacity to move, most adult neurons stay put; they simply extend leg like extensions called axons outward (figure 2.3). While multiple fibers called dendrites may extend from a neuron, each neuron has only one axon. Axons only connect with dendrites; dendrites don't connect with each other. To connect with thousands of other cells, the axon splits - subdividing itself - and branches out in multiple strands over and over again. Neurons only serve to pass along information; none of them is just a receiver alone or the end of the connection.

The axon has two essential functions: to conduct information in the form of electrical stimulation and to transport chemical substances. The longest ones may be up to a meter long. The thicker the axons, the faster it conducts electricity (and information). Myelin is a lipid (fatty) substance that forms around well-used axons. All of the larger axons are myelinated. This seems not only to speed up the electrical transmission (up to twelve-fold), but also to reduce interference from other nearby reactions. Nodes along the axons, along with myelination, can boost electrical impulses to speeds of 120 meters per second or 200 miles per hour. The smallest ones probably have no advantage in being myelinated.

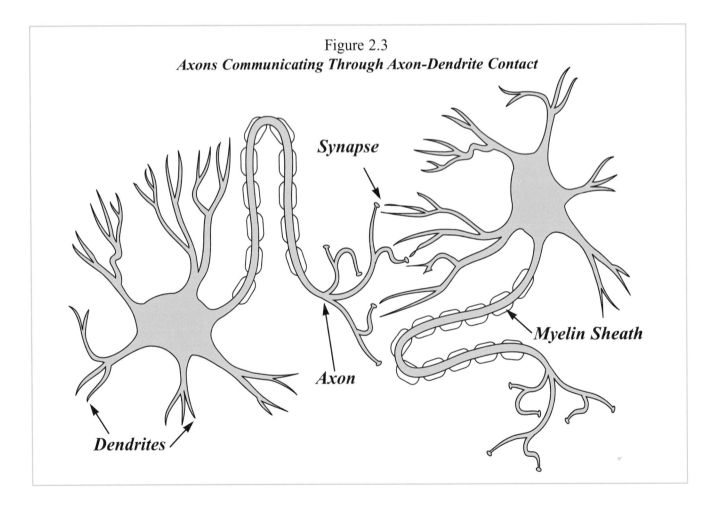

Figure 2.3
Axons Communicating Through Axon-Dendrite Contact

How We Learn

What this complex organ, known as the human brain, does best is learn. Learning actually changes the structure of the brain as it rewires itself with each new reception of stimuli. Scientists are unsure precisely *how* this happens, but they have an idea of *what* happens. First, a stimulus to the brain starts the process. This stimulus can be internal (a brainstorm) or it might be a new experience like solving a jigsaw puzzle. Then, the stimulus gets sorted and processed at several levels. Finally, the result is the formation of memory potential. Simply stated, now the pieces are in place so that memory can be formed and activated.

The Stimulus

To our brain, we are either doing something we already know how to do or we are doing something new. If we are repeating a previously learned task or activity, there's a good chance the neural pathways will become more and more efficient. They do this through myelination which is the process of coating axons with a fatty substance. Once myelination occurs the brain becomes more efficient. Washington University School of Medicine researchers Hanneke Van Mier and Steve Peterson discovered that while many areas of the brain will "light up" on a PET scan when stimulated or when a new task is initiated, the better the task is learned, the less the brain "lights up" when the test is repeated. Simply stated, novices use more of their brain, and experts use less of their brain more efficiently.

Stimulation of the brain usually occurs when one does something new - sees a new movie, listens to new music, learns a new song, visits a new place, solves a new problem or makes a new friend. Novel mental or motor stimulation produces greater beneficial electrical energy than the "old hat" stuff. This input is converted to nervous impulses which travel to extraction and sorting stations like the thalamus located in the mid-brain area. When an intentional behavior is initiated a multi-sensory convergence takes place and a "map" is quickly formed in the hippocampus. From there, signals are distributed to specific areas of the brain.

Once this input is received, each brain cell acts as a tiny electrical battery powered by the difference in concentration of sodium and potassium ions across a cell membrane. Changes in voltage help power the transmission of signals for dendritic growth. Chemicals called neurotransmitters are stored in the ends of the cell's axon which nearly touches the dendrites of another cell. When the cell body stimulates the axon with electrical energy, it initiates the release of those stored chemicals into the synaptic gap (the space between the end of an axon and tip of a dendrite).

Once this chemical reaction is triggered (or inhibited) in the synaptic gap, a new electrical energy in the receptors of the "contacted" dendrite is generated. This electrical-to-chemical-to-electrical loop repeats the process with the next cell. In this way, the original electrical stimulation is eventually converted to cell growth in the form of dendritic branching and new synapses. When we say cells "connect" with other cells, we really mean that they are in such close proximity that the synapse is easily, and almost effortlessly, "used" over and over again. Whole "neural forests" may be intact in the brain of experts in a topic.

The Formation of Lasting Learning

Learning and memory are "Siamese twins" to neuroscientists. You can't talk about one without the other. After all, if you have learned something, the only evidence of the learning is memory. Learning occurs when a post-synaptic cell subsequently requires less input from another cell the next time it's activated. In other words, it has "learned" to respond differently. A research team at Massachusetts Institute of Technology led by Nobel laureates Susumu Tonegawa and Eric Kandel (1992) have identified a single, specific gene that activates this critical memory formation. This breakthrough may explain why one person may have a better memory than another; it's partly gene controlled.

Lasting learning or long-term potentiation (LTP) has long been accepted as the actual physical process that stores learning. Since its discovery in 1973, countless experiments have defined its intricacies. Briefly, here's the process: a cell is electrically stimulated (over and over) so that it excites a nearby cell. If a weaker stimulus is then applied to the neighboring cell some time later, the cell's ability to get excited is enhanced. In other words, cells change their receptivity to messages based on previous stimulation. In short, our learning is done through the strengthening of synapses.

When Have We Really Learned Something?

While it's exciting to make some sense out of the actual cell-to-cell connections, learning and behavior are often different. For instance, you might have learned from a book how to teach a better class, but your behavior may remain the same. Why does this happen? Certainly, we can point to outside circumstances (like excess stress or a student's behavior). Yet our behaviors are more likely governed by our complex emotional states and memories. The daily chemistry of our brain adds great complexity to the question of how we learn.

Our everyday behaviors like attention, stress or drowsiness are heavily impacted by "floating" chemicals known as peptides which are present in the brain and throughout the body. These chemicals such as serotonin, dopamine, and noradrenaline, are the cause of such things as "gut feelings." The interaction of sensory data input and peptides give the brain more than its eyes, ears, taste and smell together. In short, learning happens on many levels at once, from the cellular to the behavioral, from the emotional to the physical.

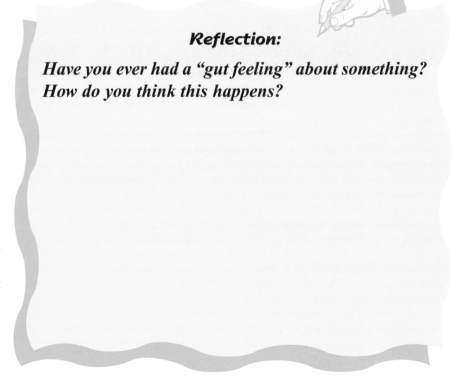

Reflection:

Have you ever had a "gut feeling" about something? How do you think this happens?

How We Get Smarter

The end result of learning for humans is intelligence. Regardless of how you define intelligence, having a bigger brain or more brain cells per cubic inch doesn't help. A dolphin has a bigger brain than we do, and a rat brain has more cell density than a human brain; however, humans have more dendritic branching and more neurons overall. We grow new connections with novelty, interactions, feedback and practice. A primary key to getting smarter is growing more synaptic connections between brain cells. A knowledge base of learning is defined as a "pattern of neural connectivity" (Black, 1991).

The brain is what we have; the mind is what it does. In other words, the "mind" is not a thing; it is a process. What percentage of your physical brain do you use? On a given day, most areas are used. That is because it has been customizing itself for your lifestyle since the day you were born. It generally works well for you because you have encouraged it to develop for your precise world. If you're good at music, you're likely to sing or compose or play an instrument. If you're good at sports, you're likely to participate in them. If you're good at numbers, you're likely to do some computation daily. In the real world, your brain is just right for you.

On a more theoretical, mathematical basis, the story is much different. We use less than one percent of one percent of our brain's processing capacity. Each of your 100 billion neurons ordinarily connects with 1,000 to 10,000 other neurons. But they could theoretically connect with far more. Since each has several thousand synapses, your entire brain has trillions of them. Your brain is capable of processing as much as 1,027 bits of data per second. However, Paul Churchland (1995) postulates that the total possible configurations is 10 to the 100 trillionth power. That number far exceeds the number of known particles in the universe. Our brain is, indeed, quite miraculous.

Could this potential neural connectivity be responsible for so-called "genius" behavior in isolated individuals? We don't know yet. Almost 10 percent of children under five have a photographic memory as do one percent of adults. Savants can calculate huge amounts of data, and in some cases, do it as fast as a computer. There are documented cases where subjects have demonstrated such genius as competency in a dozen or more languages, musical proficiency at a very young age, thought transference from one individual to another, highly efficient speed reading, or photographic recall. Could such genius potentially become commonplace in our classrooms? Could we engineer the development of another Albert Einstein, Maya Angelou, Wolfgang Mozart, Martha Graham, or Bill Gates?

Finally, if learning is what we value, then we ought to value the means or process of learning as much as the end result of learning. Though we don't possess an efficient brain, it is highly effective and adaptive. Our brain, which comprises just two percent of our weight, consumes 20 percent of our energy. What insures our survival is adapting and creating options. A typical classroom narrows our thinking strategies rather than expanding them. Educators who insist on singular approaches and "right" answers are ignoring the very qualities that have, in fact, insured the survival of the human species. Humans have thrived because they have been willing to experiment and adapt, *not* by always getting the correct tried-and-true answer. Growing a smart brain requires the exploration of alternative methods, multiple answers, critical thinking, and creative insights.

The notion of narrowed standardized tests to get the right answer violates the law of adaptation in a developing brain. The process is often more valuable than the end result. In essence, the *pattern* of learning is as important as *what* is learned. One of the ways that our brain makes meaning is by eliciting and forming patterns. Brain theorist Leslie Hart (1983) reminds us that "pattern recognition depends heavily on the experience one brings to a situation." These patterns must continually be revised as new experiences add information to the equation. In fact, Hart suggests that "learning is the extraction of meaningful patterns from confusion." Humans don't really understand or learn something (with the exception of motor or procedural learning as an infant) until they create a personal metaphor or model for that learning.

Guidelines for Better Learning

How much do you need to know about learning to be an effective teacher? By understanding the brain's natural operating principles, you will be better able to teach to the brain. Learning will increase dramatically, discipline problems will be reduced, and the joy of learning will permeate your classroom. The basic equation for how we learn best can be illustrated as follows:

Personal History
(beliefs, experiences, values, knowledge)

+

Present Circumstances
(environment, feelings, people, context, goals, moods)

+

Input (5 senses)
(visual, auditory, kinesthetic, olfactory, or gustatory)

+

Processing (learning preferences)
(states, left/right hemisphere, limbic, abstract or concrete)

+

Meaning
(Connecting experience, data and stimuli to form conclusions and create patterns that give our lives meaning)

+

Response (7 intelligences)
(verbal-linguistic, spatial, bodily kinesthetic, musical-rhythmic, intrapersonal, mathematical-logical, interpersonal)

=

Optimal learning!

Volumes of literature have been written on the theory of learning. It is not the purpose nor the scope of this book to duplicate or illuminate all of the learning theories ever proposed. However, you may find it quite valuable to discover some of the key concepts derived from the current brain research that illuminate how the brain learns best.

Key Brain-Based Learning Concepts

Our Unique Brain

Your brain is soft and pink, and is generally about the size of your two fists held together at the knuckles. Comprised mostly of water, it weighs approximately three pounds, and is a one-of-a-kind design. Consider that the brain of each of your learners is as individual as a fingerprint. In fact, even its weight and size varies. It contains a lifetime of unique experiences, meanings, beliefs, models and data. The acknowledgment of such diversity represents a considerable teaching challenge, and highlights the limitations of uniform group instruction. This unique brain develops in recognizable stages which on average can fluctuate between normal individuals by about three years. One child, for instance, may learn to read at age three, and another at age six; however, both brains are, nevertheless, developing at a completely normal rate.

Our Biological Imperative

Is the human mind a blank slate at birth waiting to be inscribed as the eighteenth century philosopher John Locke claimed? Or are we born with innate knowledge that supports our survival? Based on what we now know about the brain, much of our survival learning is pre-programmed and instinctual by nature. As Michael Gazzaniga, author of *Nature's Mind* (1992) points out, "Learning may be nothing more than the time needed for an organism to sort out its built-in systems in order to accomplish its goals."

Perhaps, more surprising though, is the finding that our basic learning skills for math, language and physics may also be "hard-wired" into our brain at conception. The word "education" comes from the Latin word "educare", meaning to draw out. Considering that learning may be no more than forming patterns and understanding out of confusion, perhaps, our role as teachers ought to be more about nurturing or drawing out learners innate abilities. Joseph Pearce, author of *Evolution's End* (1992), says that we really can't teach to the learner; we can only put them in environments which stimulate their pre-programmed learning.

Quotable

Lock-step, assembly-line learning violates a critical discovery about the human brain: Each brain is not only unique, but it develops at a rate that can fluctuate between normal learners by as much as three years.

Our Unlimited Potential

Your students are far more capable than you might have ever imagined. Each successive study of the brain's potential has documented that previous studies were often too modest. The brain has about one hundred billion (100,000,000,000) cells! When linked together, the number of connections our brain can make is variously estimated to be from 1014th power (one hundred trillion), to 10800th power (more than the estimated number of atoms in the known universe).

It is not the quantity of brain cells, however, that is most significant, but the complexity of the connections between the cells that activate learning, consciousness, memory and intelligence. Ground-breaking research by Marian Diamond (1988) and continued by William Greenough and B.J. Anderson (1991) has determined that the brain can literally grow new connections with stimulation at any age. The fact that we can "grow" our brains means that nearly any learner can increase their intelligence without limits using proper enrichment.

A Biochemical Factory

Our cognitive activity is regulated by neurons and glial - the two types of cells found in the human brain. Though 85 percent of these brain cells are glial which support, insulate, and nourish the neurons, it is the remaining 15 percent of brain cells, the neurons, that give us our brain power. When stimulated, neurons grow branch-like extensions known as dendrites. Each cell also has one extending "leg" called an axon. The axon has two essential functions which it accomplishes by connecting with dendrites: to conduct information in the form of electrical stimulation and to transport chemical substances. The split second chemical reaction of sodium and potassium at the moment of cell-to-cell interaction is the physiological trigger to learning. The particular combination of nutrients, chemicals and hormones interacting in an individual's body is the primary determiner of their quality of learning. Bigger brains are not necessarily better. In fact, Albert Einstein's brain was average sized; however, his autopsy did reveal more connections and more glial cells than the average brain.

Enriching the Brain

The brain is quite malleable throughout life. It can be nourished and developed well into old age. In fact, there's no reason to ever stop growing it. Even at age 80 and 90, your brain can still be youthful and quick if you exercise it and challenge it. The more we use it, the better it gets.

The structure of the brain can be changed in as little as one week's time by exposing it to enriching experiences. Such enrichment ought to include multi-sensory experiences, novelty, challenge and feedback. Our brains are also enriched by specific nutrition and by positive social bonding experiences in our learning environments. The effects, however, of enriched brain development often diminish after two to four weeks unless challenge and novelty are maintained. Hence, dull classrooms are out! And multi-sensory, colorful, intriguing environments are in!

Feeding the Brain

There are specific conditions that the brain needs for maximum learning. For starters, these include sufficient water and physical rest. In general, the brain also loves exercise, fresh water, oxygen and protein. Some important nutrients the brain needs are tyrosine-rich protein, selenium, boron, B vitamins, fructose and omega-3 fatty acids. These can be found in fish, eggs, wheat germ, brazil nuts and cottonseed oil.

Excessive carbohydrates can negatively impact learning as they trigger the release of serotonin, a relaxant. In addition, some studies have shown that learning drops by 20 percent when learners have a diet rich in saturated fats or high in sugar.

Left and Right Brain Revisited

Though left/right brain theorists originally emphasized compartmentalized functioning of the two hemispheres of the brain, this theory has been updated by new research. We now know that *both* sides of our brain are used simultaneously in nearly every activity we engage in. Although the left and right hemispheres have some clear-cut specialization to one degree or another, one side still requires the other to complement its overall functioning; and these specializations can vary widely between individuals. For example, most people process music as a dominant right hemisphere activity while musicians, on the other hand, usually have left side domination due to the fact that they are analyzing the composition, as well. Though in general, the left brain prefers things in sequence and the right brain is best with wholes and random learning, it is best to avoid gross generalizations. It serves us and our learners better to think of the brain as a highly interdependent system that is much more complex and overlapping than previously thought.

To illustrate the complexity of the human brain, consider that we all have 90-minute sleep cycles for deep and light sleep which continue throughout the day. Known as ultradian patterns, these rhythmic learning cycles move us from low to high energy and from relaxation to tension. Each peak in the cycle signifies more dominant left or right hemisphere activity. This means that every 90 minutes some of your learners are more left hemisphere dominant, while others are more right hemisphere dominate. This highlights how students' timetables vary; and why we need to be careful about generalizations such as "Johnny is right-brained." Even individual timetables aren't static; they can be modified to a degree through engagement of emotions and physical activity.

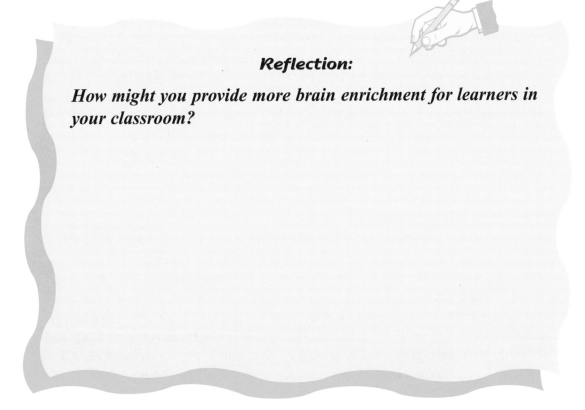

Reflection:

How might you provide more brain enrichment for learners in your classroom?

Hormonal Influences

Our brain cannot maintain learning attentiveness continually. Ultradian patterns, for one, cause normal fluctuations in nutritional and hormonal-related brain chemistry. At night we all experience periods of "deep sleep," Rapid Eye Movement (REM) time, and light sleep. During the daytime, these cycles continue, but at a level of greater awareness. Even animals have these periods of basic rest and activity throughout the day and night.

A woman's 28-day menstrual cycle may also impact learning. During the first half of the cycle, the hormone estrogen alone is present. Estrogen specifically promotes more active brain cells, increases sensory awareness and increases brain alertness. The brain, flooded with this hormone, experiences feelings of pleasure, sexual arousal, well being, enthusiasm and self-esteem. Researchers suggest, therefore, that this may be the optimal time for learning in females.

Resting the Brain

For the brain to experience its best performance it needs deep physiological rest, the kind in which you are "dead to the world." Students who are living with high stress are probably not receiving this kind of rest. Especially impacted are students who live in abusive families, overcrowded homes, or in areas with high crime. Those affected by divorce, the death of a loved one, violence or poor nutrition are also at risk. Research indicates that sleep time may affect the previous day's learning, especially of complex material. When nighttime sleep is reduced, even by as little as two hours, recall ability has been shown to be impaired the next day. Some scientists speculate that sleep gives your brain time to do some "housekeeping" and rearrange circuits, clean out extraneous mental debris, and process emotional events.

Stress and Threat Impair Learning

When we're happy, sad, stressed, fearful or experience any other emotion, our body releases into our bloodstream various chemicals to help us deal with the event. For example, when feeling fearful, it typically releases adrenaline to prepare us for the fight or flight response. When threat is perceived, excessive cortisol is released into the body causing higher-order thinking skills to take a backseat to automatic functions that may help you survive. Your brain's first priority is always survival! Because our brain is run by chemicals, it's impacted dramatically by changes in our moods. Non-receptive moods reduce our brain's capacity for understanding, meaning, memory and higher order thinking skills. In short, a stressful and threatening class climate dramatically impairs learning. Learners may feel threatened by loss of approval, helplessness, rewards, criticism, lack of resources, and what the learner perceives as a hopeless situation, as well.

Emotions and the Brain

Learning is not just a mental function; our feelings impact learning as well. Bad feelings that are ignored can thwart all attempts at learning. Good feelings, on the other hand, create an excitement and love of learning. Hormones, which regulate our emotions, are the dominant determiner of our behavior. Emotions determine why we learn and if we are confident of the learning. We only believe something and give it meaning when we feel strongly about it. Our brain gives an attentional priority to all emotionally-charged information. Our emotional brain tells us what is true and what is not true. Candace Pert (1997) discoverer of opiate receptors goes so far as to say that our whole body acts as a kind of brain. Information is carried via peptide molecules to receptor sites all around the body.

Multi-modal, Multi-path Learning

The brain simultaneously operates on many levels, processing all at once a world of color, movement, emotion, shape, intensity, sound, taste, weight, and more. It assembles patterns, composes meaning and sorts daily life experiences from an extraordinary number of clues. This amazing multi-processor is typically starved for input in the traditional classroom. Why? It's capable of processing far more information, experience and stimuli than it can usually find in school. In fact, a slower, more linear pace actually inhibits learning. An enriched environment that engages all of the senses, and includes consistent feedback from teacher and peers helps feed the brain's enormous appetite for stimulation.

Our Brain and Rote Learning

Far too often, teachers are still using the old model of "stand and deliver" - teachers talk and students memorize for the test. The brain is very poorly designed for this type of learning or for traditional textbook memory approaches. Learning is visual, auditory, kinesthetic, conscious and non- conscious. The brain is rarely over-stimulated in a classroom. The brain learns best on many pathways at once. Maximum learning takes place when learners are engaged in rich, multi-sensory, real-life stimulation. Your classroom will provide this when it is interesting, noisy, busy and provides choices for learners. For this reason, the best classroom is the outdoors, field trips, excursions and special events.

Our upper brain, the neocortex, does what we call the "higher order" thinking skills. Yet it needs something very different than other parts of the brain. It is a pattern-detecting and pattern-making organ that is continually seeking meaning by organizing words, shapes, numbers and ideas into meaningful patterns.

Consider how much you learned and retained from high school or college. The things you did learn are probably things that held strong personal meaning for you, or they were fun, or evoked other strong emotions. Our brain is genetically programmed to learn the behaviors necessary for our perceived survival. Survival learning can be on a physical, social, intellectual or emotional level. Naturally, our brain learns best when we feel strongly about the learning. We ought to keep the focus, therefore, on learning rather than instruction or teaching. Students who learn how to maximize learning and to develop better thinking skills will have the edge necessary for thriving in the midst of the information age.

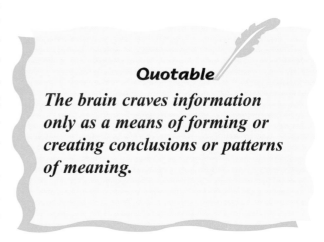

Quotable

The brain craves information only as a means of forming or creating conclusions or patterns of meaning.

Maximizing Natural Memory

Learners may seem to forget a great deal of what is taught, but much of the problem may be an over-reliance on a singular memory system. Multiple memory systems can be activated by providing activities that cover all the learning styles. Reading, storytelling, games, holding a group discussion or sharing time and seeing a video are activities that cover the various learning styles: i.e., auditory, visual, kinesthetic. Then follow up with projects that include experiential activities like role-playing, dance, drama, singing, stretching, and the incorporation of real-life activities.

Since our "thinking cap" (the neocortex) is strongly influenced by patterns, not facts, remembering information is maximized when it is provided in contextual, episodic event-oriented situations which include motor learning, location changes, music, rhythm and novelty. Primary school teachers ordinarily maximize this type of learning, but it makes sense for learners of all ages. We learn best with larger learning themes, fuller, complete patterns and interdisciplinary relationships. We do poorly when we piecemeal learning into linear, sequential facts and other out of context information lists. In short, any lesson which is designed as a simplistic, fact-oriented lesson plan is poorly designed for today's learner.

All Learning Is Mind-Body Linked

The old model of education maintained that learning was a mental function separate from our bodies. Researchers now tell us how important our whole self is in the learning process. Our mood, eye patterns and diet, for example, strongly affect learning, as do our physiology, mind state, posture and breathing. Learning to learn better must include the awareness that the mind-body relationship is integral. Mind states are as important as IQ. The best teachers will know how to influence learners' states and moods; and how to better manage their own feelings. To ignore the body in learning is to ignore the fact that this highly complex organism known as the human being possesses an integrated system of cells, molecules, muscles and organs that are completely interdependent.

Our Cycles and Rhythms

As discussed earlier, our brains are influenced by ultradian patterns and other influences, such as hormones, diet, emotions, and chemistry which continually trigger fluctuations in attention. Expecting to hold a learner's constant attention is, therefore, not only unrealistic, but unproductive. The terms "on" or "off" task are irrelevant to the brain. We learn best with multiple choices and flexibility since individuals maintain different chronological, biological and hemispheric timetables.

Recent brain research suggests we are far from a "learning machine." Instead, our learning and physical performance are dramatically affected by our biological rhythms. Carol Orlock (1993) says that we have temporal cycles of the mind and body that correspond to lunar and solar cycles. We have a 24-hour solar cycle and a 25-hour lunar cycle that affect us in countless ways, including cell division, pulse rate, blood pressure, mood swings, concentration and learning ability. In addition, these cycles influence memory, accident rate, immunology, physical growth, reaction time and pain tolerance.

The brain also seems to have a natural learning pulse which affects how long is best for a focused activity like a lecture. Use the age of the learner in minutes to determine the appropriate focus time. For example, a six-year-old is best with about six minutes of focus time; and will need

Quotable

Learning is maximized by alternating focused attention and diffused activities. Constant focused learning is counterproductive since the brain needs quiet periods to process its newly obtained information.

about one to three minutes of diffusion time (play time). A 10-year-old is good for about 10 minutes of focus time and will need 2 to 5 minutes of diffusion time (group work, individual time). The maximum focus time, even for adults, is about 20 to 25 minutes, say researchers. The brain learns best when the learning is interrupted by breaks of one to five minutes for diffusion or processing stimuli.

Assessment

Most of what is critical to the brain and learning is tough to assess. The most valuable and best learning is often the creation of content, working models, weighted values, complex patterns, learning-to-learn skills and interdisciplinary relationships. These are rarely evaluated and rarely included in traditional assessments. In chapter 23, we will examine what the brain is really learning and how to more effectively assess students.

Relax-to-Energize

Our perception of ourselves and our learning fluctuates as our ultradian patterns move us from low to high energy and from relaxation to tension throughout the course of the day. Some research suggests that these patterns result in learners being able to focus better in the late morning and early evening; and learners being more pessimistic in middle to late afternoon. This helps explain why our thinking can get unrealistically negative at certain low times and positively high at other times.

Other research suggests that the activation and suppression of cerebral/limbic structures is a key element to the success of a learner. In a positively suggestive learning climate vigilance intensity is reduced to an optimum level by activating the serotonin-energetic systems or suppressing the catecholaminegetic systems. Translated, this means the brain stays alert and relaxed for learning but not anxious and hyper-stressed in a safe and positive learning environment.

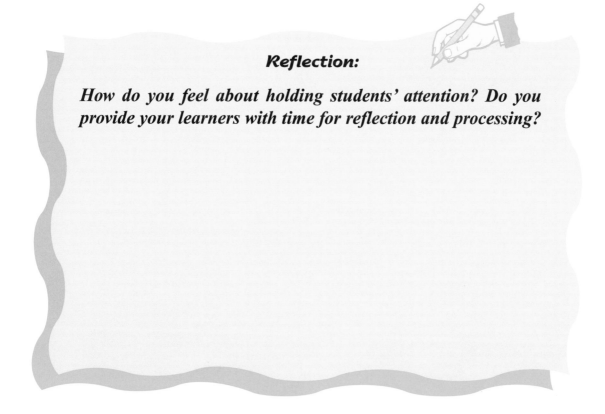

Reflection:

How do you feel about holding students' attention? Do you provide your learners with time for reflection and processing?

Summary

The concepts in this chapter ought to provide you with a little better idea of what the brain is like. Not at all like a computer, but maybe more like a rain-forest. The brain has no central command center, no boss or ultimate authority. Rather, it has overgrown areas of "intellectual weeds" and can be encouraged to grow in many new areas. It has its own seasons, own systems of parasites, and a whole set of complex interdependent relationships. Our brain is quite complex and the better we understand the complexity of it, the easier our job will become.

Quotable

All learning involves our body, our emotions, our attitudes and our health. Brain-compatible learning addresses all of these variables.

We are learners, yes; but we are also people with feelings, beliefs, food cravings, personal problems, attitudes and various skill levels. While the old academic model addressed primarily the intellectual aspect of learners, the new prevailing model points to a holistic approach that acknowledges we learn with our minds, heart *and* body. Brain-compatible learning also suggests that the better we deal with the whole learner, the more effective we'll be in teaching and learning.

Mind-Map

Using various colored felt pens, draw your own interpretation of how you, personally, learn best. There are no rules. Organize your mind-map any way you like!

Reactions:

What are your feelings about the topics presented in this chapter?

What are some practical applications for what you're learning?

What do you want to remember from this chapter?

After all, knowledge about the brain and standard education practices have traditionally been born of different worlds. It's time for a marriage.

Eric Jensen
Brain-Based Learning

Chapter 3

Learning Styles Made Easy

Chapter Preview:

- ✦ **How Important Are Learning Styles?**
- ✦ **Learning Style Models**
- ✦ **The Global Learning Profile**
- ✦ **Contextual Factors**
- ✦ **Input Preferences**
- ✦ **Processing Format**
- ✦ **Response Filters**
- ✦ **How to Reach All Learning Styles**
- ✦ **Lifelong Learning Style**
- ✦ **Detection and Diagnosis**
- ✦ **Culturally-Reinforced Learning Styles**

How Important Are Learning Styles?

A learning style is a preferred way of thinking, processing, and understanding information. If you were going to learn about biology, would you rather watch a video, listen to a lecture, or work in a lab? Researchers have found that learners score "significantly higher" on tests when learning in the way that fits their preferred style. A report of the New York State Board of Regents' Panel on Learning Styles says that it is essential to alter teaching strategies to meet the needs of a more multi-cultural global society. As a teacher, you may have been taught to present information in sequential order. It turns out, however, that this "logic" may, in fact, be the "kiss of death" for many learners.

The easiest way to reach all of your learners is simple: provide both variety and choice. Open presentations with a global overview followed by a more sequential presentation style. In this way you'll cover students who learn best with a more holistic, random approach and those who learn best with a sequential, ordered approach.

There are many learning style profiles available today. Each of them has their own strong points. The reason that they are so different is that they are assessing different aspects of the cognitive process. The story of the six blind men who each give a different description of an elephant depending on their point of reference, is a good analogy for learning style profiles. Each reflects a different reference point. Some are assessing contextual factors and input preferences, while others might be assessing processing formats and response filters.

Five of the most well-known learning style models are: 1) Bandler-Grinder; 2) Herrmann; 3) Dunn and Dunn; 4) Gregorc-Butler; and 5) the 4-MAT System (figure 3.1). Listen to your students to help determine what their dominant learning style preference is. Following are some typical responses that might illuminate what your students' preferences are: "That *looks* great!" "That *sounds* good." "I *feel* tired." "Can we *touch* it?"

Figure 3.1:
Learning Style Models

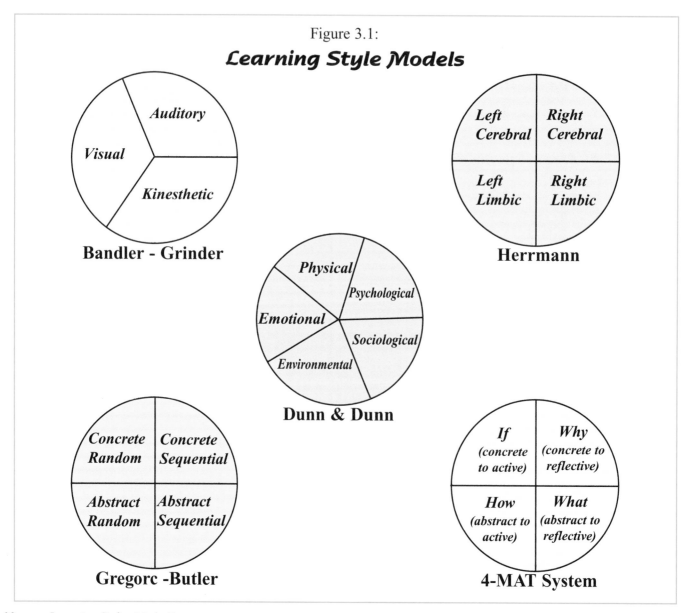

Bandler - Grinder

Herrmann

Dunn & Dunn

Gregorc -Butler

4-MAT System

The human brain actually does not just have a single "learning style." Humans are far more complex than that. We use many styles, depending on the circumstances and our survival needs at the time. To get a more accurate understanding of how we actually learn, it makes more sense to sub-divide the learning process into the following four categories:

1. Context

The circumstances surrounding a learning environment provide important clues about what will happen during the experience. Has the teacher taken into consideration the temperature of the room, social conditions or relationships? The learning style profile developed by Rita and Kenneth Dunn best addresses the importance of context in learning.

2. Input

All learning requires some input to initiate the process. Input is gathered from one or more of our five senses: visual (eyes), auditory (ears), kinesthetic (body), olfactory (nose) or gustatory (mouth). Although all two-month-old babies are gustatory learners, less than one percent of all other learners rely on gustatory input for their dominant style. Reliance on olfactory input is rarely a dominant style either. Input is either external (from an outside source) or internal (created in your own mind). Visual-external is you looking outward; visual-internal is you visualizing or using your imagination. The approach that best addresses this aspect of learning is the Bandler-Grinder model.

Bob Samples, author of *Open Mind/Whole Mind* (1987), says that humans have access to other senses, as well, including: vestibular (repetitious movement), magnetic (ferromagnetic orientation), ionic (electrostatic atmospheric charges), geogravimetric (sensing mass differences), proximal (physical closeness) and others. He suggests that as infants we actually maximize all of these senses; however, early conditioning tells us which ones are "socially correct" or "culturally appropriate." Perhaps in other societies people use a wider range of their senses.

3. Processing

The way a learner handles the actual input of data or their manipulation of it is what processing refers to. Processing can occur in frameworks of global or analytical, concrete or abstract, multi-task or single-task, etc. The way a learner processes information may be dependent on relative hemispheric dominance - either right or left brain. The two models that address this aspect of learning best are: Ned Herrmann's Brain Dominance model and the Gregorc-Butler model.

4. Response Filters

Once learners have taken in the information and processed it, the mind's intuitive response filters will influence what is done with the information. This process of reasoning will consider factors like: the time, the risk involved, and internal/external referencing points. The model that examines this aspect of learning is the 4-MAT system.

Each of the five dominant learning style models has its positive qualities; though, separately, none of them fully explains the learning process. When combined, however, a useful new format called The Global Learning Profile™ presents a holistic and comprehensive view of learning styles. The following variables are acknowledged in The Global Learning Profile™:

The Global Learning Profile™

Contextual Factors

Field-Dependent
Field-Independent
Flexible environment
Structured environment
Independent
Dependent
Relationship-driven
Content-driven

Input Preferences

Visual-External
Visual-Internal
Auditory-External
Auditory-Internal
Kinesthetic-Tactile
Kinesthetic-Internal

Processing Format

Contextual/Global
Sequential/Detailed/Linear
Conceptual/Abstract
Concrete (Objects & Feelings

Response Filters

Externally-Referenced
Internally-Referenced
Matcher
Mismatcher
Impulsive/Experimental
Analytical/Reflective

Don't worry right now if the above variables of The Global Learning Profile™ seem meaningless to you. We're about to take a closer look at them. After each area is described, you will have an opportunity to reflect on the relationship of it to your own learning style and that of your students, family or own children. This reflection process will make the information far more meaningful to you, and will aid in your recall of it.

Contextual Factors

Field-Dependent Versus Field-Independent

Learners who are field-dependent dominant (also called "street learners") prefer contextual cues: natural contexts like field trips, experiments, real-life experiences, not artificial or isolated settings. Learning is optimized in situations where the learning would naturally occur. They like to learn about science, for example, by going to museums, doing outdoor experiments, and taking field trips. On the other hand, learners who are field-independent dominant are apt to excel in "irrelevant" contexts: using computers, textbooks, audio tapes, videos. They are generally comfortable with second-hand and third-hand learning; and can learn well in environments like libraries or classrooms.

Flexible Versus Structured Environments

Some learners prefer a flexible environment where they have options and can make decisions for themselves regarding variables such as: lighting (natural or fluorescent), sound/noise level, temperature, furniture and seating arrangements. Other learners prefer a more structured environment, and usually like very detailed directions, rules, conformity and authority. Such learners usually have a very particular idea of how they like to learn, and will have little tolerance for variation.

Independent Versus Dependent

Independent learners generally prefer to learn alone; they can learn with others but when they do the effectiveness of their learning is usually decreased. Dependent learners, however, prefer to learn in pairs, groups or teams; they can work alone but when they do, their learning is less effective. Dependent learners generally learn best in a busy, noisy, talkative environments where interpersonal relationships are valued.

Relationship-Driven Versus Content-Driven

Relationship-driven learners usually feel that *who* delivers the information is more important than *what* the information is. Such learners like to build a relationship of trust, credibility and respect *before* listening or learning. Content-driven learners, on the other hand, usually feel that the information itself is *more* important than the carrier of it. Even if the learner dislikes the teacher, learning will still likely take place.

Input Preferences

Visual-External Versus Visual-Internal

Visual-external learners usually prefer visual input. They will generally maintain eye contact with a teacher, their posture is upright, they create mental pictures or models, they may talk fast and in monotones, they like handouts, and use visual terminology like, "See what I mean?" A visual learner is usually a good speller, would rather read than be read to, enjoys writing, prefers neatness, is organized, chin is up, and is less distracted by noise. Do you get the picture? They have a "personal space" and don't like others standing too close. If asked, "Are you hungry?" They might check their watch to "see" if it's time for them to be hungry! If we were to describe habits, we might say that visual-external learners prefer colorful, thinner clothes. They love books, computers, overheads, art, and photos. They buy a car based on its looks, rather than its feel. If you're in another room talking to a visual-external learner, they want to come into the room to see you as they talk. They are good at visualization and have trouble with verbal instructions.

Visual-internal learners, on the other hand, prefer to "see" things in their mind's eye first. They want to visualize the learning before it's presented. They tend to daydream, imagine things, and create mental pictures and models prior to more formal learning.

Auditory-External Versus Auditory-Internal

Auditory-external learners prefer input to be auditory. They talk a lot (either to self or others), they are easily distracted, and they memorize by steps and procedures. Auditory learners also often exhibit head bobs and maximize tempo, tonality, pitch and volume in their speech patterns. They like to answer rhetorical questions, they want test questions presented in the order they were learned, they can mimic sounds of others' voices, they talk to themselves at night and before they get up in the morning, and they often replay conversations in their head. Math and writing are likely more difficult for auditory-external learners. In class you will recognize these learners as they speak rhythmically, like class discussion, dislike spelling, like to read aloud, enjoy storytelling, remember what was discussed, and often mimic the tone, pitch, tempo and pace of the teacher. They like social occasions more than others and often are better at recalling jokes and conversations.

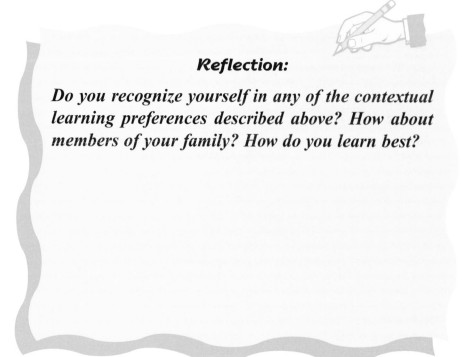

Reflection:

Do you recognize yourself in any of the contextual learning preferences described above? How about members of your family? How do you learn best?

Auditory-internal learners, on the other hand, prefer to talk to themselves during the learning process. For example, they might ask themselves quite unconsciously, "What do I know about this? What do I think? What does this mean to me?" They often hold nearly endless conversations with themselves and have difficulty making up their minds. They are also very strong in metacognition.

Kinesthetic-Tactile Versus Kinesthetic-Internal

Kinesthetic-tactile learners prefer physical input. They want to learn about something by manipulating things or by touch, feel, and activity. They're a "hands-on", try it first, jump in and give it a "go" type of learner. They're in touch with their feelings and their body, they generally have minimal facial expression when talking, they use measured words with pauses, and have slower breathing. Kinesthetic-tactile learners are usually physically active, and their spaces are often unorganized. They often say things like: "This feels good", or "let's get a handle on this." This learner is more likely to be right-hemisphere dominant. Teacher proximity, attention, and personal contact influence this learner to a large degree. In a nut shell, learning by doing the task is more interesting to them than reading about it or hearing about it.

Kinesthetic-internal learners, on the other hand, prefer inferential input; and want to experience feelings about something before learning about it. They are intuitive by nature, they like stories and movies, especially those with a great deal of "heart" and feeling in them. Kinesthetic-internal learners value strong non-verbal communication (tonality, tempo, posture, expression, and gestures). They tend to place a greater emphasis on *how* something is said rather than on *what* is said. They need to have positive feelings about the task at hand before initiating it. Kinesthetic-internal learners are less verbally expressive, more physically expressive; and less likely to be the first to raise their hand in class because they need to go "internal" to check out their answers before offering them. To sum up this modality, one can either feel their way into doing (internal) or act their way into feeling (tactile).

Processing Format

Contextual/Global Versus Sequential/Detailed/Linear

Learners who process information in a contextual/global style prefer seeing the big picture, an overview, key concepts, and how the concepts relate before putting all the pieces together - holistic, gestalt. This learner wants first to understand the relevance, the thematic vision and purpose of the learning; and is more likely to prefer multi-tasking - to work on many problems simultaneously. For example, this learner likes to tend to one task for awhile, then switch to another, then back to the same or even another. He/She is more likely to be inferential and intuitive - inferring meaning, and using kinesthetic internal cues to relate the learning. Contextual/global learners also prefer quick and simple approximation rather than exact measurement; they often have a "feeling" for the information. She/he might ask the question, "Why be so exact?"

Contextual/global learners are sometimes referred to as "right-brain" learners. A more visual right-brain dominance translates to a preference for processing in pictures, symbols, icons and themes. This learner has external focus tendencies with a high degree of distractibility. This sometimes results in the mistaken "at-risk" label; in truth, this learner simply needs to be reached with more multi-tasking, non-verbals, global overviews and stronger relationships in learning.

Reflection:

Have you ever been expected to learn in a way that does not feel natural to you? What strategies can you use to help reach all of your learners?

The sequential/detailed/linear learner, on the other hand, prefers things to be sequenced, to take small steps, and to focus on one task at a time. When this learner is ready for the next task, they'll ask, "What's next?" He/she wants a menu, formula, or list of upcoming events and lessons; and can work on several tasks only if done in order. This learner is more likely to be analytical and word-based - measuring, analyzing, asking questions, comparing, and contrasting information. She/he wants to know the why and how of something - to fully understand it before doing or deciding on it. To this sequential learner, words have very specific meaning; and what the teacher says will be held onto - word for word.

The sequential/detailed/linear learner is often referred to as left-hemisphere dominant. Preferring the world of the written word, this learner wants clear, detailed instructions and structured lessons. Since they tend to focus internally, they possess a lower level of distractibility. They are oriented for the long-term and prefer to know what's coming up each day, hour-by-hour. These learners excel in math, language, computers and other sequential work.

Conceptual/Abstract Versus Concrete

The learner whose style is conceptual/abstract prefers the world of books, words, computers, ideas, and conversations. This learner enjoys talking or thinking but is less of a "doer." He/She is probably thought of as very much "in their head." This learner is attracted to abstract professions such as writing or accounting, or may become a college professor.

Concrete learners, on the other hand, prefer the world of objects and feelings - things that can be touched, jumped over, handled and manipulated. This learner likes a hands-on experiential approach, to learn by doing, to try things out. She/he seeks action, games and movement; and is likely attracted to work where the body and hands are used extensively - for example, dancer, sculptor, truck driver, or actress.

Reflection:

Are there times when you process information one way, and other times when you process it another? Does it depend on the type of information?

Response Filters

Externally-Referenced Versus Internally-Referenced

Externally-referenced learners primarily respond based on what others think. The question they often ask themselves is "How are others expecting me to act, or to think or to say?" Society's norms and rules are very important sources of information to them and their behavior is greatly impacted by such. Before responding, externally-referenced learners will likely consider questions of etiquette and family values.

Internally-referenced learners, on the other hand, respond using themselves as the primary judge for their behaviors and choices. Their own set of rules may differ from society's. This learner is a very independent thinker and will likely act accordingly.

Matchers Versus Mismatchers

Learners who are matchers respond by noting similarities; they agree more easily, like consistencies, find sameness in relationships, prefer things that belong or go together. They like things that make sense and enjoy consistency and habits. This learner will more likely approve of something that has been done before, that fits into an overall plan, and that is generally consistent with the rest of the learning.

Mismatchers, on the other hand, respond by noting differences; they notice what's off, missing, wrong or inconsistent. They say, "But, why not?" or, "What if?" They find flaws in arguments, discover exceptions to the rule, and prefer variety and change; they are not necessarily negative, simply contrary. Mismatchers are skeptical of words like: always, everyone, all, never and no one. Hence, you'll hear more responses like, "Yes, but... " This learner wants more variety, enjoys experimenting and abhors traditional lesson plans, predictability, and doing what everyone else is doing.

Impulsive/Experimental Versus Analytical/Reflective

Impulsive/experimental learners respond with immediate action to thoughts and experimentation. Their pattern is to do it, then keep doing it until it is figured out. The impulsive/experimental learner is more likely to be oriented in the present.

Analytical/reflective learners, on the other hand, respond internally. They take in information and process it by reflecting on it. The analytical/reflective learner stays at a distance - the classic passive; they are the "stand back and watch" learner, the pragmatist. More likely to be oriented in the past or future, this learner wants to reflect on the possibilities.

How to Reach All Learning Styles

The Global Learning Profile™ highlights the numerous variables that influence the teaching and learning process reflecting the variety of ways the brain is naturally inclined to learn. Don't we all use all of these, at one time or another? Yes, we do. That's why, instead of trying to teach every learner in their dominant learning style, we must remember to offer our students both variety and choice. It's that simple. The human brain is a multi-processor. It learns many ways, usually at the same time. Offer your students a variety of learning experiences, from computers to group work, from field trips to guest speakers, from independent work to role play. Variety and choice are the key when it comes to learning styles.

Reflection:

Which of the above response filters do you identify with? Do you think you have qualities from each of the modalities?

Lifelong Learning Style

Another researcher, Michael Grinder (1989), says that while you might use several styles, your preferred (or dependent) style will stay with you for much of your life. Why? It is the one that you learned to use for survival as an infant, so your brain always gives it first priority whenever survival is threatened later on in life. For example, let's say a fire breaks out near you. Your immediate, first reaction will be one of the following: 1) visual - you quickly size up the situation and look for exits and others in need, etc.; 2) auditory - you start yelling "fire!", giving directions or screaming; or 3) kinesthetic - you start running for the exits or grabbing others to help them get out. While you may do all three, one response will be an instinctual first reaction.

Learning preferences are age-dependent. As babies, all of us were gustatory. Then, as toddlers, ages two to five, most of us became more kinesthetic. All preferences are learned early in life. In fact, researchers believe that between the ages of two and five, our dependent profile is sealed. As a young child, ages five to nine, most of us become more auditory. About 40 percent of learners develop into visual learners by the time they reach secondary school. The learners that remain kinesthetic often fall behind in instruction or are labeled a behavior problem, developmentally delayed, or hyperactive. More often than not, this learner's brain is *not* delayed. It's just fine; however, what is true is that there is simply a great range of what ought to be considered normal development.

Detection and Diagnosis

One of the most often asked questions by teachers is, "How can I discover a student's preferred learning style?" There are two very simple answers to this inquiry: 1) provide choice and they'll choose their favorite modality; and 2) learn to pay attention to student responses. Each one of the learning styles discussed in this chapter provides obvious clues. For example, visual learners follow you with their eyes as you move across the room - they watch for visual cues and want notes and handouts. Mismatchers find differences in what you are doing versus what they think you should be doing or what should have happened. To increase your effectiveness with various learning styles, start identifying students who have a particular learning style. Then pick another and work with it. Over time, you'll have the process down to an art. As you develop your own eyes and ears for identifying various learners, you'll find it increasingly easy to teach to all of them.

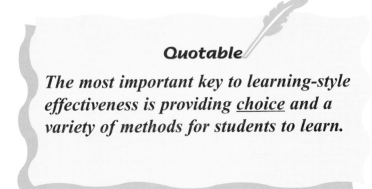

Quotable

The most important key to learning-style effectiveness is providing <u>choice</u> and a variety of methods for students to learn.

Any time you get the least bit frustrated with an individual student, take a moment to identify what their learning strategy is. Ask yourself the following questions to help you uncover it:

✦ What skills, concepts, or values are attempting to be learned?
✦ What are the essential components or micro-steps of it?
✦ What are similar or parallel learning activities to the one being conducted?
✦ Is the activity one that the student has been successful at before?
✦ What strategy did the student use before to succeed?
✦ What resources were used with the earlier success?

The following dialogue provides an example of how a teacher might uncover a student's learning strategy. The setting is the playground. The problem is that a student is afraid to climb up a tall tree on a "ropes course." Even though the climbing is probably quite safe, he is afraid to leave the ground.

Teacher:	Is there a reason why you don't want to climb the ladder? (information gathering)
Student:	Yes, it's too dangerous.
Teacher:	But I'll help you so it will be safe. (attempts an obvious rebuttal to gather more data)
Student:	It's still too dangerous. (discovers it's not a matter of logic, it's something else - teacher needs more data)
Teacher:	Have you ever done anything else that was dangerous? (notice teacher has quit insisting that it's not dangerous; it is to the student. The teacher attempts to find a past parallel activity which included danger, but ended up being fun)
Student:	Sure, I ride my skateboard pretty fast. (just the reference the teacher had hoped for; he's a kinesthetic-tactile learner)
Teacher:	Okay, lots of kids say they ride fast, but *how fast*? (teacher challenges student in an attempt to elicit risk-taking, braggart behavior)
Student:	Really fast! (strategy worked)
Teacher:	How in the world did you ever do that? (teacher affirms student as a dangerous risk-taker in another context, then asks for the strategy)
Student:	It's easy. I start out slow, then just do it. (Jackpot! Student has given you the learning strategy, but teacher elects to verify)
Teacher:	You mean you learned how to do it by starting slow and working your way up? (he's a sequential learner, teacher realizes)
Student:	Sure, it's easier that way. (strategy verified)
Teacher:	If you were to climb up just part of the ladder, how far could *you go* (emphasis on these two words) and still feel safe? (teacher asks student to participate in selecting chunk size)
Student:	About two steps. That's all, no more! (chunk size given)
Teacher:	OK, but do you have enough nerve to do even that much? (challenge issued to complete first chunk, that appeals to mismatchers)
Student:	Sure, anybody could do that. (student completes the first part of the climb and returns to the ground)
Teacher:	You did great! Now that you've conquered that, how far can you go next time? (reinforcement, further challenge issued)
Student:	Well, about to there. (Student points to new goal, process continues until student successfully reaches top of ladder in four chunks)

This student's style is linear, kinesthetic, mismatcher. He likes challenges and physical activity, but prefers to take one step at a time. How did the teacher figure this out? By asking the right questions. How did she know which questions to ask? She knew the possible choices of learning styles, so she simply asked the ones that might fit.

Once you identify what dominant style you use when you teach, you can begin to expand your repertoire. Most commonly, teachers present in a way that fits their own preferred learning style. In order to reach more students, you will need to present in a multi-dimensional, multi-sensory mode that includes many of the major modalities. Experience, trial and error, and questioning can help shed light on the mystery of learning styles. When the most common questioning tactics and strategies fail, your experience will guide you to try some of the other possibilities.

Culturally-Reinforced Learning Styles

All learning styles are culturally reinforced. While a specific culture, of course, does not guarantee a particular learning style, it can provide reinforcement for it. There are many ways to define culture - by wealth, color, origin, religion, genetics, values or gender, just to name a few. Cultures can be as specific as the middle-aged lumberjacks of Astoria, Oregon or as general as all women. A culture of any type maintains some common values and experiences that influence its people. Similarities within groups are, therefore, not uncommon. It is important, however, to recognize that there are always exceptions to the norm. So then, how can we use these generalities to improve classroom learning?

For the sake of example, let's consider that American Indians *tend* to be past-referenced, right hemisphere learners, and you are teaching a class with a large population of American Indian learners. Translating what you know about the American Indian culture and learning styles, you choose teaching strategies which build heavily on tradition - that focus on the past and what we have learned from our ancestors. Further, you emphasize wholes, rather than parts; feelings, rather than facts; and music and ideas, rather than texts and lists. Your chances of success have now dramatically increased.

In another example, consider the "mañana" or "no worries" attitude exhibited by many societies, especially island cultures. Inferring a "take it easy" approach to life or a "we can always do this tomorrow" pattern, learners from such cultures would logically benefit from a teacher who helps focus them on the immediate value of a learning objective versus its long-term benefit. The teacher might also want to engage the learner in more "hands-on" learning and less lecture.

When used in this manner, the following broad cultural implications can help teachers analyze individuals' learning styles in an effort to maximize learning. They ought not, however, be considered the gospel. There are many variations along the continuum in each modality; and people, even of the same culture, vary along the continuum, as well. Ultimately, the most important things to remember are: 1) to provide a climate where every learner is respected and nourished; 2) to avoid homogeneous ability groupings; 3) to encourage multi-status and multi-age teamwork; and 4) to offer choices that make sense for all learning styles.

It is critical that you work as a partner with your students in discovering and eliciting their learning styles. Follow through with appropriate recommendations; and offer them the opportunity to not only try out compatible strategies, but to understand how they can optimize learning with the knowledge of their learning style. Teaching students to teach themselves is a long-term benefit that will impact students for the rest of their lives. In fact, there may be no more valuable or empowering a lesson than the awareness of how one learns most efficiently.

The brain learns many ways at once; we do not have a single, dominant lifelong learning style. Provide a variety of learning methods; allow learners to choose how they wish to learn at least 50 percent of the time. Discovering your students' learning styles and following up with them is one of the most valuable learning benefits a teacher can provide.

Reactions:

What are your feelings about the topics presented in this chapter?

What are some practical applications for what you're learning?

What do you want to remember from this chapter?

Learners aren't navel oranges being prepped for market on a conveyor belt; learners are, rather, as diverse as all the produce in the world. To prep them adequately, we must tend to them individually and with respect for their differences.

Eric Jensen

Chapter 4
Diversity & Differences

Chapter Preview:

✦ **Learners Who March to a Different Drummer**
✦ **Matchers and Mismatchers**
✦ **Multi-Cultural Diversity**
✦ **Male and Female Differences**
✦ **Different Developmental Stages**
✦ **Gender Differences in Thinking**
✦ **Problem-Solving Differences**
✦ **Attention Deficit Disorder**
✦ **Dyslexia**
✦ **Drug Abuse**
✦ **Gifted and Talented Learners**
✦ **Is There a Better Way?**

Learners Who March to a Different Drummer

This chapter is about the student who is exceptional; that is, they catch our attention because they are not your "average" learner - the square peg in the round hole phenomenon. The educational conveyor belt moves quickly. Teachers have only so much time in the course of a school day; and students who don't move along at the pace expected of them, often feel lost and lonely and uncared for. They may be gifted learners who are bored with the standard. They may be learners who process information differently. Or perhaps, they're dyslexic. Chances are that their difference, whatever that is, if not attended to sensitively, will manifest as a classroom discipline problem. This learner is less likely to feel comfortable in a traditional group setting, and less likely to get good grades. This does not mean, however, that the exceptional learner cannot succeed in school. It probably does mean, however, that you will have to shift your point of reference when judging this learner's abilities and progress. Learners aren't navel oranges being prepped for market on a conveyor belt; learners are, rather, as diverse as all the produce in the world. To prep them adequately, we must tend to them individually and with respect for their differences.

Matchers and Mismatchers

As discussed in chapter three, our brain tends to either match up information input with familiar data, or it mismatches it, looking for what's different. Or, more often than not, it functions somewhere along a continuum between the two processes. The degree to which a student learns by noticing similarities versus differences is highly individual. Virtually no one does either type of information processing 100 percent of the time, but tendencies do exist. About 50 percent of Americans match and mismatch evenly - they do both with the same frequency. On the other hand, about 10 percent of the American population mismatches constantly. And about 40 percent are habitual matchers.

The degree to which a society or culture matches or mismatches is culturally reinforced. In some countries, like Japan, it's simply bad etiquette to mismatch, so you have a nation which has a high percentage of matchers. In Israel, on the other hand, you have a majority culture that encourages questioning and critical thinking; thus, mismatchers make up a high percentage of the population there. Because Australia was used as a penal colony by England, it has a higher percentage of mismatchers to a small degree than other countries. The "California greener grass syndrome" also influences the balance of matchers and mismatchers in a particular area. For example, those who tend to emigrate are mismatchers, "different thinking" individuals who are comfortable with change. This is partly the phenomenon that has influenced California's diverse self-selected population. In America, more matchers live in the Midwest than in any other part of the country. On the other hand, states with relatively high percentages of mismatchers include Vermont, Oregon, California, and Washington.

Matchers likely work at the same job for years, keep the same friends, eat at the same restaurants, and do many of the same activities year-after-year. It would not be uncommon to hear a matcher make generalized statements using words like: everyone, always, we, never, all.

Mismatchers, on the other hand, tend to prefer change over sameness. They like trying new things, going to different restaurants, taking an alternative route home, and generally experimenting more. They find exceptions to the rule. It would not be uncommon to hear a mismatcher use words like: but, and not always. If a sign says "No Trespassing," a matcher will likely obey, while a mismatcher will wonder, "What's in there?"

Those who are matchers tend to:

✦ Agree with you more often
✦ Prefer the familiar, tried and true
✦ Be uncomfortable with novelty
✦ Follow rules, stay with the group
✦ Learn by similarities
✦ Do what is expected by others

Those who are mismatchers tend to:

✦ Disagree more often
✦ Prefer novelty, change, a bit of risk
✦ Sometimes ignore rules and boundaries
✦ Need differences to understand content

Quotable

We have probably labeled countless learners, "troublemakers" when, in fact, they are simply learning by divergent thinking.

Mismatchers are not being negative or obstinate for the sake of being difficult, nor are they trying to prove you wrong; they are merely processing information in the way that is natural for them to do so. Mismatchers do, however, pose particular challenges in the classroom (unless you recognize this as their learning style and have a strategy for dealing effectively with it). The good news is that mismatchers are not particularly difficult to identify.

Do any of the following scenarios sound familiar? You've told your class that you'll be ready to start the next lesson in 10 minutes. Inevitably, a student raises his hand and says, "It's been 11 minutes, teacher." Or let's say you've distributed a hand-out that contains a misspelling; a student raises her hand and says, "How come this is spelled wrong?" Or you ask your students to begin an activity and one chimes in, "Why aren't we doing this the way Mr. Jones's class did it last year?" If you say to a mismatcher, "You've got two choices", he/she is surely thinking, "Why not three?" You might also notice that though most students respect classroom rules, mismatchers often break them. It is almost as if they are obsessed with trying to find an exception to the rule. These kinds of responses can drive teachers (and other students) who are matchers crazy if they don't understand that this is a natural and normal way for some people to filter information and develop patterns.

Key points for dealing effectively with mismatchers:

◆ Don't try to "fix" them; they're not broken.
◆ Appreciate and respect their alternative point of view ("Thanks for pointing that out, Katie. I hadn't thought of it that way.")
◆ Make sure that they follow the same rules as everyone else.
◆ Avoid labeling learners since their preferences may vary depending on stress levels or circumstances. It's best to use "match" and "mismatch" as active, flexible verbs (i.e., "He was mismatching me again," or, "Good mismatch."
◆ Privately, tell them, "Creativity is wonderful. If you are creative in areas other than discipline, it'll keep us both happy, and you out of trouble."

We have probably labeled countless learners, "troublemakers" when, in fact, they are simply learning by divergent thinking. Think of the question, "Is this person filling the mold (matching) or trying to break the mold (mismatching)?" The next time a student says, "Hey, you misspelled a word on this worksheet," say "Thanks for finding that. If you'd like, you can be in charge of proofreading handouts." Learn to appreciate that mismatchers love to learn, they simply learn by differences, not similarities.

Multi-Cultural Diversity

Many learners feel like they don't fit in the system. It's easy to feel that way when the system has been designed by a different culture than our own. As our concern has grown for meeting the educational needs of an ever increasing multi-cultural society, so has our awareness of distinctive patterns, expectations and needs within cultures. These patterns significantly affect the way students' communicate and the learning styles they develop. Although it's critical to avoid generalizations, knowledge of cultural patterns can be highly useful for problem solving in the classroom. Use the following chart as a guide but use your own experience as a rule.

Examples of Culturally Reinforced Conversational Styles

	Blacks	Hispanic	Anglo	Am. Indian	Asian
Conversational Eye contact	Low	Low	High	Medium	High
Assertiveness	Moderate	Low	Low-Mod.	Low	Low
Ways to Align	Call for unified expression	Call for silence	Call for silence	Call for silence	Ask for silence
Conversation Style	Direct personal truth-issue oriented	Passive containment	Non-confrontive representative compromising peace-oriented	Direct combination issue/truth compromise	Casual calm, historical
Use of Emotions	As a valid source of expression	To be held back until confront point	To be managed	To be contained as much as possible	To be avoided
Reaction to Heated Dialogues	As long as talking is going on, it's OK verbal threats rarely serious	Extremes: withdrawal or high response to verbal can lead to pent-up violence	Discomfort: threats taken seriously	Discomfort: avoidance	Discomfort: keeping emotion out

As always, ask students for clarification. Check things out. Avoid assuming that everyone within a cultural group is the same. The patterns outlined here are only that - general patterns. There are always exceptions. And there is a great deal of variance within cultures, as well. Being aware of cultural patterns can help us increase our sensitivity to another person's frame of reference - to more fully understand another's point of view or experience. Most of us have limited exposure to other cultures and backgrounds. Due to this, it is easy for us to be ethnocentric in our thinking and problem-solving strategies.

Today's culturally diverse population is a demographic reality. In 1995, one-third of all students in American schools were non-white. This rapid change in demographics has created new economic and social problems in schools. Let's take a look at some of the issues educators are trying hard to remedy.

✦ There is a disproportionate school failure rate among students of color.
✦ There is a disproportionate school drop-out rate among students of color.
✦ The dominant educational and social-cultural structure is Anglo.
✦ Students of color often feel disenfranchised in school.
✦ Society either reaps the benefits of educated citizens or pays the social and economic price for those who are disenfranchised, unemployed, and/or institutionalized.

Some of the arguments that are posed by those opposed to updating our educational system and meeting the needs of our changing demographics are:

◆ The movement is motivated by those who are out of power and simply want more power at the expense of others.

◆ Things are not perfect the way they are, but they don't need an overhaul.

◆ It's just a big political strategy to gain a political base.

◆ The United States is designed to absorb other cultures, not to adapt to them.

◆ Those who don't learn or stay in school are simply not motivated, or they are of weak character, or their values are wrong.

◆ We are lowering the standards, not improving the system.

What is the right approach to take? First, how do you feel about the issue? Get informed and learn more about the history, customs and issues of other cultures. Second, find out what your school's policy is regarding multiculturalism? Find out how textbooks are selected, how curriculum is created and what the state mandates are. What structures have been put in place to help you respond to diverse demographics? Key into your students. Are they thriving in school? Or are they barely surviving?

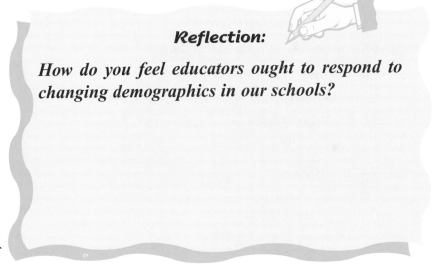

Reflection:

How do you feel educators ought to respond to changing demographics in our schools?

There is new evidence that what we call "race" is very different than what race is genetically. The landmark book on the topic, *The History and Geography of Human Genes,* Cavalli-Sforza, et.al. (1994), concludes that once human genes are removed for skin coloration and physical stature, "races" are nearly identical! In fact, the variations among individuals is so much greater than those among races, that the whole concept of race is genetically meaningless. Surprisingly, sub-Saharan Africans are closer to Southern Europeans than they are to Australian Aborigines. Native American tribes were of three blood lines, genetically, not one. Caucasians are genetically in between the Mongoloids and the Africans.

As discussed in chapter three, a culture can be any group of people that shares common values or experiences. Therefore, cultures can exist within cultures. For instance, the anglo culture might share certain general characteristics; and within that culture, i.e., rural, urban, liberal, conservative, female, male, Catholic, Jewish, middle-, lower- or upper-income subgroups may share other cultural traits. So then, the question becomes, to what degree are people influenced by their culture(s) and what sub-cultures do they identify with? It logically follows then that there is no one "black" culture, just as there is no one "white" culture or any other culture. Even in a school that was racially homogenous, you would have different cultures: the upper achievers, the socialites, the athletes, etc. Thus, the automatic grouping or stereotyping of people by color represents faulty thinking. The Chinese student in your classroom who was adopted by Caucasian parents at birth will most certainly have very different cultural attributes than the student who is a Chinese refugee.

Male and Female Differences

If a single culture based on race does not exist, then certainly a single culture based on gender does not exist either. Cultural attributes by gender are influenced by many things. The two most important distinctions, however, are sociological and biological. Our discussion here will be limited to the biological distinctions, since many volumes have been written already about the sociological implications of gender. *You Just Don't Understand*, by Deborah Tannen (1991) and *Men are from Mars and Women are From Venus*, by John Gray (1992) are two very popular ones should you care to study this topic further.

Obviously, there are noticeable biological differences between the sexes; but are there differences inside the brain, as well? Many researchers have reported clear-cut brain differences between men and women. Although some things can safely be said about certain differences, there is still some dispute over the scope and magnitude of other differences. Taken altogether, the evidence suggests that male and female brains are organized along very different lines from very early in life. Variances within the same sex do exist, but certainly not to the same extent as those found between the opposite sex.

Quotable

While each brain will have varying amounts of sexually differentiated characteristics, some generalizations can still be made about the differences between males and females.

It seems that post-conception hormonal influences are the primary difference-maker between the genders. Not all females are five-foot-five and not all males are five-foot-nine. But on the average, males are taller than females. The range of differences listed below should be viewed like a continuum. In the same spirit of averages, neuroscientists have found many sexually determined differences in the biology of females and males. Some of these differences are:

- Length of the nerve cell connectors
- Nucleus volume in hypothalamus
- Pathways that the neurotransmitters follow
- Density of nerve cell strands
- Shape of the nucleus in the hypothalamus
- Thickness of left and right side of the cortex control centers
- The number of vasopressin neurons in the hypothalamus
- Thickness and weight of the corpus callosum
- Location of control centers for language, emotions, and spatial skills

Different Developmental Stages

Children's' brains develop at varying rates which can differ from a few months to three years and still be considered "normal." In addition, differences have been found in the developmental rates of boys and girls. This makes the assessment and grouping of children by age problematic. We don't group teachers or business people at their jobs by age; why should we group children in school this way?

In a study of two hundred right-handed children, the boys outperformed the girls on spatial tasks. But linguistically, the girls show earlier dominance than the boys. Boys often have trouble in learning to read early in life because of right brain specialization. Since reading is both spatial and linguistic, it makes sense that girls generally learn to read earlier than boys.

The brain not only grows differently, it decays differently. We now know that the right brain of females has longer plasticity than that of males. This means it stays open to growth and change for more years in girls than in boys. The degeneration of nerve cells in the male brain precedes that of females by 20 years. Although the rate of loss by females is greater than that of males, it is still not enough to overtake them. The researchers say that their estimates of cell loss are conservative.

Quotable

Developmentally, girls learn to talk and read earlier than boys on the average. Does this make it right to label the boys "slow learners" or "hyperactive?"

One of the reasons why adolescent boys are more physical than adolescent girls is that the part of brain used for such is more developed at that time in their life. On the other hand, in females, the part of the brain used for interpersonal skills is more developed and plays an integral role in teenage girl culture.

Gender-Differences in Thinking

Researchers report that female and male brains function quite differently with regard to sensory perception. In fact, when we say that the sexes live in different worlds, we may be more right than wrong. Females often report having experiences that males don't understand, such as intuition, food cravings or social interaction clues. Some of the differences, of course, are related to our social conditioning. The challenge for researchers is conducting experiments that have been controlled for cultural and social bias so that biological differences can be isolated. Some of the differences that have been documented follow:

Hearing

The female ear is better able to pick up nuances of voice, music and other sounds. In addition, females retain better hearing longer throughout life. Females have superior hearing, and at 85 decibels, they perceive the volume twice as loud as males. Females have greater vocal clarity and are one-sixth as likely as a male to be a monotone. They learn to speak earlier and learn languages more quickly. Three-quarters of university students majoring in foreign languages are female. Females excel at verbal memory and process language faster and more accurately. Infant girls are more comforted by singing and speech than males.

Vision

Males have better distance vision and depth perception than females. Females excel at peripheral vision. Males see better in brighter light; female eyesight is superior at night. Females are more sensitive to the red end of the spectrum, excel at visual memory, facial clues and context; and are better able to recognize faces and remember names. In repeated studies, females can store more random and irrelevant visual information than males.

Touch

Females have a more diffused and sensitive sense of touch. They react faster and more acutely to pain, yet can withstand pain over a longer duration than males. Males react more to extremes of temperature. Females have greater sensitivity in fingers and hands. They are superior in performing new motor combinations, and in fine motor dexterity.

Activity

Male infants play with objects more often than females. Females are more responsive to playmates. The directional choice, called "circling behavior," is opposite for males and females. In other words, when right-handed males walk over to a table to pick up an object, they are more likely to return by turning to their right. Right-handed females are more likely to return by circling around to their left.

Smell and Taste

Females have a stronger sense of smell and are much more responsive to aromas, odors and subtle changes in smell. They are more sensitive to bitter flavors and prefer sweet flavors. Females are more susceptible to the damaging effects of alcohol than males.

Problem-Solving Differences

Males and females have very different ways of approaching and solving problems. The following is a summary of the differences found in problem-solving tasks between genders.

In general, females do better than males in the following areas:

✦ Mathematical calculation
✦ Precision, fine-motor coordination
✦ Ideational fluency
✦ Finding, matching or locating missing objects
✦ Use of landmarks to recall locations in context, on maps

The problem-solving tasks that favor males are:

✦ Target-directed motor skills (archery, football, baseball, cricket, darts, etc.)
✦ Spatial: visually rotating objects
✦ Disembedding tests (locating objects, patterns from within another)
✦ Mathematical reasoning, word problems
✦ Use of spatial cues of distance, direction in route-finding

There are many activities in which females excel over males: assembly, needlework, precision crafting, micro-production, communication, sewing, nursing, pharmacology and many of the arts. On the average, girls read earlier than boys. And in general, females are more intuitive and multi-tasking, they relate better interpersonally, they score higher on matching exercises and on non-verbal skills, and are more likely to attribute failure to lack of ability rather than effort.

In general, males are more: single-task, issue-oriented, visual-kinesthetic, inductive or deductive and more likely to attribute lack of success to opportunity or effort, not ability. Though it is true that more boys than girls are identified as "developmentally slow," if we were to account for natural differences in developmental stages between girls and boys, we'd suddenly find that up to 75 percent of these boys would immediately be reclassified as normal. In addition, the areas in which males excel: gross motor skills like sports, mechanics, construction and sculpture, aren't always graded or valued in our traditional school setting.

So, we know that these differences are both environmental and genetic, but what can we do about them? Should education try to be culture or gender-bias free? There are real differences among cultures and between the sexes, does equal education mean that everything should be done the same for all individuals? These are complicated questions. And unfortunately, there is no single absolute good answer for each of them.

What we can do, however, is become more aware and informed. Learn the differences between culturally-reinforced stereotypes and physiological or genetic differences. Open up discussions with colleagues about the research and its implications. In the classroom, keep expectations high and avoid stereotyping. However, modify your expectations about an individual's behavior and learning based on what you know about them. Be holistic and ecological, using a "systems" approach to insure greater success. Educate others about differences. Many problems may not be problems at all. They may simply be an expression of the "natural" way in which a particular sex or learning style generally operates. Eliminate groupings by age or grade. They tend to cause feelings of inadequacy. Learners may be being measured erroneously against others at a different developmental stage, rather than by the effort they extend. Instead, students can be better clustered by age ranges, (i.e., 5 to 7 year olds, 8 to 10 year olds, 11 to 13 year olds, etc). The bigger your bag of response strategies to deal with the exceptional student and the variety of learning styles they rely on, the more successful you will be.

Attention Deficit Disorder

Attention Deficit Disorder (ADD) and Attention Deficit Hyperactivity Disorder (ADHD) are related conditions that fall under the rubric of learning disorders. At this time, there is no consensus about the definitive cause of ADD/ADHD, but there are numerous theories. ADD/ADHD is most typically characterized by learners who are easily distracted, talkative, forgetful, have poor concentration and productivity and are low in achievement. Additionally, ADHD is also characterized by hyperactive behavior. As quoted by authors Judyth Reichenberg-Ullman and Robert Ullman (1996):

> *At least two million children in the United States are currently taking stimulant medications (including Ritalin, Dexedrine, and Cylert) for ADD. That is more than 1 in every 30 children ages 5 to 18. In 1988 half a million children were being prescribed stimulants for ADD. The number has quadrupled in only eight years and is doubling every two years.*

The latest theories on the causes and remedies for this problem that has become all too prevalent among American youth. Let's take a look at the parts of the brain that regulate attention are the brain stem and limbic system. The influence of complex variations in the efficacy of chemical neurotransmitter molecules determine our attention patterns. Norepinephrine and dopamine (both catecholamines) are the principal neurotransmitter systems that process attention. Some researchers say that an insufficient number of these molecules may cause hyperactivity (Barkley, 1995). It is thought that learner attentiveness may be optimized with a "normal" middle level of these catecholamines. But is there more to it?

Other researchers believe that ADD/ADHD is a combination of conditions: a "rule-following disorder" (a dislike of following rules); a genetic disorder (in the linguistic-motor system where words and actions match up poorly); a high motivational threshold (it takes a great incentive for seemingly simple tasks); and a problem of self-regulation (a disturbance in the child's ability to use self control with regard to the future). The disorder is so situational, that if we take an ADHD child out of school and put him/her in a different setting, the symptoms often disappear (Barkley, 1995).

By using Magnetic Resonance Imaging (MRI) scans, it was discovered that ADHD children had a smaller corpus callosum, particularly in the region of the genu and splenium and its anterior. Therefore, some researchers suggest that deviations in normal corticogenesis may underlie behavioral manifestations of this disorder. Translated this means that children with attention deficit disorder may suffer from a right hemisphere syndrome. Simply put, the left and right side of the brain don't talk to each other as well as they should. Another theory holds that many learners labeled ADD/ADHD are really normal; and simply exhibiting learning styles that can be disruptive in the classroom setting (Grinder, 1989).

Very often problems associated with ADD/ADHD are treated successfully by drug therapy. While sometimes vitamin B-6 works, Ritalin™ and Cylert™ are the most popular drugs prescribed. Stimulant drugs like Ritalin™ work to normalize the brain's reaction to distracting stimuli, improving concentration and focus. While the drug seems to work miracles for some, a growing contingency of parents are concerned about the principle behind prescribing behavior-altering drugs at an early age. Some people are worried that serious other problems are being masked by drug therapy. Some are concerned that drugs for the treatment of ADD/ADHD are over prescribed when alternative therapies (like homeopathy, psychological counseling, and diet changes) might be effective. (Reichenberg-Ullman & Ullman, 1996). Others are concerned about the side-effects of prescription drugs or a lifelong dependency upon them.

The best recommendation for treating learners who exhibit symptoms of ADD/ADHD is to start with the simplest things first. Begin eliminating variables. Discover if the student is more kinesthetic or has a rule-following cognitive disorder. Then focus on diet changes. Stay open-minded about symptoms and treatment. If one classroom strategy or method of treatment is not working, it's not a hopeless case. Switch to another. Seek professional advice; and get as many opinions as possible.

It is true that many more boys than girls are diagnosed as ADD/ADHD; however, since most hyperactive behavior disappears in boys over time, it's a dubious sex-based label. When differences are factored in between normal male and female developmental stages, the label and condition gets diluted even more. There is a considerable movement developing worldwide that is focuses on creating appropriate gender-based learning models that consider developmental stages, and other differences, between genders.

Michael Grinder, author of the book *Righting the Educational Conveyor Belt*, says that some students diagnosed as hyperactive may, in fact, simply be expressing their particular learning styles. A kinesthetic learner may want to move around, touch, tap, hit, try out and engage his/her body in almost everything.

This learner is more likely to be male. If the teacher is visual, the movement may be attention-getting and, at times, annoying. To the teacher, this is a "problem student" but, in fact, the student may be perfectly "normal."

Dyslexia

Dyslexia, a reading disability, in individuals with apparently adequate intellectual and perceptual abilities, has also become a subject of great debate. Perhaps the most promising research on dyslexia (and hyperactivity) comes from researchers who have made strong correlations to inner ear problems. It seems that infection-related fluids (effusion) interfere with hearing which interferes with auditory perception and processing. Some studied have shown an incidence of cerebellar-vestibular dysfunction in dyslexics which has been successfully treated in many dyslexics with a combination motion-sickness drugs and repatterning exercises.

Some research correlates dyslexia to factors like: excessive lead in the water supply, emotional problems stemming from inadequate family stability, food additives (especially red dye, aspartame, preservatives and artificial flavors), excess sugar, a couch-potato lifestyle, refined carbohydrates, and excessive television watching. Whichever turns out to be the cause, it will be some time before we know for sure. There is understandably enormous difficulty in isolating specific behaviors and testing all the variables that could possibly influence them. Unfortunately, as difficult as it is to find a definitive cause for dyslexia, it is just as difficult to determine how to effectively deal with this troubling reading problem. Various strategies, however, have been suggested; and each of them uses brain research applications to help the learner *manage* the disability. For treatment options, contact www.fastforward.com.

The Influence of Color

Researchers M. Livingstone, et. al. (1991) say that our brain processes sensory information on two separate parallel paths. The faster sensory system notes the location in the background. The slower system, in the foreground, processes what the objects are. In dyslexics, the faster system is sluggish and doesn't delete quickly enough the previous word or words seen. As a result, when eyes move from word-to-word, the reader experiences blurring and fusing of words. Special colored lenses (called Irlen) can help the reader successfully deal with this problem.

On the other hand, others disagree with this approach. They say that the supposed benefits of tinted lenses are unsubstantiated. They also contend that recent experiments have proven that the intervention of colored lenses is insupportable.

The Influence of Sounds

Since dyslexics are frequently right hemisphere dominant, they miss out on many key sounds. In addition, a split second delay in the routing of information within the brain, when it has to cross hemispheres twice, creates a time delay in understanding oral instructions. This makes super-attentive listening a requirement for dyslexics. But that can get exhaustive when it has to go on for more than a few minutes. As a result, the dyslexic child tends to lose attention and fall further behind in learning.

Re-training the Eyes

Some researchers suggest that dyslexia has to do with spatial orientation. They have defined a point of perception in space which is called the "visuo-awareness epicenter." The location of this epicenter varies among individuals. For example, a boxer's epicenter is 16 feet above his head; a race car driver's, 30 feet in front. For best reading, the epicenter may need to be within inches of the head - above and behind. When the brain is re-trained to be in control of this roving center of awareness, reading improves dramatically. This method is not a panacea but a learning process."

Inner-Ear Problems

Some researchers have made strong correlations of dyslexia to inner-ear problems. It seems that infection-related fluids (effusion) interferes with hearing which interferes with auditory perception and processing. That would make sense, since Many dyslexics have hearing difficulties. Why? A hearing defect in the range of 500-cycles-per-second prevents hearing the quieter, more easily-confused voiceless consonants, such as M, N, P and B. The left hemisphere is specialized for hearing clicks and other closed sounds, while the right is more sensitive to vowels.

Prenatal Influence

Some research suggests that dyslexia may be influenced by prenatal affects. It is thought that during key times of cell migration in the developing embryo, certain groups of neurons end up in the "wrong" areas causing poor reading but encouraging mechanical or creative abilities. Many creative people, (i.e., composers, painters, producers, athletes, singers, and musicians) confirm that they are dyslexic, including: Cher, Mohammed Ali, Madonna, and Dustin Hoffman, just to name a few.

A large number of students who are having a tough time in school have learning disabilities that can be successfully treated and/or managed. Stay informed. The information available on learning disabilities is growing.Find out what school and community resources are available to assist you. Keep a printed list of your findings available for easy access when necessary. Share your information with others.

Drug Abuse

The problems of drug abuse are surprisingly widespread; not only with regard to the types of drugs used, but who is affected. Suffice it to say, anyone, even students from "functional" families in good neighborhoods, can have problems with drugs. The diverse panel of drugs being widely used by students in most schools today include the following:

Common Drugs Used Today:

- *Alcohol*
- *Marijuana*
- *No-doz, Vivarin™*
- *Ritalin™ crystals*
- *Glue, paint, and other inhalants*
- *Cocaine, crack*
- *Methamphetamines, speed, crystal*
- *Cold remedies*
- *Valium*
- *Pain narcotics*
- *LSD, mushrooms, acid*
- *Poppers*
- *Ecstacy*
- *Angel dust*
- *Heroin*

Learn to read the behaviors of habitual drug users. Have someone from the local police department come to your school and talk to your staff and students about the appropriate steps to take when you suspect someone is a drug abuser. Find out what your school's policy is on drug use and be ready to act on it. When you have a student who you think is involved with drugs, seek intervention. You may be the best hope he or she has in getting help with the problem. Ask for assistance from your school's psychologist, nurse or counseling department. Ignoring the issue will not chase it away. Be proactive. don't wait until a student overdoses and everyone says, "Why didn't anyone do anything?"

Gifted and Talented Learners

Are there learners who are "more intelligent?" The way this question is answered depends on what you mean by intelligence. If you buy into the notion of a fixed intelligence, you could say that some learners are more intelligent. But our intelligence is not fixed and can develop in many ways with proper enrichment. Howard Gardner's theory of multiple intelligences (1993) suggests gifted and talented programs are, at their best, ignoring what we now know about the brain. At worst, they are very elitist and damaging. Why? The determination of who is gifted and who is not is based on an outdated model. The following reflect some of the false assumptions gifted programs make:

False: Giftedness can be measured or predicted.
True: The majority of society's greatest contributors were *not* identified as gifted in school.

False: So-called average (or below average) students do not benefit from an enriched gifted program.
True: Research suggests that all learners benefit from enriched programs.

False: There are only a few truly gifted learners.
True: Master Japanese violin teacher Suzuki proved he could teach competent-level violin playing to any child. Glen and Janet Doman of the Institute for Human Potential in Philadelphia have been teaching babies math and reading skills before age three. Unless there is brain damage or a specific disease preventing it, each of us can develop some form of genius.

False: Special talents and abilities are genetic.
True: Research suggests that genetics account for about 30 percent of the special talents of individuals. This means that the majority of our talent, intelligence, and ability is up to us and our environment.

False: There is something special about gifted learners (Those who are dominantly visual learners are more often labeled as "talented and gifted").
True: Visual learners are often quieter, read better, focus longer, and pay attention to the teacher. For many teachers, having a student like this is a real "gift" in their class! The irony in this is that many individuals who have made major contributions to science and society (i.e., Steven Hawking, Steven Spielberg, Walt Disney, Martin Luther King, Albert Einstein, Stevie Wonder, Ray Charles, Spike Lee, and Quincy Jones, just to name a few) were all labeled "problem" students at one time or another. What does this tell you about the value of labeling? Maybe it's time to re-examine how we assess learners. Creating enriched environments for some and not others (based on somebody's erroneous declaration of giftedness) is not only unfair, it is illogical.

How about pullout programs for students with special needs - are they ineffective, as well? The key to answering this question is understanding that there is a difference between teaching content and process. Many pullout (special education) programs teach primarily content. They simply teach it slower, using more flexibility, and stronger relationships. By itself, that's not bad. But in the larger context of education, it does more of a disservice (unless it is done "right") than a service since students then become stigmatized as "slow learners." The impact of this label on a student's self-concept can be devastating and lifelong.

Is There a Better Way?

Should we end all pullout programs? No. However, doing it "right" means that all pullout programs should be teaching process and values, *not* content. For example, rather than teaching students to spell particular words, teach them a system of *how* to spell. Rather than always facilitating the learning activities, teach students *how* to facilitate their own learning. Teach them about eye-accessing cues, learning-style profiles, graphic organizers and mindmaps, communication and social skills. Help them gain increased self-confidence through mastering skills and strategies rather than content. These students should be out of regular classes just long enough to receive the additional training they need to return comfortably to the mainstream classroom.

Reflection:

What kinds of process skills do you currently teach? Can you think of any process skills that you were taught or somehow learned that have been especially valuable?

Reactions:

What are your feelings about the topics presented in this chapter?

What are some practical applications for what you're learning?

What do you want to remember from this chapter?

Life is a bowl of cherries. It's full of pits. Whether you control your life or it controls you, depends, in large measure, on your ability to spit out the pits.

Richard Saunders
Jump Start Your Brain

Chapter 5

Mental Models of Success

Chapter Preview:

- ✦ **Secret to Teaching Success**
- ✦ **The Pygmalion Effect**
- ✦ **The Teacher as Catalyst**
- ✦ **The "Demand Model" Versus the "Discovery Model"**
- ✦ **You Make a Difference in the World**
- ✦ **You Have the Power of Choice**
- ✦ **It's Your Job to Enter the Student's World**
- ✦ **The Meaning of Your Communication**
- ✦ **There Are No Failures**
- ✦ **Feedback Is Critical**
- ✦ **The Primary Cause of Learner Failure**
- ✦ **All Students Are Gifted**
- ✦ **We Are Conditioned by Our Beliefs**
- ✦ **Your Conversation Affects Your Results**
- ✦ **A Low Ego Works Best**
- ✦ **Authenticity Works Better Than Acting**
- ✦ **The Tao of Teaching**
- ✦ **The New Role of the Super-Teacher**

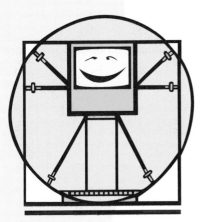

Secret to Teaching Success

The secret to successful teaching is contained in "mental models." Mental models are the frameworks, belief systems, thought patterns, paradigms and sets of operating principles upon which our thoughts and behaviors are based. We all have mental models - even if we aren't conscious of it. A mental model that inspires a teacher to make smart decisions most of the time, build or preserve student dignity, and spark motivation in a way that appears to be almost magical, is the mark of an excellent teacher. This chapter illuminates the "right stuff," the key factors that successful teachers seem to possess. How important are these factors?

The *Harvard Educational Review* discussed students educated in a poor neighborhood of Montreal. Despite the likelihood to the contrary, two-thirds of the former pupils of "Ms. A" achieved the highest level of adult status, while the remaining third were classified as "medium status." None of her former students fell into the "low" group. Years later, the students remembered her unshakable faith in their ability to learn and the extra time and attention she provided them. Both the students and the teacher remembered one another well and their special times together. Another teacher in the Washington D.C. area has had, among his students, four who later became Nobel Prize winners. One would be a coincidence, two would raise an eyebrow, but four is simply stunning.

To have that kind of long-lasting influence, a teacher needs even more than great lesson plans, subject mastery, and well-polished presentation skills. One study asked individual teachers to describe values, beliefs, attitudes, and their correlation (if any) to results in the classroom. It demonstrated conclusively that teachers with better classroom results had a certain set of attitudes about themselves, learning, and their students.

The Pygmalion Effect

In the classic book on teaching, *Pygmalion in the Classroom*, authors Robert Rosenthal and Lenote Jacobsen remind us of the power of our own beliefs. The book is based on a study where a teacher was told that a group of students were highly intelligent. In fact, the students had tested well below normal and often displayed behavioral problems. However, the unknowing teacher who believed these were gifted students treated them like gifted students. The more the teacher treated them that way, the more they responded that way. She literally created gifted students. This study, 40 years old, is still the most eloquent statement about the power you have over the success of your students. What you believe, you will create. Do you think you were given a class of "low ability" kids? If so, you will prove your beliefs to be true.

Remember a time when you thought someone was prowling around your house. You probably felt fear. Then, later, you discovered that it was only the wind or the neighbor's pet. The "prowler" caused your reaction of fear, even though he didn't actually exist! Although it was an illusion, your mind and body reacted as if the prowler was real. The "as if" principle asserts: act as if something is true and you will get the same effect as if it is true. Thus, teachers who believe that every one of their students is gifted will get the same results as those teachers who, in fact, teach officially gifted students.

What's Changed?

Old:
Teacher teaches, students perform, teacher assesses.

New:
Teacher is a catalyst for student learning and student self-assessment.

The Teacher as Catalyst

Indeed, the times, they are a changing! Many teachers today think of themselves as "learning catalysts." A whole paradigm shift is taking place. Where once teachers were perceived as the "controllers" of a classroom and authority figures to be obeyed, this image is outdated and not effective in today's public education environment. The old definition basically implied a top-down power structure — "I'm in charge, you are less than I." Instead, a learning catalyst sees their role as promoting learning in whatever form is appropriate. They are fully skilled in the use of multiple intelligences and the learning styles models. They are skilled at reading and managing student's states. They utilize and integrate technology, mind-mapping, accelerated learning, peripherals, music and art across the curriculum. They give learners choice and variety, with plenty of feedback. And more importantly, they've not only had exposure to these methods, they use them consistently and with confidence.

The "Demand Model" Versus the "Discovery Model"

A common method of teaching, known as behaviorism: 1) determine desirable student behaviors; 2) measures learner's behaviors; 3) rewards the positive behaviors; and 4) punishes the negative ones. This model of teaching which is based on operant conditioning is attributed to psychologist B.F. Skinner. It might also be called the "demand model"; and it is basically outdated. The climate of the classroom today is rather one of student empowerment, honoring the individual, and encouraging critical thinking and expression. Teaching with a heavy hand does not facilitate such values. The new model presumes that students want to learn, that learning can be joyful, and that learning how to learn and having a love of learning is more important than drilling, knowing rote facts, and testing well.

You Make a Difference in the World

You are a biological miracle. Unless you are an identical twin, there has never been, nor will there ever be, another person like you in human history. You bring a unique bundle of mind, heart, spirit and skills to your learners. No one before you and no one since will offer what you have; and therefore, you have a responsibility to share it with others. You are a once-in-forever celestial event. Be responsible and bring forth your gifts to others.

Some people have the erroneous attitude that only *certain* people really matter, and that the rest are simply pawns on the chessboard of life. Upon closer inspection, every so-called important person has many others who support and make possible what he or she does. Every one of us does matter and because of that, everything we do, large or small, adds to the sum total of contributions. We are the pebble that redirects the flow of water, that then alters the flow of a stream, that then changes the riverbanks, that then alters the landscape, that then fills the lakes, that then provides water for thousands, that then evaporates into clouds, that then changes the weather, and that then ultimately affects the fate of humanity.

What's Changed?

Old:
Behaviorist theory: student as subject; teacher identifies, measures and demands desirable outcomes, based on reward and punishment.

New:
This approach asks, "How does the human brain naturally learn best; and what can we do to provide it the optimal environment?"

Because you do make a difference, every part of your life is worth attention. For example, does it matter if you say "hello" to the student in the back of the room? Absolutely! Does it matter if you take the extra time to better prepare your lesson plan? Everything you do, in some way, contributes to your students, as well as to the educational system. This attitude also says that the value you add to the lives of your students will also enrich your own life.

Here's an example. As a teacher, if you excite and inspire just 10 students from your class, and each of those kids relates their enthusiasm to 10 other kids, how many have you actually affected? The answer is obviously 10 times 10 or one hundred students! Can you imagine the cumulative effect over a period of years? That's why every student is valuable, unique, and important. Each student is deserving of both your time and respect.

You Have the Power of Choice

Top performers in any field have the attitude (whether true or not) that they are free to feel and experience exactly what they choose. After all, if we're not in charge of our own thoughts and experiences, who is? There are people, however, who believe that someone or something else is responsible for the way they think and feel as evidenced by expressions like: "You make me so happy!" "You make me mad." "You frustrate me!" Or "The way you do that makes me nervous." All of these statements are born out of a belief that someone else can force us to have certain feelings or experiences. A super-teacher chooses his or her own feelings, and chooses the appropriate ones for the situation. Instead of "you make me so frustrated," a super-teacher accepts responsibility by saying "I feel frustrated at this moment." In order to be able to manage a productive classroom, we must have control over our own attitudes and responses.

The essence of our humanity is our power of choice. That power resides in the moment between a stimulus and our response. In that split second (what may seem like an eternity) we either have a knee-jerk reaction or we react responsibly. We also have a choice over both what we experience externally and internally. This means that you can choose how to feel regardless of whether you are in a traffic jam, a rainstorm, or a class of so-called problem students. This means that it is your choice to feel frustrated, happy, sad, or peaceful. You are choosing your job, your friends, your spouse, and how you spend your free time. You are not a helpless victim. At any point on life's merry-go-round, you can change horses, enjoy the one you're on, or get off the ride completely.

An interesting corollary to this attitude is it can allow you to make the shift from considering yourself responsible-guilty (as in "Who's to blame?") to being responsible-accountable (as in "I'm here to create opportunities for you"). If every year you have lazy unmotivated students no matter what school or grade level you teach, guess what the common element is in all of these situations? The teacher makes it possible for motivation and high energy to be present (by creating opportunities) *or* makes it impossible for success qualities to manifest (by not creating opportunities). Accountability is one of the most important qualities a teacher can have.

It's Your Job to Enter the Student's World

Successful teachers consider the student's point of view. If a student's interest is motorcycles, the teacher might relate the course materials, in some way, to motorcycles. If the student does not understand the material, the successful teacher adjusts his/her approach. Does this sound like more work? Initially, it is. Does it work? Dramatically well. As students start taking responsibility for their learning, learn how to learn, and enjoy learning, your job, in the long run, becomes easier.

What's Changed?

Old:
Teacher presents his or her viewpoint of the world as the truth; students are expected to conform to this view.

New:
Teacher finds out from learners what their preferred learning style is, what their mental model is, and enters the student's world to optimize communication and learning.

The Meaning of Your Communication

If you explain photosynthesis to your students and they don't understand it, you might be inclined to make a quick judgment. You might assume, for instance, that they are a bit slow, that they didn't do their homework, that the topic is too tough for their level of understanding, or that it's an off day for them. The problem with any of these choices is that none will accomplish the objective of insuring that your students understand photosynthesis.

The solution? Acknowledge that regardless of how clearly you *think* you explained the material, the students didn't understand it. Remember, your commitment is to do what will make the students successful. Then "repackage" or reformat what you just said until your students get it. If you say "green" and they hear "red," simply try another approach until they receive the meaning you intended. The meaning of your communication is the response you get. This approach is known as "flexible teaching."

The only problem with this belief is that it means that you will be constantly reformulating what you say because you have ceased to blame it on the students. Yet something exciting happens when you adopt this belief: the quality of your communication increases along with student rapport and respect. The shift is from blaming others and justifying poor results to being accountable for results which is a much more exciting way to teach. The side effect is not bad either — better learning is achieved.

There Are No Failures

Okay, so let's say a teacher accepts responsibility for their communications as well as what goes on in the rest of their class; after awhile, they might begin to feel that they fail a lot. That is, unless they hold to the belief that each time one "fails" at something one learns something; and that each learning experience is valuable and needed. If a teacher believes that learning something new is more important than "looking good" or avoiding failure, they begin to enjoy the former so-called failures and see them as gifts. Or, at worst, see them as simply a result or outcome from which to learn.

So then, what's a failure? Only a learning moment! What if each time you had a so-called failure, it actually provided you with a valuable and useful lesson which made you a better person? That's exactly what top teachers believe. They believe that regardless of what happens in their classroom, they and their students can learn, grow, and excel from the experience.

What's Changed?

Old:
Avoid mistakes - they're bad. Mark students down for poor results.

New:
Mistakes provide valuable feedback and an opportunity to grow. We can use them positively and learn from them.

In this sense, a "failure" then is as good as success. Each and every experience builds knowledge, and increases the chances of the next event being more closely aligned with the desired results. Are we turning lemons into lemonade? Absolutely! This approach is highly effective in attaining personal excellence because it forces us to learn something from every experience. There's nothing wrong with "failures" - it's only when you don't learn from them that an outcome is truly a failure.

Imagine how much fun you'd have in life if you held the belief that every adversity carries with it the seeds of an equal or greater gift! It's a well-worn cliché, but it's as true as ever: what you look for, you shall find. Look for the negative and you'll find it. Look for a gift in your mistakes, and you'll find it, too. Welcome mistakes knowing that any person who doesn't make them is certainly risking very little.

Feedback Is Critical

If mistakes are really opportunities to learn something, then feedback is absolutely essential to self-correction and classroom mastery. One's progress towards mastery ought really be measured by one's willingness to be coached. To the degree that you allow input from qualified others, and apply the input, you'll improve. Teaching means you must be willing to be a student yourself. In fact, your students will learn from you at the rate that you learn from them.

If you're trying out new things in the classroom, you can expect to have many learning experiences. With each new class, teachers start the learning process all over again to determine how individual students think and organize their reality. The best way to get to know your students is to ask them, or to try a new method with them which naturally leads to some unsuccessful outcomes.

A more useful label for failure, hence, is feedback. Success then comes easier knowing that failure is no longer possible, only outcomes or feedback. Correction, without invalidation, is indeed, one of the real keys to mastery. Masters use such phrases as "Wow, I learned how not to do it that time!" or, "Wow, this is an apparent mess. What can I learn from this?" Reframing the meaning of the word failure, therefore; and replacing it with the word lesson or gift will move students closer to their goals.

The Primary Cause of Learner Failure

With so many types of learners in the classroom, flexibility on the part of the teacher is essential. In fact, inflexible teaching is the primary cause of learner failure! Now, you may be saying "Wait a minute, I know how important planning is, how can I plan and be flexible at the same time?" And you're right, this takes more time initially. But remember, if you believe it is your responsibility to get through to students in whatever way you have to, you will become a better teacher. However, if you claim that your responsibility is only to present the information and then it's the student's responsibility to understand it, you might as well just mail them a book.

It is far more productive to suspend judgments about your students; after all, they are merely responding to your leadership. Students don't get up in the morning and say to themselves, "I think I'll resist learning today." The natural tendency is to want to learn since most learning occurs nonconsciously. Our job, as learning catalysts, is to make learning as much fun for our students as it was in kindergarten. As you implement greater flexibility in teaching strategies, you will also likely eliminate tracking, grouping, and hierarchies of "intelligence." In the extreme, inflexible teaching has led at times to the labeling of some students as "untrainable." With flexible teaching strategies, even students with IQs below 50 have been taught and trained for jobs. This represents super-teaching!

What's Changed?

Old:
Some students are going to fail no matter what is done. That's just the way it is.

New:
Instill an attitude of success. Increase your own flexibility and your students' success rates will soar along with your own.

All Students Are Gifted

The work of Harvard Psychologist Howard Gardner (1993) suggests that we have not one or two, but multiple intelligences. He says each of us has our own unique package of intelligences that are definitely worth developing. It is interesting to think that rarely does a kindergarten student fail. Why? Because kindergarten teachers think of their children as potential astronauts, writers, dancers, fathers, scientists, engineers, nurses, teachers, designers, mothers and leaders. Their classrooms are usually full of music, movement, storytelling, art, interacting and role-playing. How often do we see all of these multiple intelligences reflected in a high school science, English, math, or history class? Not enough!

The same student who flunks a math test at school may be a star surfer, socialite, or car mechanic. The student who writes poorly may be a good video game player, actress, or chef. The student who is doing poorly in all of his or her classes may be the most creative, resourceful, and powerful neighborhood gang leader. When you treat your students as if they are gifted - you'll make enlightening discoveries about their resources and abilities in creativity, flexibility, social skills, leadership, and problem-solving.

All of our students have talents and gifts, our job is to find useful applications for them in the classroom and to create mechanisms for responsibility. Some students, for instance, may just need an opportunity to use their "street skills" in an academic setting. Soon your students will feel like they have a purpose, and will begin to reassess their potential to succeed in a scholastic setting. Students want to succeed. Give them the chance by letting them use, inside the classroom, what they already do well outside of school.

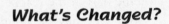

What's Changed?

Old:
Let's test students to find out if they are gifted or not.

New:
Let's bring out the giftedness in every learner we can.

The rural student who does home chores and looks after his/her siblings has developed the attributes of perseverance, commitment, dedication, and loyalty. Enhance these qualities in the classroom. The best teachers assume that every student is gifted. They simply act "as if" and as a result they get better performances from their students. And ultimately their students enjoy learning, leading naturally to stronger self-esteem.

We Are Conditioned by Our Beliefs

Over time, each of us has learned what can be done or what is possible, and what cannot be done. Yet each person seems to produce different results. This tells us that our beliefs and attitudes, which have conditioned us very powerfully, vary widely from person to person. This variance about what we believe we can and cannot do is subtle, but easily measured in the classroom. When translated into teacher expectations of student performance, these beliefs can dramatically affect behavior. When you believe your students will do better, they usually do.

As teachers, we are all biased. There are no "objective" teachers. In an exhaustive review of teacher behaviors, the following subjective biases were discovered which have a powerful effect on student performance:

✦ *Unconscious Reactions:* You may dislike or like a student simply because he or she unconsciously reminds you of your own child or a neighbor's. All it takes is an action, a comment, or a look that you associate with another child, and the instant association is made.

✦ *Cognitive Dissonance:* We often have a tendency to ignore evidence which is inconsistent with our expectations or prior experience. Your least-liked student can make a brilliant deduction and you're much more likely to ignore it than if it was from your class "genius."

✦ *Halo Effect:* We often allow one characteristic to overshadow others as an umbrella or behavioral "halo." For instance, if your favorite student has a small annoying habit, you are more likely to discount it and be more forgiving.

✦ *Projection:* One tendency is to see in others the things we like or dislike the most about ourselves. This creates a strong subjective "filter" through which you evaluate behaviors.

These influences make it difficult to single out a particular variable as the reason for a student's change in performance. As a top teacher, your goal is to reduce your bias and subjectivity as much as possible. Although many factors are present, at least start with the awareness that you are likely to be biased! The bottom line is that teacher subjectivity is a dominant influence in student performance.

Your Conversation Affects Your Results

It is interesting to note that one distinction between average and true master-level teachers is reflected in their conversation styles — both internal (what you say to yourself) and external (what you say to others). The single greatest difference is that master teachers have conversations about possibilities while less effective teachers talk about complaints, problems, and limitations.

In other words, top teachers talk about how they want things to be, what might happen, openings for success, student breakthroughs, new ideas, untapped potential within students, and opportunities for their work. The less effective teachers have conversations about the limitations of their students, how bad things are, how no one listens to them, how they were right all along, what's wrong with education, and who is to blame for the problems at their school.

Possibility or complaint? That's the distinction to be made in your conversations. What's the possibility that your students are actually twice as smart as they appear to be, but you are actually stunting their growth? What's the possibility that homework can be joyful instead of a drag? Or that learning can be fun instead of a rut? Super-teachers converse with students about their potential, rather than complaining about their failures. Very few people feel empowered by complaints about them. Begin to monitor your conversations with students, and others. You may be surprised to discover how powerful your thoughts are, and how they impact your reality!

There Are No Unresourceful Students

Every teacher has encountered the student who appears to be slow, unmotivated, or incapable; yet, that same student can rebuild a motorcycle from the ground up or write magnificent love letters. A key principle, one that super-teachers know and live by is this: all behavior is state-related. What your students do has more to do with their momentary state than their abilities or capacity. All of us go through moments when we are exhausted, tired, depressed, or doubtful. During such times, even the most well-trained educator can be as unresourceful as the student in their approach. To change the behavior, however, the teacher needs to influence the state of the learner. Some strategies for altering student's states are presented in later chapters.

What's Changed?

Old:
Label students based on their classroom performance.

New:
Treat negative class behaviors as temporary and every student as having unlimited potential.

Each Person Does Their Best

Evidence shows that successful teachers are compassionate and understanding. How can you acquire such traits? The answer is simple. It's a matter of whether or not you believe that every student is doing his or her best. Super-teachers, those who teach with compassion, understanding, and know how have a different belief about people than average or below-average teachers. The belief is this: Each person's behavior makes total and perfect sense when understood from the context of that individual's reality.

Since each student has had a different upbringing, different parents, different information to access, different experiences and in fact, lives in a different world than you, their behavior is totally appropriate, regardless of how illogical, bizarre, stupid, crazy or sick it might seem to you. If you had the exact same everything (parents, home, history, etc.) as your students, your behavior would have to be very similar to theirs. In reality, we'll never know if this belief is true or not. We don't have a control group to study. But if you follow this belief and its implications, you'll be much more successful.

The expression that a student is "doing their best," refers to the best for that student, not for you or anyone else. There should be something more added: "Everyone is always doing their best given: 1) the context; 2) the perceived choices available; and 3) the intended outcome. Considering these three qualifiers, people are always trying to, meaning to, and actually doing the best that they can. *You* might be able to do better, but your students are not you. If you keep reminding yourself of this, you'll gain much peace of mind and compassion for others in a world of seemingly wacky behavior.

> ### Quotable
>
> *The super-teacher's mission is to rediscover the childhood joys of learning with their students as their partners.*

When you understand that each student is always doing their best, their behavior is then viewed with positive intent. You may ask, "But what about the student who defaces school property, assaults others, or just doesn't show up?" The answer is the same: the intent is positive, even though the method used to achieve that outcome is deplorable. When a student assaults another or defaces property, the positive intent may be to clear his/her anger, resolve a feud, gain peer acceptance or build a sense of importance. When you ask why a person exhibits delinquent behavior, there's always a good reason, to that person. Super-teachers try then to create outlets, avenues, and alternative methods for the positive intents to be transformed to positive behaviors.

A Low Ego Works Best

Your teaching methods and strategies may follow many different paths. There are many good options. A very important addition to the mix, however, is to maintain a low ego investment in your work. Teachers whose egos aren't in check often exhibit these behaviors:

✦ Wanting to let students know when they make a mistake
✦ Resisting picking up the trash on the floor in your room
✦ Wanting students to remember you at the end of the year
✦ Wanting to be right about something in debate or discussion
✦ Hoping students will like you and think highly of you

- Having it be important to look smart, witty, or charming
- Making students wrong for forgetting something
- Having your own life be more important than your student's
- Keeping things the same, protecting the status quo

The above actions all radiate from the point of view of a super-ego, rather than a super-teacher. The ego is the part of us that tries to protect us from looking bad, being wrong, or being at blame. Having a big ego should not be mistaken for having high self-esteem or self-confidence. Rather, it reflects an elevated concern for what others think, and an effort to cover oneself from being accountable. There is a better way.

Keeping your ego in check means that you are more concerned about what is true to yourself and your own integrity instead of what others think. Having a low ego means others come first, not in the sense of harming oneself, but in the sense of allowing others to be "the star." The list described above looks different when it reflects the behaviors of a low ego person:

- Letting your own humility and mistakes set an example
- Never being too proud to do "whatever it takes" to help
- Wanting to allow others to be heard and acknowledged
- Wanting students to experience how great they are
- Having it be important to make others look good
- Making it safe for students to admit their own mistakes
- Getting satisfaction by helping others make their life a success

One of the easiest ways to measure your ego is to ask yourself a simple question: "What am I committed to, getting credit or having my students get credit?" Also, note the amount of change you are comfortable with in your life. The ego wants to protect status quo, hence, resists new ideas and change. But quality teaching requires risk-taking and change.

Authenticity Works Better Than Acting

All of us have our acts. These are roles that we play, hats that we wear, and personalities that we exhibit. Acting provides us with great flexibility in our behaviors. Acting can also protect us, in a sense, because if someone rejects us, they are really only rejecting our act. The danger comes, however, when we start believing our acts and thinking that we *are* our acts, or when we hide behind our acts. Sometimes our act is an attempt to be interesting, cute or theatrical instead of being genuinely interested in others. If you act aloof or "cool" when it's time to admit a mistake, the risk is that students will never get to know who you really are, and the example being set is not one of accountability or personal responsibility.

What's Changed?

Old:
The teacher as the boss, the star, the autocrat of the classroom.

New:
The students as proactive, responsible, capable stars of the classroom.

Trying to be perfect or totally "together" for your students is not necessary; in fact, it is detrimental. Rather, make it okay for your students to make mistakes by admitting your own imperfection. The solution is to be authentic. Your students ought to be able to recognize when you're acting and when you're not; and they are learning from your responses. What are you *really* teaching?

The Tao of Teaching

As a super-teacher, there is no big "ta-da" or end point to celebrate your arrival. Teaching, as a profession, requires continuing education to stay in tune with its changing nature. One strategy for staying motivated and committed to the profession is to attend professional development trainings, classes and workshops. You have probably developed a wide-range of motivational techniques to use at your disposal. The writings of Lao Tzu have been one such motivational strategy for me. Translated, Lao Tzu's, *Tao Te Ching* means "the book of how things work." Written in the fifth century BC., it has long been a classic in both Chinese and world literature. Its much-loved wisdom has well withstood the test of time.

It is likely that many of Lao Tzu's sayings are familiar to you. For instance, "The journey of a thousand miles begins with a single step" is one. Not surprisingly, the best teachers seem to include ancient wisdom as well as modern devices in their teaching toolbox. Included in the bibliography is a book that is an adaptation of Lao Tzu's work, entitled *The Tao of Leadership* by John Heider (1985). The following is a synopsis of its philosophy:

A wise teacher lets others have the floor. A good teacher is better than a spectacular teacher. Otherwise, the teacher outshines the teachings. Be a mid-wife to learning - facilitate what is happening, rather than what you think ought to be happening. Silence says more than words; pay much attention to it. Continual classroom drama clouds inner work. Allow time for genuine insight. A good reputation arises naturally from doing good work. But do not nourish the reputation, the anxiety will be endless; rather nourish the work. To know what is happening, relax and do not try to figure things out. Listen quietly, be calm and use reflection. Let go of selfishness; it only blocks your universality.

Let go of your ego, and you will receive what you need. Give away credit, and you get more. When you feel most destroyed, you are most ready to grow. When you desire nothing, much comes to you. The less you make of yourself, the more you are. Instead of trying hard, be easy: teach by example, and more will happen. Trying to appear brilliant is not enlightened. The gift of a great teacher is creating an awareness of greatness in others. Because the teacher can see clearly, light is shed on others. Teach as both a warrior and a healer; both a leader and a yielder. Constant force and intervention will backfire as will constant yielding. One cannot push the river; a leader's touch is light. Making others do what you want them to do can become a failure. While they may momentarily comply, their revenge may come in many forms. That is why your victory may be a loss. To manage other lives takes strength; to manage your own life is real power.

Much of an ineffective teacher's time is spent trying to *make* things go differently or *disputing* what actually is occurring. An unwise teacher pushes or forces people and situations; and as a result, is annoyed a lot. For you to grow as a master teacher, you must know what teaching really is about. It is about serving others, facilitating the discovery of each person's highest self, humility, acknowledgment, and allowing others the respect and love they need to grow.

The New Role of the Super-Teacher

The old model of a classroom teacher "filling up" students with knowledge is obsolete. The role which is more effective in today's changing world is that of a coach - one who uncovers talent and learning, and instructs and inspires in the fundamentals. This represents a delicate but essential shift in thinking. The top names and biggest winners in sports coaching history all taught much more than the sport, itself. The legends, Vince Lombardi, Don Schula, Red Aurbach, Don Coryell, "Bear" Bryant and John Wooden, for example, each believed in building character, as well as technical skill. And all of these coaches had a powerful affect on the personal lives of their athletes.

Coaching means that the teacher is more interested in providing direction in learning than in the learning itself. It means that the teacher is a guide, not an authority figure. It means that the personal, philosophic, and emotional part of the learner is coached and directed as much as the intellectual part. Yet, in order to do this, the teacher must have his or her own life in order. That's a tall order for any occupation, much less one that puts personal growth at the bottom of budgetary priorities.

What's Changed?

Old:
Like an empty container, the teacher's job is to fill students up with knowledge.

New:
The teacher's job is to serve as a catalyst so learners can develop a love of learning and the knowledge of how to learn optimally.

Super-Teaching Requires a "Seize the Day" Attitude

Many students find school boring and tedious. This might be reinforced by their parents who find their jobs stressful or unfulfilling. But with student's academic (and sometimes, personal) lives at stake, teachers must role-model a "carpe diem" attitude. This means making the most out of today, finding the jewel or the gift in every opportunity; and if life gives you lemons, learning to enjoy making lemonade. Life isn't a certain way. Life is created, on the spot, every day, by real people who build it their way. Why is it that something disastrous can happen to two different people and one falls apart while the other grows stronger? The difference is in the individual's mental models. One believes life is a wondrous gift; the other believes it's a kick in the butt. The results reflect their attitudes.

Teaching Is an Inherently High-Risk Job

The notion of teaching as a safe, comfortable easy-going job has changed. Many years ago, elementary education teachers simply needed to have a lot of love and a desire to teach; and secondary and college teachers needed lecture skills. Elementary teachers still need a lot of love, but that's about all that's the same. Teaching today is far more rigorous than it has ever been before.

Today's teachers are front-runners who are courageous and committed learners, willing to take risks and make mistakes. It's a dangerous job because to succeed teachers must confront whatever ideas, systems, or relationships are not working in their personal or professional lives, and change them. It's a place where consistent performance breakthroughs are required just to survive. This intense on-the-edge line of work requires that you set a public example of integrity, love, commitment, and awareness for up to six hours a day. Just as teaching is a coaching job, it is also critical to have a willingness to be coached yourself. One of the greatest baseball players who ever lived was the Japanese legend Sadahara Oh. In spite of his unparalleled success, Sadahara was so committed to growth, that he went to his teacher to get coaching after each ballgame. This meant being up, after a day's workout and a night game, from midnight until two in the morning to get tutored!

Ask yourself what you do that acts as a stand for your commitment to being coached and learning new things. How do you respond to suggestions, changes, and new policies? When was the last time you tried out (and committed to mastery) an entirely new teaching methodology? It takes that kind of openness in order to be effective. It takes that kind of role-modeling to be respected by your students - the more willing they find you to be coached, the more willing they will be.

Teaching Is a Fully-Paid Personal Growth Seminar

No other occupation requires such rigor and such exemplary behavior as teaching. There is also no other occupation which has provided such possibility to our children and the planet as a whole. In your classroom, you can create a microcosm of the world. You can break the back of classroom boredom. You can put an end to dreadful learning and inspire joy, instead. You can build nurturing relationships that last a lifetime. You can overcome personal limitations by learning something from every student. You can expand yourself in ways that allow you to live with more love, integrity, and vitality. And for all this, you will be fully paid.

The flip side here is that you need to consider very seriously whether or not you want to play this game because once you call yourself a "teacher" you must, out of fairness to yourself and your students, give 110 percent. Your students may become a success or failure in life dependent upon how they were regarded and treated by you as their teacher.

This chapter has provided the prototype of the "Super-Teacher." It offers a variety of ways to think about yourself, others, and the teaching profession. Though you may not agree with all of them, don't "throw out the baby with the bath water." Rather, take what does

What's Changed?

Old:
Teaching is a safe, easy, low-risk profession.

New:
Successful teaching in today's climate requires vigilant personal growth and professional risk-taking.

work for you and apply it gently. One way to do this is to simply "act as if" something is already true. If you have the desire to expand your skills and abilities, it will happen. To remind you of your goals, you might write affirmations on index cards and keep them handy for daily review. Use mental pictures to rehearse the way you would like to be allowing yourself to become more comfortable with the image. This practical method of learning offers a way to practice something without risk.

Finally, and perhaps most importantly, use your knowledge. The investment you make in yourself will pay lifelong dividends. Integrate these patterns of success into your behavior and you'll be pleased with the results. You can begin the path to mastery with these simple steps. Now is a good time to start. The affirmations on page 107, 203, and 204 might help!

Reactions:

What are your feelings about the topics presented in this chapter?

What are some practical applications for what you're learning?

What do you want to remember about this chapter?

Glass, china and reputations are easily cracked, and never well mended.

Ben Franklin

Chapter 6

Taking Care of Business

Chapter Preview:

+ **The Business of Teaching**
+ **Building Positive Parent Relationships**
+ **Assessment Success Tips**
+ **Presenting Your Best Self**

The Business of Teaching

The multifaceted profession of teaching requires the right attitudes, skills, knowledge, experience, relationships and, yes, business acumen. This chapter focuses on the business role you play as a teaching professional. The more you think of yourself as a professional, not unlike an attorney, doctor, counselor, engineer or producer, the better prepared you'll be for the business of education.

Like a businessperson does when they accept a new position, make it your job to learn as much as you can about your school. Learn about the various cultures represented in your classroom. Discover what has been done by other teachers in the past. Look through school archives, read old newsletters or newspaper articles. Ask your colleagues and students about the traditions and rituals. Who are the legends, the key people of yesterday and today? Find out who has power and who doesn't. Observe who plays the role of "victim" and who plays "hero." Meet other teachers and key people at the school, like secretaries, cafeteria workers, custodians, etc. Locate and utilize your resources, including sources for supplies.

The True Professional

Those who complain about "getting no respect" might be served by respecting themselves first. If you want to be treated like a professional, act like one. Dress professionally. Be on time. Read professional journals. Stay current in your subject matter. Get on school staff development committees. Invite other teachers to read books that have inspired you. Obtain other people's business cards; and if your school does not provide you with one, have one made. Full-service copy shops can make a simple, cost-effective business card for you within a week. List your credentials and specialty on the card and carry it with pride. You never know when your contacts are going to come in handy.

Support

Find a true friend who is also a great mentor teacher in your school. Sign up for every workshop you can. Be a hungry learner. Get specific feedback from the principal and other teachers. Audio tape or videotape yourself. Teach your students how to give effective feedback and then have them provide you with evaluations periodically. The key to good feedback is that it be specific, accurate, and shared in a caring and kind environment that supports the goal of growth and learning.

Building Positive Parent Relationships

Handling Parent Conferences

Show parents how they can be allies. Ask questions. Be affirming, rather than adversarial. Ask for their opinions (you don't have to take their advice, just listen!). Stay calm when confronted with anger. Take three deep breaths and work to preserve the relationship you have with them. Keep your integrity.

When meeting with parents, be prepared. Do your research and homework before the conference. Have notes and test scores available to support your concerns. Make them available for parents to see on the spot. Include work that students have done recently to support your concerns or praise. Have copies done if you wish for the work to remain in the classroom and with the parents, too. Parents are generally interested in what is best for their child. Approach parent conferences with this in mind. Consider them a great opportunity to develop a teamwork approach. Have your school calendar available so that you can talk specifics when addressing dates for goals, student commitments, and follow-up meetings.

Nurturing a good relationship with your student's parents will serve you and the students throughout the school year. Start with comfortable and familiar territory. Small talk is most important during the first 60 seconds of a conversation. Purposely make eye contact and smile. Create and maintain rapport. Use words like "we" and "us" instead of "I" and "me." Talk at approximately the same pace, tempo and volume as the parent. Find areas of common agreement. Match conversational predicates like "I see what you mean." Learn as much as you can about the particular culture of the family, regardless of the ethnic background. Everyone's learning is affected by their culture. Avoid judging. Your goal is to gather information to help you problem-solve at a later time.

Smart Ideas

If you have limited time available for the meeting(s) be sure that you have a clock in view but outside the view of the parents. This creates a natural way for you to monitor the time. Start and conclude the conference at the scheduled time. You have a busy schedule, as do the parents. Have a list prepared with about a half-dozen positive things you have observed in the student, and want the parent to reinforce. Then, address the challenges and your suggestions for improvement. Be willing to listen and ask questions. Avoid comparisons with other students.

Quotable

The most irrelevant information to a parent is how their son or daughter compares with someone else's son or daughter.

A relevant question, however, is "How is my son or daughter doing compared to six months or a year ago?" When the scheduled closing time of the meeting is near, say to the parents, "We have two minutes left. Here are the issues I heard us talk about, here's what we discussed and here's what we agreed to do next." If it is necessary to continue the dialogue, schedule another meeting then and there.

Building Parent Rapport

Areas for discussion might include: proper home study environments, optimal brain food and nutrition, respective discipline policies and the student's goals. The parent-teacher conference provides a golden opportunity to impact the student through the parent. Take advantage of it! Maintain your values, poise and integrity. Regardless of how frustrated a parent is, never promise to change anything that would violate your personal or professional standards. If you ever feel pressured or uneasy with a parent, ask to take a fresh air break or say you'd like to think about it and schedule a follow-up meeting, or simply say you'll get back to the parent later (and then do it).

Assessment Success Tips

The most important aspect of grading students is to make sure that you are basing their grades on a variety of assessment forms. Students ought to be provided a chance for their strengths to shine in the various areas of intelligence. To determine the broad abilities of a student use a variety of assessment mediums such as: learning logs, drama, debates, music, role-plays, models, mindmaps, presentations, journals, and poetry. Have students create their own test questions. Plan some ongoing activities so that students receive continuous feedback. Avoid last minute situations where you may be too rushed to complete an accurate and fair assessment. Keep a file on each student. And have students maintain a portfolio of their work.

Teachers can help prepare parents for report cards. Take the opportunity to talk to parents about the role of assessment and your approach to grading. Encourage them to avoid giving rewards or bribes for grades. To avoid "parent-shock", make sure that they know in advance if their child's grades have dropped significantly. Talk to your students about your grading policies from the onset of class. Have a written grading policy posted in the classroom. Make it as specific and positive as possible. Refer to it throughout the semester. Students can't possibly meet teacher expectations if they don't know what those expectations are.

Quotable

The key to good feedback is that it be specific, accurate, and shared in a caring environment that supports the goal of growth and learning.

Avoid Labels

Use positive language with parents when referring to their child. Remember, this child is their life! Avoid labels. Instead of saying a child is a trouble-maker, say "Susie often disrupts her classmates." Start each report card with a strength. Even if it is, "Mary has such a great sense of humor." Refer to specific assignments, actions, and classroom behaviors when at all possible. Avoid generalizations like, "Joe has a bad attitude."

Distribution

If you pass out report cards in your classroom, do two things. First, talk to the students about what grades are for. Set it up as a positive experience by telling them that we all need feedback in life and that report cards are just one form of feedback. Explain that the purpose of feedback (and report cards) is to enhance their learning. Secondly, pass report cards out at the end of class. Make sure that students know what to do if they feel they've been treated unfairly or have questions. Students ought to feel free to discuss their grades with you. Such conversations can be instrumental in building trust, rapport and motivation for future learning.

Follow-up

If a parent contacts you about the assessment and is unhappy, it's more important to be a good listener than a strong debater. Insuring future success with the child is important, so if the phone call is unsuccessful, meet with the parent in person. Try to focus your conversation with parents on ways student learning can be optimized, rather than on what's wrong.

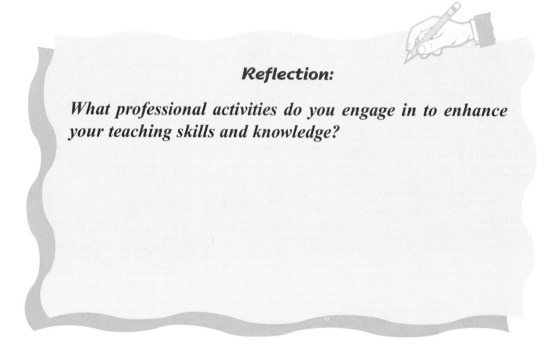

Reflection:

What professional activities do you engage in to enhance your teaching skills and knowledge?

Presenting Your Best Self

Your Health

Are you healthy? You can be sure your students are getting subtle messages about how you care for yourself, treat yourself, and your overall self-esteem. Good teaching takes energy! Make sure you have an overall health and fitness program that includes stress reduction, relaxation, nutrition, cardio-vascular training, stretching and muscle toning. Being health-conscious sets a good example for your students. Group interactions, personal relationships, energy levels, and self-esteem are all affected by your health. When you feel better, you teach better.

Physical Messages

As you become increasingly aware of your own powerful influence on student behaviors and attitudes, you will also discover just how many messages have been communicated unconsciously by you. Your posture is one such communication vehicle. How you move and hold yourself gives an uninterrupted stream of messages about your sense of joy, self-confidence, and energy level. You may be pleased to know that your posture is a mutable thing - you are not permanently stuck with it. Many techniques work for altering posture, including yoga, physical therapy, exercise, Tai Chi, meditation, massage, etc. to name a few.

It has even been determined that people whose posture is tentative, stooped and tired-looking are more apt to be attacked. Known as "mugger susceptibility," this concept when translated to the classroom means that your posture could be inviting student attacks - whether physical, verbal or mental. The question to ask yourself is, "Am I presenting myself with dignity, pride, and energy?" And, "Does my posture reflect this?"

Attitudes like: "TGIF" and "I just want to make it through the day" will be reflected whether you realize it or not in your teaching. If you want your students to enjoy the process of learning, it is incumbent upon you to enjoy the process of teaching. Don't forget, students learn more from you, the person, than they do from the lesson plan.

Dress Standards

Your clothing, like your posture, is a very visible reflection of your attitudes and feelings. Your dress is also a very simple thing to change. John Malloy, author of *Dress For Success* (1975) and a well-known image consultant, was a teacher at one time. This helps explain his interest in a research project he conducted on the effects of clothing on learning in the classroom. The results present a powerful argument for carefully selecting what you wear. His work suggests that clothing worn by teachers substantially affects student attitudes, discipline, and work habits. In his experiments, Malloy chose two different teachers who were matched for style, delivery, and course content. Then each teacher was asked to conduct sessions with the same group of students who were then tested respectively. The study showed that the more professionally dressed teacher got better student outcomes than the casually dressed teacher.

Malloy's Conclusions:

- ✦ Neatness counts; even dirt, spots or food marks on your clothing can be a source of unwanted judgment.
- ✦ See yourself through your audiences' eyes. What looks great from 2 to 3 feet away may be quite ineffective at 10 to 20 feet away.
- ✦ Avoid bold patterns as they distract your audience - studies showed increased audience blink rates when exposed to loud patterns.
- ✦ Try to contrast your clothing with the background. Ideally, you will stand out just enough to be noticed easily.
- ✦ Avoid things which jingle, crackle, scrape, or make other distracting sounds.

All of the things that influence your image (neatness, odor, cleanliness) have the capacity to create or destroy your rapport with students.

Your Self-Expression

Like posture and dress, your language is also a powerful medium for expression - consciously or unconsciously. The super-teacher is very aware of this both in front of the room and in informal settings. As a role-model, it is inappropriate for teachers to use foul or abusive language, even when provoked. It is unprofessional (and not useful) to criticize (ever!) or to make critical value judgments about your students or other people. The following examples help make the important distinction here between a judgment and an observation:

Judgement: Johnnie is a real jerk; he doesn't want to learn.
Observation: Johnnie is talking in a raised voice and is not completing his assignment.

Judgement: Susie is the brightest kid in our class.
Observation: Susie has received the highest test score twice this year.

Judgement: That stupid assembly was a waste of my time.
Observation: I don't recognize any immediate value from that assembly.

Notice the shift from "it's out there" to "it's within my power."

Affirm the Positive

At the beginning of a class, it's common for students to say, "I'm awful at this." When learners affirm these thoughts, it negatively impacts their progress. A more productive affirmation is "I'm not real comfortable with this yet, but I know with practice, I will be." Though you may think the difference between the two affirmations is trivial, over time, the brain responds appropriately to the messages we program it with.

The difference between using words like "awful" and "not comfortable" can have a dramatic impact on our consciousness. Our mind reacts to the word or feeling that is dominant. For example, when the mind hears "awful" in the first example, the influence is much greater than when the student hears "not comfortable" in the second example. Which influencing words would you rather your students hear? Obviously the one that builds self-esteem is better. Students usually adopt self-talk that is similar to that of their family.

A student who is made aware of their self-talk and how it impacts their learning will have been given a powerful lifelong learning tool. If negative self-talk has ill effects on learning, you can imagine how damaging negative teacher-talk is on a student's psyche. Once a teacher calls a student slow, rude, disrespectful, stupid, lazy, or a pain in the neck, the damage cannot be erased. What you affirm you reinforce. Rather than complaining about students, simply tell them how their behavior affects you. You're perfectly within your rights to say:

"I'm frustrated and irritated when you're late."
"I'm really disappointed when you let us both down."
"I'm hurt when you say that."

A student who is made aware of their self-talk and how it impacts their learning will have been given a powerful lifelong learning tool.

Learners need to know how they affect you. If you are embarrassed and hurt by their actions, tell them. However, you do not have a right to call them names. One harsh word from a teacher can have a life-long negative impact on a student. Is it a double standard that students call teachers names all the time, and yet, teachers can't do it back? Of course. No one ever said teaching was easy. It takes a thick skin and a heart of gold to teach. If you're unable to bite your tongue and keep negative comments to yourself, you have two choices: either work on your own negative behaviors or leave the profession. If you can't take criticism, find a job where you'll never be criticized. Your students deserve a fighting chance to make it in this world. They need all the positive affirmation they can get.

Take Acting Lessons

Taking acting lessons might sound like a funny recommendation, but it is amazing how much "star" is bottled up inside every teacher. You have your own kind of charisma and electricity that, as of yet, may not have been fully tapped. Acting encourages a form of self-expression which can ultimately serve you well in the classroom. For example, you might learn a simple facial expression which will create suspense, another which creates surprise, another which expresses appreciation and so on.

Another valuable lesson borrowed from the theater is to align your intended message with your body language. For example, though a teacher may say they care about their students, their body language may show otherwise. Or, a teacher may say that they are really interested in the material they are presenting, yet their students are bored to tears. This is one of the most common problems teachers face. However, a good acting coach can help you learn the subtle art of communicating dramatically with an audience. The key here is that the more flexibility you have, the wider range of learners you will reach. For most teachers, acting expands their choices and gives them new possibilities for getting the results they want. If you have three ways to respond in class, you are likely to be less effective than someone who has ten ways. Behavioral flexibility is one of the most important keys to classroom mastery. Acting skills expand behavioral choices.

Set an Example

Teachers are observed, heard, felt and interacted with hour after hour. Every facet of a teacher's personality has an opportunity to surface, and it usually does. Why pay attention to such detail about your personality? Because you, the teacher, are the single greatest determiner of your student's success. You are so much more important than the textbooks, the video, the room, or the lesson plans. Because of that, the three most important keys to producing better students are:

1. **Set an example**
2. **Set an example**
3. **Set an example**

In the late 1960s, Marshall McLuhan popularized the expression, "The medium is the message." It may apply better to the teaching profession than any other. Although ultimately technology will augment or replace much of your impact, today you are the carrier of the message. Because you have your own personality with attitudes, feelings and opinions, you will "package" your message uniquely. In short, there is no objective teacher. You are as much a packager of information as a television set or videocassette player.

Because of this enormous influence, your own beliefs and values in education will filter and flavor your teaching. Take this as an opportunity to re-examine your "medium" more closely and make sure it represents you in the best possible way. In the moments before class begins, many details require your last-minute attention. These can make the difference between an average class and a great one. Superteachers take the time to do their homework, just as they ask their students to do. For teachers, as with students, the payoff for being prepared is enormous.

Mind-Map

Using various colored markers, represent who you are as a teacher. What's important to you?

Reactions:

What are your feelings about the topics presented in this chapter?

What are some practical applications for what you're learning?

What do you want to remember from this chapter?

Education is basically an art, and the teacher expresses the highest concept of this art when he or she keeps it from becoming routinized and lethargic.

Howard A. Ozmon, Samuel M. Craver
Philosophical Foundations of Education

Lesson Planning

Lesson Planning Versus Planning Learning

Traditionally, teachers were taught to develop lesson plans based on *what* they planned to teach. New thinking suggests that we ought to be planning *how* to best approach the teaching. Planning learning versus lesson planning suggests that our plans include strategies that make the most sense for the material and the learners with whom we are working. Plans that will work best will be flexible, interdisciplinary, and true-to-life. They will also incorporate strategies that encompass multiple learning styles. This chapter will examine the various influences that distinguish average-teachers from super-teachers when it comes to planning learning.

One of the first teachers to popularize the learner-centered approach was the humanistic psychologist Carl Rogers who coined the term "client-centered therapy" in the 1960s. Rogers believed that it was more productive to focus on the needs of the client or student than on the needs of the system. Although this change might seem subtle, the impact is powerful. Lesson plans by themselves mean nothing. Even well-designed lesson plans will fail without the skill and knowledge of an artful conductor who understands his/her audience.

A super-teacher navigates the course of learning. This means that you are ready, at every moment, to add or delete things from your plan, or if necessary, to change courses completely. A teacher cannot be certain how their students will respond to a lesson. Draw on your own experience and the student's in the moment. This is what you, as a navigator, have to offer beyond what can be gained from a textbook.

Covering the Content Versus Uncovering the Learning

Our profession is *not* about filling up students with facts, but rather opening up students to learning. Start with the premise that your students *can* learn and *will* learn. Avoid labels and make their genius your self-fulfilling prophecy. We're in the business of creating environments where exciting, fulfilling, and empowering learning events can occur. We are in the service business and it is our job to make it work for students. If you maintain this attitude, your approach to teaching will be student-centered.

Course objectives are important, but *how* the objectives are achieved should allow for infinite possibilities. A good lesson plan will not make a poor teacher into a star. But a poor lesson plan *can* make even a well-intentioned teacher look bad. Contrary to the popular misnomer that "the better you are, the fewer notes you need," the most competent teachers plan well and usually keep and use frequent notes. Creating the lesson plan provides clarity; and clarity leads to better orchestrated classes. Masters can fail successfully, but the master always plans to succeed. Remember the saying, "If I fail to plan, I am planning to fail."

In essence, the process of planning is more important than the plan, itself. The process insures that you have determined the objectives, thought out the salient points, and developed a road map for the trip.

Translation and delivery of your plan are also critical. The success of your lesson plan has more to do with the way in which it is delivered (rapport, presentation skills and learning environment) than how it is structured. In fact, how you structure your lesson plan is a personal thing - what works for you is what matters. Super-teachers, though well prepared, always make room for the spontaneous to occur. It is not a contradiction of terms to have both a structured plan and, at the same time, be open to spontaneous learning moments. There is value which can come from each.

A Strong Learning Plan:

+ *Allows you to stay focused on outcomes*
+ *Gives you added confidence*
+ *Allows for creative ideas to surface*
+ *Gives you a place to make notes, corrections, and additions*
+ *Provides class structure and coherence*
+ *Provides concrete visuals*
+ *Provides the teacher with a sense of organization and completion*
+ *Provides a permanent record of your lessons (what, when and how)*

Clarifying Your Outcomes

Identifying intended results or learning objectives are an aspect of teacher training that has traditionally been emphasized. Teachers, therefore, don't usually have a hard time accomplishing this task. Some questions that you might ask, however, while reviewing your lesson plans are:

✦ Does the lesson plan have integrity? Are the objectives consistent with the big picture - your plan for the year, the school's plan, the district's?

✦ Does your plan "dovetail" with your learner's goals? Is it a "win-win?" Is it learner-centered?

✦ Have you designated a time for completion? Are the goals measurable? Is your plan realistic? Are the short-term and long-term objectives consistent?

✦ Are your objectives stated in a positive way? Have you asserted what you want to happen, rather than what you don't want to happen?

✦ Do you have an evidence procedure? How will you know when your outcome is reached? Do you have the resources to succeed? How will it look, sound, or feel when the goals have been accomplished?

✦ Are the objectives valuable to your students? Do they represent a breakthrough, a challenge, a growing experience or a "stretch?"

Some examples of outcomes that are more difficult to measure than the ones above are:

✦ *Positive bias:* A student's "good relationship" with the subject or liking of the material is important and sometimes hard to measure. Objectives that are linked to positive bias are things like: the student's curiosity in the subject was peaked, the student understands the lesson's relevancy, the student is gaining an appreciation of the learning process as a lifelong endeavor.

✦ *Learning styles:* A student's understanding or awareness of their own preferred learning style(s) is often more valuable than learning the specified material. Have your students learned anything about *how* they learn?

✦ *Patterns of meaning:* A student's ability to process and connect interrelated facts and identify patterns is a very valuable learning objective. Can your learners identify models, themes, and commonalties?

Since most textbooks maintain only content-related objectives, rather than process-related objectives, to achieve the kinds of outcomes like the ones listed above, you will, personally, have to provide the material. The best methodology you can use to encourage these outcomes is classroom discussion. The best material you can use to achieve them is your own personal examples and experiences. In any case, it is important to keep in mind that the purpose of the lesson plan is secondary to the purpose of the class/course. Though specific objectives related to individual lesson plans are important to the process, the bigger picture - that of course intended outcomes - ought to take precedence.

An important first step in creating measurable outcomes is to make them clear and objective. For example, the objective: "To be able to write the chemical formula accurately for photosynthesis" is clear, measurable and objective. The teacher's opinions, interests, or judgments are irrelevant; the student can either write the formula or not. If the objective, however, read "To be able to understand photosynthesis well", the outcome would be subjective and unmeasurable. What "well" means to one person, of course, may be different than what it means to another. Some examples of clear objectives are listed below, along with their unclear counterparts:

Unclear: To learn the key parts of the class novel.
Clear: To role-play two characters, then submit a one paragraph summary on the experience by next Tuesday at 2 p.m. - may be done in the form of a mindmap, essay, audio tape, video tape, or medium of learner's choice.

Unclear: To understand the United State's role in the Arab-Israeli war.
Clear: To write an analysis of the conflict which includes: 1) the major ways that the U.S. aided Israel; 2) theories about why the U.S. aided Israel; 3) speculations about the future of the region; 4) recommendations for our involvement in the region; 5) a comparison of our current involvement with the historic role we have played in the past; and 6) a discussion of how the subject relates to your own life.

Three Major Learning Areas

Students not only vary from one another on learning style preferences, they differ in terms of the three major learning areas, as well. The three learning areas are: cognitive (what we know), psychomotor (what we do) and affective (what we feel). To reach the broad base of students you are assured of having, make sure that each class has elements that address each of the learning areas.

1. Cognitive:
Commonly known as what we know, but better defined as:

✦ *Knowledge* - being able to recall and define.
✦ *Comprehension* - being able to translate into own words.
✦ *Application* - using tools outside original context.
✦ *Analysis* - being able to note strong and weak points.
✦ *Synthesis* - to create from other parts.
✦ *Evaluation* - to compare and contrast.

2. Psychomotor:
Commonly known as physical skills, also:

✦ *Accuracy* - to be able to hit a target.
✦ *Coordination* - to be able to move within parameters.
✦ *Manipulation* - to create cause and effect.

3. Affective:
Commonly known as values, feelings and attitudes, also:

✦ *Attending* - participation and commitment.
✦ *Responding* - intensity and quantity of response.
✦ *Valuing* - importance and worth, biases.
✦ *Values expression* - to be willing to share freely.

Quotable

Super-teachers, though well prepared, always make room for the spontaneous to occur. It is not a contradiction of terms to have both a structured plan and at the same time, be open to spontaneous learning moments. There is value which can come from each.

Accelerating the Learning

The book *Superlearning* by Sheila Ostrander and Lynn Schroeder (1979) attracted a great deal of attention a couple of decades ago to exciting new ways to learn. The concept they coined "accelerated learning" was popularized by Ostrander and Schroeder in the United States, as well as by Bulgarian educator Georgi Lozonov (1975) who identified a similar learning paradigm he called suggestopedia. Whatever terms are used, the principles of accelerated learning embody many separate but interrelated disciplines. This makes it difficult to define because accelerated learning, rather than being a small fixed body of knowledge, is a dynamic, growing and inclusive domain. It synthesizes the research from fields as varied as psychology, cognitive science, communication studies, systems theory, management, and physics; and it applies its principles to subjects as varied as music, theater, storytelling, rituals, and teaching and learning. Also impacted by the principles of accelerated learning are strategies such as: total physical response, nonconscious learning, alpha states, suggestion, multiple intelligences and Neuro-Linguistic Programming (NLP).

Georgi Lozanov documented that by utilizing more of the potential of the human brain, we are able to accelerate learning from three to ten times over the results of more traditional methods. No one in the Western world has duplicated these amazing results. However, many teachers and trainers have reported that they have doubled the standard predictable gains and done so with much greater student enthusiasm, a deeper understanding of the material, and greater long-term value.

Ingredients of Success

So, how is accelerated learning accomplished? The common element of the approaches is to provide a stimulating environment that facilitates positive, multi-modal joyful engagement. The primary medium is the teacher's artful use of positive suggestion. The accelerated learner becomes intrinsically motivated towards achievement, self-confidence, and mastery of content. As the student feels competent in the process, a love of learning emerges. Amazingly enough, much of the time, the learner is unaware of exactly how *much* is going on. Only that a lot is going on and it is fun!

Though, accelerated learning is not a recipe that requires exact measurements and cooking temperatures, there are essential ingredients. For the synergy to occur, the following seven elements must be present.

1. Sensory-Rich Immersion Environment

The learning environment must be *full* of sights, sounds and things to do. Affirmations on the wall like, "Your Success is Absolutely Assured" is one example. Others are: good aromas (i.e. from flowers, food or potpourri), comfortable seating, plenty of natural lighting if possible, large mind maps or memory maps previewing upcoming content, uplifting music, and colorful intriguing peripherals. A sensory-rich environment provides stimulation to the brain, creates novelty, and encourages the learner to enter "another world."

2. Learner Preparation and Conditioning

A traditional teacher hopes that students come to them motivated and ready to learn. An accelerated learning teacher, on the other hand, assumes that students come to them with many barriers to learning; therefore, artfully plans an assault on those barriers. Typical learning barriers include:

- ✦ *Intuitive-Emotional:* the fear of failure, embarrassment or even success. Fear can be overcome by warm, positive teacher interactions and early successes in the subject area.
- ✦ *Critical-Logical:* the critical self-talk by students who believe they aren't smart enough or the subject is "too hard." Self-imposed limitations can be overcome by affirmation, significant successes, reframing, or teamwork.
- ✦ *Ethical-Moral:* the belief that learning is "hard work" or that it's "no pain, no gain." Limiting values originating from parents, the church, etc., can be overcome through cooperation and communication.
- ✦ *Biological-Medical:* the lack of learning efficiency due to inadequate nutrition, or intake of food additives, drugs, or other toxins. Poor nutrition can be overcome through education, support, and modeling healthy alternatives.
- ✦ *Cultural-Social:* the barriers reinforced by negative peer pressure, outdated cultural or ethnic customs, and unproductive learning styles. Such challenges can be overcome by inclusion and communication. Insure that the medium used to deliver the content is full of the participant's own cultural icons, myths, stories, and meaning.
- ✦ *Institutional-Physical:* the challenges triggered by large bureaucracies or those suggested by television, radio, or movies. Such barriers may include a dislike of authority, an irreverence towards school, or an approval of socially antagonistic behaviors.

Address student concerns explicitly in your curriculum planning. For example, with math, anticipate the following perceptions and head them off by talking about them in advance:

- ✦ I can't understand it.
- ✦ It's too hard.
- ✦ It's too boring.
- ✦ It's for geniuses or nerds.
- ✦ I'll never use it anyway.
- ✦ I'll forget it in no time.

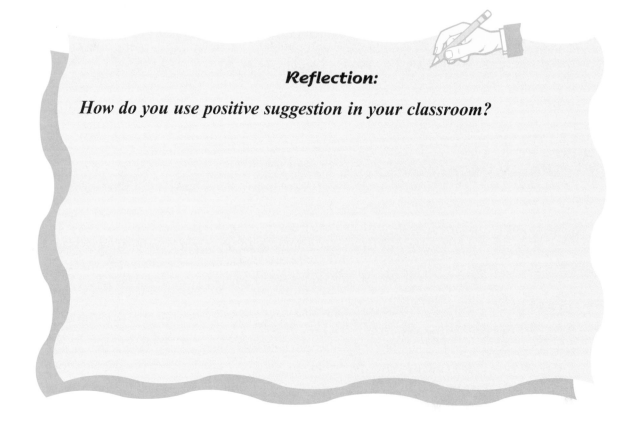

Reflection:

How do you use positive suggestion in your classroom?

Once you have identified the negative beliefs common to your subject, and you have addressed them, you can determine strategies for offsetting them. For example, set up a simple mnemonic device to insure that students remember each of the key points from the learning. Put up posters or peripherals to help address those negative beliefs: "Math is easy" or "Math is a big part of my everyday life." Use positive suggestion in your language, for example, "After you've *successfully* completed your group project, raise your hand, so I'll know you're all done."

3. *Multiple Learning Styles/Intelligences Implemented*

Present material with multiple learning styles in mind. As discussed in chapter three, use as many of the following strategies as possible:

✦ Visual, auditory, kinesthetic, olfactory and gustatory
✦ Abstract, concrete, global, and linear
✦ Inductive, deductive, intuitive, match, and mismatch
✦ Field-dependent and field-independent
✦ Past, present, and future referenced

Also use memory keys such as:

✦ *Musical:* Use of songs to learn (i.e., the alphabet song)
✦ *Linguistic:* Use of humor, mnemonics, rhyme, puns, sequencing
✦ *Motor:* Use of body to learn (i.e., role-play, hands-on activities)
✦ *Contextual/Spatial:* Based on location and circumstances (i.e., various corners of the room, the outdoors, desktops, costumes, varied lighting, sound, colors, and seating, etc.)
✦ *Sensory:* Use of intense visual, auditory, kinesthetic, olfactory and gustatory approaches (i.e., intense aromas, food, specially-anchored sounds, costumes, props, etc.)

Using multiple intelligences means creating a context in which every student can succeed. There are many ways to be smart and the context determines the evidence. Chapter 15 will elaborate on this important concept first presented by Howard Gardner (1993). Gardner says there are seven or more ways to learn:

✦ *Verbal-Linguistic:* lecture, tapes, sharing, and reading
✦ *Interpersonal:* group work, partners, and cooperative work
✦ *Bodily-Kinesthetic:* action, movement, and simulations
✦ *Spatial:* artwork, mindmaps, and re-design of environment
✦ *Intrapersonal:* self-assessment, intuition, and metacognition
✦ *Mathematical-Logical:* problem-solving, math, and prediction
✦ *Rhythmic-Musical:* patterns of music, sound, and meaning

4. *Student-Centered Learning*

As discussed earlier, student-centered learning is an approach that involves learners directly in the decision-making process. Student-centered learning is valuable because it develops responsibility in students; students become more motivated and participate more in decisions when they are involved in making them; achievement scores increase; and students enjoy class more. Ways to implement this approach are:

✦ Ask for student input on content.
✦ Give students a subject and ask them to create a game with it.
✦ Give students a choice about doing something now or later.

- ✦ Have a suggestion box and act on useful ideas.
- ✦ Allow students to teach, present, and interact with each other often.
- ✦ Give students an opportunity to co-create rules.
- ✦ Use teams, partners, groups, and classroom buddies.
- ✦ Model empathic listening and respect.
- ✦ Provide acknowledgment, praise, and acceptance.
- ✦ Honor cultural diversity and incorporate diversity into learning.

5. Positive Suggestion

Everything we do reminds our brain of something. In fact, everything is suggestion. This means that the clothes we wear, the materials we use, the seating arrangements, the tonality of our voice, volume, and tempo all give signals. Some ways to use positive suggestion are:

- ✦ Post positive affirmation posters.
- ✦ Greet students at the door with a smile, handshake, or kind word.
- ✦ Stay committed to totally positive interactions.
- ✦ Play music in a major key depicting positive messages.
- ✦ Offer congruent gestures, tonality, volume, facial expressions.
- ✦ Use stories with themes or myths that reach the unconscious mind.
- ✦ Provide continual verbal, visual, and kinesthetic affirmations about the student's potential and efforts.

6. Engage Emotions

Providing purposeful play and spontaneous celebration is a critical factor in learning acceleration for several reasons: 1) the emotions can only be engaged if the learner has been prepared for learning; 2) the emotions are one of the keys to engaging long-term memory; 3) the learning often becomes peripheral or secondary to the activity, hence perceived by the learner as less stressful and easier; 4) emotions trigger the positive brain chemicals which may lead to a future love of learning. Following are some examples of ways to engage emotions:

- ✦ Simulations (i.e., cities, stores, restaurants, newspapers).
- ✦ Modify popular games into academic games using cards, ball toss, puppets, commercials, and school situations.
- ✦ Music, especially for rituals.
- ✦ Contests which are a win-win for the players.
- ✦ Theater, role-play, costumes, and props.
- ✦ Concert-readings (reading fiction or nonfiction to the interplay of classical music).
- ✦ Celebrating milestones or end point successes.
- ✦ Fun rituals to mark opening, closing, and transition periods (i.e., music, drum rolls, "Oooohhhhs and aaaahhhhs" and class cheers).
- ✦ Cooperative team games (i.e., New Games).

7. Orchestrated Learning

All learning is state-dependent. If students are not in the appropriate state for learning, you're both wasting time. Therefore, this is the most important element in accelerated learning. Artful management of student states requires experience; the more you observe and work with student's states, the more efficient you will become.

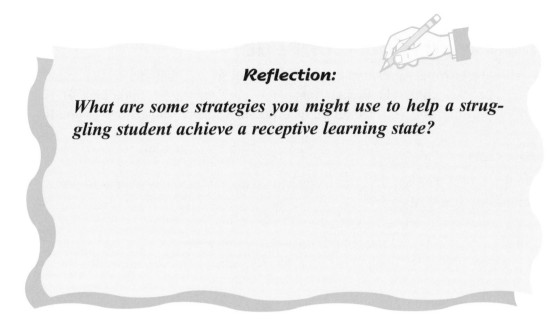

Reflection:

What are some strategies you might use to help a struggling student achieve a receptive learning state?

Do the strategies you've listed evoke a state of enthusiasm, excitement, flexibility, love, caring, interest, curiosity, confidence, attentiveness, joy and relaxation in your student(s)?

Skills Mastery Model

For each skill set to be taught, consider whether the following steps or considerations have been implemented:

✦ Have you created the proper state? Are your students excited, attentive, relaxed, and ready to learn?

✦ Have you established rapport with the students on both the conscious and unconscious levels? Have you shown your learners how the skill is relevant to them?

✦ Have you identified learner outcomes? Are they measurable in observable behavioral terms? Do the students know what's in it for them? Are they in alignment with the students personal goals, ethics, emotions or personal history? Have they bought into the outcomes?

✦ Do your students have a model of the "parts" and the "whole" of what they are learning? Did you use a historical or literary metaphor? Can the model be internally accessed or is it relevant to them?

✦ Have you created a reality bridge for the skill to be learned? Have you asked learners to celebrate in advance the successful mastery of the skills?

✦ Have you provided learners with an accurate demonstration of the new skill? Do they know what to watch for?

✦ Have you presented the activity in micro-steps so that each step is understood and repeated by the group? Did you have students *show* you, *tell* you, and *do* the skill to insure that they know each of the steps?

✦ Have you shown your students how to practice the skill with partners or in small groups? Are your directions specific and clear?

✦ Do you have adequate supervision to insure that the skills are learned? Have you incorporated peer teaching or group work if not?

✦ Have you provided a closure or check-in for the learning? Have you answered any questions, addressed any concerns, generalized the information to other areas, globalized its importance and reviewed its relevancy?

Planning Learning Content

The following outline provides an example of a lesson plan format that can be generalized to any skill area. The seven stages include: 1) Preparation; 2) Globalization; 3) Initiation; 4) Elaboration; 5) Incubation; 6) Verification; and 7) Celebration. Incorporate as many suggestions as you find helpful.

1. Preparation

+ Pre-expose learners to the big picture or a conceptual map of the subject or skill area.
+ Teach learning-to-learn skills.
+ Address topics like: nutrition, self-esteem, coping and other life skills.
+ Create a strong immersion learning environment that is interesting!
+ Reinforce your credibility by being organized and well-versed on the subject.
+ Be aware of the best time of day for learning based on brain cycles and rhythms.
+ Discover your students' interests and background.
+ Provide brain "wake-ups" (cross-laterals or relaxation-stretching exercises).
+ State strong positive expectations; allow learners to voice theirs also.
+ Create relationships and encourage strong positive rapport.
+ Read learner states and make adjustments as you go.

2. Globalization

+ Provide the context for learning the topic (background).
+ Elicit from learners what possible value and relevance the topic has to them.
+ Provide physical or concrete evidence of the subject or skill to be learned.
+ Provide a "hook" for the learning that is novel or meets strong personal learner needs.
+ Use puppets, flip charts, slides, videos, music and/or other special effects and visual aids.

3. Initiation

+ Immerse your learners in the topic instead of the singular, lock-step, sequential, one-bite-at-a-time information approach. Expect a sense of temporary overload in learners. This state will be followed by anticipation, curiosity, and a determination to discover meaning for oneself. Over time it all gets sorted out, by the learner, brilliantly.
+ Provide concrete learning experiences such as a problem-solving exercise, a field trip, interviews or hands-on learning. Learners ought to have some choice in which experience they choose. Employ as many senses as possible in the process.
+ Allow learners to discover, build, find, explore, and design.
+ Incorporate well-designed learning software if possible.

4. Elaboration

+ Tie things together thematically.
+ Ask learners to write questions, explore data bases, construct models.
+ Have learners read up on a topic, watch a video, or write a creative piece.
+ Address student questions.

- ◆ Facilitate group discussions or team forums.
- ◆ Students can sort, analyze or make mind-maps of the material.
- ◆ Students can play a leader role - ask, interpret questions, and ideas.

5. *Incubation*

- ◆ Provide for unguided reflection or "down time."
- ◆ Provide space of several hours to several days between topics so that the brain gets time to subconsciously sort, process, and connect ideas.
- ◆ Provide extra personal time (either active or passive) for silence, journal writing, relaxation, movement needs, or simply a change of subjects.

6. *Verification*

- ◆ Have students present a lesson to the class.
- ◆ Have students design test questions.
- ◆ Use both written and verbal assessment strategies.
- ◆ Have students create a project, a working model, a mind map, a video, a newsletter, etc.
- ◆ Have learners act out a skit or role-play.
- ◆ Have students complete a self-corrected quiz that is not collected.
- ◆ Incorporate group discussions, interviews, games, physical movements, a dance or a quiz show.
- ◆ Students evaluate their own work and tell each other how they did.
- ◆ Review and wrap-up.

7. *Celebration*

- ◆ Engage emotions; make it fun, light and joyful.
- ◆ It's bragging time; have students show off their work to the class or in groups.
- ◆ Provide acknowledgment and compliments.
- ◆ Use music, streamers, horns and other special effects.
- ◆ Provide positive feedback. It can be as simple as giving a "high-five" or as complex as a class-designed and produced celebration party.
- ◆ In this step create, the all-important love of learning. Encourage students to shake hands, laugh, and have fun. Never miss it!

Linking Subject Matter

The old way of teaching a subject like math, science or history was to divide it into smaller chunks called units. Then the teacher would sub-divide the units into daily and weekly lesson plans. Each day, the teacher would present a micro-chunk of the whole. It sounds logical. But it is not the way our brain is best designed to learn.

Imagine yourself as a four or five-year-old child and you just received your first bicycle for your birthday. You're all excited and you want nothing more than to jump on it and go! But, your parents have decided that you should learn to ride a bicycle the "proper way" in the right "order." So, they will teach you to ride your bicycle based on the following units:

How to Ride a Bicycle
(Old Model)

1. History of the Bicycle
    A. Inventor(s)
    B. Evolution of
    C. Transportation niche
        a. Advantages and disadvantages of usage
        b. Comparisons with other modes
    D. Mechanical/product specifications
        a. Materials used

2. Safety
    A. Personal safety
        a. Proper signals
        b. Defensive attitude
        c. Permission (when, length of time, etc.)
    B. Neighborhood safety
        a. Possible hazards
        b. Neighborhood culture
        c. Storage of bicycle (locks, garage, etc.)
    C. Sidewalk and Road safety
        d. Laws, customs, and bicycle maintenance

3. The Skills of Riding
    A. Posture
    B. Balance
    C. Purpose of training wheels
    D. Advanced riding skills

4. Benefits of Riding
    A. Social advantages
        (visit with friends)
    B. Exercise and fresh air
    C. Transportation

Naturally, by the time your parents have completed unit one, you have lost interest and gone on to something else. The brain is far more capable than the sequential "lesson plan" above reflects. Obviously, a more typical child's approach is to get a few bits of important information, then hop on a bike and give it a try.

Quotable

The brain learns best in real-life, immersion-style, multi-path learning; fractured, piecemeal teaching can quickly kill off a love of learning.

Amazingly enough, most kids learn to ride a bike just fine. And if you think about it, you learned some of the most complex things in your life including your native language without formal instruction. Did you learn the rules of grammar before you started writing? Of course not! Much of our learning is just "picked up" over time.

Interdisciplinary Approaches

Is it possible then that our brain can "pick up" subjects like science, history, geography, math, life skills, literature and the arts? Of course it is! That's the way our brain is designed to learn: multi-path, in order or out of order, many levels, many teachers, many contexts, and many angles. We learn with themes, favorite subjects, issues, key points, questions, trial and error, reflection, and application.

Quotable

Interdisciplinary learning is a process closer to the way the human brain is naturally designed to learn best.

One of the greatest gifts you can offer your students is an awareness of the relationship between classroom learning and the real world. An interdisciplinary approach urges you to weave common threads through your student's learning instead of using a single subject approach or textbook. Textbooks present a single viewpoint or approach which the authors have chosen. In this fast-moving information age, your preferred sources of information ought to be the student's real-life experiences, magazines, computers, videos, television, journals, and libraries.

In planning for interdisciplinary study, it is important to:

✦ Be certain that the theme is worthy of extensive time invested, that there are plenty of materials and resources available on the topic, that it has application to student's real world, that the pattern and rationale is clear and compelling for learners.
✦ Incorporate student ideas, situations, events, and contributions.
✦ Present various angles and views.
✦ Present sub-topics that are interrelated. Some examples based on a zoo theme, for example, might be: Geography of the world's zoos, animal types/species, systems involved in running a zoo, economics of a zoo, endangered species, colors of animals, foods eaten, the food chain, etc.
✦ Identify weekly topics. Use newspapers, television shows, kid's examples and school issues to tie into each of the components.
✦ Identify relevant key points: Concepts, skills, knowledge, attitudes, values, models, and patterns.
✦ Brainstorm outcomes or essential things you'd like students to learn.
✦ Identify your resources: field trips, CD-ROM, library, school sites, guest speakers, computers, etc.
✦ Incorporate learning styles, multiple intelligences, and Bloom's Taxonomy into your lesson planning.

Using a zoo theme, for example, Bloom's Taxonomy would suggest students exhibit:

✦ *Knowledge* - by listing and describing all the animals in the zoo.
✦ *Comprehension* - by grouping them into categories and discussing the rationale for the grouping.
✦ *Application* - by building a model lion enclosure that lions would like.
✦ *Analysis* - by writing and singing a rap song about the daily life of animals in the zoo.
✦ *Evaluation* - by creating a checklist of desirable enclosure qualities; visit your own zoo and evaluate 10 animal's quality of life there.

✦ *Synthesis* - by pretending visitors from another world came to earth and wanted to make a zoo full of humans. What would that "zoo for humans" be like? Students would be encouraged to draw it out on a huge piece of paper and describe it to the class.

Conceptualize your theme as a spider web. The title is in the center. If you have nine months, you'd have nine threads coming out from the center of the web. Then branching out from the monthly threads, you'd have four weekly threads. Certainly flexibility should be maintained though your plan is specific. This thematic style of teaching and learning has been demonstrated far more effective than the traditional unit, chunk, unit, chunk, piecemeal approach.

The classroom becomes a living, learning laboratory. The learning is connected and the themes are relevant. Think of the classroom possibilities for discussion, projects, plays, and writing! Give your students a list of at least 10 addresses where students can write to for free information including US. Government agencies, the Chamber of Commerce, as well as state agencies. Better yet, help them discover for themselves how to locate addresses, phone numbers, and contact persons for each unit. This is a terrific way for them to become lifelong learners.

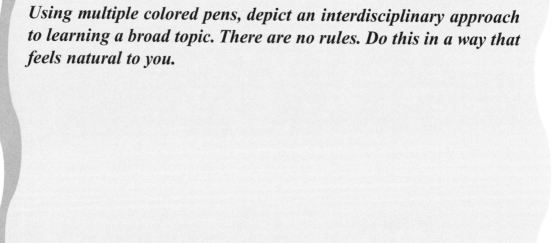

Mind-Map

Using multiple colored pens, depict an interdisciplinary approach to learning a broad topic. There are no rules. Do this in a way that feels natural to you.

Reactions:

What are your feelings about the topics presented in this chapter?

What are some practical applications for what you're learning?

What do you want to remember from this chapter?

The brain is continuously making sense of experience. When we understand this deeply, we will begin to perceive that everything in the classroom is "experience." The presentation, the activity, the silent reading, the cooperative group, the worksheet- everything is being processed by the brain and is given a unique set of meanings.

Geoffrey & Renate Caine, Sam Crowell
Mindshifts

Chapter 8
Learning Environment

Environments Can Teach

With all the hours spent in a classroom, the cumulative environmental effects on both students and teachers have tremendous impact. Many consider the traditional classroom a "primary obstacle" to learning. What can be done to change the negative associations that many students have about classrooms? A lot. An artfully designed and carefully planned positive-suggestive environment can do 25 percent of your teaching for you. Conversely, a poorly-designed learning environment can significantly detract from the learning process.

Every moment the student's eyes are not on you, they are taking in the classroom - sometimes in parts, sometimes as a whole. The environment they take in must reflect your end purposes or you risk getting poor results. A well-designed learning environment can do many things.

At its best, a favorable learning environment can:

✦ Encourage a positive relationship between the student and the subject matter.

✦ Create rapport between the teacher and the student.

✦ Stimulate thought, creativity, and curiosity.

✦ Build self-esteem, confidence, and self-worth.

✦ Inform, influence, persuade, and excite.

✦ Add to your student's level of responsibility, sense of justice, and positive feelings about school.

✦ Help make your classroom a cool place to be.

Read This First

Your classroom structure obviously needs to reflect your subject matter, grade level, personality and objectives, as a teacher. If you are a science teacher, of course, your classroom will look different than that of the humanities class next door. If you're teaching at the elementary school level, your classroom needs will be dramatically different than if you're teaching high school. This chapter provides some general guidelines for providing positive learning environments. You will need to make the distinctions, deletions, and modifications necessary to make the information compatible with your specific situation. In spite of this, it's likely that you'll find this information to be extremely valuable. Simple classroom modifications can dramatically impact student behaviors and learning results.

Regardless of the room you're assigned, the possibility exists to make it work well. Though you probably won't be able to turn your classroom into a *Better Homes and Gardens* award winner or an *Architectural Digest* showcase, it can be made bright, nurturing, expressive, useful, and humane. To make a classroom look right, it usually takes some money - though, much can be done for $50 or less. Paper, art objects, plants, and other classroom items that cost nothing or next-to-nothing can be acquired with a little imagination. Most beautiful classroom environments are put together using a combination of donated, disposed, or borrowed items. Small or nonexistent classroom budgets do not justify an ineffective classroom.

The research on the human brain in regards to enrichment is very persuasive. More challenge, novelty, engagement of emotions, color and feedback are ideal for the growing brain. This means an environment that is interactive, interesting, personalized and relevant. In order to maintain these qualities, the classroom must be changed often. Keeping interest high can be achieved by changing things such as bulletin boards, seating arrangements, furniture, pillows, colors, etc.

Quotable

Everything that we have discovered about the brain in the last 20 years suggests that we need more stimulus, more change, more movement, and more perspectives in the classroom.

Everything that we have discovered about the brain in the last twenty years suggests that we need more stimulus, more change, more movement, and more perspectives in the classroom. The most unproductive arrangement possible is the standard, rigid sit-still format that is driving most students and therefore, teachers, crazy. Of course, whenever weather or finances permit, work with your students in the less traditional environments. Take field trips, teach science in a nearby field, and use the rest of the school or neighborhood as a place to learn.

How to Get Help

Most teachers find themselves doing things that are actually the responsibility of others. The job of teaching is so big that without the support of other teachers, you can feel like you're sinking into a snake pit at times. The best way to get help is to give it. And the best way to get appreciation is to give it. Teaching can feel like a thankless job. When it does, stop and think for a moment when the last time was that you complimented or left a thank-you note for the janitor, the school secretary, the cafeteria crew, or the principle? Remember, too, that sometimes we must do what is necessary for the result we want, regardless of our job description! Winston Churchill said, "It is not enough that we do our best; sometimes we have to do what's required."

Keeping the classroom environment fresh does not have to be your sole responsibility. Set up a system where groups of students rotate the responsibility for it. With some guidance, they can contribute their individual talents (drawing, painting, synthesizing, giving advice, or scavenging for useful items) to achieve a mutually agreeable environment. In this spirit, it is possible to have a beautiful and functional classroom which is maintained by your students who get to feel some ownership in the process. If you have to move from room to room, make up a "kit" or "portable environment" that goes with you.

Safety Is Paramount

Above all else, safety is a primary consideration for teachers. Each teacher should be familiar with how to prevent and deal with any type of emergency. Teachers must know where the fire extinguisher is and the nearest phone. In addition, you should keep a current list of doctors, police, and fire numbers close by and a first aid kit which includes plenty of gauze, tape, and band-aids. Also keep a broom for cleaning up broken glass and cloths and rags for spilled items accessible. Know how to contact the building administrator or manager if necessary. Other necessities include knowing emergency procedures for fires, earthquakes, floods, hurricanes, windstorms, power failures, and blizzards. These are all part of the overall safety of your students and they are just as important as anything else a teacher does.

Room Preparation

Always include a check of your classroom before class starts. The following checklist may help you do this quickly:

◆ Is the room neat, clean and organized?
◆ Is trash disposed of properly?
◆ Are chairs arranged in the way you need them?
◆ Are the day's materials and handouts organized?
◆ Have all materials been checked for accuracy?
◆ How's the room temperature and humidity?
◆ Do you have your lesson plan(s) ready?
◆ Have you prepared the chalkboard? How about a greeting and any pre-class directions the students need?
◆ How do your bulletin boards and walls look? Do you have happy, thought-provoking posters or peripherals up? Have you changed the peripherals lately to keep the atmosphere fresh?

Many teachers have a checklist that they use each day, but many don't; and they begin their classes in the same way they end - in chaos. It takes a purposeful commitment to prepare your class for super-results each day. When your class starts chaotically, students are put into a confused, disjointed state of mind and the learning effectiveness drops dramatically.

Temperature Is Critical

The first thing a person will notice when they enter a room is the temperature; and this consideration is often overlooked by teachers. Classrooms kept between 68 and 72 degrees Fahrenheit seem to feel most comfortable for the largest majority of students. Often a teacher becomes so engrossed in what they are doing that they forget to check the temperature. For this reason it is suggested that you leave your classroom during breaks to get a sense of the outside temperature. If at all possible, a teacher should find a way to provide good air circulation - windows are easiest if the weather and building design permits. Many teachers have found it helpful to attach a small indicator piece of cloth next to a window or air conditioner so that they can tell at a glance if the air is circulating.

For teachers who are interested and have access to them, ionizers and humidifiers have been found valuable for student and teacher comfort. About 20 percent of the population is affected adversely by atmospheric electrical charges. Many experience great discomfort when the weather turns super dry and static electricity is prevalent. A negative ion generator can be useful in such cases.

Use of Color

Your classroom walls can support learning. Consider color. The shades, tones, and hues on the walls are so important that entire businesses have been created to do color consulting for optimum work environments. If your walls are not a pastel blue, light green, or aqua, find out about the possibility of painting them. Some teachers have found certain yellows to work well also. Other colors create reactions, whether conscious or subconscious within many of the students. A wood paneling or brick-face can create a warm, home-like feeling in many cases, and the cost of paneling is reasonable.

Power of Peripheral Stimuli

While the front of room is best kept aesthetic, simple, and clean, the sides of the room should have your most important instructional visual stimuli posted. How often do you see your student's eyes wandering around the room? In most cases, very often! In one study, it was found that while the recall of lecture material went down, the recall of peripherals actually increased! Do not try to draw attention to peripherals since they are meant to impact at the subconscious level. Peripheral messages are often more powerful than standard front-of-the-room instructional strategies. Be sure your messages are positive.

The positioning of visuals on the wall can make a major difference in how they impact the student. The direction your eyes look indicates an access to a certain physiological mode such as visual, auditory or kinesthetic. If you want the item to evoke good feelings, put it below your students' eye level. When the eyes are looking down and to the right, the body can most easily access the kinesthetic mode. If you want students to talk about an item on the wall, put it at eye level, since your body accesses constructed or created sounds with the eyes looking to the left or the right. This area is for communications and upcoming events. If you want students to simply notice the information, as in the form of review, put it above eye level which stimulates the visual mode for recalling the information.

Peripheral stimuli can effectively achieve the following purposes:

✦ *Communication Board:* to post assignments, messages, lost-and-found, resources, and other pertinent bits of information. Put items you want students to talk about at eye level.

✦ *Results Report:* to chart the progress of the class as a whole than to post individual test scores or well-written papers. Possibilities include putting up collective mindmaps of the week in review, group art projects, or presentations or even a large graph or thermometer showing the progress of the entire class as a team. Student work ought to be posted at a lower level to access feelings of pride.

✦ *Inspiration Area:* to post bright colored posters affirming positive messages, poetry, or quotes of famous people.

Be aware of how messages might be perceived by your students. For example, a teacher of learning disabled students (an excellent one in every other way) posted a nature scene picture with the message, "Things take time." What came across to some of the students was actually the message, "You learn slowly, so don't expect too much, too soon." A poster which says, "You Can Do It" is much more useful, for instance, than one that reads, "Hang In There, Baby."

Affirmations

Your room should be a fertile source of confidence, information and good feelings for your students. One of the best ways to do this is to put 5 to 15 posterboards up 16" X 20" up to 22" X 28" in size. Use light colored boards such as white, natural, canary, pink, powder blue or light gray. Then in simple, easy-to-read letters, paint or print in reminders for your students. Put them in the first person so that the student reading them knows that they apply directly. Put these signs up high, on the sides, and back of the room. One above the door is especially potent. Change them often, and use them to refer to or repeat in class. Some useful affirmations, regardless of whether your students are four or forty follow:

Useful Affirmations:

✦ *I am a bright and capable learner.*
✦ *If you learned something new today, give me five!*
✦ *Learning is fun, easy and creative.*
✦ *I do things simply, easily and playfully.*
✦ *I am healthy, happy and wise.*
✦ *I am the change I want to see.*
✦ *For things to change, I must change.*
✦ *I am a unique and precious being.*
✦ *I can do magic.*
✦ *I enjoy reading and using affirmations.*
✦ *I love myself just the way I am.*
✦ *Every problem offers a gift.*
✦ *I am a resourceful learner with many choices.*

Flip Charts and Markers

Most teachers use their chalkboards a great deal; however, the ceramic boards now available are a great improvement, as are flip charts. The benefit of using a flip-chart with large sheets of paper is that you can save what you write for posting. With both the flip-chart and the ceramic board, brightly-colored markers can be used which increase visual impact. When making lists, for instance, alternate colors increase visibility. If you need to use a chalkboard, colored chalk can improve readability, provide more choice of expression, and improve recall. Many teachers who don't have access to metal chalk-holders wrap the base of the chalk with masking tape to prevent breakage and reduce chalk dust.

Lighting

Though classroom lighting seems to be a controversial subject among teachers, one point which most agree on is that indirect or natural lighting is better than fluorescent lighting. Some areas of the room have greater need for light than others. A well-lit front of the room (spotlighting you, the chalkboard and flip chart) is critical. In many cases, you are not given much of a choice, so whether one kind of lighting is better than another is a moot issue. However, you can bring in inexpensive lamps to augment your lighting scheme.

Room Arrangement

Another area of physical environment is the arrangement of the room itself. Unattached chairs and moveable desks are best for maximum comfort and flexibility. Carpeting, if possible, creates a much warmer atmosphere. If this is not possible, provide a throw rug at the front of the classroom. The room needs to meet the needs of the subject matter, the students, and the teacher. To accomplish this, first notice what the course content demands are. They are obviously different in a woodworking class than in a speech class.

In general, position yourself at the front of the room in a way which puts the least depth from front to back with your students. In a rectangular-shaped room, be at the center of the longest side. It's far better to move from left to right across the stage than front to back. Decide what kinds of student-to-student interactions will be needed. Most teachers, perhaps unconsciously, have set up the class in a way that discourages student interaction. However, student disruption and behavior problems are not greater when students are allowed to interact with each other. Students need teacher-student and student-student contact for the best learning. Super-teachers arrange their classrooms to accommodate this important need. In fact, you might even want to encourage students to sit next to others they haven't sat next to before. Switching seats is a good idea because where one sits does change one's perspective.

Open Space

Room size is a critical factor in the world of first impressions. Most teachers do not have a choice about room size, so it is suggested that you use available resources to create the illusion of the room being the size you desire. The apparent size of a classroom can be altered by using such things as dividers or mirrors. In a standard classroom with desks, students should have 10 to 15 square feet of space each; and about 5 to 8 square feet without desks. The chairs and desks that are used in most classrooms are an unfortunate compromise of price and quality. Most of the chairs used promote lethargy, back aches, poor breathing, neck pain and sore bottoms.

Learn about anatomy so you can support the postures which are physically healthy. Here are some simple suggestions:

♦ Keep the knees higher than the hips.
♦ Support the arms and shoulders.
♦ Get up and stretch often.
♦ If you *have* to have desks, your chair should be three inches or less from your belly button.
♦ Your chair seat should be from 16 to 22 inches from the floor depending on your height.
♦ Make sure that your chair or a pillow provides lumbar (lower back) support.

Seating for Success

The key for seating success is variety and appropriateness. Seating is an excellent way to vary stimuli. Where a student sits in the class affects his/her learning experiences so flexibility is important. There is some strong research by Rita Dunn and Kenneth Dunn (1989) that suggests that many students will learn substantially better when given a choice of seating (i.e., sitting on the floor versus standing or occasionally walking around). Forced "frozen" seating can impair learning!

This means you may want to allow students to choose a different seat each time they enter the room and make sure that they are in a different part of the room, too. Remind the students that the room looks different from each section and that they can gain additional insights and experiences by changing their viewing points. It's true in a sports situation and true in a room. The whole notion of switching seats helps students find fresh, unconditioned situations, leaving old fixed, limiting patterns behind. If at all possible, set up the seating so students can see and interact with each other. The novelty of it will wear off soon and the effectiveness will far outweigh any conversational distractions.

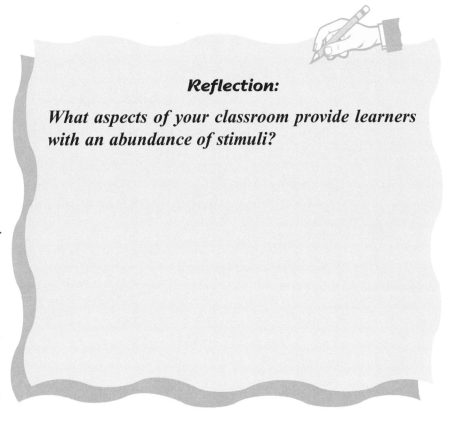

Reflection:

What aspects of your classroom provide learners with an abundance of stimuli?

The Sounds of Learning

The amount of stimulation that the human brain desires and has the ability to integrate is astonishing. The sounds present in your room are just as important as how it looks and feels. While your room may be visually attractive, 40 percent of your students are auditory learners. Students love music, and thus, it can be used very effectively to enhance the classroom atmosphere and student attitudes. Music when used appropriately can evoke specific desirable mood changes.

One way to use music in the classroom effectively is to have it playing at the start and close of class and to mark transitions or breaks. Music selection should be based on the state of your learners. Observe them closely. Are they distracted, over-active, lethargic? If you want them upbeat, put on faster-paced music such as exciting movie themes. If they are restless, put on slower-paced music with 40 to 60 beats per minute. Many teachers play lively classical music at the outset, slower music during moments of relaxation or test-taking, and up-beat music during activities. Other specific suggestions for the use of music in the classroom can be found in chapter 16 on Music in Learning.

Breaking the Ice

Greeting students at the door is a simple and effective way to set the stage for a productive class session. This is also a good time to plant seeds for the day's learning, and to make a positive personal impression with each student.

Pre-class mingling is also a good time to enjoy students and learn about their interests. A classroom that is bright, playful and happy will evoke a friendly state in your learners. Breaking the ice with learners will be simple if the classroom feels comfortable, sounds joyous, smells good, and looks interesting.

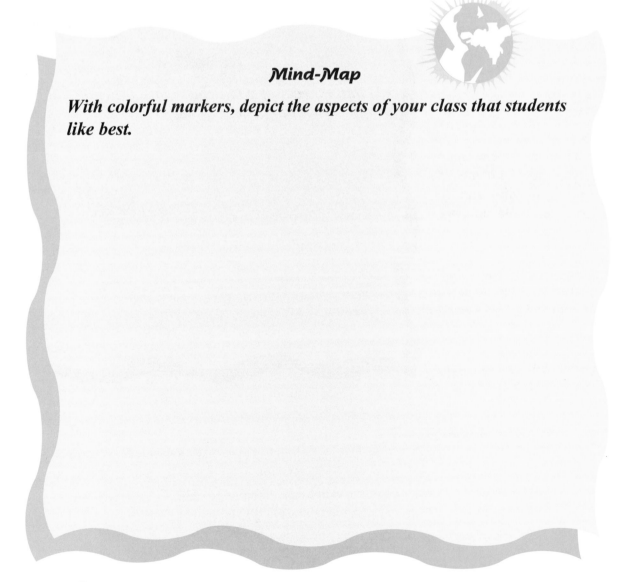

Mind-Map

With colorful markers, depict the aspects of your class that students like best.

Reactions:

What are your feelings about the topics presented in this chapter?

What are some practical applications for what you're learning?

What do you want to remember from this chapter?

Teaching is a skill so complex that no single factor can fully explain or describe the qualities of an effective teacher.

Allan C. Ornstein & Daniel U. Levine "Teacher Behavior Research: Overview and Outlook," *Phi Delta Kappa*

Chapter 9

Presenting Skills

Chapter Preview:

- ✦ **Communication Defined**
- ✦ **Planning and Organization**
- ✦ **Notes and Prompts**
- ✦ **Openings: Well Begun is Well Done**
- ✦ **Four Keys That Open Doors**
- ✦ **Attention-Getters**
- ✦ **Connecting the Group**
- ✦ **Addressing Student Fears and Concerns**
- ✦ **Making Your Point**
- ✦ **Different Voices**
- ✦ **Positive Wording**
- ✦ **Let's Get Physical**
- ✦ **Closings: Parting is Such Sweet Sorrow**
- ✦ **Key Points for Closings**
- ✦ **Review and Evaluation Strategies**
- ✦ **Presenter Feedback**
- ✦ **Preview of Coming Attractions**
- ✦ **Congratulations, Celebrations, and Closing Rituals**

Communication Defined

The definition of communication is simple: the transfer of meaning. The meaning of your communication is the response you get! Let's say, for instance, that your classroom is burning down so you yell "fire" but some people don't take you seriously, they think you are joking. At this point, it is obvious that you had better change your communication strategy. It's not enough that what you say works for most people most of the time. What's "enough" is determined by your resources and commitment to the outcome. If 90 percent of your students understand your message about the fire and leave, are you committed to the outcome enough to insure the "safety" of the other 10 percent? Similarly, is it enough that 90 percent of your students in reality are getting your message, while the other 10 percent are getting "burned?"

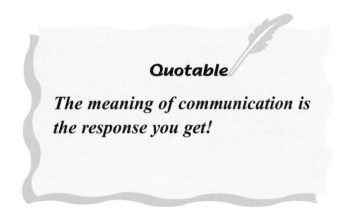

The meaning of communication is the response you get!

A strong commitment to effective communication does not mean that you will always get 100 percent understanding, but it does mean that you understand the complexity of the task. Most of us grew up believing that if someone else doesn't get the meaning of what we say, it's their fault. When we shift the responsibility of communication to ourselves rather than other, we take a step closer to being a super-teacher. When you approach your students with the perspective that the meaning of your communication is the response that you get, your classroom results will increase dramatically.

The communication process includes three essential elements: content, delivery and context. When you do not get the expected results from your communications, ask yourself the following questions: Is it *what* I'm saying? *how* I'm saying it? or Is it the *circumstances*? Focus on what's going on for the learner. Evaluate their understanding by asking questions such as, "Could you re-phrase what I just said?" "What's not clear to you?" "How do you know you don't understand?" "What would it take for you to really understand this topic?" "When you say you're not sure, what parts are you sure about already?" Just by asking useful questions such as these, you'll begin to understand how your students think, learn, and draw conclusions. You'll also learn more about your own instructional style. As you gather information about your students and your own communication patterns, keep in mind the three elements of communication influence:

1. Content or *what* you are saying:
This is essentially your subject matter. It is also includes your ability to build relationships, add value, create motivation, elicit promises, and prompt requests.

2. Delivery or *how* you are saying it:
This includes your posture, eye contact, positioning, expressions and gestures. It also includes the school's dress code, grooming, and especially, your voice qualities: tonality, volume, pitch, tempo, and rhythm.

3. Context or the *conditions* and *circumstances* involved:
This area includes class mood, rules, prior learning, etc. You have within you, at any time, in any place, both the ability and the responsibility to create favorable learning conditions.

When you teach with an emphasis on people, rather than on curriculum, your communications will be student-centered. This means that the focus is on the effects of your communication, not the generation or creation of the communication. Communication is a two-way conversation with your students. The meaning of your communication is not what you intended, but rather the response you get. To succeed at the game of communication it takes the following:

✦ Clear, well-defined outcomes for the interaction, presentation, or conversation.
✦ Well-developed perception and sensory acuity skills to be able to know what responses you are getting.

✦ Enormous flexibility so you can keep changing what you are doing, if needed.

✦ A personal commitment to the listener and the outcomes - you are willing to keep trying until you are successful.

To communicate at this level requires commitment. It requires your best self each time you interact. Being "purposefully present" for your students means being mindful of your mutual objectives, being caring, fully awake, clear, and patient. It means you are doing what you are supposed to be doing: listening, speaking, being "in the moment." All of this requires integrity, honesty, truthfulness, and a commitment to your values.

Express yourself more than you think you need to. Make every day a challenge - stretch and try to grow to a new level. Be yourself and let your good qualities come through so that the class can relate to you as a real human being, not a "teacher." Super-teachers use a vast array of specialized communication tools. When these tools are used as part of a presentation, the result is magic - a special kind of charisma. Yet, in reality the magic is actually many small things done well. Some of the key components of an effective presentation are: planning and organization, notes and prompts, opening remarks, attention- getters, connecting the group, addressing student fears, making your point, and closings. Let's take a closer look at how these components influence your communication with students.

Planning and Organization

In planning your presentation always keep the learner in mind. That's right, the learner. For a moment forget about all the great and wonderful things you want to teach. What you are about is learning, not teaching. Powerful presentation skills require asking the right questions before you even go into the classroom. What will the learner's mindset be? What does he/she already know? What does the learner bring to this topic? What are the biases, the beliefs, and prejudices? What will the circumstances be? What two or three things do I want to make sure are learned? What resources do I have at hand? How much time is allotted? The more questions you ask and the better the quality of questions, the greater the likelihood you'll discover what you really need to know to achieve success.

Notes and Prompts

How can you present new material with a minimum of notes and prompts? Don't bother trying. Many of the very best presenters in the business use them. The key is using them unobtrusively and flexibly. If you follow the three steps outlined below, you will succeed. They work!

1. First, create a mind-map that outlines the key points of your presentation and the interrelated aspects of it. See the chapter on lesson planning for ideas. You can keep this for your own reference, display it on an over-head projector, or copy it as a handout for the class.

2. Next, write out a more detailed outline for yourself on a sheet of paper or note cards. As you write it, talk yourself through the lesson. Visualize yourself doing it. Be specific. This is where the real planning for the lesson takes place.

3. Now, write out a general outline on paper large enough for posting up on the back wall of the room. This way, you'll have all your key ideas right up in front of you for easy reference. And the students can refer to it later if necessary.

Openings: Well Begun Is Well Done

There is enormous potential for creating classroom magic during the first moments of class when students are in a distinctive first-time state of mind. A presentation opening serves many purposes, including: to orient the audience, to preview material, motivate, inspire, and gain rapport. Your students begin class with their own "mental set." Your job is to unsettle their existing mindset and create a new, more resourceful one. A carefully designed and artfully orchestrated introduction can make possible a significantly better class. Therefore, the purpose of an introduction or "set induction," as it is often called, is to maximize the effectiveness of the forthcoming presentation.

The length of an introduction, in general, ought to be proportional to the presentation length. For example, a ten-minute speech might need only a one-minute introduction; whereas, a one-hour presentation might have a ten-minute introduction. In a two day workshop or seminar, the first couple of hours might be allotted for the introduction.

Four Keys That Open Doors

Many factors influence the planning of a good opening depending on the particulars of the situation. Some of the questions you need to ask yourself at this stage are: How much time do I have? Who are these students? What do they know about the subject? What is the purpose of the presentation? What credibility do I have with this group? And what is my relationship to the group? Once you have answered these questions, develop your opening with the following four objectives in mind:

1. Get Attention

If you don't get the attention of the group at the beginning of your presentation, you probably aren't going to get it at all. The audience is ripe for contact and influence at this point. They are forming first impressions. To capture the interest of the group, you may need to create a state-change. This can be accomplished by engaging the group's emotions - curiosity, humor, fascination, novelty, or challenge.

2. Build Rapport and Trust

Some learners are not receptive to learning until a relationship with the teacher has been established. Create a connection with learners. Show concern for them as individuals. Follow through with your promises. If you say that the group will be given a break at noon, do this. What might seem like a trivial promise becomes an important marker when students are trying to determine how much they can trust you. Always open the class and introduce yourself on time even if you don't actually start the formal presentation. Your time, as well as that of the other students, is valuable and deserves to be respected. Being on time is also a way that you honor your agreements and create a context of worthiness and importance.

3. Establish Relevancy

The best way to establish relevancy is to provide some building blocks for the process and then ask students to build it. It can be done on an individual basis, with partners, or in small groups, depending on the time allotted and the particulars of the situation. Answer questions that come up for students like, "What's in it for me?" by providing essential information. They need to know what they can expect from you, what the big picture is, what your objectives are, and how you plan to reach the objectives. Then give students some say and ownership in their learning by asking them to think for themselves.

4. Create a Learning Climate

Much of this book is about establishing a receptive learning environment. Doing this is a long-term proposition that includes many things. To begin the process, make a commitment to eliminating high stress, threat, anxiety and learner helplessness in your classroom. Keep your promises. Build a structure that supports individuals. Encourage a sense of joy in class. And continue to learn new things yourself.

Attention-Getters

There are, of course, countless ways to get attention. You have to find the ones that work best for you. But some general guidelines and suggestions will help as you make your way down the sometimes unsettling path towards effective communication.

When getting started be generous with your eye contact. Enjoy "taking in" all of your students for a moment so they know you have personally seen them and acknowledged their presence. Let them know by your facial expressions and body language that you are happy to have them in class and that you are excited about the upcoming lesson. Make sure your posture and positioning say you are open to your students. Avoid starting out behind a desk or table. This softer, gentler manner "invites" rather than "demands" student attention.

Bring a boom box or CD and play exciting upbeat music such as a movie theme from a big hit. If a movie production company has already spent millions creating a favorable public impression, you may as well take advantage of it!

Suggestions for Nonverbal Attention Getters:

- Make eye contact
- Raise your hand
- Hold up an interesting object
- Motion towards the clock
- Open your mouth and pause
- Have a student get the attention of others for you
- Move to the center of the room
- Stand in a designated spot
- Stand in an unusual spot
- Look anxious and ready to start
- Hold up your finger to your lips vertically
- Conduct a transition event
- Play an instrument
- Give a drum roll
- Put on a special hat or other prop
- Pass out a book, a handout, or novelty item
- Use noisemakers
- Do charades or mime
- Do a magic trick
- Give a coded message
- Use puppets
- Hold up an unusual object
- Change lighting
- Begin clapping

Connecting the Group

Whatever greeting you use in your presentation, put energy into it! It might be "Good morning", "Hello, boys and girls (ladies and gentlemen)!" or "Hi, and welcome to...." Congruence is critical at this time. Make sure your verbal message is also conveyed by your body language and gestures. Project your voice and make sure you are talking to each and every student. After you have greeted your audience, a direct call to action will engage your audience. Possibilities include:

✦ "Please turn to the person sitting nearest you and welcome them."
✦ "Everybody take a deep breath, please."
✦ "Please say hello to three other people around you."
✦ "Eyes and ears up front, please."
✦ "You sssshhhh-ould find this class very interesting today."
✦ "Please find the best colored pen you can from the tray in the back."

Any request is best stated with a tone of respect, support, and expectancy that the call to action will be met. If your efforts at building rapport have been successful, your audience will follow through with the request. Now the intent is to build audience rapport. Rapport, a distinct physiological state of positive responsiveness, is necessary to lead your students effectively. As a teacher, it's critical that your audience feels comfortable responding to you. Your students do not need to like you for you to establish rapport with them. Rapport equals responsiveness, not affection. As a teacher, you can do just fine if others dislike you - but you must have responsiveness. The favorable relationships you develop with your students will mark the degree of your influence. Quite simply, rapport is the ability to enter a student's world to see things the way he/she does, to hear what he or she hears and to feel what he or she feels. A class with good rapport consists of students who feel validated and important.

There is a difference between building relationships with individuals and with groups. When a group reaches a size of between 10 and 15 people, it takes on a life of its own. It becomes over time, as Author Michael Grinder (1989) says, the "group's group." In other words, the group has it's own energy and culture separate from you. Learn to understand the group's culture as quickly as you can. If it's your class, and it's the first day, and they are all from diverse backgrounds (they have not been together before as a group) you can strongly influence the norms of the group. But you'll never completely control the group, nor would you want to. A resentful group can be your worst nightmare!

Quotable

Some learners are not receptive to learning until a relationship with the teacher has been established.

To develop positive relationships within the group, be interested in your students instead of trying to be an interesting teacher. Greet them at the door with a smile, handshake or hug, whichever is appropriate. Give warm, sincere and authentic greetings that convey caring and interest in every student. Repeat the dose daily throughout the year. Be sure to respect the emotional, physical, psychological, and spiritual mood of the students. Be sure to respect the beliefs, opinions, prejudices, attitudes, and experiences of them, as well. Be sure to ask permission of the group for anything you need that requires the trust of the group. More than anything else you can do, being a caring and genuine teacher will build relationships.

Addressing Student Fears and Concerns

Each student comes into your class with many questions. Some of them seem trivial, some are obviously more critical. "What's coming up?" or "What do I do if this happens?" or the most common one, "What's in it for me?" "Will this be on the test?" "Will I be embarrassed, threatened or pressured today?" You must answer these questions soon, so that learners will be able to focus on the learning.

The three biggest fears of students are that the class will be boring, that they won't learn anything, and that they won't be treated fairly. Let's take a closer look at these fears and what to do about them:

1. *Are you interesting?*

One of the biggest fears of students is boredom. Regardless of the value of the course, students want to know right up front if you are interesting, fun, and can make class go quickly. Every student has had the misfortune of suffering through a slow and uninteresting class and the last thing they want is to do this again. Assure them either verbally (you can say, "What I've found is that students learn more when they enjoy what they are doing. This class will be a lot of fun."); or non-verbally by being very expressive and engaging.

2. *Are you competent?*

Maybe the second greatest fear is that they won't learn anything. It's important to establish credibility and professionalism so that students have confidence in your ability. Here are some possible ways to state your competence:

A new teacher: "My name's Eric Jensen and I've been interested in science for over six years. I did successful graduate work in environmental science with an emphasis in systems thinking. You'll find I know my subject well, I teach it in a fun and new way, and I love sharing as well as learning with you."

A veteran or tenured teacher: "My name's Eric Jensen and I'm pleased to have you in class. I've worked successfully with over 10,000 students in the last 15 years and am confident you'll do well. Because of the new way this class is organized, you'll not only learn a lot, but have fun doing it."

3. *Are you fair and trustworthy?*

This question is prompted by the thought of being evaluated and the fear of failure or, just as bad, not getting what is deserved. It's important for a teacher to give the students some assurances or a sense of fairness. A possibility is: "In the past, other students have found me easy to talk to and my evaluation methods fair. I'm sure you will too."

Make sure that your students know what they need to do in order to succeed. This must be made explicit; and ought to be either in writing for each student or posted in a highly visible place in the room. The more specific it is the better; however, depending on the nature of the class, it maybe as simple as the following:

◆ Participate
◆ Take notes
◆ Review notes two times per week
◆ Follow directions
◆ Set goals
◆ Ask questions

The important thing for students to know is that they have control of the class outcomes. In other words, give them your specific procedure for determining if they have met your evaluation criteria. This should include what you expect them to learn, by when and in what form they will be required to demonstrate competency. Share your expectations with them and ask for their expectations, in return.

Students also need to know the ground rules. Can they talk in class, move around, go to the bathroom or sleep? What happens if they're late, chew gum, eat in class or disrupt? What about listening to pocket stereos? Is there a dress standard? Any area which is the least bit uncertain needs to be taken care of in the introduction. Each student brings expectations into a learning situation and the more you handle them ahead of time, the fewer problems you'll have later.

Students need to know the location of the pencil sharpener, the bathroom, the trash can, the resources, the drinking fountain and the clock. They also want to know when breaks are, where they are allowed to go on breaks, what they are allowed to bring back into the classroom, and what time to return from a break. Make sure students know what forms to turn in, where to put them, and the deadlines. Usually there are a dozen bits of data that students need to know the first time they are in your classroom. Having logistical information allows students to relax and become involved with the process of learning.

Students need to know the benefits of taking your class. What will a student "get" by being in your class? Spend a few moments learning about your student's needs. The more a student perceives need for your material, the greater the motivation. The following questions elicit student need for learning study skills:

✦ How many of you think your studying takes too long?
✦ How many of you fall asleep sometimes while doing your reading?
✦ How many of you have had the experience of studying for a test, thinking that you know it, then blowing it at test time?

Possible benefits are suggested in the following questions:

✦ Who would like to know three ways to cut study time in half?
✦ Is there anyone who'd like to be better at (any subject)?
✦ How many of you would like to have a choice of colleges to go to?
✦ Who in here would like to learn more ways to earn a living?

Then, ask students what they think they might get out of learning better study skills. This quick activity creates immediate recognition of students' needs and offers benefits for taking your class. By hearing responses to these questions, students get a sense of the mutual needs of their classmates. They begin to see themselves "in the same boat" which may help to reduce lingering fears.

A similar tool that can work, depending on your audience, is the certainty affirmation. Tell your students, with certainty and congruency, that they will learn and remember the subject you teach. It might be something as simple as: "I've taught this course many times and my students always get it. I am certain that each of you will master this subject, as well." It's easy for them to feel like they'll succeed in the midst of certainty.

The possibility of failure should not deter your confidence. If you communicate uncertainty and hesitancy in your students' learning ability, it will impact their ability to learn. In short, any doubts on your part become a self-fulfilling prophecy. As a professional, you can't afford a negative thought.

The research is compelling - what you think about a student affects his or her chances for success. You have a moral and ethical obligation to believe in the ability and positive chances for success in every single student. If you don't believe that they can succeed in your class, you may want to: 1) have the student transferred to another class with another teacher; 2) learn the teaching skills to help them succeed; or 3) consider whether teaching is right for you. Now that you have prepared your students for success by using effective communication "stage-setting" techniques, let's examine the ways to get your point across.

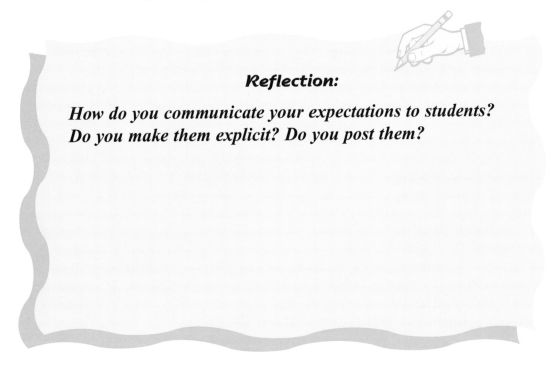

Reflection:

How do you communicate your expectations to students?
Do you make them explicit? Do you post them?

Making Your Point

Have you ever noticed the catchy headlines of the publication, *The National Inquirer*? "Five Ways to Improve Your Marriage," or "Why Single People Are Less Lonely," or "New Diet Amazes Even Scientists!" As much as tabloids are criticized, people buy them! Why not catch your student's attention using the same proven technique? Some examples of "catchy headlines" follow:

◆ *Biology:* "Today we'll be learning about DNA. We'll find out how nature has put enough information in your genes to fill up 10,000 volumes of *Encyclopedia Britannica*."
◆ *Ancient History:* "How would you like to have 20 slaves working for you, for 20 years? What would you have them do? Today we're going to talk about a civilization that had 20 slaves per citizen."
◆ *Health:* "In a few moments we'll learn why you can't catch a cold at the North Pole during the winter."
◆ *Geography:* "Next we'll discover how there are pieces of matter on our earth that are older than the earth itself." Or, "We'll discover which country has sand dunes as high as a 35-story building."
◆ *Literature:* "One of the things we'll find out today is what author wrote a 6,000 word poem when he was twelve years old."

If you can say a paragraph in a sentence, do it. If you can say a sentence in a word, do it. Generally, the shorter the phrase, the more powerful. Say it, then pause; let it settle in for a moment and then continue on. Long-winded sentences lose audiences. If you have a list of items to read off, make sure that you read only a few items at a time before stopping. Then break the pattern and continue. Here's a great way of delivering lists - interrupt yourself to remind the audience to focus. Say: "You'll need to know this for the exam" or "Wow, get this!" or "everyone focus on..." This keeps the audience from simply checking out because they know what is expected of them. Here's an abrasive slogan from the advertising business regarding the attitude of the consumer towards information: "Tell me quick, tell me true, or else my love to heck with you!"

Different Voices

As a presenter, you'll want to use several distinctly different types of voices. Each has a different body physiology and each creates a different result. Michael Grinder, author of *Envoy* (1993), calls two of these the "credible" and the "approachable" voices. The first is for sending, the second is for feedback. These are very culturally dependent. Culture can mean gender, nationality, geography, circumstances, etc. Traditionally in male circles, in sports and the military, you'll hear much more of the "credibility" voice. Among women, you'll traditionally find more use of the "approachable" voice. Both have important roles in the classroom. Learn the culture of your audience and use the one that's appropriate for the group. If you consistently use the same one, you limit your own choices and the ability of the audience to respond to you differently.

The decision, regarding which voice pattern to use, is easy to make. Ask yourself what you want. Am I sending information or do I want to receive information? Do I want to make an impression with my agenda, or do I want to discover another's agenda? Do I want my audience to laugh, to be introspective or to be impacted? It doesn't matter as long as you're purposeful about it.

Quotable

What you __think__ about a student affects his or her chances for success.

The credible voice has less variance, less inflection and ends the sentence on a lower note with the chin down. The credibility comes from the fact that your statements end with the finality and authority which says, "This is a fact!" Use this voice when you are telling it like it is, giving commands, facts, calls for action and strong opinions. There are many legitimate times to use this voice, and the larger the group, the more you're likely to need it. It is the voice of control.

The "approachable" voice is used for the times when either the group is smaller (15 or less) or when you want feedback from a larger group. This voice of yours is higher, has more variance and regardless of where the tonality starts out, it ends up higher at the end. You have more of a bobbing, up-and-down head movement. It's the voice that you use when someone has just given you a surprising bit of information and you respond by saying "Really?" Your voice goes up, and the other person is expected and invited to respond. To be successful as a presenter, you need both voices, the credible one and the approachable one.

Positive Wording

A common pattern of ineffective teachers is the use of negation - they spend more time telling their students what *not* to do, than what to do. The best teachers put most of what they say in the positive form. Negation exists only in our language, not in our experience. If you say, "Don't do that!", it doesn't tell the person what to do, it only says what to avoid. Therefore it creates no action, involvement or empowerment.

If someone says, "Don't think of the color purple, think of any color as long as it's not purple", you have to think of purple to know what not to think of! In the same way, if you say to your students, "Don't be late", they have to think of what lateness is like in order to understand the sentence. Why would you want to remind them of what lateness is like if what you really want to do is remind them of timeliness?" It makes more sense to say, "Be sure to be on time." Simply word your sentences so that students know what you want.

Let's Get Physical

Students need and want physical movement to be at their best. They love to get up and move around: the mind can only absorb what the seat can endure. Part of the reason many students don't participate is that they sit slouched over, with poor breathing, and limited circulation in a stuffy room. Be responsive to your students! Watch them closely to see what they need. Give them a 60- second stretch break. Have them walk around the room or do an assignment that requires them to move. Be sure to refer to the chapter on energizers which offers more than one hundred ways to get up and oxygenate!

Closings: Parting Is Such Sweet Sorrow

What's the best way to end a class? For some teachers, the bell does the job. For others, class is over when they run out of material. One of the best opportunities for learning can take place during the last few minutes of class. If you design your class well, you'll look forward to the feelings of completion and satisfaction that can accompany your closing. Ideally, your entire class will feel an inner sense of accomplishment at this point.

Class closures belong in the category of completing unfinished business. A well-taught class needs an ending to tie pieces together and relate the parts to the whole. This simple act insures that the value students receive remains intact. Even if you are rushed and running out of time, closures ought not be neglected. If you are doing a 10-minute presentation, do a closure during the last couple of minutes. In a 50-minute presentation, do a closure in the last five to eight minutes. In a one-day course, allot 30 to 45 minutes for a closure. Closure is the last word, the final thought, the ribbon around the package!

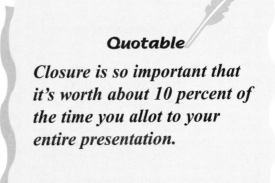

Quotable

Closure is so important that it's worth about 10 percent of the time you allot to your entire presentation.

Closures offer time for students to integrate the course material in a way that truly adds to their resources. It can afford an opportunity to ask some important questions: What was the point? Did I learn anything? Have I enhanced my sense of myself? How can I grow from this experience? An effective closure will encourage students to make useful conclusions about what was just taught. Students seem compelled to be clock-watchers as a class nears end! Make it your personal challenge to create a kind of closure that will capture their attention and imagination well enough to make it a memorable experience.

Key Points for Closings

A successful closing includes five elements: 1) a sense that something was accomplished - movement occurred; 2) that it was worthwhile both internally and externally - validation; 3) that it was understood and believed - internalized; 4) that the audience knows the next step to take - follow-up; and 5) that it is complete at least for now - wholeness.

Quotable

A good closure is not an after thought. It deserves equal time, if not top billing, with the presentation and introduction.

Learners like to know progress was made and have that acknowledged. Validation can come from many sources including a review or test. It can come from the student's own introspections or self-discoveries during the class. Or it can come from a sharing with each other in the group. Facilitate a group sharing by asking students to think about such questions as: What happened today? What did I learn? How does what I learned affect me? Or how do I feel about it? This is a great time for you to get some feedback on the value of the class.

A good closure offers a sense of completion. Students like to know that a section or part of something is done. They need to have their questions answered, their upsets handled, and their excitement shared. Completion also means that you have led students into the future with the information or "future-paced." Make sure you congratulate or thank students for their attention and presence. The closure may also need to provide information for the student such as scheduling, announcements, or assignments. Finally, students should leave your class with an excitement and curiosity to learn more.

There's a saying that goes something like this: "It's not what happens, it's what you do about what happens." A variation is: "It's not what you learn, it's the conclusions you draw about yourself that make the difference." If a student has come to a potentially damaging conclusion in response to a learning activity, you'll want to lead him/her to a more resourceful one. For example, if a student says that what they just learned is that they "don't work well with others," ask some clarifying questions such as:

Sample Closing Questions to Address:

✦ *Does anyone else feel the same way I do?*

✦ *Was this worthwhile for me?*

✦ *What do I do with what I've learned?*

✦ *What's next?*

✦ *How can I continue to learn more on this subject?*

✦ *Do I really understand what was taught?*

✦ *Will I remember what was taught?*

✦ *How does this fit in with everything else I know?*

✦ *What if I can't use any of this information?*

✦ *What is coming up next?*

- "I appreciate your sharing that. What do you think, specifically, causes you to not work well with others?"
- "Thanks for letting me know. When you say others, I wonder if anyone, specifically, comes to mind?"
- "I respect you for expressing this. Could you imagine what it would take for you to be able to work well with others?"
- "It's great you shared that with us, thanks. I was thinking, if you were to solve this challenge, how would you go about it?"

With each question you ask politely and respectfully, you are helping that student reach inside themselves to discover resources they didn't know were there. You also have an obligation, as a learning coach, to make sure that any conclusions drawn are useful for the student's life. This intervention is not only preferred, it's the reason that you are in the classroom - to shape beliefs, attitudes and values.

Review and Evaluation Strategies

An aspect of the closure process that is generally much enjoyed is the open oral recall drill. This activity generates a great deal of energy and confidence in students. To start an open review, begin with a sentence such as:

Today we started with the concept of _____ and how it affects the _____. Then we learned another form called _____.

As you ask the question, the students answer orally in unison. This type of review requires mostly simple recall skills. Ask for items you are confident students know. The oral recall drill reinforces that they know the material, and they have a lot fun doing it together. Most of this review is structured as a sentence completion exercise. Make sure the answer is clear, singular, and something that was discussed in class.

Mind-mapping is an organizing tool used for note-taking and recall. Mind-maps can also be effective in the closing process to review and evaluate student learning. In groups of three or four, have students create mind-maps of the lesson presented. While they recall, organize, plan, and think about the material once again, the material gets arranged in such a way that makes sense to them. Usually a group can put together a well-designed mind-map in 10 minutes or less. You might also have teams plan a mind-map for the course. Display completed mind-maps around the room so each group's work can be admired, reflected upon, and reviewed.

Quotable

There are no failures in the classroom; there are, however, often unrecognized gifts.

Facilitating a class discussion on a topic presented is another common and useful way to review and evaluate a group's learning. This can be done in small groups or pairs or as a class. If possible, use group leaders previously trained to help facilitate the discussion. Some examples of questions you might ask to open a discussion follow:

- How do you feel about this subject today compared to before?
- What was the best way for you to learn this?
- What points interested you the most?

- What did you learn about yourself today?
- How might what you learned, and how you learned it, affect your life?
- Why do you think this was taught today?

Presenter Feedback

Even if you only have three minutes, you can get reasonably accurate and useful feedback on how effectively you communicated. Super-teachers are committed to improving, no matter how experienced they become. Ask your students for written and/or oral feedback. It can be formal (evaluation survey) or informal (show of hands or foot stomping to vote). Be specific with your questions. Remind students that the best feedback is stated, personally. For instance, when you said _____, I felt _____. Or when you demonstrated such-and-such, I got confused. Not only will you be getting valuable feedback, but you'll be teaching your learners how to give productive feedback - a life-long skill worth learning! A simple example of a written evaluation form is provided below.

Class Evaluation:

Date: Class:

Directions: No name, please. After each thought, please comment.

1.   *What I enjoyed most about class was:*

2.   *What I disliked most about class was:*

3.   *Class would have been better if:*

4.   *What I discovered about myself today is:*

5.   *I had a change of attitude or perspective regarding:*

6.   *I describe my attitude now toward this subject as:*

7.   *What I'd like to know next on this topic is:*

8.   *Other comments:*

Once evaluations are collected, you must read and do something about them! Look for areas you can improve on; notice the feelings and moods of your students. If a student is troubled, you might mention to the class: "Some of you expressed some concern over how things are going, and I'd like to invite you to meet with me for a moment after class."

Preview of Coming Attractions

As you close an ongoing class session, tantalize your students with tidbits of learning to follow. Figure out what would be interesting to your students and turn it into a commercial for the next class. This can be done in the form of posing a question or challenge. In a study skills class, for example, you could say, "Next class we'll be learning how to reduce study time and increase reading comprehension. Anyone interested...? Great! See you next time!" Or, in other classes, it might be:

+ Next class we'll learn ten new words in Spanish that could help you out of a jam.
+ When we meet again, we'll find out how learning about rock formation has made millions of dollars for some enterprising people.
+ At our next meeting, we'll learn to use a power tool that can save you dozens of hours of valuable time.
+ Next time, we'll discover who was the only president in our history to never marry and why.

Congratulations, Celebrations, and Closing Rituals

The close of class is the perfect time to acknowledge and appreciate your students for their participation. For every single class, regardless of what was taught or how well the students learned, find something that you can sincerely appreciate or acknowledge. Make sure that your comments are congruent with your posture, voice, words, tonality and gestures. Learners especially remember openings and closings. Make the closing memorable! Ask students to:

+ Complete their learning logs.
+ Put a learning thermometer on the wall to jump up and touch.
+ Do a self-assessment.
+ Post a personal hand print above the door. Put a poster up that says, "If you learned something new, high five!"
+ Take a walk outside with a partner and discuss what you learned.
+ Play a game involving the key points of the class.
+ Bring in something relevant to the class to share with others.
+ Write a poem about their learning or feelings about their learning.
+ Offer a verbal word of thanks for something you received from the class or a classmate.
+ Create test questions for the next class.
+ Celebrate - use music, streamers, and party favors. If it's worth learning, it's worth celebrating!

Every teacher can immediately add to their effectiveness by establishing a closing ritual. A closing ritual serves to integrate the conscious content taught in the class with the student's unconscious experience. Some examples of strategies that will accomplish this objective follow:

+ Everybody repeats the class theme (it could be any one that you select, maybe the thought of the week such as "It's in every one of us").
+ Everyone sings a class song.
+ Students give all the others a standing ovation.

- ✦ Incorporate a class mascot.
- ✦ A student shares/the class philosopher.
- ✦ Clapping/a tai chi clap/dancing.
- ✦ Simply standing up and taking in a deep breath of energy.
- ✦ Pointing out or noticing the class accomplishments.
- ✦ Conducting a class cheer.

Whatever the closing ritual, get class buy-in before facilitating it. Or if your students are able, have them design the closing ritual. Introduce the ritual with energy and enthusiasm. Be consistent and have fun with it. If some students are slow to join in, be patient; some people are slower than others to warm up to activities that involve expressing emotions. The closing ritual is the final experience students will have in your class so its importance can't be overstated! Have fun!

Mind-Map

Using colored markers, depict the ideal learning environment. Remember, there are no rules, or right or wrong ways to do a mind-map.

Reactions:

What are your feelings about the topics presented in this chapter?

What are some practical applications for what you're learning?

What do you want to remember from this chapter?

Being open and being attentive is more effective than being judgmental.

John Heider
The Tao of Leadership

Chapter 10

Powerful Listening Skills

Chapter Preview:

- ✦ **Two Ears, One Mouth**
- ✦ **Worst Listening Mistakes**
- ✦ **Listening Is a Learned Skill**
- ✦ **Use a Listening Voice**
- ✦ **Learn What the Speaker Needs**
- ✦ **Many Ways to Listen**
- ✦ **How to Create a Listening Environment**
- ✦ **Empathetic Listening**
- ✦ **Here's the Real Skill**
- ✦ **Avoid These Listening Mistakes**
- ✦ **Listen to the Person First**
- ✦ **Reading Non-Verbals**
- ✦ **Precision Listening**
- ✦ **Clarifications**

Two Ears, One Mouth

Should we be listening more than we are speaking? In the best classrooms, you'll find teachers who do just that. Regardless of the effectiveness of your presentation or teaching skills, you may be ineffective as a teacher unless you have strong listening skills. Listening to others inspires, compliments, enriches and nurtures. The dictionary defines listening as "to hear with thoughtful attention." It also means being fully present with the intention of receiving the intended meaning of the communication.

Worst Listening Mistakes

There are many more ways to listen poorly than to listen well. What often occurs in a conversation is one or more of the following:

- ✦ Trying to figure out a way of leaving the conversation.
- ✦ Wanting to impress the other person.
- ✦ Trying to find flaws in the other person's argument.
- ✦ Forming judgments about them.

- Preparing your next statement.
- Trying to avoid or prevent rejection.
- Figuring out how to make the other person wrong.
- Trying to buy time until you have a clever response.
- Checking your watch or the scenery.
- Pacifying the speaker.
- Thinking of what advice to give, then giving it.
- Drifting off or daydreaming.
- Listening only to what applies to you.
- Pretending you know what the other person is thinking.
- Continually changing the subject or controlling it.

It's surprising how many ways there are to *not* listen. But if you think about it, most people talk *at* each other. There is very little genuine listening. In fact there's a whole movement going on now (out of the Boston area) called the Dialogue Group. They are encouraging people to learn to really listen and really talk in a way that generates honest communication. The list we started above is continued below:

- Rebutting, arguing, and debating with the speaker.
- Constantly bringing up your own story.
- Agreeing with the listener when you really don't agree.
- Providing solutions before the speaker feels heard.
- Preparing to "top this" with a comment about how you did something better, cheaper, easier, smarter, etc.
- Over-identification: "Oh, you know the same thing happened to me, except.." And the attention is switched.
- Giving advice (most of the time, the speaker doesn't want it).
- Lecturing the other person.
- Asking trivial questions that interrupt the essence of the speaker.
- Constant reassurance that everything will be fine.
- Ignoring while still pretending to listen.
- Listening as if you have to defend or justify your own position.

Quotable

Listening means making a commitment to understanding another's reality. It often requires detachment so you can hear without becoming emotionally engaged.

The only task you really have while listening is to understand the speaker's world from their point of view. Receive, understand and appreciate the communication, then acknowledge that fact by providing feedback to the speaker.

Listening Is a Learned Skill

Effective listening is a skill you must develop as a presenter or teacher. Listening means making a commitment to understanding another's reality. It often requires detachment so you can hear without becoming emotionally engaged.

Unfortunately, our society offers few role models for effective listening. Communication models depicted by the media, for instance, often have speakers competing to be heard. For an exercise in awareness, listen to several television sitcoms. Notice how often the listener communicates with a put-down, then the canned laughter begins. Put-downs are a poor source of humor and should be banned from your classroom. Show a videotape of a typical program and ask your students for an analysis of the communication skills used. Each time a put-down is used, ask the questions:

◆ What was the put-down?
◆ Who laughed?
◆ How did the listener feel?
◆ How would you feel?
◆ Does the put-down add to another's life?
◆ Eventually, how might the listener feel about him or herself?
◆ Could the speaker have said something funny and still be fair and respectful to the listener?

Use a Listening Voice

Some voices are termed heavy and authoritarian. Other voices are labeled easy to listen to and more approachable. When you want to be listened to, or to listen to others, use your "approachable listening" voice. This voice has more variance and regardless of where the tonality starts out, it ends up higher at the end. It's the voice that you use when someone has just said something and you respond by saying "Really?" Your voice goes up, and the other person is expected and invited to respond. To be listened to and to be good at listening, listen to your own voice and ask yourself, "Am I ending the sentences on an 'up' tonality or a 'down' tonality?" The 'up' tone invites questioning, responses and doubt. The 'down' tone says "This is how it is."

Learn What the Speaker Needs

A good listener knows that when the speaker is talking, the subject matter is often of secondary importance. Speaking is an act of personal disclosure and sharing. To the speaker, what's important is himself: needs, feelings, attitudes, observations and opinions. The topic of the conversation is simply a vehicle. Few speakers feel genuinely listened to and as a result, it is a rare honor for them when you are a good listener. To be listened to is to be validated. It says your thoughts, feelings, observations and needs are important. Hence, most of the time the speaker simply needs to know that they have been heard. The listener's actual response is secondary.

Many Ways to Listen

Surprisingly, there are many kinds of listening styles. This means that people develop a filter through which messages are processed. Here are six different kinds of listening styles.

1. The *leisure listener* has an acute ear for what pleases him/her. He/she listens for the non-verbal messages, enjoys stories, is present in body but not always in mind, is seldom intense and listens as if it's a ride at an amusement park.

2. The *inclusive listener* has a wide listening band of interests, relies heavily on the key idea, is widely accepting, at times even gullible, and notices non-verbal messages well.

3. The *stylistic listener* evaluates the message by the medium, is fully tuned to the physical presentation of the speaker, watches for non-verbal messages, evaluates speakers for credentials, listens for style and flair, or gets bored.

4. The *technical listener* listens to those who have a track record or who are "qualified" to use up precious listening time. He/She is interested mostly in how and why something works, has a narrow listening band, and is often a detached and unemotional listener.

5. The *empathetic listener* listens for the emotional state of the talker, detects voice fluctuations, tempo, tonality, etc., is sensitive to physical touch, and often becomes part of the drama of the conversations.

6. The *non-conforming listener* is most attentive to information which directly affects him/her, has a narrow band of listening interests, and is excellent at sniffing out the story behind the story.

Did you identify yourself with a particular style? If so, you are "receiving" on only one band of a multiple-band radio station. It's important to recognize your own style, then you can expand your listening skills by exploring other styles and using them when they are appropriate to the situation. Quite simply, the two most important listening styles for teachers are: 1) empathic listening as a response to emotionally-laden speaking; and 2) precision listening as a response to content-oriented speaking. In both modes the outcome is discovery. What works consistently is knowing which one to use and using it effectively.

How to Create a Listening Environment

The prerequisite for any effective communication is the fostering of a safe listening environment. The first condition is trust. Only after you have consistently demonstrated that your students can trust your responses and openness, will they feel safe and willing to take the necessary risks that precede learning. To increase class trust among students, model a style of communication which "responds with respect." Thus, never put a student down, *even as a joke*. Never, ever be sarcastic to a student or use a belittling remark. You must set the tone of love, safety, and respect in the classroom.

If one of your students makes a habit of responding with "put-downs", use a nonverbal signal as an alert. It may be some theatrical sign such as a line drawn across the throat with the wave of the finger. This signals an inappropriate response and requires a respectful one. With increased feedback, the quality of classroom communication will improve.

In addition, each person must agree that active listening requires commitment to the "work" of listening. This means more than silently pointing eyes and ears toward the speaker. Rather, it requires your fullest attention to the speaker. Actively hear all of what is being said.

Your own mood is important to monitor as a way of preparing the listening environment. Before you put yourself in the position of listening, ask "What am I feeling right now?" If there's an unexpressed emotion inside you, it may create a distorting filter for the message. For example, an angry person will hear differently than a person who just won the lottery. Find a way to move through your feelings so that you can go on and listen without the added filter.

Quotable

To increase class trust among students, model a style of communication which "responds with respect." Thus, never put a student down, even as a joke.

Listening also requires a certain amount of clarity of intention. Do you need to be in a closer place to hear better? Are you willing to say, "I'm sorry, I didn't get that; would you repeat it, please?" Being ready to listen means that you are in a receptive state, committed to listening, and clear that you are ready to discover, not preach. Let's take a closer look at the two styles teachers use the most.

Empathetic Listening

When you detect an unusual emotional response from a student, use the empathetic listening style. It works well under circumstances like the following. When a student is:

✦ Angry, frustrated or upset
✦ Hurt, saddened or worried
✦ Jealous, bitter or sarcastic
✦ Excited, happy or enthused
✦ Hopeful, uncertain or tense

Empathic listening engages the listener very little in terms of auditory responses. It *does* engage the listener non-verbally. Try to put yourself in the shoes of the speaker. This style of listening encourages the listener to simply "be there" in partnership as a friend. The following scenario exemplifies this approach:

Speaker: "I am so sad; my best friend was hurt and is in the hospital."
Listener: "Oh, I'm so sorry; this must be very painful for you, too."

This style of listening centers the focus on the speaker rather than the content. Notice the listener did not say, "Which hospital?" or "When are visiting hours?" The following tips will help ensure success:

Tips for Listening With Empathy:

✦ *Listen for the feelings behind the message.*
✦ *Let the speaker know you are listening and care.*
✦ *Avoid interruptions or lengthy comments.*
✦ *Listen for the relationships in the speaker's world.*
✦ *Be an "invisible" listener; make the speaker visible.*

Listen in silence with full attention on the speaker. Listen with an ear for the relationship of what they say about their own lives, not yours. Most listeners are so "into" their own world, that they rarely experience the speaker's world. Untrained communicators have only one mode of communication, that of relating the message in terms of their own lives. Resist that temptation and listen to the speaker as if you were in his or her shoes living the experience yourself. Only then can you truly be empathic.

Live the expression: "To walk a mile in another's moccasins." It is difficult to over-emphasize the importance of learning to get the message from the speaker's point of view - his or her experiences, feelings and meaning. Yes, you may have your own point of view which filters the message, but the skill is in being able to let that go so that you can really shift your frame of reference.

Listen with respect. Every person who attempts to communicates has a message they want to send. They do not always know what their message is, and they do not always communicate their message well; however, their communication is a way of including you in their world. Show respect for that.

Non-verbal communication provides powerful cues that will help the listener understand the full message. It will reveal things about the speaker that the voice will not. Listen for feelings and voice changes. As valuable as the content of the message may be, learn to tune into the feelings of the sender. Often feelings are a more accurate clue to the speaker's meaning than the words he/she chooses. Emotions are not easily hidden and there are many ways to spot them. As children, we became very good at tuning into differences in our parents' voices. There are obvious ranges of volume, but the most useful ones in listening for emotions are the cracking of the voice, the drop in energy level, and change of tone.

Here's the Real Skill

What *isn't* said can be as important as what *is* said. There are three ways to listen for what isn't being said: generalization, deletion, and distortion. Speakers often generalize; this statement, itself, is a generalization. A typical generalization is making a blanket statement based upon a single incident. For example, after one upsetting incident at school, a student might say, "School is stupid." The student may have liked school yesterday, but at this moment, he/she is not enjoying it.

Deletion is information left out so that you get an inaccurate picture. Let's say that a student is doing well in a class until the latest exam. Upon receiving a lower than normal grade, he says: "I'm doing lousy in this class." The deletion, of course, is that all of this student's successes before the poor grade are forgotten. In addition, he has deleted any productive observations, needs, and feelings.

Distortion is a change in the meaning of the information. For example, let's say a student is doing well in a class and the teacher makes a supportive comment. The student's distortion might be: "You are just saying that to be nice. I'll bet you say that to everyone." The student takes the message and distorts the meaning to have it fit their perception.

If we listen carefully, we can find that a speaker often has a strong bias in one direction or another. For example, if a speaker is continually saying what an awful job another teacher is doing, you may suspect some ulterior motives. If you hear a teacher complain about a fellow teacher, you may want to reply with, "I'm sorry to hear you're not happy with him/her."

Avoid These Listening Mistakes

A common listener reaction is to divert attention from the speaker or topic. This is frustrating to the speaker because it prevents him/her from truly being heard. The three most common mistakes poor listeners make are: 1) offering similar stories; 2) proposing unsolicited advice or solutions; and 3) taking the message personally.

While offering a similar story may seem like empathy to an untrained listener, what is really being said is, I don't really care about *your* experience. If the speaker is sharing his/her troubles, don't jump in and try to make him/her feel better by telling about your own troubles. This tactic shifts the attention from the speaker to you, the listener; and doesn't allow the speaker to feel heard and understood.

While proposing a solution may seem like a positive approach to the untrained listener, most people don't want or like to "be fixed." This means there's no need to start a "Dear Abby" in your mind where you are trying to fix, advise or correct the supposed ills of the speaker. If the speaker wants your advice, they will ask. Instead, relax and be an empathic and caring listener, giving the speaker the same attention and respect you'd like if you were speaking. They will likely come up with their own very effective solution to their problem themselves; and in the process, will feel empowered by their resourcefulness and coping skills.

While likely done unconsciously, taking a speaker's message personally changes the listeners ability to hear objectively. Receive the communication with detachment. It is a rare speaker who can deliver a message from a perspective other than his/her own. Each message is colored by a lifetime of values, perceptions and personal experiences. For example, a student may say to you, "I don't like this class. You like the other students more than me." In fact, the student is really saying, "I don't experience feeling special, having self-worth or well-being in this class. I feel inadequate; and would at least like some more attention and recognition in class." The only way to find out for sure is to ask. But the important thing is to not engage in the message emotionally, but to focus on the meaning of the message to the speaker.

Compare and contrast listening with ease to listening on edge. When the listener is eagerly ready to respond, either verbally or mentally, the speaker cannot relax and communicate optimally. Instead, give the speaker "permission" to simply speak. This means that you don't need to placate the speaker by constantly saying, "I know what you mean." Or, "You're right as always." It does mean you can respond appropriately: "Hmmm. Yes, I see." Or, "You bet." To listen with ease also means to accept what the speaker is saying without making judgments.

Super-teachers make the speaker more "visible" or more complete in their sharing. Since much of a speaker's world is often masked, the above tools serve to recover lost, deleted, or modified information. To be a good listener means to stay out of the boxing ring and courtroom. The "communication boxer" is the listener who chronically spars with the speaker, either verbally or mentally. You may have met such a person - they constantly interrupt or argue, and in so doing, miss the point of your communication. For example, if your comment is: "Whew, it's hot. It must be over 90 degrees today!" The boxer is likely to say, "Yeah? I heard it was only 86 degrees at noontime!"

> **Quotable**
>
> *Untrained communicators have only one mode of communication, that of relating the message in terms of their own lives. Resist that temptation and listen to the speaker as if you were in his or her shoes living the experience yourself.*

Listen to the Person First

Suppose a student says, "I didn't do my homework because there's no place to study in my house." You can listen with the reaction of: "That's just an excuse," or "Why don't you study elsewhere, then?" But to actually enter the student's reality would be to listen carefully to find out more of what's going on. In other words, if the student avoids doing homework, it's not because the student is lazy or stupid. This doesn't mean that the act is justifiable, just that students are only going to do what they feel their best choice is, not what your best choice is for them.

For example, a student may say: "I feel like everyone in class is doing better than I am." Your first reaction might be to jump in and say, "No, that's not true, Kenny. You did better than a third of the class on the last test." In so doing, however, you have missed the point of Kenny's communication. What he is really saying is that he is dissatisfied with his academic performance. He wants to be heard. Other conclusions you might draw from his statement are your own opinions and should be checked out with the speaker.

Reading Non-Verbals

Pay attention to body language and calibrate it! Gross generalizations are common with regard to the meaning of body language. For example, just because a person's legs are crossed, it is inaccurate to conclude that this person is closed or guarded. It could be that the person is merely resting one leg or foot. So be careful about over-generalizing in this way. Rather, consider the information you gather from body language as part of the equation. Below are some of the commonly given explanations for gestures. You'll notice that some of the explanations are contradictory:

+ *Legs uncrossed:* openness, receptivity, macho, cool
+ *Scratch head:* puzzled, nervous, impatient
+ *Tug on the ear:* ready to interrupt, lending an ear
+ *Touch nose or jawbone:* doubt, contemplation
+ *Open extended palms:* generous, openness, disbelief
+ *Hands on lips:* impatience, silence, deep thought
+ *Hands on knees or leaning forward:* readiness, stretching, attention
+ *Clenched fist:* power, anger, control
+ *Hands in pockets:* hiding meaning, relaxed, cold atmosphere
+ *Shrugged shoulders:* uncertainty, negative, tight neck
+ *Hands clasped behind back:* authority, humility, service
+ *Looking downward:* deep in thought, bored, feeling emotions
+ *Steepled fingers:* confidence, boredom, scheming, a barrier
+ *Holding up objects:* reaching out, hostility, distance
+ *Closed palms on the chest:* struck by a thought, honesty, defensive
+ *Both hands clasped:* grief, anticipation, confidence
+ *Eye contact:* interest, anger, boredom, distrust

Use all of your sensory acuity skills to listen. Pick up on a flush in the face or the neck, or a dilation of pupils. It could be the texture of the skin changes, as in getting "goosebumps." The ear, nose, throat, hands, or legs may twitch as a response to an emotion filling the body. An obvious visual clue is tears, which might be signaling sadness, anger, relief, frustration, or joy.

The eyes may have an increased blink rate or twitch when the speaker moves into either highly emotional messages or they are reliving an experience, or even lying about it. The eyes may also squint when the intensity of the message goes up. The mouth gives excellent messages because it is also delivering the content. Watch for tightened lips, narrowed jaws, frowns, smiles, held-back laughs, or lifted lips. An astute observer will also notice the breathing rate of the speaker. As the breathing rate quickens, you may guess the speaker is experiencing some anxiety, excitement, or other stimulating emotion.

The key to reading body language is calibration. Observe, then check it out. Avoid assumptions; ask questions. Don't blindly follow rules about what certain gestures mean. Calibrate, calibrate, calibrate.

Precision Listening

Precision listening involves gathering information from the speaker. The listener asks questions such as, "How exactly did that happen?" Or, "When, specifically did you do that?" This style of listening seeks to gather more content and to better engage the speaker. For example, let's say a student says, "Boy, am I in trouble; I'm flunking geometry." The listener would ask, "Do you mean you did poorly on the last test or are you saying that you are likely to get an "F" in the class?" Then, once more information is elicited, the listener might ask questions such as, "Well, what do you plan to do about it? When will you start?"

This style is best used when the emotions are calm and the content is the most important matter at hand. In this case, it's important to make the content more visible so that misunderstandings are reduced. Precision listening is really listening with a commitment to understand "and resolve" what the speaker is saying. It means that you become actively engaged in drawing out the details of the content in a way that insures you understand what the speaker is saying.

Many speakers haven't the slightest idea what they really want to say - they talk around the subject, but not directly of it. They mask or exaggerate their fears and often present to you what they think you want to hear. It takes legitimate desire and commitment for the listener to read through all of their distortions, deletions, and generalizations. Many speakers omit the obvious and it's your job to elicit the message as best as you can. However, give speakers the opportunity to deliver their meaning. Do not put words in their mouth.

Precision Listening Tips:

- ✦ *Listen fully without interrupting.*
- ✦ *Give feedback to the speaker on what was said.*
- ✦ *Ask for relevant details.*
- ✦ *Clarify and elicit requests and promises, retrieve deleted information.*
- ✦ *Appreciate and respect listener.*
- ✦ *Elicit speaker's next step.*

While precision listening is an active, challenging role, keep this in mind: It is unfair to others and is counterproductive to constantly monitor or challenge another's communications. If you do feel puzzled, unclear, or something doesn't sound right then ask for a clarification, but always with respect and politeness. You are doing both yourself and the speaker a real favor when you use these tools politely, as they are intended.

Understanding is important, so paraphrase if necessary. Restate in your own words what you think someone just said. This does not mean repeating the exact words like a pet shop parrot, but rather how you have translated them. When you paraphrase correctly, the speaker is reassured that you really understood what was said. Here's an example of paraphrasing:

Speaker: This has been one of the longest weeks I've ever had in school.
Listener: It sounds like you are going through a really rough time, David.

Paraphrasing, done incorrectly, can be aggravating to the speaker. What has been referred to as "parroting" is a case of the listener sounding like a tape recorder rather than a compassionate and empathic human being. The following is an example of how *not* to paraphrase:

Speaker: I'm real happy with the score I just got on my test.
Listener: So you're real happy with the score you just got on your test, Huh?

Complete communication provides the listener with the big picture. It includes feelings, needs, thoughts and observations. When the listener gets incomplete communications, the mind has a tendency to "fill in" the missing information. This can lead to inaccurate conclusions. Here's an example:

Speaker: My notebook was stolen - I can't believe someone would do that! (includes an observation and a thought; lacks a feeling and a need)
Listener: Sounds like you're really upset; I'm sorry it happened. Do you need some help with your notes?
(listener tries to fill in missing items - the feeling and the need)
Speaker: I'm so sad.
(feeling expressed, what's missing is thoughts, needs and observation)
Listener: I can tell it's really brought you down. Tell me what else has been going on?
(listener asks for deleted information)

If you would like to encourage trust, safety and rapport, make sure that you always acknowledge and appreciate the speaker for sharing. Say with sincerity, "Thank you for sharing that with me." Or, "I really appreciate you being willing to share that with me; I feel honored and privileged." Or, in another example, you might say, "Thank you for letting me know that; it must have taken a lot of courage to share it with me." Notice that in each of the examples above the listener always acknowledges that the communication was received before addressing any of the issues.

Clarifications

Most of what is understood is different from what is sent and we have become accustomed to living with the chaotic results. In order to communicate more successfully, you must train yourself to become more precise and insist on reciprocal clarity from the speaker. As you might guess, some tact is required to do this successfully. When you ask for clarification, first acknowledge the speaker. Effective questioning is used by the teacher in the following examples:

Student: I don't understand this.
Teacher: I'm sorry I wasn't more clear for you. What specifically don't you understand?

Student: I don't want to do this.
Teacher: I appreciate you telling me. Exactly what is it that you don't want to do?

Student: I'll bring my homework to you later.
Teacher: Thanks for the offer. What time were you thinking of?
Student: I'm ecstatic.
Teacher: That's great; tell me more.

Student: He ripped me off.
Teacher: What a bummer! Exactly what happened?

Student: I feel scared.

Teacher: I appreciate your sharing that. What is it that you feel scared about?

Generalizations Corrected

Student: Geography is a pain in the neck.

Teacher: I'm sorry it's not more fun for you. Specifically which part of it is tough for you?

Student: Teachers are really supportive here.

Teacher: I appreciate that information. Which ones come to mind?

Student: Everybody knows it's a big waste.

Teacher: Thanks for sharing that with me. Who are you referring to specifically? What do you mean by a waste?

Limits Clarified and Exposed

Student: I can't tell you that.

Teacher: I appreciate your honesty. Have you thought about what would happen if you did?

Student: I can't do this.

Teacher: Sounds like something's in the way. Can you imagine what would happen if you did?

Student: I have to be this way.

Teacher: I respect your choice. You must have a good reason for saying that. I was wondering what would happen if you changed it?

Absolutes Exposed

Student: I can never do anything right.

Teacher: Thanks for telling me. What you said is possible, but can you think of a time when you did do one thing right?

Student: Nothing good ever happens to me.

Teacher: Sounds like you're pretty down right now. Can you think of something good that you'd like to have happen today?

Imposed Values Made Evident

Student: Assignments are a waste.

Teacher: I'm sorry. Is there any way I can make them more meaningful for you?

Student: It's not good to keep us late.

Teacher: I appreciate you keeping track of it. Whom do you think it's not good for?

Student: It's rude to say that.

Teacher: I appreciate your sharing your thoughts. It's rude to say what, according to whom?

Student: That's a waste of time.

Teacher: Sounds like you are frustrated. Anything you can do to make it worth your time?

Distortions Challenged

Student: I know you won't accept this paper.

Teacher: You sound hesitant to turn it in. Can I ask why?

Student: He should know better than to say that to me.

Teacher: I respect your opinion. How would you guess he'd know?

Distortions Clarified

Student: If David didn't have to leave early, I would have my assignment.

Teacher: It sounds like you feel things were out of your control. How, specifically, did you put yourself in a position where David had control over your assignment?

Next, discover if there are any additional steps to take. Most of the time, as soon as the sharing and disclosure is complete, the speaker is usually satisfied. The solution to the problem, in other words, is just listening. Sometimes, we just have to get something "off our chest." In other cases, the speaker's interest in the topic goes beyond "venting." As a listener, the most appropriate action you can take is to ask the speaker if there is anything that can be done. If, and only if, the speaker gives you permission, should you shift from being a listener to being a problem-solver.

Quotable

Two primary issues exist for people when they're speaking: the primary one is self. We want to be paid attention to. The secondary issue is other. We want our meaning to be understood by the listener.

The key to empowering your speaker is simple: meet the speaker where he/she is "at." Accept their reality as true for them (it is!), then allow the speaker to hear or feel their own inner experience. Find a gift in every problem, a jewel in every situation, and appreciate something sincerely about that person, regardless of what was discussed. You will excite, inspire and motivate your students and they will feel cared about. Can you imagine how much more willing your students would be to communicate if you responded this way? Isn't it worth trying?

Reactions:

What are your feelings about the topics presented in this chapter?

What are some practical applications for what you're learning?

What do you want to remember from this chapter?

It is essential not to lose sight of the fact that we are intensely social animals who can exist only in a complex web of relationships. Our ability to think and share our thoughts and ideas has played a vital part in the human success story.

Susan A. Greenfield
The Human Mind Explained

Chapter 11

Successful Interactions

Chapter Preview:

- ✦ **It's All About People**
- ✦ **Let's Process**
- ✦ **Body Language That Invites Interaction**
- ✦ **Questioning Strategies**
- ✦ **Should You Interrupt?**
- ✦ **Framing Your Interaction**
- ✦ **Reflective Responses**
- ✦ **Handling Hostile Questions**
- ✦ **Asking Content Questions**
- ✦ **Choosing a Responder**
- ✦ **Types of Questions**
- ✦ **Handling Right and Wrong Answers**
- ✦ **Student Sharing**
- ✦ **Responding to Creativity**
- ✦ **Discussion and Inquiry**
- ✦ **Pre- and Post-Class Dialogues**

It's All About People

Teacher/student interactions impact students' lives more than you may realize. This is likely the most important aspect of a teacher's job; and the part for which the teacher is usually least trained. Interaction happens when a student asks questions, when the teacher asks questions, during discussions, when ideas and feelings are expressed and even during pre- and post-class encounters. Many students have made major life decisions based on conclusions drawn from teacher/student interactions. You might hear a person say something like: "Oh, I could never do that. I don't have the talent." It is possible that this person had a fourth-grade teacher that said as much to them. Another person says, "I'm thinking about becoming an attorney." Her tenth-grade teacher said she had an aptitude for business, legal and communication work.

When was the last time you heard a student talk about a lecture they heard a year ago? Students don't generally remember things like lectures, or classroom activities. They remember things that impacted their emotions. A teacher has a lot of influence. Be careful what you suggest. Every single interaction matters, no encounters are wholly useless, there are no insignificant people! It's been said that "we are all therapists, whether we know it or not." In other words, with each and every interaction, there is an opportunity to heal or damage. There is no middle ground. Students aren't left feeling neutral after an interaction because it's human nature to draw conclusions. Every interaction is initiated with the intention of accomplishing a result. The outcome is important, but so is the vehicle for that outcome. When a student asks a question, he or she will either feel good for asking it or not.

Let's Process

Since learning happens when students are receptive to it, we want them to feel good. If their state of mind gets clouded by negativity, embarrassment, hurt, or rejection, they are likely to shut down. The process, therefore, becomes as important (if not more) than the product or end result. If you say, "Who knows the answer to this question?", for instance, an inherent assumption exists that the answer is the most important part of the interaction. There are two items as important as the answer, however: the process and the context. Process involves: 1) how the student arrived at the answer; 2) the way in which the question is asked; and 3) the way in which the teacher responds or acknowledges the answer. The context refers to the circumstances surrounding the asked question. If you ask the question with an intention to empower and support, you will come across in a different way than if you ask the question to determine who has the correct answer.

Successful interactions have three qualities. First, each person feels respected and treated fairly. Second, both people receive desirable outcomes. Third, each person experiences a sense of completion or closure. Successful interactions are not accidents. They are a result of your creation of classroom conditions which make it safe and worthwhile for students to interact openly with their teachers.

If your students don't participate, share, or ask questions, you can be sure that it's not that they have nothing to say. Classes naturally generate lots of questions and responses. Expression is a natural human trait and it is an unnatural circumstance which suppresses it. A classroom that encourages interaction and, at the same time, structures it into appropriate formats, will have some guidelines. The following suggestions will help set the stage.

Class Agreements or Groundrules

When a person is speaking, others are expected to remain quiet. Encourage students to share from their own experiences or creations rather then telling others how "the world is." This allows students to learn to validate, honor and respect themselves as well as their thoughts and feelings because the teacher is placing a priority on what the student says, not what some textbook says. Of course this also means that an answer that the student comes up with, or figures out is perfect for sharing, too.

Time

Be sure to allow sufficient time for interactions. Class allotments may vary from as little as 10 percent of class time to as much as 80 percent, depending on the nature and circumstances of the course. If the teacher rushes interactions, students will withdraw from contributing.

Role Modeling

You can encourage students to open up and share about themselves by doing it yourself - self-disclosure. Or ask students to share how they feel about interacting with other students, their parents, their teacher, etc. Tell your students that questions are appreciated and that it's safe to ask them. Tell them that you always support them, and you will not use interactions as a way to make them wrong or to pick on them. Let your students know that their questions don't have to be the "question of the year" to be worthy of asking; and that it's better to ask it than to let it go unanswered.

Remember you are the one who creates a sense of openness in the classroom. It's not the students, the administration, or the outside world. You have the power and the ability to make your classroom perfectly safe. Develop a procedure for scanning the room for raised hands whether it's going row by row or section by section. One of the most frustrating experiences for students is to have something well up inside of such importance that they are willing to risk sharing it with the group, only to have a teacher miss their hand. Again, it's easy to blame the student for not raising their hand high enough, but blaming doesn't serve you as a master teacher.

Look, listen, feel, see, notice, scour, perceive and search the room constantly for cues that a student is ready to share something. Your students will give you non-verbal clues more readily than the verbal ones. You have got to begin to notice the raised eyebrow, the shift in posture or breathing. For some students, it's very invalidating not to be recognized.

Body Language That Invites Interaction

Once you have recognized a student and they begin to speak, move further away from them. This encourages annunciation and a sense of inclusion for the rest of the class. Make eye contact with the speaker. Shift your physiology from stance of presenter to stance of listener. Shift internally, as well, from a visual mode to an auditory or kinesthetic mode. The listening role is softer and more receptive and relaxed.

Quotable

One of the most frustrating experiences for students is to have something well up inside of such importance that they are willing to risk sharing it with the group, only to have a teacher miss their hand.

The proper physiology is the one that gives the message to the student, "I'm interested in you, your question, your well-being, and I respect you." This means an erect but not rigid posture, full face-to-face attention, with shoulders facing the student. It means both hands are at your side or clasped behind you. Anytime your communications seem to be off, check your physiology. Is it possible that you look bored, hostile, aggressive or close-minded?

When you want to invite participation, nod your head and end your comments or questions on an 'up' voice tonality. Then, indicate with a nod of the head or eye contact or with a motion of your hand that it is time for the student to speak. Instead of pointing, gesture towards the student with an open hand, palm up. This is usually accepted by questioners as less intimidating or confrontational. Hence, they feel their comments are more likely to be welcomed in the future.

Questioning Strategies

So far, we have mentioned several steps for inviting interaction: 1) keep your eyes open for signs of a question or comment; 2) check your physiology before you recognize the speaker; and 3) indicate with an outstretched arm and open palm gesture that it's appropriate to speak.

Also, make sure the speaker has the attention of the class. If not, have them wait a moment until the rest of the class is ready. Be sure each person has heard the question. If necessary, have it repeated. Be sure you ask in a tone that lets the class know that the question is worth hearing. For example, "John, that question is important, and I want everyone to hear it. Will you please repeat it?" Avoid blaming; rapport will be lost by making comments such as, "The class was being rude, please ask the question again, John."

If you want the student to adjust the volume of their voice, you might use your hands like a movie director, raising them from low to high or from high to low. Of course, you can also cup your ear or lean towards the speaker to indicate your need for greater volume. Maintain rapport with the speaker by being ready to match tonality, tempo, volume, gestures, posture and breathing. When the student is done talking, thank or acknowledge them. This reinforces student respect and encourages contributions.

Should You Interrupt?

Ordinarily, students are best served by being allowed to speak uninterrupted and without corrections or changes to what they are saying. There are three instances, however, when you ought to interrupt a student; and those three exceptions are: 1) if the interaction is extremely unclear or dragging on when the attention of the class has dissolved; 2) if the question contains an initial premise which, as stated, makes the rest of the question invalid or inappropriate to answer; or 3) if the comment contains any damaging, profane, critical or hostile language which you cannot, in good conscience, leave uncorrected. If you need to interrupt, do so respectfully, let the speaker know why and then allow them to continue.

While a student is asking their question, quiet your mind. A tendency exists to either "check out" or begin daydreaming or to be overly engaged and reactive to the question. Let the student complete the question without being corrected for errors if it doesn't affect the essence of the question. If the student asks a question to which your response is anger or other strong emotion, pause for a moment, allow yourself to relax and get centered before answering.

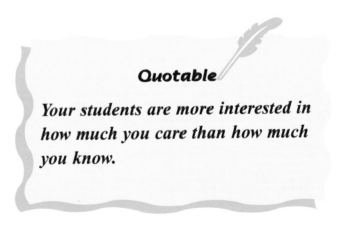

Quotable

Your students are more interested in how much you care than how much you know.

Framing Your Interaction

When answering a student question or dialoguing with them, it's important to have a framework for your responses. Some suggestions follow:

◆ Let the rest of the class know if the question is extra-important or critical to their success. This can serve as an attention-getter.

- If you are unprepared to answer a question, let the student know this. Don't make up an answer. Instead, give the student a suggestion on how they can find the answer; or tell them you will have the answer for them tomorrow; or offer how you might come up with the answer together.
- If the question is inappropriate to answer, invite the person to "stay with" the question and explore the nature of the question instead of giving a pat answer. Another possibility is to express that now is not an appropriate time to answer the question; however, acknowledge the speaker for asking it and let them know that you can answer more fully at a later time.

Reflective Responses

When a student asks a question or makes a comment in class, they risk being thought of as wrong, stupid or inadequate. One of the biggest reasons students don't ask more questions in class is most have been embarrassed at one time or another. Reinforce the student by giving immediate acknowledgment for asking the question or for asking a certain type of question. You might say, "Thanks for asking, Joe. The answer is...", or "I'm glad you brought that up, Joe..." Or you may simply thank the student for asking and answer the question. After this, however, you must decide which answering technique will best serve the student and their question. Some strategies and examples follow:

Student: "What's the real cause of a recession?"
Teacher: "I like your question, thanks for asking it. Some say it's related to interest rates, employment rates, and the overseas value of the dollar. Would you agree or disagree, and why?"

Notice that you have opened up the possibility that the student may already know the answer. It's a form of acknowledging the awareness and reservoir of information we all have. Another possibility is to turn to the group and ask, "Who would like to offer some possible answers to Katie's question?" Here you are using the question as a way to empower others and to invite participation.

Respect the student and the question. This means avoid jokes about it or making light. Stay with the sincerity and intent of the question. Avoid judgments about what the student should have known and studied, or about the quality of the question. Use the student's name when responding. For example, "Good question, Jenny. I like questions that deal with central core issues."

An excellent way to encourage future questions is to make sure that the answer you give is brief. First, give the big picture overview, then the specifics. Students get turned off by long-winded answers. They're often boring and it defeats the purpose of involving the students. Remember that an important objective when answering student questions is to build rapport.

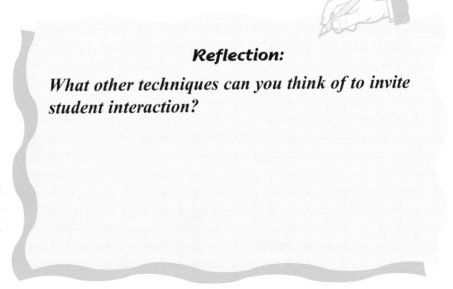

Reflection:

What other techniques can you think of to invite student interaction?

The way some students learn is by mixing and contrasting. If you ask, "Why is the ocean blue?", you may have a student who says, "All oceans are not blue. What about the Red Sea?" Respect each person's style of thinking. The way some students learn best is to find exceptions to the rule. They are not being negative or sarcastic. Others, of course, will do the opposite. If you ask, "How are these cars different?", you may have a student who says, "They're not, they're practically the same." It's quite possible that a student learns best by matching and comparing. Trying to discover the thinking style of others, rather than showing them how they are wrong, is important when wording a reflective response. Once you understand how each student tends to process information, you will be a big step closer to consistently successful outcomes.

Handling Hostile Questions

One of the most critical things a teacher does is to maintain rapport with their students. When you get a hostile question, it is because the rapport has been broken. The moment you hear a hostile question, relax, center yourself, and re-establish rapport. Then discover the student's needs and do whatever is necessary to re-create a new alliance.

Matching a student's body language is one easy way to encourage rapport. For example, if a student is sitting down, lower yourself to their eye level. A student's verbal cues can be matched by listening to the content of their message. Ask yourself what is going on in the student's world to cause such action. What does the student believe in order to ask that particular question? Place yourself in the student's shoes to understand it from their point of view. Listen for predicates such as "I feel that..." or "I hear that..." or "The way I see it..." Match the predicate used by the student and/or their tone, tempo, and volume. If a student is aggressive, your calculated response might start off somewhat aggressive becoming softer and more receptive as you continue to speak.

Open your response with one of these three rapport-builders, "I appreciate..." or "I agree..." or "I respect..." Complete the sentence as you and the student move towards co-creating a mutually satisfying solution. As an example:

Student: You don't know what you are talking about. This is really stupid!

Teacher: Maybe you could help me out a little. What doesn't make sense to you and what are some things we could do about it?

What's Changed?

Old:

"Raise your hand if you can tell me how the United States might decrease unemployment?"

New:

"Everyone get ready to answer this question: What are some of the ways that the United States might decrease unemployment?"

Listen, empathize and respect their point of view. Repeat back to them what you think their point is so they know they have been understood. Always handle an irritated participant completely so that the rest of the group can relax and move on with the day. Even if you need more time with them later, ask for an appointment with the upset person from the front of the room so that they know you care and are willing to work things out. Never leave someone upset, hurt, or brooding in your audience or classroom. Never make fun of anyone except yourself from the front of the room. And never embarrass others or you risk shutting down the rest of the group and reducing positive interactions.

Asking Content Questions

Check your intention when you ask questions of others. An optimal outcome for each question that you ask is to empower the student who answers it. Thus, make sure that your questions are asked with compassion and that they can be easily answered by the student. It is your job to build students' self-worth; and this is not done when students feel unsuccessful. Therefore, eliminate trick questions unless used in the separate context as a learning tool. Ask questions with the full expectancy of engaging the class in a productive way. The new way engages the whole class in the learning process and encourages the student to contribute. It's an old idea and a simple one: Involved students are more successful!

Choosing a Responder

How do you decide whom to call on? This depends on what you want to occur in the classroom. What outcome do you want? Do you want everyone kept on their toes? Do you want to work with a few students who need extra help? There's no one answer. Successful teachers match their methodology to the desired outcome. Consider the impact of the following decisions:

✦ Choose a volunteer. As you create an open class atmosphere, you will see many hands up when you ask for volunteers. Be aware, however, of the possibility that you will get the same volunteers each time.

✦ Choose a student who you feel can use a boost in self-confidence. Be sure they can "win" before asking them.

✦ Call on the student you have selected as a class consultant for the day. Every student has some special or unique knowledge or talent. Make it your job to discover students' aptitudes.

What's Changed?

Old:

"Today we'll be discussing history, so open your books to page 20. Now, who has something they'd like to share about what they've learned?"

New:

"Kevin, you know a great deal about guns. Since we're discussing the civil war now, I'd like you to be a class consultant in that area for today. Just signal me when you have something you'd like to add."

Teacher Response Tips:

✦ *Provide a "mistakes okay" climate for questions and answers.*

✦ *Assert that there may be multiple answers to your question.*

✦ *Check in with audience before asking question to insure readiness.*

✦ *Everyone gets a partner or learning buddy to serve as consultant.*

✦ *Utilize response cards, signals, cues.*

✦ *Give a multiple choice menu with the question.*

✦ *Ask who is ready and has the answer.*

✦ *Provide more wait time - respect learning styles.*

✦ *Use selective calling - choose only those who know it.*

✦ *Utilize team and group cooperative responses.*

✦ *Develop a signal for students to use when they're ready.*

✦ *Role reversal - have students check your work.*

✦ *Tell students all the questions that will be asked in advance.*

✦ *Do Jeopardy turnaround - the students have the answers and they ask you the answers.*

Types of Questions

There are many ways to ask useful questions in the classroom. Let's take a closer look at three of them: the recall question, the analytical question, and the application question. The recall question is intended to elicit stored data from prior knowledge or experiences. The best description is that it's close to a stimulus response mechanism. The recall question draws from students the kind of information that a card file or computer might store. Here are some examples of recall questions:

Identifying: Which one is your favorite book on teaching?
Completing: This chapter is on successful classroom _____.
Matching: What other books are similar to this one?
Listing: Name all of the important chapters in this book.
Observing: What subtitles do you see on this page?
Reciting: Earlier I said there are how many types of questions?
Describing: Describe the cover of this book.
Defining: What's the definition of a successful interaction?

The analytical question requires processing and is usually associated with cause and effect. It requires different thinking skills than recall questions. Some examples of analytical questions are:

Comparing: What do you and your students have in common?
Sequencing: In what order should you call on your students?
Inferring: What can you infer from the first sentence on this page?
Classifying: How would you rate this book so far?
Contrasting: In what ways is this book different from the last one you read?
Analyzing: What could you say about that answer?
Organizing: How could you arrange this information better?

Analytical questions also include those which require distinguishing, grouping, explaining and experimenting.

The application question requires the student to move beyond the immediate information to arrive at their own constructed knowledge. In this creative thinking process, students have to use fantasy, make-believe, and invention. Examples are:

Applying: What would happen if you learned all the tools in this book?
Generalizing: Now that you're a better teacher, what can you say about your self-esteem?
Speculating: What would happen if every teacher knew what you now know?
Modifying: How quickly can you adapt this book to your own classroom?
Forecasting: Based on last year's growth, how good will you be next year?
Distorting: After you teach one great class, are you the best teacher ever?"
Deleting: What is it you want to ignore about this book?
Inventing: I wonder how many ways you could tell others about this book?

Application questions also include those which require theorizing, stating examples, judging, imagining, and extrapolating.

Handling Right and Wrong Answers

When you get an answer you like, use the opportunity to follow up. You might say to the student, "Can you tie that excellent answer into what others have said?" Most importantly, remember to always acknowledge and thank the student for their contribution.

Many educators are fanatic about students exhibiting the "right" answer. They reward students who know it and penalize those who don't. These educators argue that either a student knows the answer or doesn't, but that there's no in-between ground. In this massive technological and information age, ask yourself, "Is it more useful to teach students facts or to teach them strategies for finding and creating information when they want it?" To be successful in modern day life requires that students know how to arrive at an answer, and how to apply information from various angles for problem solving.

It ought to be permissible for your students to fail momentarily with a "wrong" answer. Draw their attention, at this point, to the process that will lead them eventually to a successful answer. Failure is encouraged in the larger context of being successful; and in fact, failure is the information needed to become successful. Lead students to ask the questions: Was the strategy I used useful? Would I use it again? If not, what's an alternative strategy? In this framework, a wrong answer is not a failure.

Some educators believe that our handling of wrong answers had led to an artificially low ceiling on performance. In a direct, single-answer recall situation, the student who offers the wrong answer may actually be using a higher order, more successful strategy for learning than the student who comes up with the correct answer. Many students read more ambiguity into a question than is usually intended, leading them to wrong answers.

Quotable

"Wrong" answers can sometimes be more useful than correct ones. The process by which the student arrived at the answer is what is most important.

Yet the strategy for most teachers is to encourage the simplest or most efficient path to the answer rather than stressing that there are many paths. The real problem with this strategy is that you end up with inflexible learners. It has been declared that teachers listen for expected answers rather than hearing the ones they get. The student who does not frame their ideas the way the teacher does fails. As you increase your awareness of multiple learning strategies, you'll discover that your students may show dramatic gains in test scores, enthusiasm and even IQ!

Tips for Handling Incorrect Answers:

- ◆ *Prompt them for a better answer; do the "hotter and colder" game.*
- ◆ *Ask them to say more about their answer to clarify what they mean.*
- ◆ *Ask for a repeat performance in 5 minutes; then check back.*
- ◆ *Give more non-verbal or verbal clues to coax them.*
- ◆ *Walk them through the steps of learning or logic to get to a better answer.*
- ◆ *Say your answer is a "good contribution" or "good effort" and move on.*
- ◆ *Change the question to make the problem more understandable.*
- ◆ *Put the answer on hold and ask if others would like to add or comment.*
- ◆ *Change your question to make their answer right.*
- ◆ *Give the correct answer indirectly within 30 seconds after attention is switched.*
- ◆ *Express humor at the situation; but never at the student.*
- ◆ *Use confirmatory phrases such as "so your answer is... so that means..."*
- ◆ *Offer a "break state" to shift the attention away from the student.*
- ◆ *Offer a course rule: all answers are temporary until we validate them.*
- ◆ *Give credit for saying "I don't know" or suggesting a possible answer.*
- ◆ *Have them find two others who agree with the answer and add to it.*
- ◆ *Re-assign the problem again, change one variable.*
- ◆ *Always acknowledge and thank them for the contribution.*

Make sure to use your senses to find out if the student feels complete with the interaction. Does he/she feel good about what was contributed or learned? You can tell by their physiology, posture, expressions and voice. If a student feels successful, they will beam with confidence and self-worth. If their eyes are dropped, shoulders are slumped and voice is lowered, you can be sure the interaction did not achieve the intended result of empowering the student. If you are the least bit unsure, check with it out with the student: "Jane, now that we've talked about this for a moment, what are you feeling or thinking?"

Student Sharing

Sharing is just as important for tenth graders or college students as it is for second graders. It's valuable for many reasons. One is that everyone is on equal footing. If this activity is handled properly, it can be an opportunity to: 1) learn about others; 2) gain confidence in speaking to a group; 3) gain acceptance from the group; 4) learn and discover something about oneself; 5) gain a sense of self-worth.

If you notice others are losing attention while a student is sharing, you may need to refocus the class and encourage the speaker to include classmates in the sharing process. You may also have to remind students that what's being shared might relate to them.

Student Guidelines for Sharing:
- *Speak from your own experience.*
- *Be considerate and respectful - no put-downs, profanity or pre-judgments.*
- *Be respectful of the time available.*

The teacher's primary role during student sharing is to stay "in relationship." Be sure you provide eye contact and create rapport through either nodding or matching some of the gestures. The way to respond is to put yourself in the student's shoes for a moment, suspend judgment, and join his or her reality without being caught up or paralyzed by it. When a student shares something, simply respond with comments such as, "I appreciate your sharing, thank you." Or, "I enjoyed what you had to say, thank you." Or, "Thank you very much for sharing yourself." Or, "Great, thank you." Or, "I respect what you have to say, thanks." In that way, the student knows he or she is appreciated, heard and respected.

If you want to validate a student's contribution further, this can be done by referring to a student's sharing at a later time in class. For example, "As Johnny said earlier...." This technique is extremely powerful, because it is a major boost for a student to be quoted by the teacher! Another tool for validation is to write student comments on a flip chart or the chalkboard, saving them for the whole class to see.

Responding to Creativity

Imagine a student coming up to you and saying, "I made up a new theory on why the Civil War happened." Or another student saying to the English teacher, "I have a new kind of poetry." Or a math student saying, "I am making up a new way to find square roots." While some teachers would respond receptively, others might raise eyebrows skeptically and ask for proof. If your outcome is to foster self-esteem and creativity in the thought process, you'll respond with enthusiasm and support. Say to that student, "That's terrific. Tell me more." These brief moments can make a big difference in a student's life. Be ready for them.

Discussion and Inquiry

Teacher-led discussions have the capacity to enliven, inform, inspire and, perhaps most importantly, allow students to understand how others think. If done poorly, students will be resentful and unwilling to participate in the future. If you plan to have a discussion or inquiry process, first get clarity on your intended outcome. If your outcome is to pursue the truth, you are in trouble! After all, whose truth are you after, yours or a student's?

Nobel prize-winning physicists David Bohm, Niels Bohr and Albert Einstein have all said that there is "no fixed reality." Reality is constructed from the point of view of the observer. We each participate in the momentary creation of our own experiences, our truths and subsequently, our universe. Therefore each of us has a different, yet equally valid, truth. The quest for a single "truth" in the classroom is not useful. It is only useful to evaluate the relative merits of a point of view or a suggestion. Be open to alternative ideas.

Pre- and Post-Class Dialogues

One-on-one contact is important for both teacher and student. If the interaction is positive, just listen; If there's a problem, however, be extra alert. When a student talks to the teacher about something, you can be sure it is important to them. What you do or don't do in these moments is very important. Often when a student comes to you, they're feeling unresourceful and helpless. Your outcome must be to empower them, and to add to their resourcefulness so that at the completion of the interaction, they feel stronger and more able than before. These times are prime opportunities for assisting the student to think and problem-solve!

If the student's head is hung low, you've got two choices. One of them is to change their physiological state. Politely ask the student to move their head more upright to eye level. This will immediately pull them out of the "victim", or "poor me" physiology and get them into another state, probably auditory or visual instead of kinesthetic. Another possibility is to match the posture momentarily so that the student feels a commonalty with you. Assume a posture that is similar, pace your voice tempo with them and match breathing, if possible. Then lead them to a more resourceful state. The following is an example of an ineffective dialogue between a teacher and student:

Do You Make This Mistake?

Student: *Look*, I'm doing awful in this class. I don't *see* how I can get my grades up, and I just *flashed* on the final next week.

Teacher: You *sound* really concerned. Thanks for *talking* to me about it, maybe you're right, our last class was an *earful*.

Student: Well, that's not exactly it...

Notice that in the first sentence, the student used visual words: look, see, flashed. The teacher responded with mismatched auditory words: sound, talking and earful. This does not encourage good rapport!

Here's a Winner!

Student: *Get a load of this.* I keep a *stiff upper lip* when studying, but it all *boils down* to the same old thing: I'm *knee-deep* in trouble.

Teacher: Thanks for *touching base* with me. There's a couple of things that'll help you come to grips with this if you can just *hang in there* while we build a strong foundation.

Student: Good idea, I can *handle* that.

Notice that in the first sentence the student was in the kinesthetic mode: get a load, stiff upper lip, boils down to, knee-deep. The teacher matched the information modality and was, therefore, able to offer some strong support for the student in a way he could hear it.

When a student does come to you with his/her problem, that is good. They are asking for your help which is the first step towards resolving the problem. You have already established some trust with the student or they would not be approaching you. The following steps will ensure good communication:

Reflection:

How would you rewrite the example on page 156 to reflect an auditory mode rather than kinesthetic mode?

✦ Acknowledge the student's willingness to communicate.
✦ Listen without judging or solving the student's problem.
✦ Build rapport with the student.
✦ Allow silence if it arises.
✦ Keep in mind intended outcome - resourcefulness and completion.
✦ Assist the student in identifying resources for problem-solving.

Resist the temptation to offer advice, especially if the conversation is personal. Rather, stay focused on the student's ability to solve their own problem with your guidance and confidence in their ability. The following example reflects a positive outcome:

Student: I need some help. I just don't feel motivated to do my homework.

Teacher: Thanks for coming to me, I'll do the best I can to help you handle it. As far as your home work situation, what do you feel is going on?

Student: Well, I'm not sure, I'm just not motivated.

Teacher: What other possibilities are there?

Student: I guess I could... (student names choices)

Teacher: Which of those choices do you feel best about?

Student: I like the one that... (student names a choice)

Teacher: Good, I'll do what I can to help you make it work. In fact, how about if you check with me in a week? I want you to know you did great finding some solutions; you're very resourceful. I bet you'll find even more probable solutions.

Student: I didn't think I knew any solutions.

Teacher: Take a deep breath... how do you feel now? Is everything OK or is there anything else you'd like to talk about?

Student: Actually, I feel pretty good.

Teacher: Good... thanks for stopping by and good luck.

Drawing Out Information

If a student cannot offer any suggestions or solutions to their problem, then what do you do? The following examples reflect two ways to draw out information:

1. If the student says "I don't know the answer." You might respond with "I appreciate you sharing that, but I wonder, if you actually did know the answer, what would you say it is?"

2. You could say, "Do you know anyone in this class who might know the answer? How do you think that he or she might answer that question? Why don't you give it a guess!"

One of the most useful ways to help students with problems is to help them cut through the vagueness - to get at the core of the problem. Ask specific questions. The following examples reflect productive questioning responses by the teacher:

Student: This doesn't make any sense to me.
Teacher: What specifically doesn't make sense?

Student: I've always disliked math.
Teacher: Always? What about when you were in pre-school?

Student: I can't go through with this.
Teacher: What would happen if you did? ("What prevents you from following through?")

Student: They don't let me ask questions.
Teacher: Who specifically, won't let you ask questions?

Student: This is much too hard.
Teacher: Compared to what?

You can also add "softeners" in front of your questions to insure that the student receives your questions gently and respectfully. Before your question, add the phrases, "I'm wondering... Or you can say, "I'm curious. What prevents you from following through?" And, "Would you possibly be able to tell me how specifically...?" These conversation devices can reduce defensiveness and encourage positive rapport with the student.

Quotable

It's not what happens that counts, it's how we respond to what happens that counts.

In this chapter we explored classroom interactions including student questioning strategies, sharing, discussion and student/teacher meetings. Keeping your intended outcome clearly in mind - greater student self-worth, greater student resourcefulness and completion - is tantamount to success. Positive interactions are not the main course of the meal, but they are what holds it together. Good interactions optimize learning; ineffective ones poison it. Your students will be learning a great deal more than content as you help them problem-solve their way to a bright future.

Reactions:

What are your feelings about the topics presented in this chapter?

What are some practical applications for what you're learning?

What do you want to remember from this chapter?

*We are wasting valuable learning time
by having students sit too much. While standing,
even if it's just for a few moments,
your focus is stronger.*

Eric Jensen
The Learning Brain

Chapter 12

Learning Activities and Energizers

Chapter Preview:

- ✦ **We Know Better Now**
- ✦ **Experiential and Cooperative Learning Advantages**
- ✦ **Four Steps to Effective Learning Activities**
- ✦ **Activities Grouped by Multiple Intelligences**
- ✦ **Activate Learning with Energizers**
- ✦ **Energizers for All Ages**

We Know Better Now

Historically, schools have been primarily intellectually oriented. The goal was to train the cognitive mind and the lecture format was most common. In the early 1960s, however, the experiential format emerged from the genre of humanistic psychology. In the early 1970s research substantiated and validated the importance of teaching with a far greater variety of strategies such as the use of humor, music, play, games, puzzles, plays and cooperative learning. This wider "band" of teaching came to be known as "whole-brain" learning. Good teachers have known this all along and eschew lecture when at all possible. The result is a new wave of classroom activities which make learning fast, fun and effective.

Do you want validation for using games and activities? Harvard professor Howard Gardner provides a framework for understanding not only how learners can be intelligent in many ways (Multiple Intelligences), but how to nurture those seven areas. Gardner (1993) says your learners may learn best using bodily-kinesthetic, spatial, verbal-linguistic, intrapersonal, musical-rhythmic, interpersonal and/or mathematical-logical activities. A traditional classroom lecture provides for learning only in the verbal-linguistic modality. Many learners, therefore, in this environment were bypassed.

Recent findings in brain research have validated the use of many types of games which were previously dismissed as "play." Specifically, these findings include: 1) the role of emotions; 2) the library of mind-body states; and 3) the importance of low threat, high challenge exercise to the brain. First, engaging the emotions helps activate the mid-brain area. When our emotions are engaged, we better understand the learning, believe it and remember it. Second, our body has a library of memories that are activated in each physiological state. Using role-plays and other learning games creates a "body-memory" that allows us to learn with our muscles as well as our mind. Third, the body's priority is survival; therefore, in an environment of high stress or threat, the natural survival-mode responses will take precedence over higher-order thinking. And the brain thrives on multi-sensory stimulation.

Facilitating effective learning activities requires organization skills. When activities are well-run, there may be very little "down time." In general, planning activities requires as much or more time than a presentation. Activities can produce tremendous value, but only if there's a real commitment from the teacher to be fully present and alert throughout the entire activity. An "absent" teacher cannot effectively gather information about students, and provide them with feedback and support - two key roles for teachers.

Experiential and Cooperative Learning Advantages

The group process may be the best means of promoting low-stress learning in or out of the classroom. As a child, your most fruitful learning probably came as a result of actually "doing", either alone or in a group process, and by being with your family. With all the age diversity, you still managed to relate to and learn from everyone. You may have learned much from a grandmother or uncle and naturally passed on to a sibling all that you learned. The lecture format precludes student interaction, cooperation and team play. As a result, many students have learned to keep to themselves. Years of structured class discipline has made the whole notion of cooperation foreign to them. Cooperative class activities can break up unproductive cliques and create new learning opportunities. Other benefits of experiential learning include:

Strategy
Students learn how to strategize, problem-solve, and plan together. They must work as a team to accomplish the goals. Students are offered information in different formats than lecture-style.

State
For many students, it is simply more fun to learn in conjunction with others by doing an activity. The casual relaxed atmosphere is more conducive to a physiological and emotional state productive for learning.

Closeness
Students have an opportunity to build rapport with each other. Interpersonal communication is valued; and a sense of "family" where you are supported, listened to and trusted creates a sense of belonging and reduces the psychological and emotional distance between classmates.

Influence
Students receive more opportunity for sharing, persuading and self-disclosure. Many students are not comfortable speaking up in a large class. Small-group activity can encourage greater student contributions.

Creativity
Students receive validation for independent thinking and expression. It's an opportunity to break through stereotypes and self-limiting ideas about what can and cannot be done. Critical thinking and problem-solving skills are learned.

Excitement and Curiosity

Learning activities re-capture those qualities that creative children express so well - a heightened sensitivity, a value of discovery, spontaneous behavior, wonderment, and strong desire to understand and learn. The adult world is a dull gray compared to the child's world of 3-D technicolor full of new sounds, smells and feelings.

Options

There's a rich variety of ways that students learn most effectively. A variety of classroom activities provides for alternative ways to learn; and students, as a result, become better learners.

Whole-course Content

Learning activities which are chosen, planned, run and completed well have the capacity to encapsulate large bodies of knowledge and experience. They can give students a holographic sense of the entire course, thereby accomplishing something a lecture never would.

Tests and Evaluations

Well-run activities can serve as vehicles for the teacher to gather information about who needs help, who's on schedule, and what needs to be done next. Sometimes evaluative information will surface that would never have surfaced otherwise.

Lightness

For many students and teachers, activities provide an intensity "break" that doesn't occur in other methodologies. A departure from routine is always appreciated.

Self-worth and Validation

A successful learning activity can provide students with numerous opportunities to succeed and to feel good about themselves.

Integration

Learning activities offer an opportunity to interact with material in a physical sense while the unconscious mind integrates the experience into the whole life-learning of that student.

Quotable

The group process may be the best means of promoting low-stress learning in or out of the classroom.

Discipline problems may not disappear at the moment you implement more learning activities. However, discipline problems may be reduced. Many discipline problems are a result of bored, under-stimulated, and/or physically active students who need a change. Learning activities provide for more freedom to move around and talk and change. Giving students more control of their schedule goes a long way in reducing dissatisfaction. Students can take an intensity break when they need to which leads to better concentration. Perhaps most importantly, your students will benefit from having more relaxed and natural conversations about the subject matter. This casual interaction time is what shapes the perceptions, attitudes and memories of that subject in your student's mind. What has been perceived as unstructured learning or "down time", in short, is more likely valuable up time for your students.

Four Steps to Effective Learning Activities

Successful classroom activities include four important steps: 1) selection and planning; 2) set up and introduction; 3) operation and maintenance; and 4) debriefing and closure. Let's take a closer look at each of them.

1. Selection and Planning

The first most important step to facilitating an effective learning activity is to select an activity that is suited to your intended outcomes. Obviously, before you can do this, you must know what your intended outcomes are and what your parameters are. To help you determine this, ask yourself the following questions:

✦ Intended Outcome

What is the activity designed to do? What are the intended results? Are these the results I want?

✦ Numbers

How many people is the activity designed for? Does it require groups or pairs? How will I divide the students for maximum benefit?

✦ Interest

Is the activity interesting? Is it new or thought-provoking? Is it relevant to the topic at hand? Will my students make the connection to the content in our course? How will I create curiosity and interest?

✦ Manageability

Is it an activity that can be easily monitored? Can you arrange others to act as monitors? Do you need training or a prior experience to run the activity successfully?

✦ Time and Cost

Can the activity be run successfully within the time frame you have available? Is there sufficient time for the introduction and the closure? Can you afford the activity? Are you distinguishing between the actual cost of the activity and the real value to your students?

✦ Simplicity

Is it an activity that can be easily understood by your students? Is the intellectual level of the game appropriate for your students?

✦ Completion

Do you know how to complete the activity with the students? Do you have the tools and abilities to confidently lead the closure so that students understand how the activity applies to the intended outcome.

Logistical preparation and planning is as important as selecting the appropriate activity. Some questions you need to ask in the planning phase are:

✦ Will the activity create any noise?
✦ Do nearby rooms or groups need to be notified?
✦ Can the activity be interrupted? If not, make some "Do Not Disturb" signs and post them nearby.
✦ Is the room set up properly for the activity? If not, either enlist some support from other students, a set-up crew, or a janitor.
✦ Do you have all the materials necessary for the activity?
✦ Have you done a head count to make sure that you have enough materials for the entire group?
✦ Do you have some extra supplies on hand to use if necessary?
✦ How can the materials be best distributed?
✦ How will clean-up be conducted?

2. Set-Up and Introduction

For students to realize the full benefit of experiential learning, it is critical that they reach into their own experiences and discover what your proposed activity means to them, personally. An easy way to facilitate this is by simply asking questions. Some questions you might ask your students are:

✦ How many of you learned to ride a bicycle by reading a book about it?
✦ How many of you learn better by doing something yourself rather than somebody telling you how to do it?
✦ How many of you would like to learn about the beach by going there, rather than reading about it?
✦ How many of you would like a break from listening to me talk?

As you continue to elicit a show of hands, you'll be allowing the students to create value for themselves in the activity that you are about to initiate.

Encourage Physical Activity

The opening of a learning activity is also an excellent time to get students up to stretch and move around a bit. The weight of the human brain is about three percent of total body weight, but it consumes 20 percent of the body's oxygen. In order for your students to perform at their optimal level, they need oxygen! Provide opportunities for a few deep breaths or some stretching to awaken the body's senses and send extra oxygen to the brain. An oxygen break every 15 minutes is not too much.

Quotable

The weight of the human brain is about three percent of total body weight, but it consumes 20 percent of the body's oxygen. In order for your students to perform at their optimal level, they need oxygen!

Know the Outcome

You know what the intended outcome of the learning activity is for your students, but do they? The objective is very different from the purpose. The purpose is usually some open-ended statement such as "To expand..." "To increase..." But the objective or intended outcome is a clearly defined goal that can be measured and described in sensory terms. For example, "The objective is to circle the game board with your game piece as many times as you can during the 20-minute game time while following the rules exactly." Once you have told the students the intended outcome, post it. Put it up on flip chart paper or on the chalkboard so students can refer to it easily.

Make Directions Clear

One of the easiest ways to ruin a potentially successful activity is with poor directions. Most directions are C.I.P.U. This means, "clear only if previously understood." Avoid general statements such as "be fair, be responsible, stay honest, etc." These are not specific enough to elicit equal behavior from all students. Describe the directions in clear specific language and allow for questions. For example, "In this game, fairness means that you'll...." Give directions with an awareness of the various learning styles - verbally, visually, and often, kinesthetically (have students actually try them out). Then write out directions in three to five basic steps and post them or pass them out.

Also include clear time references. If it's a timed activity, let the students know whether you are using your watch or the wall clock (advantages to each). Let them know what to do if they finish early or run out of time, materials, people, etc. Explain to the students your policies on things such as noise (how much is OK?) and trash (what's messy and what's not?). Make sure students know what your role will be and if it will change throughout the activity. Also make sure they know what to do if they get lost, confused, or need help.

Quotable

One of the easiest ways to ruin a potentially successful activity is with poor directions. Most directions are C.I.P.U. This means, "clear only if previously understood."

Group Selection

One way to select groups is to use a sociogram. To do this, have each student fill out a index card with their name underlined at the top. Then have them add the names of five classmates they feel they can work with effectively. Decide how many groups you'll need in order to achieve small groups of three to six students each.

Collect the cards and sort them using your positive class leaders as the nucleus for each group. Then add one student to each group who needs support for more appropriate behavior. With your "best" and "worst" behaved students as a core, add additional students to each group keeping in mind both the male/female and the student's preferences for group members. Plan on changing the groups throughout the school year.

Other factors to consider when selecting groups are:

✦ The outcomes you want for the group.
✦ Particular outcomes you may want for an individual.
✦ Unproductive cliques or unresourceful students.
✦ The nature of the process or experience.
✦ Length of time groups will be intact.
✦ Known personality conflicts between particular students.

All of these questions need to be addressed in your mind before the activity even starts because something as simple as pairings can make a difference between success and failure of the activity. Here are some other possibilities for choosing groups:

✦ Teacher subjectively selects. In this case, the teacher would say, "You go with him, you go with her, and you two go over there..."

✦ Students subjectively select. Allow the students to get into groups on their own. Give them 60 seconds to break up into groups by finding their own team members or partners. If there are any who are left at the end who don't have partners, have them raise their hands, then let the extras pair up with each other.

✦ Counting process. Have the students count off by ones, twos and threes (or whatever group size you want) then just say all the ones go over there, etc.

✦ Arbitrary differences. In this process, the teacher simply uses arbitrary criteria to determine groups. For example, "You and the person sitting next to you are partners, the one with the shortest hair is an "A" and the one with the longer hair is a "B." Other arbitrary criteria might be birthdays, last names, street names, astrological signs, room location, clothing worn, etc.

✦ Gaming process. This sets up a completely different context for selecting groups. In this example, called "barnyard", students count off A-B-C-D-E, in maybe five or ten groups, so that everyone has a letter. Then an animal is assigned to each letter, such as all "As" are sheep, all "Bs" are pigs, and all "Cs" are chickens, etc. Have students gather in a large open space (possibly the center of the class room with the chairs cleared out) and provide the next set of instructions for forming the groups. With their eyes blindfolded or closed, students are to find their group by making the sound of the animal that was assigned to them. Naturally, you'll have a room full of clucks, moos, baaahs, grunts, etc. The goal of the game is to find all the other members in your group by the sounds alone. Once they are all in clusters, the students can open their eyes and the game is over. This is a great way to bring an element of fun into the task of group selection.

Any time a team is created, a group dynamic or group personality accompanies it. Here are some suggestions for encouraging a positive group dynamic:

✦ Allow time for team members to create rapport with each other through sharing personal information such as family background, key influences, favorite things, etc.

✦ Allow the group to create its own identity using a group name, a leader, a logo or a group cheer.

✦ Make sure that each team (and each individual team member) has a vested interest in contributing. Set up a win-win approach to competition rather than a win-lose approach. This can be achieved with cooperative games.

✦ When the activity is over, make sure that each team is acknowledged. Congratulate each team and have the team members congratulate each other.

3. Operation and Maintenance

As you monitor the activities, be sensitive to the "group energy." Is the activity being well-received? Is it too slow or boring? If you feel this is happening, do one of two things: quickly change the rules to enliven it or cut it short and keep your losses to a minimum. If the activity appears to be too lively ask yourself if the energy is creating a problem. Lots of noise, movement, and fun is not problematic unless damage is being done or students are being disrespectful of people or property. Again, if the energy of the activity is a problem, you have the same two choices as above: change the rules or stop the activity.

Stay alert to any individual situation developing such as detachment, hostility, anger or depression. This means that you must have your sensory acuity turned up to insure you catch things early and deal with them on the spot. Also, listen, watch, and feel out the situation to make sure the activity is meeting your goals. Make personal contact with students who may need an extra smile, an encouraging word, a pep talk, or just a touch on the shoulder. Be conscious of the time and make sure you give time signals so students are made aware, as well. Be sure to allow time for the process to be completed appropriately. In planning a 50-minute period, for example, you might spend 10 minutes to set up and introduce the activity, 25 minutes to run it and 15 minutes for the closing or debriefing.

4. Debriefing and Closure

The debriefing is a time to encourage student's joys, frustrations, conclusions, insights and expressions to surface and be shared. But before facilitating this aspect of the activity, it is a good idea to have students physically clear off or clean up the area in which they were working. Not only will this help prepare students mentally for the closing, it will help prepare them physically by reducing distractions.

The closure is the most important part of the activity process and absolutely should not be neglected. During this time assist the student in arriving at conclusions that demonstrate their learning. Stay focused on the intended outcome. Ideally, the results and conclusions drawn by the student will reflect an increased sense of power, confidence and knowledge. To encourage students to share their personal experience during the learning activity, you may either call on them or ask if anyone has anything they'd like to share about the just-completed activity. The following questions will help frame the learning for the students:

+ What actually happened during the activity?
+ What events took place in your group or team?
+ What went on for you, specifically? (describe your feelings, thoughts, judgments)
+ What did you learn, see, hear, do?
+ What conclusions can you draw about yourself and similar activities?
+ What other conclusions can you draw, true or not, that would add to your resourcefulness for the future?
+ What is it that you'd now do differently, given the same situation again?
+ How does this learning relate to your own life?

During the wrap-up, listen carefully, giving full attention to each person who shares their experience of the activity. Be sure to respond with an appreciative comment and an acknowledgment of the student's willingness to share. The general concepts discussed in the last chapter on successful interactions apply here, as well. During the debriefing, also be sure that students have a global sense of what the activity was for and what it accomplished. When all of this has occurred, your classroom activity will have achieved its potential.

Activities Grouped by Multiple Intelligences

Every activity will use more than one of the multiple intelligence modalities. These general categories, however, serve to remind us that the greater diversity of the intelligences used, the wider range of learners you'll reach. Your learners will be happier, learn more, and express more of what they know if they have the opportunity to learn in their preferred style.

Verbal-Linguistic Activities

Use presentations, speeches, role-play, dialogue, debate, interactive games, writing, group work, classroom discussions, guest speakers, reports, skits, listening to tapes and reading - especially books with dialogue. Other activities include: the Hollywood-Quiz Show, Secret Word, The Word in Between, The Word on Your Back, Whisper game, Question and Answer, Missing Vowels, Sale of the Century, Whiz-Kid games, People's Court, etc.

Intrapersonal Activities

These include activities of an independent nature designed to encourage creativity and stronger thinking skills. They include communication processes, creativity games, language games, self-processing, discovery processes, reading, creating tests, problem-solving, personal assessments and mind-mapping. Use solo thinking strategies, imagery, journal writing, relaxation, self-exploration, focusing and concentration exercises, self-assessment, metacognition practice, reflection and "down-time", in general.

Musical-Rhythmic Activities

Use rhythm games, hand and knee clap, foot stomp, musical instrument building and playing, learning accompanied by music, a Kazoo, write music, singing, piano, musical performances, take a popular song (Happy Birthday, A-B-C, Farmer in the Dell, Row Your Boat, Rock-Around-the-Clock, etc.) and re-write lyrics, using key words from the content of your lesson.

Logical-Mathematical Activities

Use computers, writing applications, programs, objects to sort, classifying, gadgets to take apart or fix, magnets, math, science, reading, discussion, exploring, solving mysteries, word problems, breaking codes, Dominos, Bingo, museum trips, riddles, analyzing information, outlining, grouping and calculation activities. Also includes: riddles to solve, memory games, debates, direct-recall unison drills for review, vocabulary, facts, lists, etc.

Spatial Activities

Use mind-mapping. In small groups of two to four students have learners mind-map a previous class, guest speaker or text material as a review or new learning. Then either hang up the mind-map or have the group share it with the rest of the class. Also includes: visual imagery, early memory restimulation, trance induction and psycho-kinesthetics. Use of art, building, design, changing locations, stacking objects, putting pieces together, sports, large pieces of paper, trying things from a different angle, movement, likes mind-mapping, basketball, video, ice-skating, films, skateboarding, map making, charts, snow boarding, theater, wind-surfing, sculpture, surfing, rollerblading, drawing and painting, etc.

Interpersonal Activities

Use friendships, competition, interactive games, teams, one-on-one discussion, peer teaching, group work, collaboration and empathy. Synergy games (team problem solving) are valuable for creating cooperation and team play. Also includes cooperative learning, simulations, learning teams, memory games, debates, synergy games, drills and mind-mapping.

Bodily-Kinesthetic Activities

This is the area of self-expression a la "Sesame Street." It includes: pantomime stories, puppet shows, magic acts, dances, talent shows, skits, songs, poems and role playing, ball-toss, New Games, hand-clapping, stretching, classroom demonstrations or experiments, hands-on practice, field trips, multi-media computers, mechanical instruction and building models, Simon Sez games, changing seating, exercise, crafts and hobbies, learning games and sporting events.

For games to be optimally effective in the classroom they ought to: 1) have a compelling purpose, but also be fun; 2) make learning the by-product, not the focus; 3) provide learners with choice and control; 4) keep novelty and challenge high; 5) be kept simple; 6) be a win-win situation so no one has to lose; and 7) be well organized.

Activate Learning With Energizers

Since we now know that physical activity boosts mental activity; that learning which involves the body is generally more effective; and that the engagement of emotions increases the impact and recall of the learning, we can safely declare the value of learning activities and energizers in the classroom. The purpose of energizers are primarily to "wake-up," activate and stimulate the mind and body of your learners. Although activities of this type are often used just to break up the boredom or "move the body around, that's underestimates their potential impact. "Sponges" are activities that are of a more mental nature used to engage learners for just a few moments. Originally they were used to soak up time, the way a dry sponge soaks up water, but with a deeper understanding of the importance of making learning relevant, enjoyable and multi-sensory, learning activities of all kinds are today highly valued.

Energizers for All Ages

That's right, all grade levels and all age learners can benefit from energizers. The activities listed below are the tried and true classics, plus a few new ones. Every single game was invented by someone like you, and can be adapted or changed by someone (like you!) There are hundreds, if not thousands of energizer activities appropriate for your particular class or group; however, feel free to modify the tried and true to achieve your desired outcomes.

Quotable

Teaching is a high-risk career. If you're not risking, you're not growing; and if you're not growing, neither are your students.

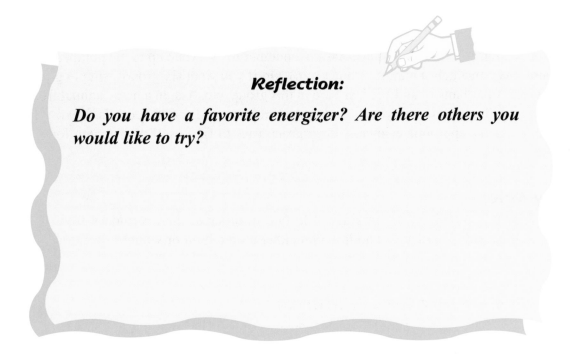

Reflection:

Do you have a favorite energizer? Are there others you would like to try?

Won't older students think the games are silly or stupid? They will, if you do. Can you play "Musical Chairs" with adults? Of course! The results you get will reflect the attitude you have. For every sponge and energizer that is done "content-free," there's a hundred variations you can add to make it doubly powerful. For example, you can either do the game "Simon Sez" as just an ordinary stretch break, or you can turn it into a half dozen fun learning activities. You may get better results if you first ask your group to take in a deep breath and stand up. Then, in this state they're more likely to feel good about participating. The following suggestions are organized in alphabetical order:

Add-Ons

Add-ons are a fun way to review a topic. Invite one person to come up to the front of the room and act out or posture something that they have learned from the course. Then another comes up and joins the impromptu living sculpture; another comes up after them, and one at a time the sculpture is added to until you have one giant human scenario that represents what was learned.

Around the World

Have everyone stand up. You or students ask a question. If they know the answer, they can take steps around the room. Each question is worth a certain number of steps depending on it's degree of difficulty. The student's goal is to move completely around the room by answering questions. Great for spatial-kinesthetic learners.

Ball Toss

Five to seven students stand in a circle facing each other about ten feet apart. One person has a ball or bean bag which they toss to someone else in the circle to start the game. The person with the ball is "on" or gets to speak. Content can be anything: "Q & A", the continuation of a story started by the first person, time for a compliment, a word association, math facts, states and capitols, etc. Keep the game fast and light. Give students some control within the framework of the clearly stated rules.

Barnyard

This energizer is a fun way to form groups. Assign a number to everyone up to the number of groups you want (6 groups, everyone gets a number from 1 to 6). Or, if you want six groups, simply go by birthdate months. Everyone from January and February are in this group, etc. Assign a noisy animal from the barnyard to each group. Then, have everyone stand up, and mix around for 30 seconds. Next, they all close their eyes and make the appropriate sounds. Each group tries to find itself by listening for their group's animal sound.

Birthday Line

Have everyone stand up and get into a single file line in order of their birthdays from January 1 to December 31. Of course! They have to do it within either a time limit or without speaking, or modifications?

Body-Brain Gym and Cross-Laterals

Especially use cross-overs, from right to left or opposite. Touch hands to opposite knees, give yourself a pat on the back on opposite side, touch opposite heels, air swimming - one arm in one direction of freestyle and the other arm swimming in the other direction, touch nose and hold opposite ear then switch, do "lazy 8s" in front of you by tracing the pattern of the number eight with your thumb ups sign. Start your eight at the center, arms length, going up and to the right, do big loops on both sides and switch sides.

Body Machines

Role play how a machine works: stand up, pair up, create and play-act like a car, truck, computer, bar code reader, etc.

Body Pass

With the exception of one person, the whole class lies down on their backs in a line. Everyone reaches up their arms while one person is passed over head down the human conveyor belt. The last person starts the new person moving along the belt without stopping the energy.

Circle Run-Ons

Everyone stands up in their own group facing the group leader. The group leader is given a topic and starts a sentence about it, leaving it hanging, such as "Energizers are best for..." The person to the leader's left (or right), continues the "run-on" sentence, but again, leaves it hanging for the next person. The goal is to keep the sentence going for as long as possible.

Clapping Games

You start a clap or rhythm pattern, then it is "passed" around the room from one student to the next. Once the first clap pattern is off and running, a student starts a clapping rhythm of their own which then gets passed to the person next to them until everyone has sent a clapping pattern around the room. Especially good for memory and music skills.

Commercial Breaks

This provides a great way to review. Each team is assigned a topic or they choose one. Throughout the class, different teams offer an impromptu TV commercial break. The point of the commercial is to review the content. Although it works well with teams, it can be done with partners, as well.

Creative Handshakes

Everyone stands up and introduces themselves to five other people using five different handshakes. This builds creativity.

Creating Ideas

Team deciders or dividers can be: birthday months, favorite seasons, male-female/boy-girl, barnyard-animal sounds, favorite desserts, favorite autos, color of eyes, etc. Or, Use "psychic handshake" method. Everyone gets a number from one to six (or however many teams you want). Then each person goes around shaking hands (their number is the number of times they shake) and meeting new people (without talking) looking for teammates by matching handshakes.

Expert Interviews

Everyone stands up. Half the audience is declared the expert in the topic you're teaching and the other half is declared the famous reporter who will be interviewing the expert. Pairs are given a time limit to get the story. Then the roles are reversed and other pairs are formed.

Follow the Leader

This can be used as a memory game, perception practice, or skills practice. A team or group leader says something, acts out something, or demonstrates something; the others follow along and repeat.

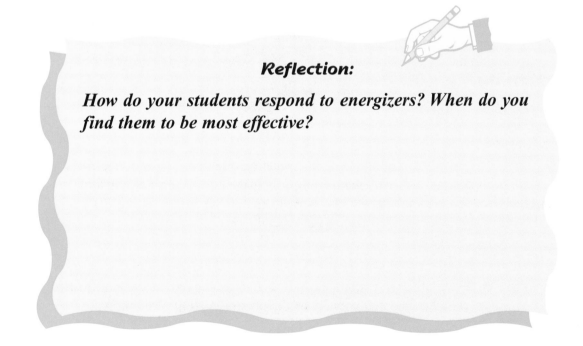

Reflection:

How do your students respond to energizers? When do you find them to be most effective?

Frisbee Review

Whoever catches the Frisbee, says one thing that they've learned in the last couple of minutes or hours, and then throws the Frisbee to someone else who does the same.

Get-to-Know-Me Charades

Tell a partner three things about yourself using no words, only charades. Then they tell you three things. Or, demonstrate three things about your school, your company, an idea, etc.

Gordian Knot

Teams of about six stand in a circle about two feet apart facing each other. One reaches across with one hand and clasps the hand of another. Each person clasps the hand of the opposite person, so both hands are connected. You now have everyone holding the opposite person's hand. Now, they have to untie themselves from this giant knot while still keeping hands clasped.

Hot Seat

Each team sits in a circle. One person is "it." Everyone else gets 60 seconds to give positive acknowledgments to the person in the hot seat. The listener has to remain silent or say only "Thank you." Rotate to the next person until everyone has had a chance to be in the hot seat..

Humor Break

Ask everyone to stand up and close their eyes. Say, "if you can think of a recent or old joke, raise your hand and keep it up. Now open your eyes. If your hand is not up cluster around someone who has their hand raised. The person with the joke tells it to the group who then applauds.

I Did It My Way

Write out the lyrics to a song and pass it out. Students revise and re-write lyrics using key things they have learned. Groups can sing or act out their new song.

Instant Replay

With a partner, one acts out something, the other replays it. You may add sounds, content, props, etc..

I Went Shopping

You start by saying "I went shopping and bought... (name something)" Then, the person next to you repeats "You went shopping and bought... (naming your item)...and I went shopping and bought..., and so on. Go around the circle giving each person a chance to remember the shopping list and add their own item to the list. This is a good game for memory and recall skills.

Lap Sit

Everyone stands in a circle with their left shoulder to the center looking at the back of the person six inches in front of them. Everyone holds onto the waist of the person in front of them. All together the group gently sits down on the person's lap behind them. If done perfectly, the group will be supported by each other like a house of cards or a domino structure.

Laughter Is Good

In groups, members get to share their favorite or the latest joke with each other. Then, each group gets to choose their favorite one to get shared with the whole group.

Let's Get Acquainted

Introduce yourself to as many people as you can in 30 seconds. Or, find someone with a birthday in your same month or year. Or find three people taller, three people shorter or the find the person closest to your exact height. Or find someone whose favorite color is the same as yours.

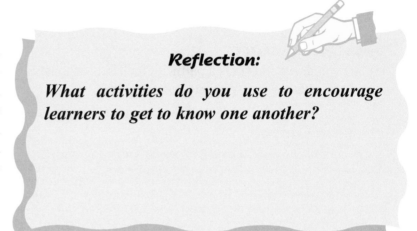

Reflection:

What activities do you use to encourage learners to get to know one another?

Magic Act

Learn a magic trick. A local magic shop can help you learn disappearing coin games or others. Use magic to make a point or teach it to the class.

Line Dancing

Invent your own words/song relating to content learned and put them to dance steps.

Massage Break

Most appropriate for adult groups. Everyone stands up and forms a circle with their left shoulders to the center. The person standing directly in front of you receives a shoulder massage from you, and you receive one from the person behind you. Can be set to music.

Movement of the Masses

Have students stand up and walk fast or run around the entire ground floor of the building to increase their circulation. As a review, they are to tell 10 others what they think has been the key word from the last half hour. Set a few rules first: safety, time, courtesy, noise, etc.

Musical Chairs

Have everyone sit in a chair which are arranged in a circle facing in. Somebody manages the music which is started in conjunction with everyone standing up and walking in one direction inside the circle. The person managing the music quickly removes one chairs while the group is walking to the music. When you stop the music, everyone has been instructed to grab a chair. The one left standing, then manages the music for the next turn; and the game is continued until only one person remains.

My Friend

Everyone picks a partner and is given five minutes to talk with each other. Then each person introduces the other to the rest of the class based on what they learned about them. Builds language, creativity, speaking and memory skills.

New York City Sounds
One team at a time assigns individual or team sounds that might be heard in New York. They begin to make their sounds, then you add another team's sounds, until you have the sound of a full city. Then a round of applause.

Opposites Attract
Everyone stands up and finds a partner. One finds or touches an object in the room, the other has to find either a "go-with" (a similar item) or an opposite.

Pair and Share
Everyone stands up and finds a partner. Share with your partner any of the following, or your own choice: 1) something you are afraid of in learning; 2) something you are unsure about; 3) something that you found interesting; Share with your partner any of the following, or your own choice: 1) something you are afraid of in learning; 2) something you are unsure about; or 3) something that you found interesting.

Retro Games
Everyone stands up and finds a partner. With eyes closed, turn the clock back 20, 30 or 100 years. How would you talk? Discuss topics you would hold conversations about during that era.

Mind-Map
Use multiple colored pens to depict how you currently use learning activities in your classroom. Remember, with mind-mapping, there are no rules.

Rock/Paper/Scissors Game

Everyone stands up and finds a partner. Match three concepts from the last hour of class to the words: paper, rock and scissors. Put the matched categories up on the board. Play the game with a partner. Each time someone wins, they get to ask the other person a question about that topic under the category of the winning object - paper, rock or scissors. This is a "quiz your partner" review game.

Role Reversals

Everyone prepares a short talk with a partner. All students (randomly or by volunteer method) come up front to teach the class for whatever period of time has been designated.

Sign Language

You teach or anyone in your group teaches a phrase or word in sign language to the whole group. Add to the phrase each day. Eventually, you learn to sing a song in sign language. An especially good one is "Wonderful World" by "Satchmo."

Simon Sez

Everyone stands and does only what Simon (you) says to do. Give instructions to follow, some of them prefaced with "Simon says," and others simply given alone. Go at a moderate pace. If they make a mistake, they keep playing. Always make it a win for all, so that no one feels left out. Many variations! You can use it as: 1) A listening game, for following instructions; 2) A get to know you game, pointing to or saying or facing a name you call out; 3) A geography game - "Simon Says, point to the direction of Alaska or point to Australia"; 4) A math game - "Simon says use your body to give me the answer to 5 plus 6"; 5) Language learning - "Simon says, point to 'su boca' or 'su mano'"; 6) A science game - "Simon says, point to something in this room made of steel, or that would not have existed 50 years ago."

Simple Observation Game

Everyone stands up and finds a partner. Take 60 seconds to observe all of the details about your partner. Then the partners turn away and change one thing about themselves. The other person then tries to guess what the change is.

Somebody's Body

Everyone stands up and finds a partner. All pairs get five minutes to use some part of the body to measure something in the room. The goal is to invent the most bizarre or fun measuring system. At the end of five minutes, the pairs report their results to the class: i.e., "This cabinet is 210 knuckles long."

Spatial Memory

Teach a move-around system using memory cue words with a different location for each word and number peg.

Stretch and Breathe

The whole groups stands and stretches. This can be done to music, can be lead by a student or done to a theme.

String Squares

Put everyone into groups of four. Each team is given 10 feet of string and asked to stand facing each other. The goal is to make the string into a large square. The group can talk, but they must keep their eyes closed until they believe they have created a perfect square.

Switch Seats

Ask students to move ten seats to their left, or three seats in a clockwise direction, etc. This is great for exploring the room from a new perspective, or changing the energy or state in the room if it's not productive. Also good for switching left and right brain hemisphere learning.

Team Affirmations

In teams, have students rotate to read aloud team-building, psych-up affirmations (found on pages 107, 203, and 204`) that you have printed and distributed to each team member.

The Good Ol' Days

Play old music from the 1920s, 30s or 40s. Do dances from different eras: Charleston, Jitterbug, big band, swing era, etc. Relate the music to history content, geography, social studies, etc.

The World's a Stage

Everyone finds three to five others to form small groups. The goal of the group is to turn the last hour of lecture or discussion into a one to three minute act (a role play). For example, they become a giant solar system, complete with the sun, planets, moon, debris and comets. Or, they might role-play a discipline policy you just mentioned. They act out a typical rule, a violation, and some solutions. They could Re-enact great moments in history, the news of the day, in poetry, character impersonations, etc.

Touch and Go

Get up, and in sequence, touch five pieces of gold, four pieces of silver, three items made of glass, two of leather, one of paper. All items must be at least 10 or more feet apart. Variations on the game can involve touching items related to content you are teaching. Here are some examples: Math: touch right angles, cylinders, cubes, rectangles, a certain total number of objects, length, height. Science: touch textures, colors, weights, rarity, solids. History: touch things that fit a certain time era or things which could be used to... English: touch objects which could make a sentence, or have double meanings, or are capitalized. Economics: touch items in order of value, cost, etc.

Traffic Light (or Mother May I)

This game can be used for counting skills, estimation and listening skills. You give directions, students ask permission to complete.

Triangle Tag

This game requires groups of four. Three students form a triangle, holding hands while the fourth stands outside the group and tries to tag whoever is "it." The triangle team keeps spinning to avoid having the "it" person tagged!

Tug of War

Everyone gets a partner and picks a topic from the content list. Each person has their own topic and their goal is to convince their partner in an argument why their topic is more important. After the verbal tug of war, a giant physical tug of war ensues with all partners on opposite sides.

What's in the Box?

You have a box up front with a secret item in it. Students try to guess what's in the box by asking questions that require either a yes or no answer. Uses inductive reasoning, problem-solving, and language skills.

Word for the Day

Announce a word for the day early in the class session. Attach a rule to it, like if you hear me use this word, yell, "Got You!" Points can be scored or a reward given, i.e. team leader, etc.

Yarn Spider (or the Web of Life)

Get one or two balls of yarn. Have the group stand in a big circle. The starter holds on to the end of the yarn and tosses the ball to someone across from them. That person holds on to the yarn and tosses the ball to another across from them. When the ball is unwound, the group has to untangle it all, in order.

Call-Backs and Bring Backs

These are actions or activities that can bring a class or group back after a break, lunch or recess. They save you having to play the role of "on-time police."

Bring-Back Affirmations

Affirm behaviors you like. At the moment it's time to start again, raise your hand and say to the group, "If you made it back on time, raise your hand and say, 'Yes!'" Use partner-to-partner or neighbor-to-neighbor affirmations as a call-back. Start out your session by saying, "Turn to the person nearest you and say, 'Welcome back!' or 'I'm glad you're here!'"

Clapping Games

Stand up in front and say, "If you can hear me, clap once." Seconds later say, "If you can hear me, clap twice." By the second clap, you've usually have everyone's attention. Variations on the clapping game: Keep saying, "If you can hear me, clap once", over and over until you get everyone focused; or face the chalkboard, overhead or flip chart. Start in the center and slowly draw small circles, concentric, getting larger and larger. By the time you get to the boundaries of the paper, you'll have the group's attention. Then say to the group, "Any guesses what I just drew?" The answer is: "Your attention."

Foot-Stompin' Hand Clappers

Use a "We Will Rock You" call back routine. One minute before it's time to start up, start foot stomping or desk pounding to the theme of Queen's classic song, "We Will, We Will Rock You." Encourage everyone to join in until the whole group is back and ready to start again.

Music Call-Backs

Use a particular song as a call-back idea. Make it a fun, upbeat catchy tune that lasts just two or three minutes and ends with a "ta-dah!" Songs like: Pretty Woman, At The Hop, Chantilly Lace and Great Balls of Fire are particularly well-suited for these occasions.

Whistles

Get a small plastic whistle from a toy store. Many of them have a fun, inviting sound. The first few times you blow it, add the "shhhhh" immediately after it. The group will give you their attention and quiet down. After a few times, you won't need to add the "shhhhh" anymore since they'll associate quieting down with the whistle. Does the name Pavlov ring a bell? Use a variety of toy store whistles. Have different whistles for different occasions. Try a classic wooden train whistle or a kids police whistle or even a circus clown whistle.

Take the list above and get together with your staff. Have a brainstorming session where everyone contributes some game ideas and the specifics of how to play the games. While it may seem better at first to have a bigger list of games, more is rarely better. More useful to you will be to have 10 games that you know well and can adapt to make 100 games. Some of the best, most adaptable games are role-plays, quiz-shows, board games, Simon Sez, ball toss and musical chairs.

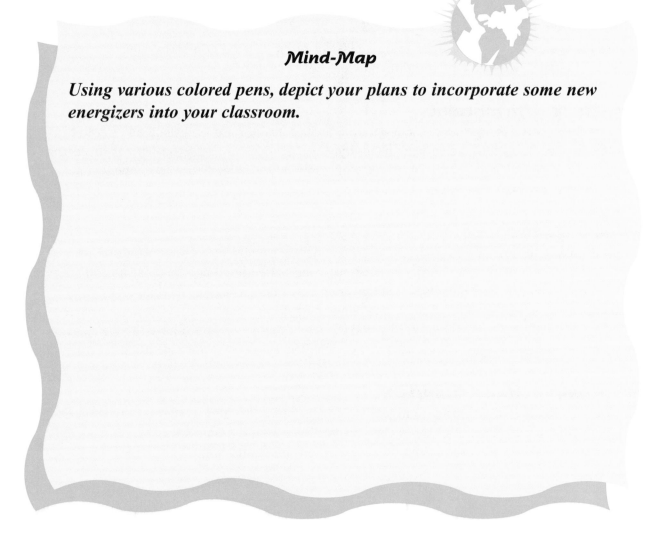

Mind-Map

Using various colored pens, depict your plans to incorporate some new energizers into your classroom.

Reactions:

What are your feelings about the topics presented in this chapter?

What are some practical applications for what you're learning?

What do you want to remember from this chapter?

Any system utilizing two or more of the brain's natural memory processes is considered a complex, and therefore successful, learning strategy.

Eric Jensen
Brain-Based Learning

Chapter 13

Learning Strategies

Chapter Preview:

- ✦ **Keep Track of Yourself**
- ✦ **Introduce and Pre-Expose**
- ✦ **Use Visualization**
- ✦ **Use Analogy**
- ✦ **Discover Learner's Prior Knowledge**
- ✦ **Goal Setting**
- ✦ **Mental Practice Boosts Learning**
- ✦ **Chunk Up or Chunk Down**
- ✦ **Relaxation Boosts Learning**
- ✦ **Isolate Key Points**
- ✦ **Chalkboard Skills**
- ✦ **Model the Learning**

- ✦ **Flip Charts and Transparencies**
- ✦ **The Benefits of Color**
- ✦ **Presentation Cards**
- ✦ **Discussion Cards**
- ✦ **Peripherals and Posters,**
- ✦ **Multi-Media Sources**
- ✦ **Guest Speakers**
- ✦ **Better Note-taking**
- ✦ **Add Music**
- ✦ **Why Engage Emotions?**
- ✦ **How to Engage Emotions**
- ✦ **The Self-Convincer State**

Keep Track of Yourself

One of the most valuable habits you can get into, as a presenter, is to keep a blank legal pad or three-ring binder close by where you can write down good ideas or comments. Always keep the notebook with you in class. Even after more than two decades in teaching, I still take notes while I teach. I learn from myself, from my students, and I generate ideas for future presentations. Never trust that you'll remember the idea or thought later. The memory is rarely as faithful as the enthusiasm of the moment. A great way to use more of these proven learning strategies is to put them on an index card, one per card. Each week, pull out a card and use that strategy. Over a period of a year, you'll have implemented many highly effective tools to boost learning and recall.

When you introduce a new idea or process, keep your stress low. Instead of following your written notes and keeping your eyes on your lesson plan, write out all the key ideas on a piece of poster paper. Post this "cheat sheet" or flip chart against the back wall. In this way, you can teach with your hands free and eyes on the group. The students can also refer to the poster for reviewing the "big picture." Most importantly, you'll have a way to present with confidence and keep your eyes and attention on your students.

Introduce and Pre-Expose

Does prior exposure to information speed up the learning? Researchers say "yes." The brain may have a way of putting information and ideas into a "buffer zone" or "cognitive waiting room" for rapid access. If the information is not utilized over time, it simply lays unconnected and random. But if the other parts of the puzzle are offered, the understanding and extraction of meaning is rapid. Learning and recall increases when a pattern is provided prior to presenting the content. Providing "post-organizing clues" is also useful. Clues related to past learning can provide a framework for recall. Make sure that you pre-expose your learners to the material starting months to weeks in advance. Some methods for pre-exposure to learning are:

✦ Mailing out a course description prior to presentation or class.
✦ Having students talk to past participants.
✦ Reading a book by the presenter.
✦ Watching a video on the course.
✦ Observing the peripherals on the walls of the classroom.
✦ Projecting a transparency or slide that previews the course.
✦ Browsing through a course workbook or syllabus.
✦ Using "previews of coming attractions."

Would it help if you put up poster-sized graphic organizers, mind maps or webbing? Yes. It worked in 135 studies that examined the effects of pre-organizers where some form of previewing techniques were used. Mapping our ideas gives learners a way to conceptualize ideas, shape thinking and understand better what they know. But most importantly, it solidifies the learning to them as "mine."

Combine pre-exposure techniques with color and you intensify the learning even more. Five hundred subjects showed greater recall of content when material was color coded. Many students who seem like slow learners may simply need pre-exposure to lay the foundation for better comprehension and recall. Visually, you can prepare them with a note before the course begins, then post mind-maps two weeks before beginning the topic. You can also prepare them for new learning with handouts, oral previews, examples and metaphors. Kinesthetically, you can offer role plays, simulations, or games.

Quotable

When it comes to learning, limit the surprises. Constant and varied pre-exposure will encourage quicker and deeper learning far better than any surprise value.

Use Visualization

Visualization can be an excellent tool for learning. Everyone visualizes, even those who are dominantly auditory, kinesthetic or have lost their sight. If a learner says, "I can't get a picture in my mind," help them learn how they do this. Ask them to use a book as the layout for their own house or bedroom. Ask them to decide where the front door would be to get oriented. Then, ask them to point to where the window is, where they keep their clothes or where there is a book in the room. These simple acts, of pointing to the layout, remind them that they do have stored pictures in their brain that they can draw upon as a blueprint for the answers you've asked for. In fact, they have to visualize to get the information!

Following are seven tips for positive visualizations and guided relaxations:

7 Steps to Guided Visualizations

1. Read Your Audience
Most of the time you'll need to prepare your learners for the learning. Get them into the state first, then start slowly by doing the least risky learning first, followed by more risk-taking.

2. Be Well Prepared
Have a pretty good idea of what you want to say, key words or concepts; have materials ready and the audio-visual equipment checked ahead of time.

3. Know Your Desired Outcome
Have a clear idea of what you want to use the exercise for. Uses can be to access certain states, pre-exposure, metaphors for resourcefulness, to connect with a particular person, idea or emotion, etc.

4. Keep the Atmosphere Low-Threat, Low Pressure
You can start by pacing the breathing, adjusting the physiology, changing your tonality, using music and building "Yes" sets. Then, you may simply ask or invite them to close their eyes to relax even more.

5. Use Multi-Sensory Terms
Use a wide range of words that appeal to the various senses like: listen, sounds, hear (auditory); or see, appear, pictures (visual); or feel, grasp, handle (kinesthetic). Match your tonality to the rate of the modality: visual is fastest, then auditory; and kinesthetic is slowest. Remember 20 percent of learners cannot visualize at all, so provide several ways to participate in the exercise.

6. Keep Reading Your Learners Responses
Keep reading the states of your audience. Watch for sighs, tapping, weight shifts, fidgeting and opened eyes. If you're off course, give them some "if/then" commands to re-gain rapport. For example, "If you're feeling ready to move on, then take in a deep breath and relax your arms and hands even more."

7. Take Your Audience Out of the Relaxation State Gently
Give them a gentle warning that the exercise is about to end a few seconds before you're done. Invite them to come back to the room slowly when they're ready. Ask them to move their eyes to each of the four corners of the room to get re-oriented. You can ask participant to discuss what they saw, heard and felt with a partner if desired.

Use Analogy
Analogy is one of the most useful of all communication tools. It can be the perfect vehicle for translating a concept in 10 seconds that might otherwise take 60 seconds or even 60 minutes. Good analogies say a lot without having to say a lot: "Like trying to sneak a sunrise past a rooster", or "Like taking candy from a baby." It causes a feeling of "Ahh-Ha!" not "Huh?" Albert Einstein had a great analogy: "When you sit with a nice girl for two hours, it seems like two minutes; if you sat on a hot stove for two seconds, it would seem like two hours."

Discover Learner's Prior Knowledge

The brain makes many more connections when prior learning is activated; thus, learning, comprehension, and meaning increases. Many learners who should do well in a subject actually underperform because the new material seems irrelevant. Brain research indicates that relating prior learning to the lessons at hand makes the current learning more memorable. Before starting a new topic, ask the students to either discuss the topic, do role-plays or skits, or make mind maps of what they already know.

Goal-Setting

You may have various types of goals for your students. Some are directed by an external agency (i.e., state standards for outcome-based learning). Others may be your own goals (I want them to develop a real love of learning). But student-generated goals are certainly the most critical. Even better are student-generated goals which are continually increased as the challenge of the work increases. Avoid giving goals too much attention, or they may become counter-productive.

The target or goal should be at an optimal level of difficulty - challenging, but attainable. Then through the process, be sure that learners have: 1) ample feedback for making corrections; 2) belief in themselves and their capabilities; 3) the actual skills needed to complete the task; and 4) an environment conducive to success.

Goals Are Best When They Are:

+ *Created by the learner*
+ *Concrete and specific*
+ *Due on a specific date*
+ *Self-assessed often*
+ *Re-adjusted periodically*

Let students generate their own goals. Have them discover whether their own beliefs can support them. Ask them about the learning environment. Is it supportive to achieving the goals? Do they have the resources to reach their goals? Most learners who want to succeed are capable of succeeding, though they often lack the beliefs to do so. Ask learners to set their own goals for today's class. Make sure the goals are positive, specific and attainable by the end of class. For example, a goal can be as simple as wanting to learn two new interesting things. You then need to provide the resources and learning climate to help your learners reach their goals and hold them accountable. Check back later to assess results and celebrate, if appropriate.

Mental Practice Boosts Learning

Research found that thinking before a learning activity improved learning. Elementary school children were asked to practice visualization, imagery and make believe. Then their performance was measured. The group that did the visualization before learning content scored higher than the other group who did not.

Before you went to your last job interview, chances are you rehearsed the interview in your mind. This kind of practicing accesses the information and "pre-exposes" your mind to it. In some cases, your learners may not be unmotivated, they may just need mental warm-ups. A few minutes invested early in the class can produce a big payoff later. Create a daily routine for your students. Before you start, have them do both physical stretching and mental warm-ups, such as mentally rehearsing a role-play, answering a question in their head, visualizing something, solving a mental problem or brainstorming.

Chunk Up or Chunk Down

A "chunk" is a computer term which means bundles of information. To "chunk up" is to find the next larger bundle of a similar kind. To "chunk down," is to break the same bundle into smaller units. This process enables you to communicate better with your students by putting information into a pattern or framework they can better digest. For example, a student says "I don't understand math." In this case, chunk down - say, "I'm pretty sure you understand addition so what specific part of math do you not understand?

Another example: The student says, "I've got to do all of this work for just 20 points? It's not worth it." In this case, you could chunk up from the level of the assignment to the benefits in life it can bring. Say, "You're right, this may require a lot of energy on your part; yet, doing it can bring you pride in yourself and better grades. Then, when you get accepted at a good university for your extra effort, you'll be glad you did it." Any time a student does not understand something, chunk it up or down until the desired outcome results.

Relaxation Boosts Learning

Many studies have shown that stress can lower your learner's intelligence. In one study, increased stress lowered IQ scores by 14 points! Chronic stress robs ones' ability to think. You may have seen this over and over. The more the stress, the more students tighten up and underperform. In other words, a relaxed nervous system is best for learning.

Take the time, before beginning each and every class, to relax your students. Here are some of the best ways to relax them:

Relaxation Ideas:

+ *Slow stretching*
+ *Laughter and humor*
+ *Music*
+ *Games and activities*
+ *Unstructured discussion and sharing*
+ *Low-stress rituals*
+ *Visualization*

Isolate Key Points

In your teaching, figure out what the two or three key points for the lesson are, the unit, or the month. Keep referring to these points; post them and weave them into your discussion every chance you get. The key concepts are like the center of a spider web connected by strings of information that ultimately create meaning.

Chalkboard Skills

For many good reasons, traditional chalkboards are quickly disappearing around the world. Chalkboards are not an easy tool to use well. On one hand, they can enliven an otherwise difficult-to-understand lecture, and on the other hand, they can put students to sleep.

When using a chalkboard, make sure you have an excellent eraser - one that's quiet, large, and effective. Make sure that you have colored chalk. At the minimum have white and yellow. If possible, get some of the other bright colors such as orange, pink, or bright blue or green. Make sure that all of your students can see the board well from every corner of the room. Make sure that you stay out of the way when you write on it. Use big letters and print as neatly as possible. Put only the most important information down. Face the group when you talk. Tell your students first what you are going to write on the board, then write it as simply and succinctly as possible. Finally, be sure to show relationships between items if there are any (use arrows and circles) and leave lots of blank space around separate items.

Symbols like arrows, faces and cartoons increase understanding and recall. Before you erase, ask if anyone needs more time to finish taking notes. Use the chalkboard only to clarify, or reinforce. Put your material on it when students are engaged in something else so that they don't have to wait for you. Keep the board clean and well-erased when it is not in use.

Model the Learning

If you are stating that a topic is interesting, be interested in it. Bring things from home, talk about them with gusto and animation. Your learners will learn more about the topic by how you do it than what you say about it. If you're talking about the use of non-verbals, prepare your own so that you are showing what you're telling. If you're talking about the importance of spelling and vocabulary, share with your students a new word *you* learned today. If you're talking about how important history is, share what you've read, heard or a historical place you've visited lately.

Flip Charts and Transparencies

A flip chart consists of a white drawing pad or newsprint attached to an easel-like stand. The flip chart's advantages are that you can use more colors, brighter ones, and that the message can be stored easily. It's often very useful to put major points (each one in different colors) down, tear it off, then post it up on the walls for easy review and reference. They can serve as unconscious reminders for your students and also serve as a conscious reinforcement of the quality and quantity of material which has been covered. Again, as with chalkboards, print legibly, use colors, and keep it simple.

For more reasons than just ecological ones, transparencies are making a comeback. Erasables can be re-used much more easily than paper from a flip chart. However, they are not long-lasting, since once they're out of sight, they're out of mind. The good things is that their size allows you to make a big impact; and they are easy to store when you're done with them. Always use color - a color printer for the transparencies or color them by hand. Use permanent markers for the best color, since the water-based ones hold color poorly and smear easily.

The Benefits of Color

A great deal of research has been conducted to study the effects of color on our attitudes and non-conscious reactions. When making murals, posters, signs or writing simple messages on the flip chart, be aware of the impact color has on learners. The following examples reflect the results of the research:

Color Meanings:

- ◆ **Red** - *urgent, present oriented, feelings, heart, important (limited usage will keep impact high)*
- ◆ **Blue** - *strong, past-oriented, tradition, factual, cold, impersonal (use when presenting controversial information)*
- ◆ **Green** - *soothing, future-oriented, relaxing, growth, positive (has widespread uses)*
- ◆ **Orange** - *active, playful, warm, assertive (could be used much more often)*
- ◆ **Black** - *dominant, dying, serious, intrusive, cold (limit usage as much as possible)*

Presentation Cards

Many successful teachers are using presentation cards (or P-cards). These are cardboard-backed visuals on 8 1/2" X 11" paper which illustrate key lecture points. Some teachers attach associated questions to the back of the P-cards and/or use them as cue-cards in a sense. This is a quick, easy and fun way to make visual associations with the topic. For example, you could hold up a math problem, and ask what theorem it represents (question and answer on the back). You could hold up the cover of a book and ask what else that author wrote. You could hold up a symbol from your lecture and ask what concept it represents. All of these are ways to increase audience participation, while at the same time, increasing the actual learning going on.

Discussion Cards

A favorite tool of many teachers are discussion cards. A key concept, paragraph of information, and a question is written on the cards which are then distributed - one to each group. The group is given a time limit and asked to read and discuss the information. At the end of the time period the team leader reports to the whole class on the nature of the discussion their group held.

Peripherals and Posters

Your students are going to spend many hours in your classroom. It's unrealistic to think that their eyes will be on you every single moment. Since their eyes will wander around the room, take advantage of that. Make every part of the room a learning experience for them and a reminder of the principles you are teaching. Use large signs made on poster board which have simple and powerful messages on them. If the eyes of a student look above me, they may find a message such as "If you can dream it, you can become it", "Learning is fun, Easy and Creative", or "Miracles as Usual." Add, "I learn quickly, easily and playfully", or "You Can do Magic." You don't need to refer to the signs directly. The messages are being picked up by the unconscious mind.

Multi-Media Sources

The possibilities for novelty and interest in your subject are high with access to CD-ROM, slides, video, film or computers. Each one of these multi-media sources has the potential, when used with the appropriate audience at the right time, to create a powerful learning experience not available through ordinary lecturing. There's no need to balance your teachings so that you have a certain number of hours which are for lecture, and a certain number that are for multi-media presentations. Your question should be "What's most powerful?" Or, "What's the ideal for this time?" Then do whatever works! One of my favorites is to double student input by lecturing on a topic at the same time as showing a film or video. This way, the students not only have a choice, but usually end up understanding both of them. It simply turns into a game and their concentration is better than ever!

Guest Speakers

One of the best (and worst) experiences for students is to have a guest speaker take over the class. It may be a bad experience for the students, if the teacher did not: 1) actually observe and pre-select the guest in a teaching situation first; 2) prepare the guest properly for the audience; 3) prepare the audience properly for the guest; 4) make sure the subject matter was appropriate; and/or 5) use the proper criteria in choosing an appropriate guest. It is very important to make sure that the guest can add something that you cannot add to the class. Students become familiar with and attached to a teacher quickly and can resent outsiders.

When it works well, guest speakers can be magic. Some of the important steps to ensure a successful presentation are: 1) review the guest speaker's presentation; 2) review with the guest what you'd like the students to learn; 3) tell the guest about the class and their needs; 4) prepare the audience for the guest and ask them to give him/her a warm welcome; and 5) give the class some direction and share your expectations with them. For example, talk about asking questions, applauding, standing up, time factors, etc. Make sure that you have anticipated many possible scenarios and planned your responses. Good preparation can make things run smoothly and insure that it provides the value you wanted.

Quotable

There is strong evidence to suggest that colored pens make information easier to recall than what's recorded by a standard thin-line ball-point pen or pencil.

Better Note-taking

To encourage more frequent and better note-taking, teach your students mind-mapping or other forms of creative note-taking. Make available a box of colored pens which opens students up to a more playful and creative learning mood. Buy the ones with a nylon or felt tip that are thinner than a magic marker, but fatter than a pencil. There's some kind of magic in colored pens that lightens up a group and invites expression and functional notes. Constantly remind them that writing down information helps them understand it better and recall it later.

There is strong evidence to suggest that colored pens make information easier to recall than what's recorded by a standard thin-line ball-point pen or pencil. Tested and proven with thousands of students over many years, they do work. The ways that they can be used in class as a form of participation are simple. After each point that you make, ask the students for a quick and simple symbol that they can use to represent it on their own mind-maps. This unleashes creativity and builds recall and understanding.

Add Music

Yes, music does belong in today's learning environments. Not just if you're a music teacher, but if you teach anything! Music is an exciting and useful addition to the classroom; however, it does take some time, creativity, flexibility and patience to bring out its full potential. Start small, then work your way up. With practice, you'll be using it just as easily as your own voice! *SuperTeaching* devotes a whole chapter to music in learning. When you're ready for it, dig in!

Why Engage Emotions?

Why engage emotions in learning? There are many good reasons. It's useful to know them in case you are asked or you need to explain why you do what you do in your classes or workshops.

1. Long-Term Memory

The more intensely that you engage the emotions, the longer you'll recall what you have learned. In fact, what you remember most from your childhood is your lowest lows and your highest highs.

2. Functionality

It meets a large part of the needs of those learners who are kinesthetic, internal feeling-type learners. This is a great way to reach those learners who are most in touch with how they feel.

3. Love of Learning

It helps instill a love of learning. The only way that your participants will develop a real deep love and passion for a topic is to access emotions while in the process of learning about it. That's how the brain creates passion for learning.

4. Fun!

It's much more fun to learn when emotions are engaged. It gets the blood flowing and makes the experience memorable.

5. New Research

Leading neuroscientist Antonio Damasio (1994) says that emotions are a key part of the logic and reasoning process. When emotions are engaged, the brain makes better decisions. The design of the brain is such that it biologically prefers integrating emotions into thinking. Damasio cautions, however, that too much emotionality can impair clear thinking.

How to Engage Emotions

1. Role-Modeling

When the teacher or presenter simply role-models a love of learning, and emanates enthusiasm about their job, learner emotions will naturally engage. Bring something you love to class. Build suspense. Smile. Show off a new pet, CD, book, clothing item, poem, etc.

2. Celebrations

Celebrations include acknowledgments, parties, high-fives, food, music, and fun! Other possibilities include showing off student work or having a student-run demonstration. Example: After students complete a project or mind-map, have them get up and show it off to each other. Create a goal like: find at least two things you like about the other person's project. The celebration music is on, the students are walking around talking about their projects, and everyone has a good time.

3. Theater, Role-Play, Drama

The bigger the production, the higher the stakes, the more the emotions engaged. Example: Your group volunteers to put on a school-wide play. You have rehearsals, stress, fun, anxiety, anticipation, suspense, excitement and relief.

4. Controversy

This can be a debate, dialogue, argument, convincing time; and it can be real or artificial. Any time you have two sides, a vested interest, and the means to express opinions, you'll get action! Example: Play tug of war. With partners, each team picks a topic from the list and their goal is to convince their partner in an argument why their topic is more important. After the verbal contest which won't likely be won by either party, the contest takes on a physical nature with a class tug of war - partners are directed to opposite sides.

5. Rituals

Rituals used on a regular basis in your class can instantly engage learners. Such rituals might include things that are done when students arrive, leave, complete a project, have a birthday, celebrate a holiday, etc. Examples: Class starts with a paired activity where everyone checks in with each other. Or class ends with a question on the board to ponder: i.e., What am I most grateful for in my life right now? Or, What am I most passionate about today?

6. Team Interplay

Teams can create an easy engagement of emotions by the nature of group dynamics. Give teams a problem to solve or a project to do together. Encourage them to develop their own groundrules and rituals. Example: Each time a team completes their task, they give a team cheer. Or team members are given pet names.

7. The Arts

Music, games, activities and energizers can get everyone going. See the chapter on learning activities and energizers for dozens of ideas. Example: The class or teams put on a play. Or, teams create fun rituals to celebrate like a cheer, a dance or a shout.

The Self-Convincer State

All learning is state dependent. If you're in a "leave me alone" state, you'll learn very little. If you're in a "curious" state, you'll learn a lot more. The better you are at observing and managing student's states, the better you'll be at eliciting the best states for learning. The "motivated" state is best for getting learning started. To bring out the motivation state in learners, arouse their curiosity, offer them challenging activities, and create anticipation or even confusion. Once the learner is motivated, you'll want to prepare the student for acquisition. This is the moment where the learner is ready to receive the data or information that will, when linked to other relevant associations, create meaning and form what is called learning.

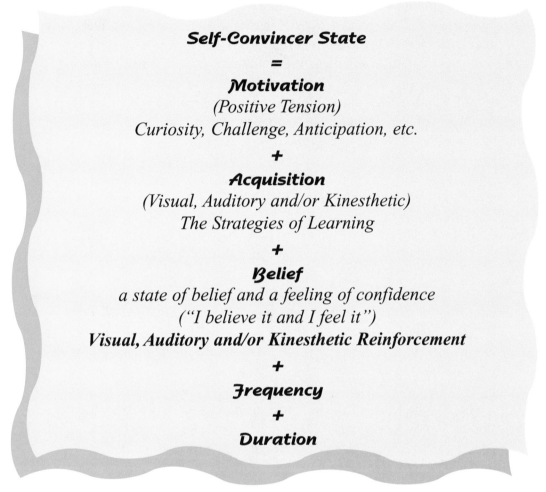

Self-Convincer State

=

Motivation
(Positive Tension)
Curiosity, Challenge, Anticipation, etc.

+

Acquisition
(Visual, Auditory and/or Kinesthetic)
The Strategies of Learning

+

Belief
a state of belief and a feeling of confidence
("I believe it and I feel it")
Visual, Auditory and/or Kinesthetic Reinforcement

+

Frequency

+

Duration

The self-convincer state follows the acquisition state. The student must *feel the feelings* of pride and accomplishment upon the reinforcement of learning. This final state is critical. It's the "Now I know that I know; and I feel good about it" state. This is the key state that creates the motivation loop for the next learning phase.

The self-convincer state is triggered by three variables: modality, frequency and duration. Modality means either visual, auditory or kinesthetic. Frequency means the number of times that the state is experienced after the initial learning. Duration means the length of time of reinforcement. Here's an example: A student comes up to you and says, "How do you think I did on my research project?" You say, "I'm real happy with it. It's your best effort yet." The students thanks you and walks away. Ten minutes later the same student comes up again. She asks a similar question about the project. This time you give new feedback. At one point, her eyes light up, and she is visibly pleased. She got what she really wanted: the self-convincer state.

Remember the movie *Home Alone?* In the movie, the protagonist, a 10-year old boy named Kevin is left home alone and burglars try to break in. He frustrates and foils their break-in attempts. His celebration state, his self-convincer, is demonstrated by the physical motion of clenching his fist and drawing it towards himself while saying, "Yes!" This is an example of the "I did it and it feels good!" state.

How We Get Self-Convinced

Have you ever gotten halfway down the road from your home and then you think, "Oh no, did I turn off the stereo, or turn on my answering machine or leave the iron on?" If you don't remember, it's because you either didn't do it or you did it but did not attach a tag to the experience. A tag is an internal feeling or self-convincer. Tags keep kids motivated. When kids know they know it and feel good about learning, they want to do and know more. This is internal reinforcement. It does not come from the teacher. You can certainly evoke it with the right activities, acknowledgement, and reinforcement, but the concept is *self*-convincer, not *other*-convincer. If you give sincere reinforcement, in the student's preferred modality, they'll often feel good and self-convince. Or, ask the student leading questions such as: "How to you feel about doing so well? Or, "How would you feel if you did as well as you wanted to do?" Or, "How did you feel the last time you did well?"

All of these are feeling questions that elicit emotions, not a yes or no answer? What you are after are signs that the learner has internalized the reinforcement you gave them. The signals are usually a nodding head, a smile, a deep breath, eyes which go down indicating a feeling state, a weight change, change in posture, skin color change or any combination of these reactions. The essence of the self-convincer state is an attached feeling (or tag) to the acquisition so that the student knows, internally, that they know it.

Remember the key to self-convincer states are simple: offer a variety of modalities, do it more than once and do it for more than just a few seconds. Have students celebrate with neighbors or partners every time they do well. Set up more opportunities for acknowledgment and celebration. End your session on a high note - a special gesture, sound, cheer, or high-five. Make sure students have emotions attached to the learning.

With the complete loop of the learning cycle accessed: motivation, acquisition and the self-convincer state, students get hooked into achievement. Unfortunately, what happens is that many students get motivated, but don't acquire the material they need because it's not presented in their preferred learning style. As a result, many learners move, therefore, into an unproductive state like frustration, irritation, or anger. These states direct the student *out* of the learning process instead of creating more motivation to get it correct. So the brain makes a critical state change when acquisition fails to occur. And the state change makes all the difference whether we eventually label the kid as a genius or not. Geniuses are simply learners who get motivated, challenged and are not frozen by "failure." Remember it was Thomas Edison, the man who holds more American patents for significant original inventions than any other human in the country, who said that "genius is 99 percent perspiration and 1 percent inspiration."

What to Do About It
So, to create motivated students who love learning, do the following three things:

1. Start a policy that every time a student doesn't learn something the first time, an effort is made to change their state into a resourceful one. Help the student recognize this important aspect of learning so that they can learn to manage their own states.

2. Set an example. Try to do something in front of the class that you know you will likely fail at. Then move into a resourceful state to solve the problem. Guess how kids acquire their behaviors? 99 percent of it is from modeling adults - nonconscious learning. You need to model how to handle failures gracefully and with ease. Plan them, set them up and repeat different variations of them so your students can learn positive ways to move through them.

3. Interruption. Anytime you see a negative state developing, interrupt it. This can be done by facilitating a physiology change. For example, have the student stand up, stretch, circle the room, play a game, listen to music, etc. Remember, you can motivate your students and you can give them a lifelong love of learning if you pay attention to states and manage them carefully to get the effect you want.

In this chapter we've revealed dozens of effective learning strategies. Add one per day or even just one per week, and you will be enhancing your student's learning tremendously. Takes notes on how and when you used the new strategy and write down suggestions for how to use it even more effectively next time. You are well on your way to becoming a Super-teacher!

Reactions:

What are your feelings about the topics presented in this chapter?

What are some practical applications for what you're learning?

What do you want to remember from this chapter?

Our visual perception is based only partly on external reality - the brain makes up the rest as it goes along.

Susan A. Greenfield
The Human Mind Explained

Chapter 14

Rituals and Affirmations

Chapter Preview:

- ✦ **Rituals Enrich Our Lives**
- ✦ **Seasonal Rituals**
- ✦ **Morning Rituals**
- ✦ **Globalization Rituals**
- ✦ **Other Ritual Ideas**
- ✦ **Affirmations**
- ✦ **Sample Affirmations**

Rituals Enrich Our Lives

Everyone already has and uses ritual. This chapter will, however, increase your awareness of how rituals can be used as powerful classroom tools to inspire, inform and energize a group. First, let's define a ritual. A ritual is an activity which is consistently triggered by an event. In other words, when A occurs, B always occurs. As an example, if you do a roll-call for attendance every time class starts, that is a ritual. If you do several things in a row consistently, that is a routine. A routine is a group of rituals clustered together. Most of us have a morning routine for getting ready to go to work.

If you chew gum often, but not at any particular time of the day or day of the week, that's not a ritual. However, if you always chew a stick of gum after lunch, that is a ritual. A ritual is predictable. That's what makes them so valuable. In today's world, with so much change happening around us constantly, it's very reassuring for learners to have some rituals to rely on. This chapter presents some ideas for classroom and/or workshop rituals. Don't be limited, however, by these examples. There are literally thousands of rituals that can be effective. Use your imagination. Or encourage your class to invent their own very personal and unique rituals.

Seasonal Rituals

Seasonal rituals can be related to one of the seasons, the solstice, the full moon, an annual event, or any of the holidays, including international holidays and celebrations. One city has an annual carrot festival. One school celebrates spring annually with "March Madness." Many schools celebrate ethnic holidays such as Cinco de Mayo. Or perhaps, it's an intellectual contest like "College Bowl" celebrated at the same time every year.

Morning Rituals

Morning rituals like greeting students at the door sets the stage for a productive learning day. Call students by name and greet them with a smile. Say something positive about them or say what a great day it'll be. Check in with them to see if they have necessary supplies, homework, etc. If they don't have them, ask what they can do about it. Set the stage for learning with a song or write something up on the flip chart or chalk board that is positive and encouraging. When it's time to start class, say to the group, "If you've made it here on time, raise your hand and shout yes!" Or you might say, "Please turn to the person sitting next to you and say, "Good morning, glad you're here!" Have students check in with their name and a review word from the lesson the day before, sing their name, stand up, say the previous person's name, use another language. Do anything but a boring routine roll-call which will put students in a state of disinterest from the start.

Globalization Rituals

Globalization rituals are a way to give students a global overview of the material to be learned that day. You might use music or make it like movie preview. Have a different student present it each day, or have students do a mind-map of the key words on the board.

Other Ritual Ideas

Stretching

Have students stand up and take a minute or so to stretch. This can also be done in teams. The team leader can lead the rest of the group in a slow stretch to wake up their body or slow it down, whatever's needed. Use verbal suggestions. Rotate leaders.

Morning Walk

In workshops, I often ask participants to pick a partner and go outside for a 10-minute walk. They can use the walk to get fresh air, meet someone new and/or to answer the three questions I gave them: What am I grateful for? What have I learned in the last day? And, what is my promise to myself today? These questions bring the learner's attention into the present, the past and the future. And a walk is usually greatly appreciated.

Mind-Mapping

Have participants get out paper and make a mind-map of the prior day's learning from memory. Allow students to talk to the people near them to refresh their memory. This exercise builds recall and memory skills, confidence and continuity.

Teaching a Partner

When a project or assignment is completed, pairs are formed, and one partner teaches about their mind-map (or project) for a particular time period, then the other one does the same. Each usually learns something new, gets a quick review and discovers that they had questions that needed to be answered.

Break or Recess Rituals

Before I send participants out to break or recess, there's a simple ritual I do. It's designed to do several things. First, it puts closure on what we just finished learning. Second, it affirms something about it or yourself. Third, it nonconsciously helps integrate the just learned material into what they already know. It's called the "yes" clap. Participants stand facing their partner, hands out to the side, palms up. I say, "In your left hand, put all of your previous knowledge, whatever you brought with you today. In your right hand, put all you have learned today. Now, when I say ready, bring them together in a simple clap, by saying the most powerful word in the English language, 'yes!'" After the big clap, they're all energized and ready for something new. I immediately have music ready to follow the noisy clap. The music is hip, upbeat and always fits the mood.

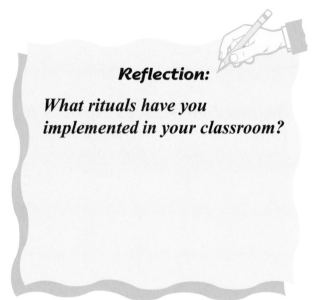

Reflection:

What rituals have you implemented in your classroom?

Music Rituals

I always play music at the beginning of my workshops. This helps develop the mood of the audience. It gets them inspired, excited, curious and ready to learn.

The Call-in Song

I always designate a "call-in" song in my classes or workshops. This is the song I always put on two to three minutes before learners are expected to return. Use songs that have a decisive ending that most people know. When the song ends, start class. Examples include: Pretty Woman, Splish-Splash, Rock Around the Clock, La Bamba, or Great Balls of Fire. I usually use certain songs for particular rituals because they have the words that are appropriate for what I'd like the participants to hear. For example, I might use the song "New Attitude" by Patty LaBelle for a song about changing behaviors, or "Hot Together" by Pointer Sisters for teamwork.

Lunch Time Rituals

At my adult workshops, when we come back from lunch the ritual is always joke time. I always read one, just to liven up the group, then I open it up to others. Naturally we want to avoid racist, sexist or other inappropriate jokes.

Learning Rituals

If you are about to start something new, or if the group has just learned a new skill, it's good to emphasize it with a ritual. Here is a simple one: have each learner turn to someone near them and say, "It's easy!" If learners are in small groups and you just gave them a project with a deadline, tell the class to turn to their team leader and say, "Let's do it!" Once the class is done with a project, topic, or skill set, I always use a transition ritual like: "Take in a deep breath." Or, "Turn to the person nearest you and tell them they're a genius!"

Afternoon Closing Rituals (Passive Review)

Near the end of class, I have everyone stand up and raise their shoulders, tighten their fists and then relax them back down again. Then I ask them to relax and allow their eyes to close. While they are still standing relaxed, I walk through the entire day's content and processes. I take just a few minutes to do this so it's a very condensed review. Relaxing music is played in the background.

Teams Self-Assess Rituals (Charts)

I often ask teams of learners to make a chart to track their progress and to self-score the charts. You can ask the team leader to report how their day went or how their team is doing overall. You'll receive valuable feedback and they will receive collective agreement, affirmation and celebration.

Closing Song

At the end of the day, I always play the song "Wonderful World" by Louis Armstrong. It's very soothing, positive and inspiring. When this is over the tape has a pause, then plays "Happy Trails" by Roy Rogers.

Final Messages

At the end of the day, I usually give previews of coming attractions for the next day. I give the learners something to look forward to and peak their curiosity with the preview.

Final "Yes!" Clap

Participants stand facing a neighbor, hands out to the side, palms up. Then, I say, "In your left hand put all of your previous knowledge, whatever you brought with you today. In your right hand put all you have learned today. Now, when I say "ready", bring them together in a simple clap, by saying the most powerful word in the English language, 'yes!'" Everyone claps.

> **Reflection:**
>
> *What new rituals do you plan to implement in your class?*

Affirmations

Our world is full of affirmations. We say, "Have a great day," or "Happy Holidays," or "Be careful," or "Have a safe trip." Why do we affirm? We like to wish the best for others. Affirmations "make firm" that which you want. It's a suggestion, a prediction, a blessing and well-wishing. The more you affirm goodness in others, the more likely you are to find goodness.

Conversely, you can also affirm negatives. If you say to another, "You are such a pain in the neck," you are simply "firming up" your impression of the person or encouraging them to "firm up" their opinion of themselves. To get the best out of learners, it's important to affirm the positives and let the negatives go. This does not mean to adopt an "I don't care" attitude. It means you do care enough to affirm the goodness in your learners. When negatives occur, deal with the problem more than the person. The chapter in *SuperTeaching* on discipline will give you some ideas.

Many think of affirmations as something that is said to another. Affirmations, however, can be visual, auditory or kinesthetic. They can encourage what is seen, heard or felt in many ways. Here are some examples:

Visual Affirmations

✦ You offer a smile, a positive gesture, an affirming written note, a special comment on paper, a positive grade or score.
✦ You create room displays for your learners: posters, signs, projects, pictures or student work.
✦ You ask your students to mentally rehearse upcoming actions. They can practice doing them in their mind successfully, over and over, until they're ready to do them in real life.

Auditory Affirmations

What and how you say affirmations to your learners depends on many things. It might be the relationship you have with them, their age, culture and even the state they're in at the moment. Other under-used types of affirmations are self-affirmation, and student-to-student affirmation. Your learners often value what their peers say as much, or more than, what you say.

✦ You say to the student: "I'm pleased with your work. It was much more detailed than what was required, more interesting and creative than I expected and that meant a lot to me." Or, you say, "Great enthusiasm, I love it!"
✦ One of the best affirmations is one a student gives to him or herself. This is the all-important self-talk. Positive self-talk is one of the characteristics of learners with strong self-esteem. You can't make a learner say to him or herself, "I'm a terrific learner!" However, you can encourage it.
✦ Ask your students to turn to their neighbor and say, "Good morning, glad to see you!" Or, at the end of the day, you might finish up with, "Turn to the person nearest you and say, 'Thanks for a great day!'" After an activity, you might say, "Turn to your partner and say, great job!"

Some criticize this as "hype" and phony, but what seems phony and contrived initially can become genuine over time. When you were three years old, your parents may have forced you to say "Thank you" each time a gift or favor was given. As a child, "thank you" felt phony and contrived. Over time, you learned the value behind gratitude. As an adult, it's worth while to learn the value of affirmation, too. It also teaches your students a powerful habit of affirming others instead of criticizing them.

Kinesthetic Affirmations

✦ The most common type of physical affirmation is the celebration type found particularly in sports. These include high-fives, hugs, handshakes and back-pats. These are great to build into a class ritual so that learning is constantly being celebrated. That affirming attitude helps reinforce the joy of learning and the "win" in it for all.

◆ Another under-used type of kinesthetic affirmation is called, "voting with your body." This is the teacher-to-student, "if, then" action request. "If you are this, then, please do that," says the affirming teacher. "If you're ready for a break, please stand up." Or, "If you learned something new, raise your hand and say, yes!" Or, "If you're ready to try out something new, please move to your right." If it's used sparingly, this technique can be quite useful.

◆ Internal kinesthetic affirmation can be learner-generated, or teacher-generated, by asking questions that elicit positive feelings. Let's say a student does well on a project. You approach individually, and lower yourself to eye level or even kneel a bit lower (bringing their eyes down to look at you at a more kinesthetic angle). Ask a question about their work that includes feeling words such as, "How do you feel about how your project turned out?" The answer forces the learner to access feelings two ways: 1) your physical position invites feelings; and 2) the content of the question invites feelings.

Wall Affirmations

There are many types of useful and affirming posters to use. You might divide them into the following categories:

Student Work

This consists of team charts, self-assessments, artwork, samples of excellent work.

Symbolic Learning

This consists of icons, logos, pictures and drawings that offer powerful symbols of meaning to the non-conscious mind. Symbols or images that have long established meaning are most effective: i.e., teams working together, sunrises, sunsets, peace signs, mountain tops, and celebrations.

Preaching

This consists of slogans and didactic messages which present powerful non-conscious messages; while learners often turn off to most verbal "preaching" messages, peripherals cut past the conscious awareness of the learner. One example is, "If it is to be, it's up to me."

Content Messages

Post up a summary of the course. Preview coming attractions. Put up key elements in graphic patterns, like mind maps. Post them well in advance of the course (2 weeks) and leave them up after the course is over.

You create the weather, the climate and the long-range forecast in your classroom. Affirmations and peripherals are part of the climate. If you want a positive climate, don't hope it will happen. Be proactive and make it happen. Ask students to brainstorm and create their own affirmations for at least part of the wall space available; and be sure to rotate them monthly so that the novelty state will remain intact and attract the brain's attention.

Quotable

Affirmation "makes firm" that which you want. It's a suggestion, a prediction, a blessing and well-wishing. The more you affirm goodness in others, the more likely you are to find goodness.

Sample Affirmations:

- ✦ Learning is fun, easy and creative.
- ✦ The future belongs to those with serious dreams.
- ✦ Act as if it were impossible to fail.
- ✦ The more you learn, the easier it gets.
- ✦ Luck is often disguised as hard work.
- ✦ All unhappiness is caused by comparison.
- ✦ You can't vote to make things the way they are, you already did.
- ✦ If life gives you lemons, make lemonade.
- ✦ If you think you can or think you can't, you're right.
- ✦ Success is a journey, not a destination.
- ✦ Inch by inch, it's a cinch.
- ✦ Failure is a success if you learn from it.
- ✦ Get an education in school and you'll have it for life.
- ✦ If you play victim, you give up your power to change.
- ✦ You can have anything you want, if you give up the belief that you can't have it.
- ✦ You're as happy as you make up your mind to be.
- ✦ If your rug is pulled out from under you, learn to dance on a shifting carpet.
- ✦ Your greatest advantage is your ability to learn.
- ✦ Nothing can hurt you unless you give it the power to do so.
- ✦ Others can stop you temporarily; only you can stop you permanently.
- ✦ Before you can break out of prison, you must first realize you're locked up.
- ✦ The biggest risk in life is not risking.
- ✦ The mind is like a parachute. It works best when open.
- ✦ No on can make you feel inferior without your permission.
- ✦ Focus, Breathe, Listen.
- ✦ I choose to respond positively, *not* react.
- ✦ If you don't live it, you don't believe it.
- ✦ If it's worth learning, it's worth celebrating.
- ✦ Breakthroughs occur when I commit myself to something I don't know how to do yet.
- ✦ Get in... Get it done... Get out!
- ✦ It's not *if* I can, it's only a matter of how.

Continued...

Sample Affirmations... Continued

✦ The difference between 99% and 100% is 100%.

✦ Live your vision with passion.

✦ Communicate to the person who can do something about it.

✦ Learning is a big part of life.

✦ Be bigger than your problems.

✦ The first step in life is getting what you want and the other 99% is wanting what you get.

✦ Who I am makes a difference.

✦ If you continue to do what you've always done, you'll continue to get what you've always gotten.

✦ I am greater than my highest thought.

✦ Get a life; get a degree!

✦ Compliments and criticisms have little to do with the listener; and more likely reflect the values and beliefs of the speaker.

✦ My success is absolutely assured.

✦ I succeed by asking questions.

✦ Reaching goals feels good.

✦ The difference between ordinary and extraordinary is that little "Extra."

✦ I rejoice in my choices.

✦ I am unique and special in all the universe.

✦ A smile is my style.

✦ It is safe for me to express myself.

✦ The more I enjoy, the more I learn.

✦ I absorb and retain with ease and joy.

✦ Don't wait for your ship to come in; swim out to it.

✦ You get in life exactly what you put up with.

✦ For things to change, I must change.

✦ To raise yourself, praise yourself.

✦ I study smarter every day.

✦ There's no such thing as failure, only feedback.

✦ Carpe diem (Seize the day!)

✦ Fear is: false evidence appearing real.

✦ I can succeed. I will. I do. It's now done.

Reactions:

What are your feelings about the topics presented in this chapter?

What are some practical applications for what you're learning?

What do you want to remember from this chapter?

When we think of intelligence, we are really talking about our ability to react intuitively, creatively and constructively to a wide range of experiences.

Robert Sternberg, PhD.
Mind in Context

Chapter 15

Multiple Intelligences

Chapter Preview:

- ✦ Teaching Content or Discovering Intelligence?
- ✦ Intelligent People
- ✦ Defining Intelligence
- ✦ Who Is Intelligent?
- ✦ The Seven Intelligences
- ✦ Additional Considerations
- ✦ Reaching All the Intelligences
- ✦ Nurturing the Intelligences
- ✦ Integrating Across the Curriculum
- ✦ Assessing Multiple Intelligences
- ✦ The Role of Gifted Programs

Teaching Content or Discovering Intelligence?

In order to boost learning and intelligence, it's useful to know what intelligence is. Robert Sternberg (1985) says, "Intelligence boils down to your ability to know your own strengths and weaknesses and to capitalize on the strengths while compensating for the weaknesses." He says that when we think of intelligence, we are really talking about our ability to react intuitively, creatively and constructively to a wide range of experiences. In other words, being "street smart" is just as important, or more so, than being "book smart."

For years, the official way to measure intelligence was the IQ test, the Stanford-Binet, or the Weschler. Using these tests, individuals would be rated at various levels. Yet researchers and educators have long suspected that something is amiss in this assessment. Often students who were assessed as "smart" or "genius" had very ordinary, if not miserable, lives. And often students who were assessed as "ordinary" or "average" had very successful and extraordinary lives. After all, the IQ test was developed decades ago as a screening process for immigrants and for sorting wartime recruits. Could it be that the IQ form of assessment is inaccurate or incomplete?

Intelligent People

Ella Fitzgerald, Carl Sagan, John Williams, Martha Graham, Bill Gates, Helen Gurley Brown, Quincy Jones, Albert Einstein, Michael Jordan, Indira Ghandi, Margaret Thatcher and Steven Segal. Which one was or is more intelligent? You guessed it! All are intelligent, in their own way! Did you know that every single one of them was labeled by their teachers as having some kind of learning problem?

Fortunately, in the late 1970s and early 1980s, with the support from the VanLeer and MacArthur Foundations a project was headed up by Howard Gardner, professor of graduate education at Harvard University, that has since widened our definition of intelligence. The project's purpose was to discover the nature of intelligence and consider alternative ways for thinking about it (1993). Because the researchers wanted to start with no prior assumptions about intelligence, it was named Project Zero.

Defining Intelligence

Gardner first had to define intelligence in order to research it. He used two criteria. The first criteria was demonstrating the ability to use a skill, fashion an artifact or solve a problem; and the second one was to do this in a way that was valued by the particular culture where one ordinarily lives. In other words, an Australian Aborigine may not be able to score as highly on intelligence if measured in Tokyo, New York or London. But he or she may be quite intelligent in the outback of Australia. The same could be said in reverse for a banker or stockbroker who succeeds in the world of global finance but, of course, might die in three days in the remote outback.

Who Is Intelligent?

Gardner's research sought to find various ways intelligence was demonstrated around the world. What he discovered was skill sets that included thing like: a Pacific Islander who can sail from island to island at night with no formal navigation system; and an equally talented choreographer of Broadway musicals. Certainly these people were succeeding in the eyes of their own culture. But there was no apparent link to formal schooling. Gardner eventually grouped the array of human intelligences he identified into seven categories. He purposely included what some refer to as "abilities" because he wanted them to get the respect they deserve. Instead of having one single figure or mark that assesses our intelligence, he believes that each of us has our own unique combination of intelligences and that these can change over time. Gardner speculates that there may be other intelligences, such as naturalist.

The Seven Intelligences

The seven original intelligence categories Gardner identified are logical-mathematical, interpersonal, spatial, musical-rhythmic, intrapersonal, bodily-kinesthetic and verbal-linguistic. Gardner first presented these ideas publicly in 1983 at the Tarrytown conference in New York. We'll introduce each of them here and discuss how they can be used to enhance student learning in your classroom.

1. Logical-Mathematical

Description: This intelligence category encompasses the ability to discern logical or numerical patterns. It includes those with the ability to solve mathematical equations or life's daily problems; one who asks many "why" or "how" questions; one who likes reasons for doing things; one who wants to classify, sort and understand information; one who wants to predict, analyze, theorize, fix things, offer advice, work in the physical and theoretical sciences or simply make sense out of their world. It's the ability to pursue extended reasoning and detailed analysis. Compatible occupations include: teaching, banking, astronomy, computer programming, accounting, inventing, engineering, mathematics, science, or appliance repair. Famous people who exhibit this intelligence: Carl Sagan, Plato, Bill Gates, Ted Koppel.

In the Classroom: This student is an effective problem-solver. He or she likes things in place and in order; and dislikes chaos and confusion. Repetitive seat work bores this student the most. Catch the attention of these students with questions like: "How would you solve this?" "What would an expert say about this?" Reach the student with challenges, problems and projects.

Can Be Developed More By: Outlining the material, doing statistical analysis, solving problems, creating puzzles and solving them, finding patterns, comparing and contrasting the material, classifying ideas or objects, exploring new material, finding locations, making calculations, computing averages, creating time sequences, using a calculator, predicting the future, creating a problem-solving guide for your subject, solving ecological problems, finding examples of how it all relates to something else. These students like computers, tangrams, inventor's fairs and science projects.

2. Interpersonal

Description: This intelligence category encompasses those with the ability to influence others, to negotiate, to listen, to resolve conflict, to persuade, to get along with others, to influence, to form teams. This student works well with diverse groups of people and enjoys the company of others. Compatible professions include: teachers, customer service representatives, therapists, politicians, beauty queens, religious leaders, actresses and actors, managers, social workers, telephone operators, salespersons and waitresses. Famous people who exhibit this intelligence: Oprah Winfrey, Sally Jessey Raphael, Phil Donahue, Bill Clinton, Mother Theresa, and Princess Di.

In the Classroom: This student prefers to work with others. Small groups and workstations attract attention. They like student council, peer counseling and service-learning projects. Working alone is distasteful. Reach this student with strong communication activities. Attract his or her attention with words like "We can do this next" or "What did we learn today?"

Can Be Developed More By: Doing more role-play, using cooperative learning groups, using peer assessment, getting and giving feedback, creating teams to solve problems, working with a single partner, doing subject matter drills with a partner, quizzing each other, reading out loud or singing, using peer coaching, organizing events, celebrations, or talent shows.

3. Spatial

Description: This intelligence category encompasses those who have the ability to judge space around them in relation to other objects or people. Gardner emphasizes that spatial intelligence is different from visual intelligence. Spatial intelligence is more three-dimensional and relational. It is not the ability to see something, but rather the ability to see things in relationship to others. A person might be legally blind and still have strong spatial intelligence.

Spatial intelligence includes the ability to: parallel park a car, fill a dishwasher, pack luggage, and design or decorate a room. One with high spatial intelligence can find a particular piece of paper even on a very messy desk. Compatible occupations may include architects, athletes (team sports), landscapers, jugglers, airline pilots, chorus line dancers, sculptors, muralists, painters, navigators, organizers, logistics people, flight deck workers on an aircraft carrier, heavy machinery construction workers or movie directors. Famous people who exhibit spatial intelligence: Peggy Fleming, Brian Boitano, Steven Spielberg, Nancy Kerrigan, Dan Marino, Steve Young or John Elway.

In the Classroom: This student often fidgets and doodles. He or she loves a picture-rich environment full of posters, mobiles and art. Reach this student with activities that allow him/her to paint, arrange, do origami, make mazes, create geo-block designs, build and draw. Catch their attention with questions that ask them to "imagine or picture something."

Can Be Developed More By: Mind-mapping, organizing, color coordinating, drawing, sculpting, rearranging the room to suit the subject, making wall displays, using guided imagery, re-setting the chairs, changing teaching locations, designing graphics, logos and flyers; by having students line up according to height - birthdays - alphabetical name order (or other combination), playing ball-toss games, circle or line dancing and human sculpture.

4. Musical-Rhythmic

Description: This intelligence category encompasses those who have the ability to translate the sounds of nature or those created in the head into patterns of music. This includes the ability to tap dance, clap in unison, dance, compose music, play music, create rhythm games and songs. Musical-rhythmic intelligence does not have anything to do with a talent for singing. Compatible occupations include: pre-school or elementary school teachers, cheerleaders, tribal cultures that use music for ritual and entertainment or communication, musicians, jingle-writers, choir leaders, theater directors and composers. Famous people who exhibit musical-rhythmic intelligence: Quincy Jones, Rogers and Hammerstein, John Williams, Lerner and Lowe, Paul Simon.

In the Classroom: This learner is sensitive to sounds and has the ability to respond to them. Reach this student by creating time for dancing, singing, listening, rapping, jingles and using instruments. This student is distracted by the teacher talking too much, repetitive tasks, scattered noise and sitting too long. Catch their attention with questions like: "How does this sound?" Use sounds or special effects to open a class.

Can Be Developed More By: Using concert readings, making class affirmations, doing "clap and slap" memory games, team cheering, having musical performances, putting information to rhythms, creating a jingle, rapping, playing instruments, making up sounds for the subject you are studying, having environmental music in background, practicing humming patterns for memory or mood changes, turning an essay, short story or movie into a musical, listening for natural sounds and then using them in learning. This student likes presentations using a musical score to highlight key parts.

5. Intrapersonal

Description: This intelligence category includes those who have the ability to think about thinking. He or she likes self-assessment, reflection, planning; enjoys tasks in solitude, uses intuition often, is a day-time dreamer, may enjoy journal-writing, meditation, focusing, self-discovery; knows their strengths and weaknesses, is likely to enjoy solitude and asking the big questions of life such as: "Why are we here?" "What happens when we die?" "Is there a God?" Compatible occupations include: authors, fishermen, philosophers, sailors, artists, farmers, spiritualists, backpackers and hermits. Famous people who exhibit intrapersonal intelligence: Simone DeBeauvoir, Bill Gates, James Michener, Socrates, Eleanor Roosevelt and Thoreau.

In the Classroom: This student likes to be left alone to reflect. He or she thrives on self-reliance and individual work. This student wants to manage his or her own work. This learner is annoyed by too many teacher-directed activities, too much structure, rules and textbook teaching. Use phrases like "What would you do if this were you?" or "How would you feel if...?"

Can Be Developed More By: Giving more silent reflection time to think about what has been learned, having students think about *how* they arrived at their solution, writing an essay on "What I have learned from life," putting themselves in the situation of a character in a play and imagining what they would do, asking them to apply what they've learned, doing guided imagery, writing in a diary or journal, meditating, doing self-assessment on personal or course goals, practicing methods for self-control (temper, breathing, focus, etc.), and figuring out how to go about solving a problem, identifying personality traits and learning styles, teaching decision-making with steps to take for better thinking.

> *Reflection:*
> **What combination of natural intelligences do you feel you have?**

6. Bodily-Kinesthetic

Description: This intelligence category encompasses those who have the ability to control body motions and manipulate objects. These learners use their body to accomplish a task, entertain or express themselves. Compatible occupations or hobbies include: dancers, actors, rock climbers, martial artists, new games leaders, gardeners, athletes, mimes, bicycle messengers, clowns, triathletes, astronauts, coaches, sheep shearers, Olympians, construction workers, frisbee players, inventors, dog trainers, bowlers, farmers or custodians. Famous people who exhibit bodily-kinesthetic intelligence are: Michael Jordan, Martina Navaratilova, Arnold Schwartzenegger, Madonna, Carl Lewis, Jackie Joyner-Kersey, Meryl Streep, Steven Segal, Robert DeNiro, Denzel Washington, and Dustin Hoffman.

In the Classroom: This student enjoys role-play, sports, field trips and manipulatives. They dislike having to sit too long. Instead, they prefer to be able to get up, (on their own schedule) and stand, walk around or stretch. Catch this student's attention by asking questions like "How does this grab you?" or ask, "How would you respond to this?"

Can Be Developed More By: Stretching, changing seats, creating a play, playing Simon Sez, using the body to learn, creating simulations, role-playing, sporting events, changing positions in the room, dancing, rearranging the room, assigning tasks in various parts of the room, forming human shapes, playing charades or Pictionary™ and other games, shaking hands, using sign languages, re-enacting great moments in history, learning each topic with a physical gesture attached, allowing students to build with Legos, weaving, working with wood and/or clay, and doing class jobs.

7. Verbal-Linguistic

Description: This intelligence category encompasses those who have a good command of the language and the ability to form thoughts. They like to talk, tell stories, argue, debate, tell jokes, shape arguments, read, discuss, interpret and re-think. Compatible occupations include: attorneys, writers, judges, editors, public speakers, translators, negotiators, comics, talk show hosts, poets, secretaries, authors, elected representatives, and teachers. Famous people who exhibit verbal-linguistic intelligence: Robin Williams, Martin Luther-King, Connie Chung, William F. Buckley, Malcolm X, Lily Tomlin, Arsenio Hall and Garrison Keeler.

Quotable

Intelligences are cultivated more than they are inherited. And different cultures tend to reinforce certain intelligences.

In the Classroom: This student prefers to have interesting graphics, posters and slogans in the environment. They are very sensitive to language, and sarcasm, especially belittling. Provide opportunities for this student to read, dialogue, use affirmations, peer teach or be involved in discussions. Use expressions like, "What's your opinion?" or "Tell me, please, why would you say that?"

Can Be Developed More By: Sharing, group interaction, listening to guest speakers, writing or giving speeches, reading, listening to tapes, creating a dialogue with partners or within teams, playing parts in a play, learning vocabulary, writing up steps to an experiment, giving instructions, creative writing, problem-solving exercises, making up puns, creating crossword puzzles on a particular subject, being an announcer or sports caster for a classroom event, impromptu speaking, using humor, joking, and journal writing.

Additional Considerations

All of us have some of each of the intelligences. We have our own unique combination of them. But the degree of expertise in each varies widely. For example you may be able to play "Mary Had a Little Lamb" on a piano, but that's very different from composing an opera. You can jog or walk, but not play professional sports.

The amount of talent you have in each of your seven intelligences does not correlate to success in society. For example, you may be the most talented basketball player in the world, but if you are unwilling to work hard, get along with your teammates and be at practice every day, you'll never become a star. On the other hand, you could be low in most areas, but have enough interpersonal intelligence to be the best customer service representative in your company. Your specific intelligence areas will change over time. For example, a college athlete may excel in three sports at age 21 and yet by age 50, be very low in bodily kinesthetic intelligence. Yes, the body will remember many of the moves, but it won't be able to perform the same.

Intelligences are cultivated more than they are inherited. And different cultures tend to reinforce certain intelligences. There are tribes in Africa in which everyone is taught how to sing and play music. As a result, all are strong in musical-rhythmic intelligence. A male Samoan or Fijian islander learns early in life that celestial navigation can save his life. Hence, he grows that particular spatial skill at an early age. Urban street kids usually find that verbal-linguistic and bodily-kinesthetic intelligences provide critical survival value for the threatening situations encountered in daily life. The better your own intrapersonal intelligence, the better you'll be at rating yourself. In other words, to even talk about your own intelligences, you'd have to have some intuition or skill at self-assessment.

You can "grow" intelligences. Most three year-olds are low in all the seven intelligences; however, years of life, social interactions, work and school experience give the intelligences a boost. The good news is that we have no "fixed" intelligence. The bad news is that the brain does have developmental stages in which each of the intelligences are more easily nurtured. The critical stage for developing a musical-rhythmic, spatial, and verbal-linguistic foundation is from ages three to six. Bodily-kinesthetic intelligence seems to be able to be developed from as early as age three up to age seventy. For developing interpersonal, mathematical-logical and intrapersonal intelligences there seems to be no age limit.

Do what you are good at and usually contentment will follow. In general, the happiest and most successful people have purposely developed areas that they were, at one time, weak in. Remember, there's always room for improvement.

Reaching All the Intelligences

So with the basics of multiple intelligences covered, let's take a look at instructional design and assessment. The ideal is to provide learning opportunities for students to be able to succeed regardless of their particular strength; this means providing learning activities in all of the multiple intelligence categories. It also means that some students may not succeed easily at everything. Some may be a bit uncomfortable. But the good news is, that over the length of the course, you'll reach your students better and reach more of them. You'll also reach them on a deeper and more profound level.

Here's the difference between an average teacher and a great teacher. An average teacher teaches so that at any given time, they are reaching 60 to 80 percent of their learners. A great teacher teaches so that at any given time, they are reaching 60 to 80 percent of their learners. So, what's the difference? With the average teacher, it's the same 60 to 80 percent of students who are doing the learning all term long. With the great teacher, a different 60 to 80 percent of students are learning every day. When you rotate learning activities that cover all of the intelligences, *all* of your students will learn over a given week.

Design your classes, workshops or trainings so that they include at least three or four of the following sub-components from each of the seven groups. You already know the basic order and the format for organizing your lesson. You may be using a model that includes: creating a certain physical environment, an introduction, the initial activation of learning, elaboration of the learning, evaluation and celebration.

Nurturing the Intelligences

Lessons can be designed that use all seven intelligences every hour, but this would involve a lot of work. If you teach elementary age students, there's an easier way to provide all seven at least once a day, probably a half a dozen times. Bruce Campbell, a third grade teacher in Washington State, has set up seven "learning stations" around his classroom.

Each station offers his students a way to learn the subject. He divides up his class into seven groups and they get time on each one, then he rotates them to the next. Bruce says that when he starts at the beginning of the year, students usually like one station. By mid-year, they like three or four of them and by the end of the year, they usually like most or all of them. Here's a perfect example of how the intelligences can be "grown."

At the secondary and/or college level, three or four intelligences may be tapped in one class and all seven within a week. Don't, however, let a week go by without reaching all seven categories or you run the risk of students getting bored and frustrated.

Integrating Across the Curriculum

The most commonly used system for implementing multiple intelligences is webbing a lesson. Put the topic or unit in the center of a piece of paper and circle it. Then make seven spokes, like a wheel, coming out from the center. At the end of each spoke, list one of the seven intelligences. Then take a few moments before you begin a unit, and list some of the ways that you could use each of the particular intelligences on the topic you have.

Reflection:

How do you teach to learner's multiple intelligences? Are you reaching all seven categories?

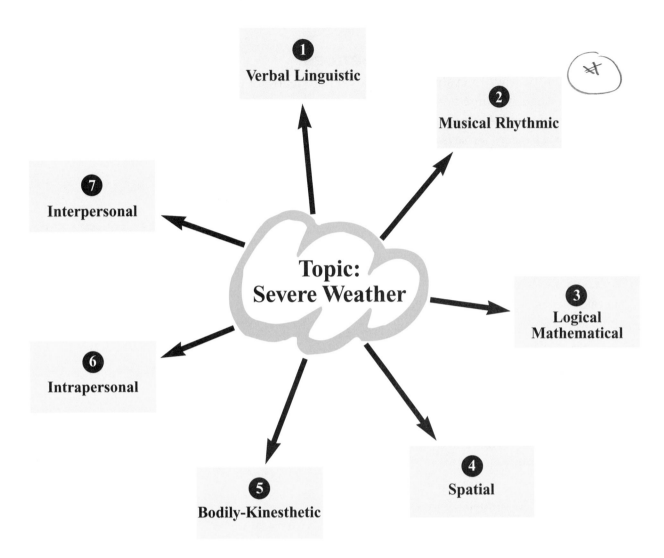

Here's an example of a lesson that teaches to all seven intelligences. Let's say it's a science topic like "severe weather."

1. *Verbal Linguistic:* You could read an opening dramatic sequence to the class or have them read to each other. They could write out their own dramatic opening using the omen of bad weather.

2. *Musical Rhythmic:* They can write a catchy jingle to warn others about a dangerous storm on the way. They could bring in music to play which refers to weather.

3. *Logical Mathematical:* They could analyze data, predict, organize information make graphs or solve logistical problems relating to a severe weather evacuation.

4. *Spatial:* Students visualize the impact of the severe weather on their own neighborhood or design a logo for the weather person. They could design a weather magazine, a mobile or TV show format.

5. *Bodily - Kinesthetic:* They act out the formation, event and dissipation of a severe storm. They could create and perform a play.

6. *Intrapersonal:* Students could read about it, write down in a journal how they would feel about it roaring through their neighborhood. They could critique the unit and their own reactions to it. How might they improve on it for next time?

7. *Interpersonal:* They can work in cooperative learning groups to jigsaw what they have learned. They could also create a play to communicate what they have learned.

Relax and have fun. Do some experimenting. What is new and a bit intimidating for you today may become comfortable, like an "old hat" by next month.

Assessing Multiple Intelligences

There are dozens of ways to evaluate students who are learning using the multiple intelligences model. Keep student's work in a large process-folio for convenient safekeeping. The old portfolio method meant keeping just samples of the student's best work to date. A Process-folio keeps the interim stages stored, too. It is important, Gardner says, so that you can better assess progress. Here are some of the possible ways to assess students.

◆ Students create jingles or songs about a unit.
◆ Give students a choice on the type of assessment.
◆ Journal or diary with reflections and personal growth.
◆ Get credit for community or business work.
◆ Create a song and sing or perform it.
◆ Produce a videotape(or audio tape).
◆ Peer assessment (with your established criteria)
◆ Build working models that demonstrate knowledge.
◆ Interviews with the teacher.
◆ Make a chart of progress in the course.
◆ Write a story or article.
◆ Perform a play, musical, or dance.
◆ Create a piece of artwork.
◆ Graphic organizers like Venn diagrams.
◆ Make an advertising flyer for the course/subject.
◆ Re-do the lyrics to a song with the new key words.
◆ Produce a large mind-map.
◆ Self-assessment using personal or course goals.

More students are assured of succeeding when you use a greater variety of assessment methods. Why? All of your students have several intelligences and are smart and gifted in some way or another. The key is to make sure you are assessing for all of the intelligences. Some pointers for observing your student's strengths follow:

◆ Students tend to do what they like or are most successful in. Watch to see who are the questioners, the hummers, the doodlers, the active learners, the talkers, the loners, etc.
◆ Provide students with a choice of games to play and watch to see which ones are picked and by whom. Pictionary, Monopoly, crossword puzzles, manipulative puzzles, charades, and music recognition games are possibilities.
◆ Have students watch a video, play, movie or musical and then do a reflection on it. Ask your students which parts were really memorable. Was it the music, the action, the relationships, etc.?
◆ Give a problem-solving exercise to a group and observe the process. For example, the one about the man and the woman starting out walking from the same place. The man takes two steps for every three the woman takes. They start out together, and immediately lose synchronization. After how many steps will they be back in synch again? This problem can be solved using just about every one of the seven intelligences. But which one is chosen by the students?
◆ Ask students to build an invention or model of something. Learners will naturally focus on a project that uses the types of intelligences that they are strongest at.

There are tremendous implications to this in the classroom. No longer can a teacher talk about "high" and "low" kids. No longer can a teacher talk about "my high achievers, my gifted kids."

The Role of Gifted Programs

With multiple intelligences there is no ability grouping. Are there ever any special education students at a multiple intelligences school? Yes, but very few. Here's why: the only way you can ability group is to first compare students; and a comparison of two students is one of the most irrelevant activities an institution can perform. How Karen does compared to Diane is absolutely immaterial. Karen's brain may be as much as three years ahead or behind Diane's in development. Karen has an entirely different multiple intelligences profile than Diane. Either of them may have a miserable and unacceptable home environment which provides constant stress and dramatic under nutrition. The only relevant bit of data about Karen is "How is Karen doing today compared to Karen's performance of a week ago or a year ago?" Now that's useful data!

The Key School is a public elementary school in Indianapolis, Indiana that is using the multiple intelligences model. The school policy is, "Every student is gifted." And they have proved it. Ordinary children act and perform like those in "gifted schools". The difference? Two things: 1) an attitude that everyone is gifted; and 2) the use of multiple intelligences by skilled teachers.

What's Changed?

Old:

The standard IQ is 100 for everybody, and you are either above the average, average, or below it. The question of yesteryear was: is this student smart?

New:

One learner may exhibit intelligence differently than another, but they are no more or less intelligent. One learner may solve a problem by visualizing it, another by talking it over, and another by reading about it, then putting a pencil to paper. The question of today is: How is this student smart?

Quotable

We are all gifted; some just haven't opened their gifts yet.

Howard Gardner says the following: "In my view, the purpose of schools should be to develop intelligences and to help people reach vocational and avocation goals that are appropriate to their spectrum of intelligences. People who are helped to do so, I believe, feel more engaged and competent and, therefore, more inclined to serve society in a constructive way." It has now been established quite convincingly that individuals have quite different minds from one another. Education ought to be so sculpted that it remains responsive to these differences. Instead of ignoring them, and pretending that all individuals have (or ought to have) the same kinds of minds, we need to ensure that everyone receives an education that maximizes his or her own intellectual potential.

It may once have been true that a dedicated individual could master the world's extant knowledge or at least some significant part of it. So long as this was a tenable goal, it made some sense to offer a uniform curriculum. Now, however, no individual can master even a single body of knowledge completely, let alone the range of disciplines and competencies.

When regular teachers are trained in multiple intelligence strategies, their students learn more effectively and efficiently. More of their students learn better and they retain the learning longer. Self-confidence is up and so is love of learning. This means you'll have fewer problems, fewer students who need special attention or special skills from a pull-out program.

Quotable

It's now time for educators and parents to quit asking the old question, "How smart are you?" The new question is, "In what ways are you smart?"

Mind-Map

Depict how you might organize a topic of learning for interdisciplinary study that incorporates the multiple intelligences. This is your mind-map, so organize it how it makes sense to you.

Reactions:

What are your feelings about the topics presented in this chapter?

What are some practical applications for what you're learning?

What do you want to remember from this chapter?

Quite simply, music is good for you -
physically, emotionally, and spiritually.
It can strengthen the mind, unlock the creative
spirit, and, miraculously, even heal the body.

Don Campbell
The Mozart Effect

Chapter 16
Music in Learning

Chapter Preview:

- ✦ **The Sweet Sounds of Learning**
- ✦ **The Role of Music in Learning**
- ✦ **Why Music?**
- ✦ **Getting Started Is Easy**
- ✦ **Sample Selections**
- ✦ **Suggestions for Introducing Music**
- ✦ **Music Player Options**
- ✦ **Suggestions Before Purchasing**
- ✦ **Duplication for Audiotapes**
- ✦ **Making the Right Music Choices**
- ✦ **Music Types: Chronologically**
- ✦ **When To Use Music**
- ✦ **Concert Readings**
- ✦ **How to Get Started**

The Sweet Sounds of Learning

Nature has provided us with such a rich array of sounds on our planet earth that for humans to copy and use them was inevitable. Most of our musical instruments are, of course, variations of animal or other natural sounds. So, the use of music as a learning aid is an ancient idea. Primitive man used it in many ways.

More recently, a great deal of research has been conducted on the effects of music on humans. Results show that music affects the emotions, the respiratory system, the heart rate, the posture, and the mental images of the listener. These effects can dramatically alter the composite mood, state, and physiology of a person. Here's the key: when you change the state of the listener, you get direct access to state changes. This means music can change the behavior of your students. Music works marvelously to energize, align groups, induce relaxation, restimulate prior experiences, develop rapport with another, set the theme or the tone for the day, to stimulate the mind, to facilitate fun and to inspire.

The Role of Music in Learning

Does music belong in a classroom where the subject is not music? Absolutely yes! There are many ways to use it. Chances are, you learned the letters of the alphabet with a song. You probably learned many words and phrases through folk songs. You learned rituals, manners and social skills with childhood songs. As you get older, you have associated many situations, feelings and people with special songs. Listening and playing music is a powerful way to learn. Consider some of the following advantages to using music:

✦ Embeds the learning faster, on a deeper level like the "alphabet song."
✦ Provides relaxation after stress or discouragement.
✦ Collects and brings whole groups together.
✦ Motivates the group to get up and get going.
✦ Builds rapport and encourages bonding.
✦ Energizes and brings new life to the group.
✦ Appeals to the particular cultural values of the group.
✦ Comforts the soul during painful times.
✦ Something to have fun with when you need a change of mind-set.
✦ Boosts achievement by activating the thinking portion of the brain.
✦ Harmonizes situations when the group seems to be on edge.
✦ Calms down hyper students.
✦ Stimulates the right brain hemisphere activating more of the brain.
✦ Increases attentiveness and concentration.
✦ Stimulates and focuses creativity.
✦ Takes some pressure off the presenter or teacher.
✦ Creates sound curtains to isolate classes or groups from distracting noise.
✦ Brings forth qualities of the music that reside within.

For most students, school is a hostile and alien environment. They're being told what to do, in cold, uncarpeted, institutionalized rooms. The one thing most kids relate to, besides their friends, is music. And music is missing from most classrooms. The first thing most kids (and many adults) do when they get in a car or arrive home is turn on music to relax, to energize, to change moods, to feel good. So, why is it not incorporated at school? It's just out-dated thinking. We decorate the walls visually, why not appeal to and utilize, the other senses such as auditory and kinesthetic? Make your learning environment much more student-friendly, build rapport with kids, and enhance the learning process with music. Do you need any other reasons to integrate music into your classes?

Why Music?

If you do need additional convincing, here are three more reasons why every teacher ought to incorporate music into their curriculum: 1) your students will love it; 2) they'll perform better; and 3) they'll feel better; plus, you will too! Music will make your work more fun, interesting, relaxing, and memorable as well.

You don't have to be a musicologist to get great results. A grasp of music fundamentals, however, may be helpful. The tapes and books recommended in this chapter are a good start; and here are some key facts:

First and foremost, all music has some sort of pace with which to measure beats per minute. The single most important question to ask about classroom music is, what's the tempo, the pacing or the beat of the music? Meaning, is it slow, medium or fast? The beat of the music affects both heart rate and breathing - the two most important determiners of mood, feelings and state. So remember, the beat is the distinction you need to be able to make. In general, your selections will be instrumental. The exceptions will include some popular music, but these may be reserved for breaks or special effects, outside of lecture time.

Getting Started Is Easy

Learning to maximize the use of music in the classroom is an on-going process. Plan to invest some time and money to make a quality presentation package. Expect to pay from $60 to $150 for a new, low-cost portable classroom music system. A medium quality stereo CD/tape player with separate detachable speakers will be adequate. As a starter kit, expect to pay about $75 to $100 for your first six-tape starter kit and CD/tape holder box. Include two Baroque, two new-age relaxation CD/tapes, and two more popular upbeat CD/tapes. Experiment with them for awhile before using them. When you're ready to expand your CD/tape collection, consider the following suggestions:

◆ 6 Baroque CD/tapes (2 of them from the later romantic time)
◆ 2 jazz CD/tapes
◆ 6 special effects CD/tapes including comedy, fanfare stretch music, TV tunes and others
◆ 3 focused slower CD/tapes
◆ 2 upbeat CD/tapes
◆ 2 popular rock n' roll CD/tapes
◆ 2 CD/tapes custom-tailored to your audience

Before you take your music to class, make sure that you have tested them and labeled them according to the situation in which they might be most useful. Try color-coding them with multi-colored peel-off dots to make for quicker in-class identification. The dots might signify classical, popular, new age or special effects. Set up your stereo in the front of the room and lay out all your cued music.

Quotable

Nature has provided us with such a rich array of sounds on our planet earth that it was inevitable humans would copy and use them.

Think about what's being taught so you know what kinds of specific music can be used and when. Prepare ahead with several CD/tape options so you can make sure that you are totally ready. Use music as a partner, an aid in the learning process. Always be sensitive to the existing mood in the classroom and respect it. If a sensitive, troubling or emotional process just took place, avoid music or use low-volume, low-key music that matches the mood. If a high-energy activity just took place, be ready with up-beat, high-energy music to match it. Music should serenade, romance and invite the audience - and maybe provide an occasional nudge. Obviously, it should never intrude. In short, use music to lead and entice.

First, cue up all your tapes by either rewinding them or fast-forwarding them to the spots where the music of your specific choice begins. Secondly, get all of the tapes out of their boxes or cases and have them easily accessible for quick usage. Thirdly, place them either in the order of projected usage or by category. You might label the categories as follow:

Sample Selections

Classical Music

Classical music is best for the active lecture presentation. Include Beethoven, Mozart and Rossini. Have available music from other classical eras for dramatics, special imaging and storytelling such as Mozart, Satie and Rachmaninoff. This can be used as a low-level background or *if* the teacher is trained in concert readings, it can be used as a carrier of dual-plane suggestion.

Slower Music

Slower music is ideal for Imagery and Relaxation. Include New Age artists such as Steven Halpern, Georgia Kelly, Adam Geiger, Daniel Kobialka, Zamfir, Ron Dexter, George Winston, and the long-time classic canon in D by Johann Pachelbel. This category includes nature music and environmental sounds, as well.

Popular Music

Pop music is great for break time or high-energy activities. Include a variety of upbeat popular songs that have a fun and energetic beat, and positive lyrics. Choose these selections very carefully picking individual songs over individual artists. Some examples of upbeat positive music for adults include: "I'm So Excited" by The Pointer Sisters; or "We are Family" by Sister Sledge. There are hundreds of good selections from Elvis to Nat King Cole. For an older group you can play older music and the audience will still relate to it. However, remember that if you're teaching adolescents, none of your audience was born *before* 1980, so be careful of the age of your music selections. Music from the 1960s, 1970s and early 1980s may be thought of as outdated unless a particular song is a classic.

Background Music

For background music, use primarily baroque. This includes: Bach, Corelli, Tartini, Vivaldi, Alinoni, Handel, Fausch and Pachelbel. Use "Four Seasons" by Vivaldi, "Brandenburg Concertos" and "Water Music" by Handel. When selecting these (often found in the "bargain bins"), make sure most of the compositions are played in the major (upbeat) key and done by a full orchestra (not two violins).

Popular Instrumentals

Popular upbeat instrumentals are fantastic for stretch breaks or welcome backs. Use exciting, fun or adventurous tunes such as movie themes (if you do, tailor them to your audience's age) or TV show themes. For a college audience, try the "Top Gun" anthem and "Beverly Hills Cop Theme Axel F" by Harold Faltermeyer. Try "Miami Vice" theme by Jan Hammer, the "Love Theme" from St. Elmo's Fire by David Foster and "Somebody's Watching Me" by Rockwell. For younger students, ask them what is popular. For your older audience, try themes from "Star Wars," "Raiders of the Lost Ark" by John Williams, "O-Bla-Di-O-Bla-Da" by the Beatles and "Hooked on Classics."

Special Effects

Special effects are great for those moments when you need a song that says it all. Try the themes from "Twilight Zone," "Mission Impossible," "Rocky" by Bill Conti, TV Cartoon themes, "Chariots of Fire" by Vangelis, "Eye of the Tiger" by Survivor, "Break on Through" by The Doors, "Mickey's Monkey" by Smokey Robinson and The Miracles, "The Curly Shuffle" by Jump'n Saddle. You can set a tone of hurry up, slow down, have fun, get confident, etc. You can also use the more standard special effects such as trumpet fanfare, applause, canned laughter, and others.

Suggestions for Introducing Music

Be sensitive to the needs of your audience. Tell them that you will be using music to enhance learning. Turn the volume up and down slowly when you use it. This makes it easier on the ear. Like the eye's sensitivity to light, it is less shocking to introduce strong sounds gradually.

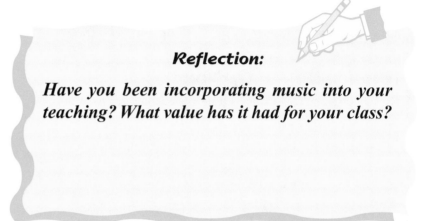

Reflection:

Have you been incorporating music into your teaching? What value has it had for your class?

In general, your audience will love music. Experiment, try recording you own. You are a pioneer in this field. Use music with purpose. Allow for quiet times for your students to breath. Avoid saturation. The effects of music are far more powerful when the freshness and newness of it is retained. Avoid rigidity with it. Be flexible, listen to your students.

If students want to bring their own tape/CDs, make two requirements. First, that you can preview the tape to insure that it is compatible with the messages and values you want for the course. Secondly, that you decide when and how to use it. In general, avoid heavy metal music, but appreciate the contributor and ask for other choices. Sometimes they'll have a second choice. The key is to stay in relationship with your students; use music as a bridge, not as a way to emphasize differences in taste. And finally, have fun with it. Music is a great team-builder.

Set the ground rules about who handles the music system and the tapes or CDs. Be consistent. If a learner complains, your volume may be too high, so turn it down a bit while that person is watching. The complainer may be an auditory learner. You'll need to move their seat position farther away from the tape player. Or, they may simply need time to adjust. Be sure to acknowledge and respect the various needs of your learners. Thank them for their input. This is your cue to do a couple of things. First, make sure that you explain, sometime soon, more about the music - why you use it and how it can assist learning. Always make it clear that learners can switch seats at any time.

Most importantly, be positive and receptive to your learner's concerns. The music has to work for both you and the audience or it isn't working at all. Allow for diversity. Respect your learner's values as well as your own. Consider visual, auditory, and kinesthetic cues and multiple cultures in your music selections.

Research by musicologist Don Campbell suggests that the right ear is better for hearing logical information and the left ear is better for feelings, emotions and pleasure. This means that the ideal in your teaching or training is to situate yourself so that you're talking more often to the left ears of your audience and playing music to the right ears. This can create a dilemma: how do you attend to your music system if it's on the opposite side of the room?

One possibility is to have detachable speakers and have the actual system with you on the student's right side with the speakers on the other side. Or, you might use a remote control. Or, plan your musical selections far ahead so that you have a few seconds of lead time to walk to the other side of the room. Or, you can simply relax about the whole thing and do it the way you want to do it.

Music Player Options

Right now, you have three choices outlined below. Each has their advantages and disadvantages.

✦ Compact Disc (CD) player
Advantages: clarity of sound, remote control option, more music storage in less space
Disadvantages: more expensive, possibly less portable, CDs more expensive, and difficult to make own recordings.
✦ Audiocassette Player
Advantages: ease in creating your own recordings, lower cost, greater availability
Disadvantages: tapes can break, get mangled and wear out
✦ CD ROM with computer keyboard
Advantages: ultimate in convenience
Disadvantages: lack of available music, more expensive, less portable

Suggestions Before Purchasing

CD Players

If you can afford it, get one that can take several discs at a time. Get a remote control. Get only the features you actually need. Think small for the player. Detachable speakers are ideal or at least good quality ones. Otherwise you defeat the purpose of getting the great quality of CD sound. The new decks let you record music onto a blank CD.

Cassette Tape Players

Get a dual deck player. It gives you much more flexibility during your trainings and you can record from another cassette tape. The "high speed dubbing" and "quick cue" are both important. Detachable speakers are ideal or at least good quality ones. Turn them up high in the store and listen carefully to them before purchasing.

CD ROM With Computer Keyboard

Make sure you buy it for the other things besides just the music. Get the one with the most power you can afford. Check the used market—you may find a great bargain. Ask around among "Tekkies" (those who are in the know about computers and ROM music) before you purchase so that you become an educated consumer.

Duplication for Audiotapes

For most of your music, use 10 to 30 minute custom tapes. These are tough to find at a regular music store or department store. Radio Shack has the 30 minute ones, but these are of low-grade quality. Look in your local yellow pages under the category of "Tape duplicating," "Recording" or "Music Production." There are usually several companies in town which specialize in duplicating. Make duplicates of every tape and keep your originals at home. Buy a box of cassette labels from either a duplication place or from a good office supply. Print or type on each label the exact content. Draw a simple symbol or tape a picture from a magazine to the cassette so that it can be identified easily from several feet or even yards away. Having a "right-brain" visual, draws attention to the tape quicker. Label each of them with your name, phone number and address, as well.

Making the Right Music Choices

Your primary decision about which music to use is answered by asking this question: "What is the 'state' of the learner I wish to evoke?" Since music affects the state of the audience you should always be asking the critical teaching question: "What is my target state for the audience and what state are they in now?" Music can be the gap-closer. Primarily, you'll be evoking the state you want through type of music, volume and beats per minute (BPM). Type of music means Classical, Jazz, Marches, Rock-n-Roll, Baroque, New Age, Romantic, Big Band, etc. Volume is important because the same composition can either be low-key background accompaniment or a pulse-quickening attention getter. Choose music carefully based on the state you want to achieve. The beats per minute provide the pacing.

Selection Pacing and Purpose:

✦ **Relaxation:** *40 to 60 Beats Per Minute (low)*
✦ **Alert:** *60 to 70 BPM (moderate)*
✦ **Active:** *70 to 120 BPM (high)*

Music Types: Chronologically

Pre-Renaissance (Composed before 1600 A.D.)

This era ranges from the early Christian music through the middle ages, Romanesque, Gothic and Renaissance periods. The bulk of this music was either minstrels with very few instruments (usually flutes, tambourines, percussion, or bells) or Gregorian chants. For centuries, African and Asian tribal music was a blend of percussion, bells and wind instruments. Pre-Renaissance music is available in the specialty section of some of the more complete music stores. Several teachers have reported successful uses of chants as a calming tool for elementary children.

Baroque (Composed 1600-1750)

Composers include: Vivaldi, Bach, Handel, Telemann and Correlli. Music of this era was simple, ornamental and regal. Best used for background, harmony and restful alertness. It is characterized by balance, unity and counterpoint. The music was all written by "house musicians," those who were permanently employed by a church, court, council or opera house. These composers wrote for specific occasions and the music usually glorified God, the king or a particular event.

Classical (Composed 1750-1820)

Composers include: Mozart, Hayden, Rossini and Beethoven. The music of this era was full of energy, surprises and contrast. Classical music hatched the modern orchestra, the symphony, themes and motives, the sonata, the concerto and the overture. It's great for creativity, background, storytelling and lectures. The composers were usually supported by a patron who financed them in exchange for the publicity, ego gratification and primary access to the compositions.

Romantic (Composed 1820-1900)

Composers include: Shubert, Tchaikovsky, Chopin, Wagner, Verdi, Dvorak, Rimsky-Korsakov, Debussy and Brahms. Music of this era is characterized by passion, suspense, wonder, impulse, ecstasy and depth. Expect it to evoke a sense of freedom with connotations of the fictitious, far off, legendary, fantastic or surreal. You've heard a great deal of Romantic music as the background for movie themes and Disney animations. The music can set the stage for emotions, clear out anger, arouse interest and curiosity. It can announce an arrival, help us to fall in love, evoke rage, depression or backdrop a chase scene.

Post-Romantic and Early American (1890-1920)

Composers include: John Phillips Sousa, George Gershwin, Maurice Ravel, Scott Joplin, Strauss. These composers stood on the shoulders of the giants of the past to create whole new music forms. The great marches, ragtime and sweeping waltzes all came out of an explosive era for music. These selections can be some of the most useful for teaching and learning. The music evokes grandeur, emotion, humor and excitement.

Quotable

Music affects the emotions, the respiratory system, the heart rate, the posture, and the mental images of the listener. These effects can dramatically alter the composite mood, state, and physiology of a person.

Big Band (1930-1955)

Composers include: Glen Miller, Dave Brubeck, Les Brown, Stan Kenton. The music was written for live audience performances as dance music for "swing" dancing. It's fun, upbeat and happy. It can be used with groups as break or recess music, or for background accompaniment during team projects.

Traditional Jazz (1920-1960)

Composers include: Dizzy Gillespie, Count Basie, Claude Bolling and Louis Armstrong. The innovator who transitioned jazz from the older style to the newer was the legendary Miles

Davis. Jazz, like other forms of music, was written as both a personal statement and a story to tell. Early jazz could be danced to or listened to at clubs. Use traditional jazz for upbeat activities, movement, and teamwork.

Modern/Popular Jazz (1960-present)

Composers include: George Benson, David Sanborn, Miles Davis, Oscar Peterson, Wynston Marsallis, Kenny G, Richard Elliot, Grover Washington, Tom Scott, Chick Corea, Joe Sample, Spyro Gyra. Written as artist's creative expression. Written primarily to listen to versus dancing to.

Modern Popular Music (1955-present)

The Nashville sound, The Philadelphia beat, the California sound, Country-Western, Motown, New Wave, Pop Rock, Soft rock, (I'll omit heavy metal), Gospel and Rap. Good songs to use from this era are the ones used for popular movie soundtracks.

New Age/Earth-Environmental Music (1975-present)

Composers include: George Winston, Paul Lanz, Dave Grusin, John Klemmer, Steve Halpern, Ray Lynch, Paul Winter, Vangelis, Kitaro, etc. Best for relaxation, uplifting, creativity, meditation, concentration or focus.

Special Effects (1950-present)

Disney soundtracks, Olympics, Movie, TV and Cartoon themes. These are best for fun, activity, suspense and celebration. Use the "Turning Point" special effects tape for these effects or build your own library of off-the-wall sounds.

When To Use Music

Use music 30 percent or less of your total class time to avoid saturation. Use in the following situations:

Background Music

Use with low volume during presentations. Four Seasons by Vivaldi, Water Music by Handel, Brandenberg Concertos by Bach.

Brainstorming, Creative Problem-Solving

Piano Concerto #5 by Beethoven, Etudes by Chopin, Claire de Lune by Debussy, Piano Concerto #26 & 27 Mozart, Swan Lake by Tchaikovsky.

Calming Music (see also relaxation music)

Amazing Grace (traditional spiritual song) Classical guitar composers, piano music, Claire de Lune by Debussy, Trois Gymnopedies by Eric Satie.

Celebrations, Successes, Wins

Celebrate by Three Dog Night, Celebrate by Madonna, Grand March from Aida by Verdi, The Creation and The Seasons by Haydn, Celebration by Kool & the Gang, Hallelujah Chorus from "Messiah" by Handel.

Closing Ritual

Use to mark a positive ending for each day. What A Wonderful World by Louis Armstrong, Happy Days theme on Vol. #3 of TV Themes by Steven Gottleib, Happy Trails by Roy Rogers on Vol. #1 of TV Themes by Steven Gottleib.

Introducing a New Student or Guest Speaker

Fanfare for the Common Man by Arron Copeland, Rocky Theme by Bill Conti, Olympics Theme-1984 Summer Games, *Star Wars*, and *Raiders of the Lost Ark* on Best of John Williams, We Will Rock You or We are the Champions by Queen.

Thinking Music

Thus Sprake Zarathrustra (2001 Theme), Blue Danube by Strauss, *Fantasia* by Disney, Suites for Orchestra by Bach, Toy Symphonies by Haydn, Musical Joke by Mozart, Desert Vision and Natural States by Lanz and Speer, Silk Road by Kitaro.

Group Singing

During games or contests. Use pop songs and traditionals. *Snow White*, *Songs of the South*, *Bambi*, Dumbo, Winnie the Pooh, Mary Poppins on Disney Soundtracks (Vol.#1,2,3) Hap Palmer Songs.

Starters or Openings

Epic Movie Soundtracks: *Chariots of Fire*, *Superman*, *E.T.*, *Rocky*, *Lawrence of Arabia*, *Born Free*, *Dr. Zhivago*. "Oh! What a Beautiful Morning" from Oklahoma. All of the James Bond 007 soundtracks, the theme from The Mission, Ravel's Bolero, Well-Tempered Clavier, Prelude in D Major by Bach, "Amanda Panda" song from Saving the Wildlife by Mannheim Steamroller or the Hungarian Dances by Brahms. Most tracks by Yanni.

Specialty Situations

Special effects for danger, fear, fun, laughter. *Jaws*, *Mission Impossible*, Comedians (Wright, Leno), Clocks, Bells, Drum Roll, Screams, Twilight Zone, Flintstones, Hi-Ho, "Zip-a-dee-do-dah..." create your own, buy a special effects tape from Turning Point or have students in class be responsible for different sounds and you call on them.

Storytelling

Also for concert readings. Classical artists: Beethoven, Mozart, Haydn, Neverland by Suzanne Cianni, Romantic music: Wagner, Dvorak, Rimsky-Korsakov.

Stretching

Also for deep breathing, calming, and relaxation. Summer, Autumn, Spring and Winter by George Winston, Silk Road by Kitaro, Barefoot Ballet by John Klemmer, Michael Jones on Piano.

Tests and Quizzes

Evoke an alert, low-stress state. Use same Baroque music used during original presentation of content or soft piano or violin concertos (with orchestras, not a solo).

Transitions

Use with activities like stretch breaks, cross-laterals, energy-builders, switch seats, etc. Hooked on Classics by Philadelphia Harmonics, 1812 Overture by Tchaikovsky, William Tell Overture by Rossini, Theme from *Rawhide*, 0 Theme by Giraldi or Benoit.

Visualization

All recordings by Daniel Kobialka, SeaPeace by Georgia Kelly, most by the artist Kitaro. Summer, Autumn, Spring and Winter by George Winston, Steven Halpern's music.

Creative Writing

Theme from *Exodus* by Handel, Nocturnes by Chopin, Peter and the Wolf by Prokofiev, The Egmont Overture by Beethoven, Environmental Music: birds, flute, waterfalls.

Concert Readings

A concert reading is the purposeful use of music in conjunction with planned content. The interplay of the music and subject matter creates an effect like a sound track for a movie, play, or opera. A pioneer in the use of this technique, Georgi Lozanov, found that well-delivered concerts can open gateways to learning, reach the subconscious, create better understanding of the subject, activate long-term memory and reduce overall learning time. Accelerated learning relies on three types of concert readings which are presented in sequence for full impact:

1. Decoding

The initial globalization period is a short, light, and fun introduction to the content using intriguing, attention-getting music. This can be achieved with a chorus, parable, chant, or poem. It builds confidence and anticipation. Decoding is done at the beginning of a new session when a fresh topic is introduced. This phase is about three to seven minutes in length. Use dramatic, light, or bizarre music to inspire.

2. Active Concerts

During the active concert stage, the content is put into context. The music is interplayed with the reading of the play, script, dialogue, or text. The music supports the absorption of the detailed material being presented, to some degree unconsciously. Learners keep their eyes open during the dramatic presentation. Use classical or romantic selections such as Beethoven or Haydn. The active concert can be done in the middle of class time or next to the last part of the session. It can be done once every 5 to 10 hours of learning time. The active concert phase is 5 to 15 minutes in length. Let the music play for 10 to 30 seconds before starting the reading. Never compete with the music. Rather, use the musical pauses, highs and lows, in time to your reading. During the louder, more active parts of the song, stop reading. Reading to the pace of the music is called "sound surfing."

3. Passive Review

This phase of the concert reading provides a low-key review of key points. It may include the same material used for the active concert phase, but the music to be used in conjunction with it is baroque. Learners close their eyes and relax. The passive review last about five to eight minutes; and is done at the end of a class session.

Presenting the Active Concert

Content

Make sure that you know your content well and are comfortable with the meaning of it. Tell the students what you'll be covering. Give them a short preview of the material verbally. Do this even when you are using handouts of the material.

Music

Make sure that you have listened to your music many times so that you know it well. How long does the introductory movement last? When does it go up and back down again in volume? How about the pacing and tempo?

Environment

You may want to change the lighting a bit. Have the learners stand and stretch, do some deep breathing. Give positive suggestions of expectancy. Allow students to sit comfortably.

Credibility

Stand with authority. Announce the name of the musical selection, the composer, and specific piece. This will prevent some listeners from being distracted during your reading trying to figure out which composer and selection it is.

Volume

Make the volume loud enough to fill in the non-speaking parts and quiet enough so that you can talk during the "down" times.

Pause

Get the attention of the audience. Create anticipation. Wait until the introductory movement of the selection is over before you begin - usually it's from 5 to 35 seconds into the piece.

Dramatic

Make large movements and gestures to emphasize key points. Think of yourself as a Shakespearean performer and enjoy creating a show. Finish with a dramatic statement or final closing remark.

Experiment! Doing concert readings is a great way to have fun, be creative and embed powerful learning. Repetition is the secret to comfort. And with comfort, you'll achieve confidence and competency.

How to Get Started

Start with just one tape or music selection. I recommend a Baroque selection, maybe Handel's Water Music or Vivaldi's Four Seasons. Get used to using it. Make your mistakes on it and your successes with it. Learn when to use it. Using just one tape will keep your stress level low. When you're comfortable and competent with that one tape, add another. Use that for awhile until you're comfortable with it, too. Over time, you'll be able to build up your selections until you can bring many of them to your place of work. I typically bring 24 tapes (over 200 selections) for a workshop. Over time, you'll get used to using all of them. And your students will, too! Take risks and have fun!

Reactions:

What are your feelings about the topics presented in this chapter?

What are some practical applications for what you're learning?

What do you want to remember from this chapter?

The human way of life is essentially social. To get things needed to keep alive we cooperate with other people. This requires special programs of the brain.

J. Z. Young
Programs of the Brain

Chapter 17 ———————————————————

Teams and Cooperative Groups

Chapter Preview:

- ✦ **Learning Can Be Noisy**
- ✦ **What is Cooperative Learning?**
- ✦ **Cooperative Learning Components**
- ✦ **Preparation**
- ✦ **The Ten-Step Process**
- ✦ **How To Create and Manage High Performance Teams**

Learning Can Be Noisy

The old way of teaching was simple. The teacher stood in front of the room and lectured. The students sat quietly and obediently in lined up rows of seats. You will *not* see such a scene today in classrooms where learning is really going on. Today's classroom is busy, interactive, flexible and the learners may be up front as much as the teacher. Why the change? Two reasons: First, we now know more about the brain and learning, so we know the advantages of interactive learning. The old model of stand and deliver is dead. Second, we now use a greater diversity of learning styles and intelligences to reach a wider range of individuals and cultures. More people learn this way.

Teams and cooperative learning are two different things. A cooperative group can have common characteristics with a team. A team can also work cooperatively. Still, they are definitively different and should be used for different purposes.

What is Cooperative Learning?

Cooperative learning is an active learning process in which academic and social skills are fostered through face-to-face student interaction, individual accountability, and positive interdependence. It is very different from other group structures - namely, competitive or individual. The most commonly group structure used by teachers is the competitive group. Nothing's wrong with this - it's a competitive world. But it ought to be used no more than 10 to 20 percent of total class time.

The competitive structure is clearly about win/lose. Basically, it's a system built on the philosophy of scarcity of goods. "There's only so many prizes, so many goodies, and if you're the best, you are the winner." Another group structure - the individual group, may not motivate by the scarcity of goods mentality, but by the sink or swim mentality. No one helps each other out or shares knowledge and skills. As mentioned, cooperative groups may work as a team; and teams may cooperate. But in cooperative learning, part of the explicit team experience is learning collaborative skills versus producing something.

Cooperative learning is being used for all age groups from elementary through college level. It also works with all ability levels. In the past, it seemed to make the most sense for kids in grades three through six because of the particular stage of social development they are at while in those grades. Now, there are so many creative derivations of it that many teachers are finding it very effective for grades 7 through 12, as well.

Quotable

Today's classroom is busy, interactive, flexible, and the learners may be up front as much as the teacher.

Cooperative learning is ideal to use when introducing challenging skills or material that encompasses more than one right answer. Allow all students to contribute; and involve as many senses as possible. Examples include research, spelling, writing, math problems, literature, language, science, reading discussion or special projects, etc.

The benefits of cooperative learning include: higher student achievement, the mainstreaming of special education students, improved social skills, increased cultural awareness and peer acceptance, a greater sense of belonging, a boost of self-esteem and greater responsibility. It's tough to find any disadvantages!

Cooperative Learning Components

Cooperative learning is *much* more than just "group work." The following five components need to be present for it to work its "magic." Make sure you use all of them.

1. Positive Interdependence

Humans have to depend on each other in order to succeed. One strategy for facilitating this type of learning is to give a group a task or problem to solve with limited supplies or materials.

2. Face-to-Face Interaction

Humans have to talk to each other or communicate effectively in an alternative way in order to succeed. Put students in groups of three in chairs that face each other. Give them a task which requires each of them to interact with the other two.

3. Individual Accountability

The best way to facilitate the learning of accountability is to give students roles and responsibilities within a group. Have the group decide who will be the recorder or secretary, who will be the encourager, the timekeeper, and the supply monitor.

4. Collaborative Skills

These are the backbone of cooperative learning. The collaborative skills you choose to teach will depend on the grade level you're teaching and what the skill level of the group is. Here are some suggestions by age groupings:

◆ *Grades K-5*

Encourage students to use each others names, look at others, share feelings, keep things calm, keep voices low, say "please" and "thank you", express themselves verbally rather than physically, repeat what has been said, stay on task, ask questions, and give ideas.

◆ *Grades 6-12*

Encourage students to paraphrase, listen for feelings, listen to learn, show appreciation, give direct eye contact, share feelings, disagree in a positive way, check for other's understanding of what's been said, give and hear opinions or feedback, and evaluate self and others.

5. Group Processing

This skill is the understanding and the true learning experience of the day. At the end of each lesson, students make consensus statements like: "What I learned... and how I felt..."

Preparation

◆ Do a lesson plan with clear objectives. Make sure you know what you want the students to get out of it - to see, hear, and experience.

◆ Carefully engineer the selection of groups so that they are heterogeneous (grouped with a diversity of abilities, gender and any other differences). Also, if you have kids who you know will fight, separate them from the outset. As your groups mature later on in the year, individuals that were separated can be placed in a group together with the hope that reconciliation will occur.

◆ Begin small. Use easy, familiar, non-content chunks. Make your collaborative objectives simple so that some early "wins" are experienced.

The following ten-step process provides a simple outline for cooperative learning success:

The Ten-Step Process

1. Context

State objectives clearly for the lesson; create an anticipatory set.

2. Task Explanation

Tell the groups exactly how to do the task at hand. Spell out your expectations. Give simple, clear instructions, both auditory and visual (and kinesthetic if needed).

3. The "Moment"

Check to see if there are any questions. Get learners thinking about the task so that they can anticipate challenges or problems. One way to encourage questions is to ask: "If you did have a question, what might it be?"

4. Introduce Collaborative Focus

Introduce the social skills to be learned or reinforced from the lesson. Be sure to model them. What does cooperation look like and sound like? Have learners practice for a few seconds with their group. Go multi-sensory for review. Also be sure to set up the rules and roles in the group. Who is the recorder, the encourager, etc.?

5. Begin Group Work

Set it all in motion with minimal intervention on your part. Provide positive strokes.

6 Group Statements

Formulate statements about how the group process can improve both academic and social skills.

7. Students Share Academic and Social Skills

Have students share statements about their particular group experience beginning with: "I felt..." and "I learned...."

8. Teacher Shares Academic and Collaborative Observations

Tell learners what you saw, felt and heard.

9. Closure and Completion

Ask students for additional thoughts or reactions to the group process. Check groups for individual accountability. Who participated? Who did their assigned job, etc.?

10. Celebration

Go around and give high fives or other acknowledgments with fanfare. Make it like a party, lots of fun for one-half to one minute. Then, have learners set new goals for next time.

How to Create and Manage High Performance Teams

If it's not right for you to use cooperative learning (especially good for K-6), it may be right for you to use teams. Here's how to make teams work like magic. Before you start with the notion of building teams, we're going to presuppose that you already assessed the need and the cooperation level of your audience and it is, indeed, appropriate to continue.

Teams work well for about four to six weeks. It takes about one to two weeks to learn to work as a team, then by the last week, members are often ready to form new teams. The best time of the year to use teams are:

✦ Weeks two through six of the school term. Using teams at the outset helps establish cooperation and reinforce other positive social values.
✦ When there is a particular project that demands teamwork and high productivity.
✦ The last two to four weeks of the year when you want tighter focus and cohesion.

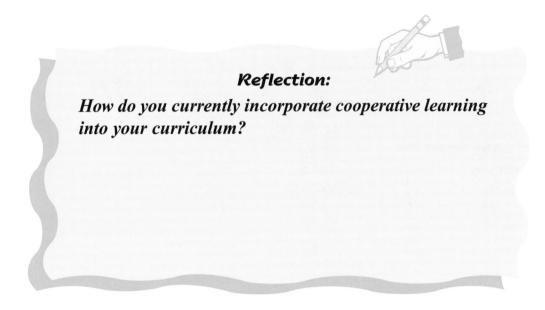

The 10 steps for creating and managing high performance teams are:

1. Engineer the Team Composition Carefully

There are many ways to select teams: randomly (count off, names in a hat, etc.), by learning style (go for diversity such as mixing visuals, auditories, etc.), by months of the year (creates an astrological mix), by participants picking their favorite other team players, by age (diversity is key), by past performance levels (careful!), by common themes at work or school (all interested in this topic), by games (close eyes, make barnyard sound and find like animals), etc. There's no right or wrong way to do this but by experimenting with the various methods, you'll soon have your favorites. If you have a specific "relationship" problem to solve or a "problem person", be willing to accept whatever happens. This person might figure that you are making a purposeful separation and get resentful. Team size is ideal at five; however, a group size of four to six works quite well. Do not form a team with more than seven members; it's just too large for fluid interaction and process efficiency. Instead, break into sub-groups if necessary.

2. Allow Team Members to Bond

A group does not a team make until the bonding and magic of synergy occurs. Otherwise, they're simply a bunch of individuals. Getting to know each other is critical. This process can be allowed to happen naturally over time, as it does in most real-life situations. However, I don't personally trust the intimacy process to occur like this. People have too many things to do and rarely share the things that truly matter with another person unless the process is formalized and time allotted for it.

Some simple team activities can help insure bonding. Before beginning, however, make sure that each group has a timekeeper and knows the signals to communicate the time. Team members should have already been coached on how to be good listeners and appropriate ground rules set for the group. Ask students to refrain from questions or comments during the speaker's sharing time. Explain that once everyone is done, questions can be asked or stories shared.

This process will help members get acquainted with each other. Give the parameters of the exercise. For example, tell learners this is an opportunity to give 90-second biography of yourself (no work-related information, only family, school, hobbies, tastes, etc.). Or you might ask them to tell about the most important things that have been going on in their life during the last seven days. Another good question is, Who was the most influential person in your life and why and how is your life different because of them? Or, what is it that you are most excited, happy or committed about? There are obviously a lot more possibilities, but the point is to get members to talk about something that creates some closeness, that requires some moderate risk without making it too uncomfortable.

3. Find Team Leaders

The team leader ought to be self-chosen, rather than appointed. The question to put out to the group before choosing is, "Who is willing to be most committed to the success of the team?" then let each person go around the circle, and share why they do or don't want to be the team leader. Discourage prompting from others in the group. If two people want to be the team leader, either they can rotate or be co-leaders. One does it for one month, and one does it for the next month or whatever. If no one wants to lead the group, provide more information about the benefits of being a leader—it's an opportunity to grow, demonstrate leadership, impact others, make a difference, etc. Usually, this solves the problem.

4. Develop Team Spirit

Team spirit can be developed in a lot of ways. Some ways will be more appropriate than others for your group's particular age-level and make up. First implement a time limit, then use any or all of the following techniques (or devise your own) for breaking the ice and developing spirit: Ask the team to pick a team name in 90 seconds. Have teams create a wild cheer in four minutes. Have the group come up with a choreographed skit with the cheer. Have them create a special gesture and saying for their team. Have them create a logo or coat of arms. Have the team read a poem together or solve a problem together or learn an activity together. Use your imagination for even more ideas. It's critical to allow and encourage wild celebrations and noise. If it's suppressed at the start, it'll disappear fast.

5. Identify Team Goals

Teams need a way to know if they are doing an effective job. Ask the team to collaborate on a set of goals together. The goals need to be specific and measurable. Ask the leader to announce their group's goals to the class. Ask the group how they will measure their goals?

6. Establish Relationships

The strength of the relationships on the team largely determine the likelihood of success. Do an initial exercise where each of the team members verbalizes to the leader their willingness to work with the leader; and the leader then verbalizes his or her commitment to the members. Encourage active listening. If each team member feels listened to and encouraged to participate the group will be strong. If a couple of members dominate the team, resentment will eventually set in and the team effectiveness will diminish. Also make sure that you develop a positive relationship with the team leaders since they are the ones you'll meet with the most often. They are your leverage, your ticket to managing the teams.

7. Create a Management System

The management system I prefer most is a self-assessment—a team scorecard. A sample team scorecard is included on page 241 to copy and/or refer to. Use a scale from 1 to 10 for scoring purposes with 1 being the lowest score and 10 the highest. Ten minutes before the end of the session, ask team members to give their team leader feedback on their performance. Some criteria will be obvious like attendance.

Other criteria, like "contribution to the group" are more subjective and require a bit more analysis. Depending on the age level you're teaching, the chart will have differing criteria. For K-3, use from three to five items. Suggestions include: attendance, enthusiasm, courtesy, safety, or new things learned. With high school-age learners, I use criteria like: contributions to the group, participation on the team, team spirit, goals reached, dependability, on time, cooperation, or respect. Assessment criteria is listed in a vertical row at left with weeks or days listed horizontally at the top of page. Have group's assess themselves frequently. The self-assessment charts ought to be interchanged with other assessment tools to keep the process fresh. Take breaks from them every other month or so.

TEAM NAME:	Week #1	Week #2	Week #3	Week #4
TEAM SPIRIT				
CONTRIBUTIONS TO CLASS				
ON TIME				
PARTICIPATION ON TEAM				
TASK COMPLETION				
CREATIVITY				
GOALS REACHED				
COOPERATION & RESPECT				
AVERAGE SCORE				

8. Discover Personal or Hidden Agendas

Every group member has a personal agenda. Elicit what they are. This can be done by the group itself with some direction by you. Or you can rotate through each group to facilitate this exercise yourself. Have group members discuss things like promises of attendance, contributions they want to make, the level of participation and/or support members want to lend to the group, etc. Group members can make requests to the rest of the group to help them stay with their personal goals. For example, a request might be: "I haven't been on time lately, could you notify me 30 minutes before our meeting?" The team leader will want to keep track of who is asking for what and who is promising what.

9. Create a Public Scorecard

Scorecards keep teams accountable and increase positive pressure. Even though each team has its own management system and scorecard for itself, you'll want a way to list all of the other teams on one major scorecard. At the bottom of each individual team chart is a place for a team average. This is the number that you'll put up on the composite chart of all teams. Then an average score for the class can be obtained. It's easy to see if the team/class is improving if it's numbers are increasing. However, make sure that the items being measured are accurately reflecting what is really happening with the team. Otherwise, the team will discount the growth and treat the scores like a joke.

Creating a scoring system is only useful if you follow-up with it. Have teams give frequent announcements about how they are doing; and encourage team cheers to celebrate progress. If you downplay the scoring and remove the celebration process, you'll regret it and the teams will cease to perform up to par. Keep the energy high, use sound effects and enlist the other teams to cheer in support. The wild, unbridled energy you can create and sustain is the fundamental key to teams working well together on a long-term basis. Any team can last for the short-term, the long-term requires emotions!

10. Relax and Play Together

Make sure that you allow your teams time to relax and play together. Ask them to do a skit, juggle, play a game, a sport, go to an event, sing, go out to eat, to drink, or whatever. This allows the team a chance to lower their guard and really get to know each other better. Generally the better your team members know each other, the more they'll accept each other and will work together to succeed.

Mind-Map

Depict how you use cooperative groups in your classroom or ways you would like to.

Reactions:

What are your feelings about the topics presented in this chapter?

What are some practical applications for what you're learning?

What do you want to remember from this chapter?

Intelligence boils down to your ability to know your own strengths and weaknesses and to capitalize on the strengths while compensating for the weaknesses.

Robert Sternberg, PhD.
Mind in Context

Chapter 18

Thinking and Intelligence

Chapter Preview:

✦ **Do We Create Intelligence?**
✦ **What Role Do Teachers Play in Learner Intelligence?**
✦ **Orderly Learning**
✦ **Understanding Your Student's Thinking**
✦ **Using Eye Movements for Thinking and Learning**
✦ **The Importance of Thinking**
✦ **Growing Thinking Skills**
✦ **Spelling/Math Strategies**
✦ **Are Questions Better Than Answers?**
✦ **Analyzing Student Answers**

Do We Create Intelligence?

We have all heard students described as: sharp, advanced, smart, gifted or high-achievers. We've also heard students described as: unmotivated, low skill, lazy, slow, disadvantaged or special education. Is it fair to label learners like this just because they do or don't exhibit certain talents? In order to talk about intelligence, it's useful to define it. Robert Sternberg (1985) says that when we think of intelligence, we are really talking about our ability to react intuitively, creatively and constructively to a wide range of experiences. In other words, being "street smart" is just as important as being "book smart."

What Role Do Teachers Play in Learner Intelligence?

You play a vital role in the kind of intelligence your learners develop because many skills and talents exist within the individual, but need to be discovered and nourished. A learners attitude about intelligence can be impacted to a large degree by the teacher, which in turn, impacts the student's abilities.

The old notion of a fixed intelligence is out of date. In fact, it has done a great deal of damage to learners, impacting their self-esteem and entire life. If you believe you're intellectually inferior, you make limiting choices. Soon, your beliefs become a self-fulfilling prophecy. Do you think this sounds far-fetched? In 1968, Harvard professor Robert Rosenthal described experiments in which teachers' expectations of student intelligence actually raised their IQ scores! How many times have we heard this? Plenty! The results from his landmark book, *Pygmalion in the Classroom* bear repeating:

- Forming expectations is natural and unavoidable.
- Once formed, expectations tend to be self-sustaining; we communicate those expectations with subtle and powerful cues.
- We are more comfortable with people who meet our expectations and less comfortable with those who don't meet our expectations.

Specifically, let's apply these results to learning:

- High expectations lead to higher performance.
- Better performance leads to more learner liability.
- We treat those whom we like better and they learn more.

You might be thinking, "I don't do these things." Are you thinking you're too experienced or too sharp to avoid doing this? Think again. Every teacher communicates expectations in some way or another. Let's say there are two groups of learners in your class, those for whom you develop lower expectations and those for whom you develop higher expectations. We'll call them the "L" (low) group and the "H" (high) group, respectively. Which of the following do you do?

- Interrupt Ls more often than the Hs.
- Give Ls less specific and less frequent feedback than Hs.
- Praise Ls for marginal or poor responses.
- Criticize Ls more frequently for poor behavior.
- Give less wait time to Ls for responses.
- Provide Ls with less academic support time than Hs.
- Seat Hs closer to you, Ls further away.
- Give Ls less challenging work.

Where do all these low and high expectations about learners come from? You'd be surprised. Most teachers think that they come from other teachers, class records, parents, socioeconomic background, or observations. Nothing could be further from the truth! Teacher expectations come from within. The potential you perceive about your learners is directly proportional to your belief in yourself. How much do you believe that you can positively influence your learners? In short, the successful teachers, the ones with consistently higher expectations and results, do not form their expectations from external prompts. They generate these expectations based on their own skill, experience and success in bringing out the potential of their students.

Quotable

The secret to classroom success with all of your learners is to treat <u>every</u> student as "gifted and talented."

Why treat everyone as gifted? Howard Gardner, Harvard Graduate Professor of Education (1993), concluded that there is not just one way to be smart, there are over 200 ways! Gardner researched the nature of intelligence and defined it as the ability to: 1) use a skill; 2) fashion an artifact; or 3) solve a problem in a way that is valued by the particular culture of that individual. In other words, a Wall Street stockbroker and an Australian Aborigine can both be considered highly intelligent in their respective cultures. If they switched roles with each other, both would have a difficult time surviving (although I suspect the Aborigine might last longer).

Gardner grouped the array of human intelligences into seven categories now known as the multiple intelligences (the subject of chapter 15). He purposely included what some refer to as "abilities" because he wanted them to get the respect they deserve. Instead of having one single figure or mark that assesses our intelligence, he says that each of us has our own unique combination of these intelligences and that they can and do change over a lifetime.

It is more difficult to assess students using multiple intelligences, but much more rewarding and accurate. A student's profile can and will change; especially over 10 years time. Over an entire lifetime, a person's intelligence profile will change a great deal, though probably none as dramatically as it will from ages 2 to 20.

Use all seven intelligences in your instructional design. For assessment, make sure that your learners have choices on how to express their knowledge through varied assessments. In a mathematics class, a learner who is average in mathematical-logical intelligence, but low in interpersonal or verbal-linguistic skills, may be poor at explaining or expressing what they know. Yet if they are strong in intrapersonal skills, they may be able to assess their

Gardner's Multiple Intelligences Review:

◆ **Verbal-Linguistic**
◆ **Intrapersonal**
◆ **Musical-Rhythmic**
◆ **Logical-Mathematical**
◆ **Spatial**
◆ **Interpersonal**
◆ **Bodily-Kinesthetic**

(see chapter 15 for complete descriptions)

own progress and troubleshoot for mistakes. If they are strong in spatial intelligence, they may be able to make a graphic of what they know. And if they are strong in musical-rhythmic, they might express ideas better with sound. Each of your students has a unique combination of intelligences and having one is unrelated to another. It is very possible, for example, to be high in both interpersonal and intrapersonal intelligence.

What's Changed?

Old:
The deficiency model: "Is he or she smart or dumb?"

New:
The empowerment model: "In what ways is he or she smart?"

If you have decided that you want to give tests, it makes sense to test in ways that reflect the real learning going on. The old, out-dated notion of testing intelligence is like a thermometer. Your temperature is either high, low or average. In the old model, you were tested for primarily writing and speaking (verbal-linguistic) or problem-solving abilities (mathematical-logical). Many very intelligent learners were labeled stupid, average or slow by this means, when in fact: 1) the presentation style of the teacher did not tap into all seven intelligences; or 2) the assessment was so narrow that it never allowed the learner to demonstrate what they really knew.

We now know that this measuring system thwarts talents and abilities. We must teach and assess in the seven intelligences to reach all learners, not just give lip service to the concept of equality. In the chapter on presenting skills (chapter 9), you'll find many ways to use the seven multiple intelligences in your presentations. The chapter on better assessment (chapter 24), will give you many assessment strategies that fit the multiple intelligences model, as well. With practice, teaching with multiple intelligences will become automatic.

David Lazear, one of the pioneers in translating Gardner's Theory of Multiple Intelligences and author of *Seven Ways of Teaching* and *Seven Pathways of Learning* (1994), talks about four levels in developing the use of them. Each level, he says, takes multiple intelligences a step further and insures that they will become a productive part of the learning process.

Level 1: **Tacit Intelligence** ("I've always used the seven intelligences, I just never called them by that name.")

Level 2: **Aware Intelligence** ("Now that I have a name for them, I'm more conscious of when and how I use them.")

Level 3: **Strategic Intelligence** ("I know when and how to use each of them.")

Level 4: **Reflective Intelligence** ("They are an integrated part of my daily personal life, as well.")

You'll get what you develop. If you have so-called slow learners who find your content a bore, look in the mirror. Ask yourself, "How can I make this subject matter come alive with excitement and challenge? How can I provide more feedback in a low stress, supportive environment?"

Here are ways to increase the frequency and value of feedback:

✦ Greet students at the door.
✦ Comment about previous learning.
✦ Allow students to peer teach and do weekly reviews with each other.
✦ Have students talk themselves (out loud) through their thinking process.
✦ Learners keep team score charts for group work and post results.
✦ Encourage the use of a journal.
✦ Have learners devise "mock tests" which they take ungraded.
✦ Have pairs prep for a test together.
✦ Have students self-correct their homework, quizzes, or tests.
✦ Learners present to the group and get oral or written feedback.

Orderly Learning

Should all learning and thinking be sequential and orderly? No. Researchers say that a climate of novelty, suspense, surprise, disequilibrium, uncertainty and disorder can lead to a richer understanding of the content. Some say the brain is designed for chaos. In fact, the behaviorist, reward-punishment, super-ordered systems attempted in most learning contexts are actually the least likely to produce the desired results. Why? The most effective learning is either real-life or patterned after real-life, and real-life is suspenseful, surprising, uncertain, and disorderly.

Most of the time, we simply repeat stored "programs." This does not represent learning necessarily, but replication of habit. The brain runs programs and patterns all day long. Only

Quotable

Some researchers postulate that learning only occurs at "impasses."

when we are stopped in our tracks by a problem or situation and forced to rethink it is there the possibility of new learning. Naturally, many times, learners, even at an impasse, will choose a prior "tried and true" path and no learning occurs. But the point here is this: the experience of chaos and confusion may be one of the few ways to naturally trigger new learning. This, of course, does not mean that poor planning is a good thing. Teachers who have sloppy lessons, with scattered thinking. and poor preparation will find that their students may begin to reflect the role-modeling. On the other hand, learners with teachers who over-structure, manipulate and control may find that learners resist by creating disruptions or detachment.

The optimal level of chaos is achieved in an orchestrated learning environment reinforced by the structure of positive rituals and infused with choice, novelty, multi-sensory input, and challenge—a sort of "orchestrated disequilibrium." Utilize learner-generated role-playing, simulations, theater, songs, experiments, field trips, extemporaneous speaking and meaningful project work in which chaos can occur naturally. Allow the activity to run its natural course when possible. Minimize intervention.

Understanding Student Thinking

When you or I say, "I am thinking," what we are really saying is, "I'm trying to manipulate internal symbols in a meaningful way." Thinking is composed of accessing prior or creating new model representations. All representations fall into the following categories:

As we learned earlier, our mind, body and feelings are all an integral part of learning and processing. There is no separation. It will come as no surprise, therefore, that *how* you are thinking can be discerned by observing the body. When we are tense or happy, others can pick up on our body language and have a good idea how we're feeling even without you speaking a word. Your eyes can provide some of the best thinking clues. Our brain's are designed so that our thinking style can often be determined by particular shifts in eye movements.

Representation Categories:

✦ **Visual** - *pictures, symbols, words or "internal movies"*
✦ **Sounds** - *voices, music, nature or technology*
✦ **Feelings** - *feelings about something is part of the thinking and decision-making process, especially for kinesthetic learners*
✦ **Others** - *other senses, which comprise a very small percentage of our thinking*

Using Eye Movements for Thinking and Learning

Eye positioning enables the brain to access certain senses. There are seven basic eye movements that relate to thinking (figure 18.1). These are useful for 90 percent of right-handed learners. Left-hand learners usually use reversed cues (but not always).

The best way to determine the particular eye (and thinking) pattern for a learner is to observe that person in a "real-life" no stress situation. The relationship between eye movements and cognitive functioning has been well documented. Cognitive activity occurring in one hemisphere triggers eye movements in the opposite hemisphere. The information below is a useful generalization, but remember, each student is unique.

1. Visual Thinking of Stored Picture Memories
Looking up and to the left allows you to access stored pictures (visual recall). Questions you can use to verify are: "What car was parked next to yours in the parking lot?" "Describe your bedroom." "Walk me through the clothes in your closet."

2. Visual Thinking of Created New Pictures
Looking up and to the right is where your eyes usually go to create new images. Questions you can use to verify are: "How would you look with a radically different haircut?" "What would you do to rearrange your living room?" "What would a dog look like with cat's legs?"

3. Auditory Thinking and Recalling Sounds
Eyes go to the left; that's the usual way we access stored sounds (what was said or heard). Questions you can use to verify are: "What did the other person say at the end of your last phone conversation?" "What's the ninth word in the 'Happy Birthday' song?" "When you were a kid, how did your mother call you when she was mad at you?"

4. Auditory Thinking and Creating New Sounds
Eyes go off to the right when new sounds are created. Questions you can use to verify are: "How would a dog sound if it had a voice like a pig?" "What sound would you get if you heard a siren and a rooster at the same time?"

5. Internal Dialogue (talking to yourself)
Eyes look down and to the left. When you see somebody walking down the street talking to themselves, notice where their eyes are.

6. Experiencing Feelings
Eyes look down and to the right. If you know another person failed to complete a task, you can ask them, "Did you complete the task?" In many cases, before answering, their eyes will go down (meaning "I feel badly about it"), then go back up to continue the conversation.

7. Digital for Memorized Information
Eyes will look straight ahead for this interaction. You are asked, "How are you?" Your polite answer is, "Fine, thank you." You probably kept your eyes straight ahead the whole time because you did not need to search for or rehearse the answer.

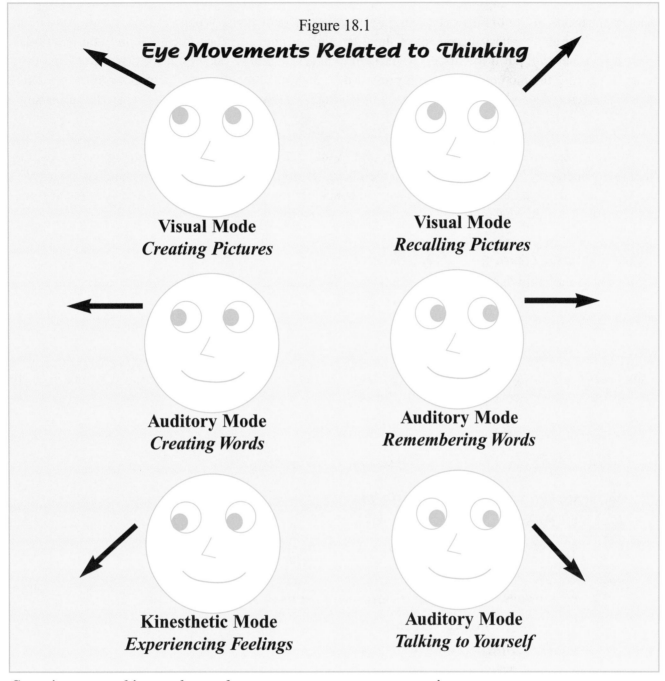

Figure 18.1

Eye Movements Related to Thinking

Visual Mode
Creating Pictures

Visual Mode
Recalling Pictures

Auditory Mode
Creating Words

Auditory Mode
Remembering Words

Kinesthetic Mode
Experiencing Feelings

Auditory Mode
Talking to Yourself

Some important things to know about eye movement or eye accessing cues are:

✦ You will not be able to determine if someone is telling the truth or not.

✦ Experienced liars will rehearse their answer so much that they can say it without having to access or create the information on the spot.

✦ A student whose eyes are roving at test time may actually be searching within their brain for the answers.

✦ Eyes to the side mean the learner is trying to recall or construct sounds.

✦ Eyes up and to the side mean they are trying to recall stored images (maybe a text, computer, chart, etc.) or is creating new images (assembling thoughts).

✦ It takes eye movement to get to the internal information.

✦ Students who have trouble spelling are very likely unaware of the value of moving their eyes to the appropriate position.

The implications of the brain's eye accessing patterns are enormous. When students create posters, art projects or murals, the best placement is shoulder high or above for best recall. When you put student work up on the wall, put it low if you want them to access feelings, head high for discussion, and overhead for storing the pictures. When you present new material, stand to your learner's right (not yours). When you review, stand to their left. This simple strategy allows your learners to learn the information easier.

At test time, let students move their eyes around. A student who is constantly told to keep their eyes on their own paper, may have limited access to their brain's storage system. Such a command will also access the "bad dog" feeling, the eyes will go down and concentration will be lost. Rather, ask students to spread out their desks so they have greater personal space at test time.

The Importance of Thinking

Biologically, the brain learns to solve problems to advance survival chances. The best thing we can do then, from the point of view of the brain and learning, is to teach our learners *how* to think. Thinking takes many forms.

We don't know how easily or quickly thinking can be taught. We do know, however, that it can be taught. Sometimes the best way to teach thinking is to do thinking. That is, walk through your own thinking steps out loud so your learners can learn from you.

Forms of Thinking:

- *Learning to gather information*
- *Flexibility in form and style*
- *Asking quality questions*
- *The ability to weigh evidence*
- *Understanding and creating metaphors and models*
- *Strategies to conceptualize*
- *The ability to deal with novelty*
- *Generating possible strategies*
- *Discussion and brainstorming skills*
- *Being effective at finding mistakes, discrepancies and illogic*
- *Generating alternative approaches outside your usual domain*
- *Strategies to test hypotheses*
- *Generalizations and identifying accurate commonalties*
- *Thinking of new meanings for things*

Thinking Skills:

+ *The ability to identify and organize information, values, and events.*
+ *Learning about something and learning to describe it objectively.*
+ *Sequencing: figuring out the logical or natural order of events.*
+ *Problem-solving: assessing the apparent problems and potential solutions.*
+ *Thematic/concepts maps: grouping, thematic information based on defining characteristics such as age, location, function, culture, value, etc.*
+ *Thinking for creativity: a twist, a turn or a new approach.*
+ *The ability to step outside your role or culture.*
+ *Composing or creating new thinking.*
+ *Learning to "reframe" the problem so that it is not a problem.*
+ *Learning to discover the source of the problem to prevent reoccurrence.*
+ *Finding ways to deal with life's difficulties.*
+ *Process/cause: discovering the flow/process and speculating on causes.*
+ *Thinking about thinking (metacognition).*
+ *Altering your own styles of thinking.*
+ *Applying your thinking skills to add value and joy to your own life.*
+ *Application of thinking to enhance others lives.*

Creativity, life skills and problem-solving are the primary skills in the teaching of thinking. Can all types of thinking be taught? Absolutely yes. It not only can be taught, it should be a significant part of any school curriculum. It's part of the essential skills package needed for survival in today's world.

What is the best way to teach problem-solving, creativity and thinking? In a brain-compatible way. That is, with real world problems and real people under authentic conditions. The brain, when faced with relevant, challenging conditions of "survival" (real or imagined, but with positive stress), will excel in learning. The brain loves to think and learn. For children, games are all about inventing new ways of thinking. For adolescents, school survival requires thinking skills. Adults need thinking skills to deal with their daily challenges.

Quotable

Being especially good at problem-solving does not guarantee success in life, but being poor at it does guarantee failure.

Growing Thinking Skills

How do you get your learners to increase their thinking power? There are many ways to learn thinking skills. Since thinking is obviously internal, the trick in teaching and learning it is to make it external so that others can discover the process. Following are some examples of how to teach others to think better.

Teaching Thinking:

- ◆ *Use examples or stories imbued with personal meaning.*
- ◆ *Give relevant examples of how others solved problems.*
- ◆ *Create team projects so that everyone feels safe to use metacognitive options.*
- ◆ *Let your learners have time to think about thinking and discuss it.*
- ◆ *Role-model: "walk" your students through the process.*
- ◆ *You and your students can solve a problem together; think out loud.*
- ◆ *Learning through debate, meaningful dialogue, or discussion.*
- ◆ *Set up a coach, a listener and a thinker to analyze a learning process; then rotate roles.*
- ◆ *Provide exercises that require introspection, reflection, and feedback.*
- ◆ *Encourage journal-writing, or writing poetry, short stories, etc.*
- ◆ *By assigning large and challenging group projects with deadlines for public display so that learners are forced to learn to "survive."*

Today's forward thinking super teachers talk about how to turn any topic or situation into a creative-growth experience. There is no need for a special course on thinking. Howard Gardner (1993) and Robert Sternberg and Richard Wagner (1994) believe that this ability, the skills to relate learning to our lives, is one of the keys to intelligence.

To the untrained eye, students are simply "thinking." The trained observer, however, can break down the act of thinking into various processes. Two highly used thinking processes are recall and creation. You either already know something and are remembering it; or you are constructing meaning in your mind. When we process information internally, we do it with our five senses: sight, sound, touch, smell or hearing. The founders of neurolinguistic programming, Richard Bandler and John Grinder, have observed that most people (especially right-handed ones) give clues through their eye movements as to which of the sensory modes they use.

The value of this information is enormous. If you know what sensory mode a person generally uses, you can better understand and communicate with them. For example, if a student's eyes are down and to the right, they may be experiencing some feelings. It's a cue for you to know that you may want to respect those sensations for a moment before you talk to them. Or, you may want to facilitate a change in thinking by asking the student to look up. This will cause them to access the visual mode thus changing the kinesthetic sensations. Here's the specific breakdown and how to access the sensory cues:

✦ Visual remembered (V.r.): eyes up and to the left for most right-handed individuals; seeing images of the past. Ask a question such as, "What color is your living room rug?"

✦ Visual construct (V.c.): eyes up and to the right; seeing newly created images. Ask, "What would your brother look like if he dyed his hair green?"

✦ Auditory remembered (A.r.): eyes looking to the left; recalling sounds heard in the past. Ask, "What was the last thing I said?"

✦ Auditory construct (A.c.): eyes looking to the right; creating new sounds in the mind. Ask, "What would your name sound like spelled backwards?"

✦ Auditory internal (A.i.): eyes down to left; talking to self. Ask person to sing happy birthday to him/herself.

✦ Kinesthetic-feelings and emotions (K.i.): eyes down to right. Ask, "How would you feel if you were sad?"

✦ Kinesthetic-external (K.e.): touching and feeling anything real from the outside world—from the feel of clothes to the feeling of clapping hands.

So, what does all this mean to teaching? The implications are infinite, but let's look at a few. Consider what would assist your students in recalling prior visual information (what was on a handout, picture, drawing or in a text) when taking a test? Quite simply, they will recall the material best by looking up and to the left. In order to construct an image of how something would look (such as if they were composing, writing, etc.), they would look up and to the right to have the best access to that information. If a student wanted to recall what you said, they would look to their left side. If a student is composing and wants to "hear" how something sounds, their eyes would go to the right.

How do you use sensory cues in conversations with students? If the student's eyes are down and to their right, it's likely that they are strongly into their feelings. If you want to communicate with them, you have some choices. Gain rapport by matching their experience; say, "You must be feeling low, David." This creates an immediate sense of rapport between you and the student. Or break the state by switching the state; say, "David, just for a moment, could you please look up at this?" These questions will pull the student out of their feeling state allowing them to access the best mode for the lesson at hand. Or pace, then lead. With this method, you begin to talk about feelings and then lead the student out by slowly having them access sounds or visuals.

Spelling/Math Strategies

A good speller (or a student recalling math formulas) uses a primarily visual strategy, while a poor speller uses either an auditory (sounds the words or letters out) or kinesthetic strategy (spells out the word by how the letters feel). The following is an example of a primarily visual strategy.

Visual Strategy for Remembering Something:

✦ *Use the eye-accessing chart to determine the direction of the student's gaze while recalling visual-remembered material. For example, "What color are the curtains in your living room?"*

✦ *Explain to the student that it is more useful to recall what something looks like when they are looking up and to the left.*

✦ *Ask the student what his or her favorite color is. Explain that it is easier to remember words in color.*

✦ *Show the student the first word or formula on the list. Have the students glance at it, as if taking a snapshot.*

✦ *Have the student look up to his or her best recalling direction and visualize a picture of that word in full color.*

✦ *Ask the student, while looking at the word in his or her mind's eye, to read the letters backward to you. (This insures that the picture is in his or her mind). Make sure that the eyes stay up in the recall direction.*

✦ *Next, ask the student to spell the word or formula forwards. Once again, make sure that the eyes stay up in the recalling mode.*

✦ *Tell the student, "from now on, you will simply remember this picture in your mind and be able to recall it perfectly."*

✦ *Repeat steps 5 through 9 for any new words, formulas or equations.*

Note: "Chunk down" longer words into three-letter units. Make sure that this method is practiced until it becomes automatic. Make sure that each of the steps are followed explicitly and that the eyes are pointed in the correct direction at the proper time. If a student has difficulty, have them create an imaginary TV set. Either way, this is a very powerful strategy when done properly.

Are Questions Better Than Answers?

The better the quality of the questions asked, the more the brain is challenged to think. The Socratic Method may have more than history going for it; it may be best for our brains. In study after study, learner performance scores improved when the questions asked of the learners improved in depth.

Useful Ideas: Instead of asking students questions that require a statement of fact or a "yes" or "no" answer, ask them more thought-provoking ones. Instead of: "What is it called when things keep falling back towards the earth?" ask, "What theories are there about gravity, which ones do you think are true, and why?" The *hots* software program succeeds precisely because it follows this methodology, rather than promoting a "math facts" type of shallow thinking. Let's say, students are asked to design a clock with no moving parts and no face. By visualizing, they may get stuck and come up with no answer. By re-framing the problem and asking new questions, however, they may come up with other solutions, such as a talking clock.

Restating questions can lead to creativity and self-confidence. It can be very empowering to reformat questions. Typically, a teacher asks a question like "What was the Berlin Wall?" or "What brought it down?" A more empowering question would be to ask learners "What interesting questions could we ask about the Berlin Wall?" Get learners involved in being a part of the solution by asking the question in different ways. If students say a class is boring, ask them, "In what ways could we make it interesting?" Of those ways, "Which ones can be done legally, affordably, within school rules, that everyone can agree with?" Have your learners make up the test questions instead of only answering them. Let students do all of the lower-level quizzing of each other on simple-answer questions.

Analyzing Student Answers

By analyzing a learner's "wrong" answers, we can discover meaningful information. Often the wrong answers fit a pattern or reveal something important about the type and style of the learner's processing. Because teachers often listen for the expected answer, they miss out on the more interpretive and qualitative possibilities. Profoundly informed people generally read more ambiguity into a question than was intended.

As an example, a student completes a multiple choice test. Wrong answers usually get a zero and are 100 percent wrong. Yet the student may have a more profound understanding of the topic than the single answer possibility indicates. What if the student made the same type of mistake 10-15 times? Does your feedback indicate that? The learner could learn a great deal by knowing this.

Another example is provided by a physics teacher. She has a test question that reads: "Using a barometer, how can you tell the height of this building?" The "proper" answer is: "Measure the air pressure at the bottom of the building and then compare it with the air pressure at the top of the building. Then use a prescribed formula to compute the difference in feet or meters." Unfortunately, a student who arrived at the right answer using a different calculation method was marked wrong—in spite of demonstrating a more creative and original way to calculate the answer. Examples of alternate methods to solve the physics problem might be: 1) Tie one end of a roll of string or fishing line onto the barometer and throw it off the top of the building. Then when it lands, measure the length of the string needed; 2) on a sunny day, use the shadow cast by the barometer and the building as a comparison and compute the ratio; 3) go to the stairwell of the building. Using the barometer as a ruler, count how many times

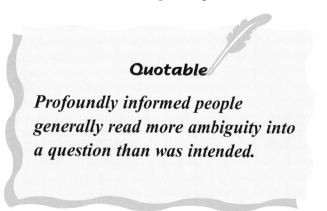

Quotable

Profoundly informed people generally read more ambiguity into a question than was intended.

you need to flip it end over end to get to the top. Multiply that number by the length of the barometer; or 4) take the barometer to the building inspector, engineer or architect and offer to trade the barometer for the exact height of the building. You get the idea.

Ultimately, learners will thrive in learning environments that encourage them to think. Allow learners to work in groups to self-assess their tests. Let them formulate rules for the patterning and understanding of their experiences and information. Have them share and shape their discoveries instead of being evaluated by a "superior" who tells them what is right and what is wrong. Encourage their critical thinking skills. After all, they may be right about something the rest of us still haven't discovered.

Mind-Map

Using multiple colored pens, depict your processes and strategies for teaching students to think.

Reactions:

What are your feelings about the topics presented in this chapter?

What are some practical applications for what you're learning?

What do you want to remember from this chapter?

There is no concept, no fact in education, more directly important than this: the brain is, by nature's design, an amazingly subtle and sensitive pattern-detecting apparatus.

Leslie A. Hart
Human Brain and Human Learning

Chapter 19 ————————————————————

Memory and Recall

Chapter Preview:

✦ **Learning to Remember**
✦ **Engaging the Emotions**
✦ **The BEM Principle**
✦ **Memories Change Because We Change**
✦ **Strategies for Increasing Memory and Recall**

Learning to Remember

One of the most common teacher and student frustrations is that much of what is learned seems to get forgotten. Is it the student's job to figure out how best to recall learning? Or is the teacher's job to teach better recall skills? The answer is both: it is your job to provide students with a framework for learning how to best learn—that is study skills or life-long learning skills. But once these skills have been introduced, it is simply practice on the student's part that is necessary.

How do your students store and recall their learning? It is becoming increasingly clear that the brain's fundamental design includes multiple memory systems. In other words, the more ways that you engage your learners, the more ways the information will be stored. Research shows that different kinds of learning is stored and recalled through various pathways. In one study, learners were asked to memorize a series of words. One group was instructed to use rote memorization techniques and the other, elaborate strategies for the task. Those using the rote method had higher forgetfulness ratios and a lower recall performance. The rote method involved simple repetition, also called "semantic" memory or "list-related" memorization. While this method is slow and often boring and requires review, it can be fairly accurate in isolated cases. But it's not very effective or efficient for 90 percent of learning that needs to happen.

Quotable

Asking students to learn and memorize material without providing them with the tools to do so is unrealistic and a set-up for failure.

We know that learners tend to remember much more when there is a field trip, a musical, a disaster, a guest speaker or a novel study location. Why? Multiple memory systems are activated. Learners often seem to forget a great deal of what is taught, but the problem may be a reliance on a singular memory system. When multiple memory systems are activated with a variety of teaching activities, such as: reading, listening to a lecture, seeing a video and follow-up activities, recall increases. Role-playing, at-home assignments, music, discussion, field trips, games, simulations or drama all provide the multi-sensory stimulation that enhances memory. Why? Researchers discovered a critical biologically-based difference between the two ways we deal with new information. Our brain sorts and stores information based on whether it is embedded in context or in content.

The difference between context and content can be described quite simply: Information embedded in context (episodic memory) means it is stored in relationship with a particular location or circumstance. Information embedded in content (semantic memory) is usually found in books, lists or other information storage devices and is memorized. Research indicates that our contextual memory has unlimited capacity, forms quickly, is easily updated, requires no practice, is effortless, and is used naturally by everyone (i.e., "What did you have for dinner last night?"). This natural memory may be based on your movement, music, intense sensory experiences, sounds, puns, relationships, and position in space and time.

The formation of this natural memory is motivated by curiosity, novelty and expectations. It's enhanced by intensified sensory input (sights, sounds, smells, taste, touch). The information can also be stored in a fabric or weave of "mental space." This might be described as a thematic map of the intellectual landscape where learning occurs as a result of changes in location or circumstances, storytelling, visualization, and metaphors.

Information embedded in content, on the other hand, is usually learned (or attempted to be learned) through rote memorization and by following lists. Semantic memory is the type of list-oriented, sometimes rote, unnatural memory which requires rehearsal, is resistant to change, isolated from context, has strict limits, lacks meaning and is linked to extrinsic motivation (i.e., she asks, "Remember that article you were reading last night, what was the name of the author?" He replies, "Gee, I don't remember. Why do you want to know?") This type of memory is unnatural and requires practice and constant rehearsal to keep fresh. That's why most people have the experience of "forgetting" so much trivia. The brain is simply not designed to recall this type of information.

What's Changed?
Learning and Memory

Old: Content	New: Multiple Systems
✦ Use of Vote	✦ Use of Location Cues
✦ Semantic Memory	✦ Episodic Memory
✦ Taxon	✦ Circumstances
✦ List-oriented	✦ Body Learning
✦ Facts	✦ Musical
✦ Texts	✦ Linguistic
✦ Names	✦ Sensory
✦ Memorization	✦ Spatial

A trip to a local science museum would provide our brain with heavy "embedding" in context. Millions of information bits, all in context, would be remembered for years. A two-week study session in science using a textbook is heavily embedded in content. And it all may be forgotten a day after the "big" test. Granted, the textbook is cheaper. But with some imagination, many teachers create much more "context" for learning. It can be done with dress, language, food, environment, and visitors.

Should we throw out "book learning?" No. Just because the brain is generally very poor at learning this way, we shouldn't discard the source. Semantic learning does have its place. When you ask for directions, for example, you want the shortest route from A to B. You don't want to drive all over the city to figure it out (although that would create a stronger "contextual map"). On the other hand, if you ask others what they have learned of significance in the last year, 90 percent of what they tell you will probably be contextually embedded information.

Engaging the Emotions

We can use emotions to get attention or to make meaning. Remember, our mental "gates" allow information either in or out of recent memory, never both at the same time. This has tremendous implications for classroom learning:

When emotions are engaged, the brain is activated. Arousal causes your body's internal "chemical cocktails" to spritz out, flooding the system with norepinephrine, adrenaline, enkephalin, vasopressin, and ACTH. Researchers think these chemicals are "memory fixatives." They signal the brain that, "this is important, keep this!" Research has confirmed that rats injected with adrenaline remember longer than those which weren't injected. Put into personal perspective, consider what you remember about your teaching career, for instance. You probably remember your lowest "lows" and your highest "highs." This applies across all areas of your life: the best and worst vacations, meals, dates, jobs, weather and so on.

Purposefully strategize ways to engage positive emotions within the learner. Without this, they may not code the material learned as important. Long, continuous lectures and predictable lessons are the least likely to be remembered. Utilize the following techniques: enthusiasm, drama, role-plays, quiz shows, music, debates, larger projects, guest speakers, creative controversy, adventures, impactful rituals and celebrations.

The BEM Principle

Research has verified that an easy way to remember something is to make it new and different. This is because our brain has a high attentional bias towards something which does not fit the pattern (novelty). Once you have read past the first item in a list, for example, the novelty effect of it has eroded. So the brain treats it differently and is less likely to re-release chemicals into the body as a response to the change. This is why you remember the first and last moments of a learning experience more than the middle.

Psychologists refer to this as the BEM principle, (Beginning, End and Middle), the order in which you are most likely to recall something. There is a distinctly different mental set at the beginning of an experience (anticipation, suspense, novelty, challenge, etc.) than the middle (continuation, more of the same, boredom, stability). The ending mental set is much different, too (new anticipations, emotions, etc.).

Your students may be able to remember much more of what happens if you provide more novelty (let them do much of it) and more beginnings and ends (and less middles). Introduce short modules of learning instead of long ones. Break up long sessions into several shorter ones. Have your students provide surprise introductions to new topics.

Memories Change Because We Change

Did you know our memory is changing all the time with new information and changes in beliefs and circumstances? Because we change, our perceptions of the event's circumstances change in relationship to our lives. Ordinarily (unless there is trauma), memory requires "repeated rehearsal in different contexts." It requires updating and new categorical input, as well as associations. This updating engages our creativity and thinking skills.

Strategies for Increasing Memory and Recall

There are many ways to help your students remember what they've learned. Teach the following techniques to your students so they can utilize them on their own:

— Attach a strong emotion to the learning by engaging the student in an intense activity.

— Repeat the learning within 10 minutes, 48 hours and then 7 days.

— Give students a concrete reminder of their learning (a token or artifact), or encourage them to make one themselves.

— Act out learning in a skit; or do a fun and engaging role-play.

— Use acrostics (first letter of key words form new word).

— Review learning on a large, colorful poster. Or, have students draw what they learned.

— Chunk information down into smaller bits to simplify data.

— Have students identify key qualities and patterns of new information.

— Personalize the lesson by using students' names, their neighborhoods, etc.

— Use a link system to link one idea to the next.

— Put learning into greater context with trips, reading, discussion, video, etc.

— Use acronyms (i.e., the space agency in America is NASA).

— Add more "what's in it for me?" to increase the incentive for learners.

— Review learning utilizing as many of the senses, as possible; sight, sound, touch, etc.

— Have learners teach each other in small groups.

— Have learners write their reactions to the learning.

— Learn contextually in different places so each location provides a key clue.

Reflection:

Pause here, and review the suggestions above once more. Check the ideas which you have not used before, but would like to try. How will you implement these ideas in your classroom?

— Use storyboards (like oversized comic strip panels) to illustrate key ideas.

— Make a class video or audio tape; the more complex the better.

— Use pegwords to link numbers or pictures to an idea for easy recall (i.e., Every Good Boy Does Fine = EGBDF - the order of the keys on a piano).

— Create or re-do a song; customize the lyrics, make a rap song.

— Make up or use a childhood story to relay information.

— Start with something exotic, then familiar, then unusual again.

— Increase accountability: have a review check-up at regular intervals.

— Hold group discussions on the material learned.

— Make learning relevant to the learner's personal life.

— Provide unguided reflection time.

— Build a working model that embodies the key elements of the idea.

— Encourage and support study groups formed by learners.

— Emphasize better nutrition: in several studies, the lecithin from wheat germ helped improve memory.

— Create a positive association with the material; emotions are best!

— Utilize partner-to-partner summaries.

— Provide learners with choices.

— Use dramatic concert readings; read key points with a music backdrop.

— Have learners mind-map what they learned and share their mind-maps with the rest of the class.

Reflection:

What strategies have you used in your own learning to increase recall?
Are there any that you have used that aren't in the above list? What are they?

Now that you see what a wide variety of strategies there are for learning, you can reduce rote learning to a minimum. By using both a variety of methods and empowering your learners to use their favorite strategies, learning will be more fun and effective. And a terrific side benefit is that the confidence levels of your learners will soar. So take the time to help students develop a terrific memory and recall system. It benefits everyone; and long after your students leave your classroom.

Reactions:

What are your feelings about the topics presented in this chapter?

What are some practical applications for what you're learning?

What do you want to remember from this chapter?

The brain does have its own built-in reward system. It's not only unique to each individual, but it also habituates to new levels. This makes extrinsic rewards unequal from the start.

Eric Jensen

Chapter 20

Motivation and Rewards

Chapter Preview:

- ✦ **Rewards in Learning**
- ✦ **Rewards Impair Creativity**
- ✦ **Rewards Perpetuate the Underachievers**
- ✦ **Rewarded Actions Disappear**
- ✦ **Alternatives to Bribes**
- ✦ **Motivation Secrets**
- ✦ **Learning Comes First**
- ✦ **Avoid Labeling**
- ✦ **Intrinsic Versus Extrinsic Motivation**
- ✦ **Sources of Intrinsic Motivation**

Rewards in Learning

The old model of teaching was to identify the student behaviors that you wanted (students on time, sitting still, being quiet, learning, taking tests, being nice, etc.), then to reward the positive behaviors and punish the negative ones. This B.F. Skinner theory of behaviorism works great on rats. But on human beings it's a disaster. Humans are far more complex than rats and while you can get humans to do almost anything to gain a reward or avoid punishment in the short-term, the qualities of creativity, civility and higher order-thinking skills will go untapped.

Rewards create uncertainty in the mind of the learner: "Will I get it or not?" This anxiety causes distress in the brain. It picks the tried and true learning and repeats the predictable, familiar paths. Under this anxiety, the brain's memory is also impaired, so are higher-order thinking skills and creativity. You get the behavior of a lower-level robot, not a magnificent, problem-solving human being. The brain operates in a lower-risk behavior mode. Some teachers use rewards. Are rewards a smart thing to do, considering the brain's natural, operational principles? Absolutely not. First, what is a reward?

A reward is defined as a compensation or consequence which is both: 1) predictable and 2) has market value. If it's only predictable, but has no market value (i.e., a smile, a hug, a compliment, a random item, an awards assembly, public approval, etc.), then it is simply an acknowledgment, not a reward. If it has market value, but absolutely no predictability (a spontaneous party, pizza, cookies, gift certificates, small gifts, trips, tickets, etc.), then it is a celebration, not a reward. If students know that by behaving a certain way, there's a chance that they might get a prize, that's enough predictability to be called a reward. The determining criteria is simple: Did the learner change his or her behavior in the hopes of getting the favor?

If you offer something that has both of those qualities, you are, in fact, bribing the learner. Rewards carry an implicit and covert threat: "If you don't meet the criteria for the reward, some opportunities will be withdrawn from you."

Rewards Impair Creativity

The relationship between motivation and rewards has far-reaching implications for the creative process. The research suggests, "extrinsic motivation inhibits intrinsic motivation." The ability to be creative is strongly linked to intrinsic motivation, since it gives the brain "freedom of intellectual expression," which fuels even more thinking and motivation.

A reward system prevents the establishment of intrinsic motivation because there's rarely an incentive to be creative - only to do the asked for behavior. Creativity is rarely part of any reward system. In fact, the two are usually at far ends of the scale. You get either intrinsically motivated creative thinking or extrinsically motivated repetitive, rote, and predictable behaviors.

Geoffrey and Renate Caine (1990) sum up rewards this way: "A system of rewards and punishments can be selectively demotivating in the long-term, especially when others have control over the system." Their contention is that the existence of any behavior-oriented threats and anxiety, coupled with a lack of learner input and control, will "downshift" learner thinking, causing learners to prefer repeated, predictable responses to lower anxiety, and making teachers think the reward system is working. This makes it harder to initiate changes within the system - since any changes in the system will create "threat and anxiety" to both students and teachers, meaning we will get more of the same.

As an example, in kindergarten, many learners get a smile sticker for good work. By third grade, it's cookies or candies. By fifth grade, the reward is a pizza for a class that behaves well. By eighth grade a student is being bribed by their parents. Is it any wonder that by the time a student reaches eleventh grade, and the teacher assigns a research paper, the student's response is, "What do I get?" Or they may simply ask, "What for?"

Learners who have been bribed for either good work or good behavior find that soon the last reward wasn't good enough. A bigger and better one is wanted. Soon, all intrinsic motivation has been killed off and the learner is labeled as "unmotivated." Like a rat in a cage pushing a food bar, the learner behavior becomes just good enough to get the reward. Some researchers, like Alfie Kohn, author of *Punished by Rewards* (1993), believe that all rewards are bad. However, Martin Ford author of *Motivating Humans* (1992), argues that it depends on whether the reward creates a conflict with the learner's existing goals. The three most likely times this occurs are:

1. If the learner feels manipulated by the reward: "You just want me to give up my guitar lessons."
2. The reward interferes with the real reason the learner started: "Now that I'm getting rewarded for getting good grades, I care only about what's on the test, not real learning."
3. The reward devalues the task and the learner feels bribed: "This class must be pretty bad if they're giving us a bribe just for attending it."

Let's illustrate the third example: a school that is having problems with truancy and low attendance decides, as an incentive, to reward those who come every day. Now, each student gets a reward for having a 100 percent attendance each month. The school has worked out an arrangement with local businesses. The reward is a free meal at McDonalds or Pizza Hut. Students immediately feel bribed for coming to school. They think, "This must be really bad for them to have to bribe us." But they still do the rewarded behavior. "It's stupid, but we'll play the game," they say. But now school is about "working the system," instead of learning.

Rewards Perpetuate the Underachievers

In stressful situations, rat behavior becomes rigid and stereotyped with repeated, predictable responses completely eliminating the participation of the local memory system. This is the part of the brain that may be responsible for certain types of memory and spatial mapping. And, we know from research that the use of rewards increases learner stress. Other researchers link up the physiological states of anxiety, negative stress and threat with thinking and human performance.

Learner Stress and Anxiety:

✦ *Reduces the ability to solve complex problems*
✦ *Reduces learner responsiveness to the environment*
✦ *Increases stereotyped, low-risk behavior*
✦ *Increases learner attentiveness to and reliance upon external systems of rewards and punishments*

There is evidence linking extrinsic motivation with work involving non-creative tasks, rewards and punishments, memorized skills and repetitive tasks. In order to get learners to be creative and have greater subject interest, higher self-esteem and the ability to be reflective, there must be intrinsic motivation. Yet, learners who are experiencing stress and anxiety in their environment will prefer external motivation, meaning a system of reliable rewards.

Paradoxically, the less support there is in the learner's environment for intrinsic motivation, the more the learner seeks rewards. Stressed, anxious learners are more likely to look to others for safe, predictable role-modeling, to listen to others for goals and to increase their own stereotyped, lower-order thinking. This creates a "Catch-22." Rewards, at a low level, work. So, the teacher continues their usage. The learner now is a victim of the "glass ceiling" principle: he or she learns to perform to the lowest level necessary to achieve the reward. The learner who has gotten used to a reward system complains when the rewards are dropped and his performance goes down. The teacher uses this as evidence to say, "I know I shouldn't bribe him, but the system works!"

Quotable

In the long-run, rewards do more damage than good towards motivating the so-called underachiever.

The problem is that the system does work - too well. Then again, holding a gun to someone's head works, too! It will get them to do all kinds of things, but it's not good for the learner's brain (among other things). Rewards lead to learners who become preoccupied with "playing the game" and not really doing quality learning. Why? The ability to alter perceptual maps, to do higher-order thinking and to create complex thematic relationships with the subject is not available to the brain when it experiences the anxiety of a reward system.

Rewards mean: 1) the psychological anxiety of performance increases; and 2) every reward carries with it an implied certainty of success or failure - but which one? The learner then wants to reduce the uncertainty, so he picks tasks that have a high degree of predictability (often boring, repetitive skills). The learner also is more likely to pick goals set by others (even the goals chosen are often the basic, overworked, media-reinforced, cliché type).

Rewarded Actions Disappear

Alan Kazdin, who once was a proponent of rewards, set up a study involving a token economy system in a health care institution in the 1960s. At first, he was excited about the behavior changes; however, in a review of the study a decade later, Kazdin (1977) changed his mind. "Removal of token reinforcement results in decrements in desirable responses and a return to baseline or near-baseline levels of performance." In other words, when the goodies stop, the behavior stops, too.

Every learner has his or her own bias which they bring to a particular context. The biases constitute personal beliefs, hopes, expectations, fears, values and emotions. These are what hold a behavior in place. In fact, Leslie Hart (1983) says, "To change the behavior, the biases must be changed, not the behavior directly." The rewards are designed to change the behavior, not the biases. Hence, any reward-driven activity is likely to fail in the long-run.

We all know teachers often offer rewards for attendance, homework or discipline. Pizza Hut had a program designed to reward students for reading by offering pizzas. The follow-up may show that the ones who read the most were the ones who were reading already; they just decided to play the game. Many of the readers who were not ordinarily reading before the promotion may not now be readers. Many learners can become intrinsically motivated if given a chance. But as long as a reward system is in place, their progress will be ultimately undermined. Reduce or eliminate all rewards and increase the alternatives of acknowledgment, celebrations, increased variety, and quantity of feedback.

If rewards are counterproductive in learning, is there ever a time or place for them? If your objective is to get people to [temporarily] obey an order, show up on time, or do what they're told, yes, rewards can work, say researchers. But, rewards are simply changing the specific behavior in the moment and not the person.

Here's an example of where a reward might be used. You have a bunch of chairs to move to another room. It's the end of the day, you're tired and hungry. You ask a couple of students who stay after class if they'd be willing to help you move them. They say, "No, not really." But you're desperate. You say, "How about if I get you both a Coke?" They change their minds and decide it's worth it. The desks get moved. Everybody's happy. The reward was appropriate. Why? It was for something physical, not intellectual.

Alternatives to Bribes

There are many powerful alternatives to bribing students for intellectual desirable social behaviors. The three most powerful ones are: 1) to make school meaningful; 2) to make it relevant; and 3) to make it fun. Beyond this, there are many intrinsic rewards that can be emphasized.

Replacing rewards with alternatives gets a bit tricky in schools where the entire system of grading is built on the concept of rewards and punishment. Good grades are a type of reward which lead to teacher approval, parent approval, scholarships and university entry. How can teachers instruct without bribes and rewards within a system that is so thoroughly entrenched? The options outlined above can have an amazing impact. Eventually they will offset the old system. Students will soon discover the value of intrinsic motivation; and they will eventually appreciate the lack of manipulation on your part.

There are, however, many "gray areas." For example, a certificate of achievement may be the form of acknowledgment you choose to give students, which is fine, until the learner takes it home and the parent rewards them with money. Then it becomes a reward in spite of your best intentions. The solution is to try to make parents aware of the destructive effects of rewards at an open house or through another form of communication like a letter home.

Intrinsic Rewards to Learning:

- ✦ *Long-term quality performance*
- ✦ *Becoming self-directed learners*
- ✦ *Developing values of caring, respect and friendliness*
- ✦ *Creativity and higher-order thinking skills*
- ✦ *Honesty, integrity and self-confidence*
- ✦ *Inner drive and motivation*
- ✦ *The joy of achieving goals*
- ✦ *Giving and receiving peer support and feedback*
- ✦ *Celebrating achievements with positive rituals*
- ✦ *Self-assessing progress*
- ✦ *Giving and receiving positive acknowledgments*
- ✦ *Experiencing a love of learning*
- ✦ *Enthusiasm*
- ✦ *Learners feel in control*

If you are using any kind of reward system, let it run its course and end it as soon as you reasonably can. If you stop it abruptly, you may get a rebellion. The learners will need a "de-tox" or "rehabilitation" time to get off the "reward drug."

Motivation Secrets

The brain loves to learn. This book is full of alternatives to bribery. One of the most commonly asked questions, from both new and experienced teachers, is: "How do I motivate students to learn?" The answer is simple. You don't. The human brain already loves to learn. Your learners have already motivated themselves for much of their life. Their brains have hungrily absorbed information, integrated it, made meaning out of it, remembered it and used it at the appropriate moment thousands of times. In short, any learner who is physically sitting in your class already: 1) motivated him/herself to get there; 2) has already motivated him/herself thousands of times; and 3) may or may not be in a motivated state at the moment. The secret is to remove de-motivating conditions and to do the little things that spark intrinsic motivation.

Learning Comes First

The question "How do I motivate students?" says more about the asker than it does the students. It also shows a misunderstanding of the real nature of motivation. All of your students are motivated to learn. In fact, the survival of your students depends on learning (though not necessarily what's taught in school). So, why don't some students seem like they want to learn in your class? William Glasser (1985) says, it's really about control.

Many teachers are really asking a different question, "How can I control learner behavior?" Is your teaching paradigm one of a learning catalyst - one who lights a fire for learning; or a traditional instructor - one who stands and delivers once the students are under control? If you're motivated by the paradigm of a learning catalyst, then how to motivate learners is a moot question. After all, in a positive learning environment, the learners are already motivated; they are naturally motivated.

Avoid Labeling

The unmotivated learner is a myth. Rarely are the most motivating conditions for learning met in a school context. This may explain why so many students have been labeled "underachievers." To arrive at school or a classroom requires some sort of motivation. It may be positive or negative, but it has gotten them there. Once the learner is in the seat, either they are exhibiting a strong motivating attitude, or the teacher needs to elicit one. The demotivated learner's negative beliefs and behaviors are usually triggered or reinforced by an artificial, unresponsive school environment. Identifying, classifying, grouping, labeling, evaluating, comparing, and assessing these demotivated learners has done little to solve the problem.

The research on motivation is both powerful and persuasive: The school environment, for most learners, is quite antagonistic towards motivated learning. Many have been astonished by the motivated learning potential in a non-coercive environment.

> **Quotable**
>
> *Learners who have been on a reward system will become conditioned to prefer it over free choice.*

> **Quotable**
>
> *There is no such thing as an unmotivated learner; there are, however, temporary unmotivated states that schools, teachers, or students themselves can trigger.*

Each learner is either motivated from within (intrinsic) or from the outside (extrinsic). All of the following de-motivate learners and drive away any possibility of intrinsic motivation:

Should the environment be all smiles, hugs and easy grades? Absolutely not. The brain thrives on challenges and variety. Stanford biologists separated amoebae cultures into three petri dishes. One was the control group, another received an abundance of food, light and heat, and the third petri dish was given just enough of food, light, and heat to survive while randomly varying the amounts. You might guess the results: the third amoebae culture developed the strongest health and lived the longest. Can you apply this to our own environment? Many successful teachers already do. They never punish the students nor do they make everything so easy that they don't grow. When learners are intrinsically challenged to develop themselves, they grow more.

Intrinsic Versus Extrinsic Motivation

Many of the characteristics of intrinsic or extrinsic motivation originate from the student's home life. Parents who bribe their children, who role-model laziness, a lack of curiosity, and avoid new learning contribute to the problem. While we have little influence on home factors, we can influence others. Many learners who appear to be "unmotivated" in the classroom excel on the sports field, or at their after-school job where individual efforts are visible and appreciated by teammates or co-workers. Though competition and rivalry are not absent in these examples, they are offset by shared goals and successes. When a student drops out of school, they are not unmotivated; they are probably seeking a more responsive environment promised by the world outside of school.

De-Motivators:

✦ *Coercion, control, and manipulation*
✦ *Weak, critical, negative, or competitive relationships*
✦ *Infrequent or vague feedback*
✦ *Outcome-based education (unless learners generate outcomes)*
✦ *Inconsistent policies and rules*
✦ *Top-down management and policy-making*
✦ *Repetitive, rote learning*
✦ *Sarcasm, put-downs, and criticism*
✦ *The perception of irrelevant content*
✦ *Boring, single-media presentations*
✦ *Reward systems of any kind*
✦ *Teaching in just one or two of the multiple intelligences*
✦ *Systems that limit reaching personal goals*
✦ *Responsibility without authority*
✦ *Hopelessness in achieving academic success*

Ways to Encourage Intrinsically Motivated Learners:

✦ *Help them learn to control their environment.*
✦ *Encourage stimulation, activity and patience for incongruities.*
✦ *Discourage feelings of inferiority.*
✦ *Provide choices that tap into learner goals.*
✦ *Build high self-concept and positive beliefs.*
✦ *Offer challenges, problems and novelty.*
✦ *Have high expectations of success.*
✦ *Role-model satisfaction from achievement.*
✦ *Create situations where learning is the by-product.*
✦ *Stimulate emotional intensity in learning through debates, music, drama, role-play.*

Other strategies can easily be developed in a learning context and many are relatively simple to do. When students are given control over the content and process of their learning, motivation goes up. But to motivate learners, it is important to allow them to make choices "about personally relevant aspects of a learning activity." Students need to be able to align self-determination goals with instructional goals.

In addition, learners who tend to focus more on fun and friendships may be able to be engaged when there are ample opportunities for self-determination and peer interaction.

These provide ways to meet personal goals and, to some, degree, instructional goals. In other words, the more ways the goals can serve the learner's own agenda, the better. Help learners to become aware of their own personal, academic, health, social, athletic and career goals. A student is often willing to work on a team project because there's another person on the project that they like and would like to get to know better. Build into your learning activities ways for students to show off, meet new people, be an expert in something, grow, get in shape or become well-respected.

Sources of Intrinsic Motivation

Give Learners Control and Choice

Let learners control as much as possible within the framework you provide. For example, allow them to choose how they will learn a topic, with whom they learn it, when and how they'll be assessed. You provide the appropriate structure and guidelines. Creativity and choice allow the learner to express themselves and feel valued resulting in less stress and more motivation.

Meet Learner's Needs and Goals

Make sure your curriculum and methods meet the perceived needs and goals of your learners. The brain is designed biologically to survive. It will learn what it *needs* to learn to survive. Make it a top priority, therefore, to discover what needs your learners have and engage those needs. For example, six year-old students have higher needs for security, predictability and teacher acceptance than a 14-year-old student. The teenager is more likely to need peer acceptance, a sense of importance, and hope. An 18-year-old learner is more interested in autonomy and independence. Use what's appropriate for the age level of your students.

Engage Strong Emotions

Engage emotions productively with compelling stories, games, personal examples, celebration, role-play, debate, rituals, and music. We are driven to act upon our emotions because they are compelling forces in our decision-making.

Provide Group Work

Use friendships, partners and group work to encourage interdependence.
Learners do better in an environment with positive social bonding and they are more motivated when they get to work with friends in groups or teams. This interdependence reduces helplessness and stress.

Engage Curiosity

We all know that inquiring minds want to know; this is the nature of the human brain. Keep engaging curiosity; it works! Newspaper tabloids and electronic tabloids have played off our curiosity for years. Witness all the stories about Elvis, aliens, celebrities, freaks of nature and UFOs. In your classroom, use leading questions, mysteries, special hooks, and experiments.

Encourage Good Nutrition

Better nutrition means better mental alertness. Provide suggestions for students or parents or both. Suggest specific brain foods (eggs, fish, nuts, leafy dark green vegetables, apples and bananas). Encourage the taking of a multivitamin and mineral supplements.

Use the Multiple Intelligences

The multiple intelligences can really hook learners in: spatial, bodily-kinesthetic, interpersonal, verbal-linguistic, intrapersonal, musical-rhythmic, mathematical-logical. When learners get to express what they know and how they know it, they are more motivated to continue to grow.

Share Inspirational Stories

Tell true stories about other students that overcame obstacles to succeed. Any famous ones? Any who have made a major contribution? These stories help form a mythology of success.

Provide Acknowledgments

These include assemblies, certificates, group notices, team reports, peer sharing, compliments, and "good job" notes. These give learners positive associations which continue to fuel further learning.

Provide Frequent Feedback

Employ lots of methods for feedback. If you rely only on yourself to provide student feedback, it's not likely that it will be frequent enough. Use peer assessment, team charts, group discussions, peer teaching, projects, role-play, non-verbals, self-assessment and oral games. Make sure that every single learner gets some kind of feedback, from you or someone else, every 30 minutes or less. The all-time best way to motivate the brain is with information - provided immediately and dramatically. That's what hooks kids into video games and adults into gambling (slot machines, horses, sports, card games, betting, etc.); they continually get feedback. The feedback motivates them to continue.

Manage Learner States

Role-model the behavior that reflects a strong, motivated state. Learn to read and manage learner's states. Even good learners have unmotivated periods which you can influence. Change activities often, use strong questions and multi-media approaches. Never let a student remain in a bad or unmotivated state for long.

Provide Hope of Success

Learners need to know that it's possible for them to succeed. Regardless of the obstacles or how far behind they are, hope is essential. Every good game show, from Jeopardy to Wheel of Fortune keeps the players hooked in with the chance of success, even when they're far behind the other players.

Role-Model Joy of Learning

Enjoy your work and come to your class ready to share what you have learned every day. Since over 99 percent of all learning is non conscious, the more you get excited about learning, the more motivated and excited your learners are likely to become.

Celebrations

These include peer acknowledgment, parties, food, high-fives, class cheers, etc. These create the atmosphere of success and can trigger the release of endorphins that boost further learning. Do not use these as a bribe; they are most effective when conducted spontaneously and randomly.

Provide for Physical and Emotional Safety

Insure that your classroom is emotionally safe—that students feel they can make mistakes and not be chastised for it. Insure student's physical safety from hazards or other students, as well. Make it safe to ask any question. Insure that physical needs are met for lighting, water, food, movement, seating.

Use Multiple Learning Styles

Do things visually, auditorally and kinesthetically. Provide both choice in how learners learn, and diversity in what's offered. Appeal to the learner's preferred learning style.

Instill Positive Beliefs

Reinforce to learners that they can succeed and can do this particular task. Discover what their beliefs are as soon as possible and work to affect them positively. Do this through affirmations, success stories, indirect references, posters, and your interactions with them.

None of the strategies mentioned above require a financial investment. You don't have to buy anything to implement them. Though, it might require more energy initially to create a climate of intrinsic motivation, it will pay off. Teachers who rely on extrinsic motivation may be vastly underestimating three things: 1) the power of their influence; 2) the desire of the learner to be intrinsically motivated; and 3) the long-term ease of instruction when learners are intrinsically motivated. Take your time. Implement just one motivator per week. Soon, you'll find miracles taking place everyday, and excited, confident and motivated learners.

Reactions:

What are your feelings about the topics presented in this chapter?

What are some practical applications for what you're learning?

What do you want to remember from this chapter?

Nothing is more absurd than to suppose that there is no middle term between leaving a child to his own unguided fancies and likes, or controlling his activities by formal succession of dictated directions.

John Dewey
The Child and the Curriculum

Chapter 21

Discipline Made Easy

Chapter Preview:

- ✦ **Discipline Can Be Simple**
- ✦ **Problems Are Just Symptoms**
- ✦ **No Such Student as a "Troublemaker"**
- ✦ **No Tips or Tools Will Replace Your Own Growth**
- ✦ **Premises of a Positive Discipline Philosophy**
- ✦ **Six Discipline Models**
- ✦ **33 Brain-Based Ways to Prevent Discipline Problems**
- ✦ **In Another World**
- ✦ **Using Rules, Guidelines, and Agreements**
- ✦ **Suggested Agreements**
- ✦ **What to Do When Agreements Are Broken**
- ✦ **When a Problem Occurs**

Discipline Can Be Simple

For many teachers, this might be the most important chapter in this book. Yet, the more you get out of the other chapters, the less you'll need this one! Therefore, it is strongly recommended that you read all of the other chapters first. As you'll be discovering, classroom management problems are usually symptoms of mismanagement elsewhere. When other aspects of the teaching process are handled well, discipline problems will be minimal.

Problems Are Just Symptoms

Discipline problems are *not* the real problem. In fact, they can be a gift to you. If you went to a physician to have an annual examination and your doctor said you have a calcium deficiency, would you be mad at the doctor? Of course not! When a student misbehaves, he or she is letting you know a "teaching deficiency" may exist. Although, you might be thinking, "No, it's a character deficiency in the student." The reality is, you have the power to influence your learners.

The "helpless victim" mentality does not solve student discipline issues. You can have a class of responsible, engaged learners who enjoy class everyday. Students who "act up" are not presenting a problem; they are simply providing you with feedback that may be essential for your success. Have you ever watched a baby play? Learning and curiosity are natural human states. When curiosity is aroused, all our senses are attentive to the task at hand. We are absorbed and nothing else is important. Discipline is unnecessary. In an ideal classroom, discipline problems virtually disappear. Guaranteed.

No Such Student as a "Troublemaker"

Now, you might be thinking, "All this sounds fine, but you haven't met so and so!" There's no doubt that some students may be acting out due to issues or influences beyond your control. The reality remains, however, that while the learner is in your classroom, you are their primary influence. Students don't get up in the morning thinking, "How can I be a real jerk today?" All behavior is state-related; and states can be managed and changed.

Using a label to describe classroom behavior does an injustice to everyone involved. There are no unresourceful people, only unresourceful behavioral states. To change the behavior, change the learner's state. In other words, your students all have the capacity to act appropriately, but sometimes they access an unresourceful behavioral state. Your job is to keep those negative states at a minimum and work towards the positive ones.

No Tips or Tools Will Replace Your Own Growth

Another assumption is that all a teacher needs is a few tips, tools, or techniques to manage the classroom better. All the tips and tools in the world won't work if you don't deal with your own biases and bad habits. Private victories always precede public victories. Learn to deal with your own "dark side" before you start telling others how to deal with theirs. The fact that you get mad or frustrated at life, a situation, or a student does not give you the right to be rude, disrespectful, or hurtful to another. Find other outlets for your stress, anger and frustration. Whatever it takes, learn how to deal with it. Everything you master in your own personal growth makes classroom management easier.

If you have problems in your classroom the first thing to consider is that you are a co-creator of the problem. If you operate from this framework, you won't be tempted to dismiss discipline problems as "those trouble-makers." This is not to say that the students don't have anything to do with it. Of course they do. But, to mobilize your own resources and make the necessary changes, you must accept responsibility for what goes on in your classroom.

Teachers who have mastered the science and art of classroom management have done it many different ways. Some follow a system, others say "do whatever works." What is most important when dealing with these issues is that you maintain an atmosphere of love, consistency, and integrity. Students need to know they are still good people; it's their behavior that is unacceptable. Students need to know what the boundaries are—a definite framework for acceptable behavior. Finally, students need to know that you will keep your word and honor your values. This sets the example for them to do the same and will reduce resentment that leads to discipline problems.

Conventional methods of discipline will fail and fail consistently because they don't provide the student with additional resources or choices. In other words, telling a student to quit doing something does not empower him or her, it only limits, negates, and frustrates them. And it ignores the source of the problem as well.

Classroom discipline is only effective in the long-term when it supports the dignity of the student. Build the learner's self-esteem, rather than suffocating it. Many students have been taught that getting mad is not an option; so they get even, instead. Your job is to expand students' choices, not shut them down. To accomplish that goal you must be flexible and learn what unfulfilled needs students have. Dovetail your desired outcomes, find common ground, then design a management strategy based on these positives.

What's Changed?

Old:
The student is the problem. Goal: to identify and measure desired outcomes and to reward the desired ones and punish the undesirable ones.

New:
Teacher takes personal responsibility and asks "How can I engage the learner naturally?" And, "What can I do to encourage more learning?"

Premises of a Positive Discipline Philosophy

Disruptions Are a Normal Part of Living

The normal class disruptions are part of school, of life and of our reality. Treat them as enjoyable challenges and sources of curiosity. It is easier to adapt your understanding of the world to reality, than to try to change the world to your point of view. The message this attitude gives to students is: School is real life.

The Classroom Is a "Learning Environment"

The classroom is a learning environment in which occasional discipline takes place, *not* a well-disciplined class in which learning better occur, or else! The least productive environment for learning is high fear, high stress. The optimal learning state is low stress, high challenge. The message this gives to students is: what we are about is learning.

Students Are All Basically Good

Students are just trying to manage their daily lives the best they can. None of us live in a perfect world. The younger the child, the fewer the resources or effective coping strategies they'll have for dealing with problems. Like you, students have normal concerns and the need to express control, attention, and love. The message this attitude gives is: "You and I are both good people, I respect and appreciate you."

The Best Discipline Is the Kind Nobody Notices

The less students know they are being disciplined, the better. Keep the focus on learning by managing states and creating constant novelty and diversity. The more outraged you become about discipline problems, the more they occur. (If you're upset, who's in control?) Remember this: "Where the attention goes, the energy flows!" Keep your attention more focused on the joy and excitement of learning. The message this gives to students is: "The teacher has things handled."

It's Never Your Class; It's the "Group's Group"

Your class has it's own culture and they act according to those rules. The rules you impose are just an aspect of the culture. Consider who the group leaders are; and work within their culture. If you over-exert power as a leader without the permission of the group, the group will sabotage you. Position gives you power, but not permission.

Problems Are Usually Spontaneous Expressions

Most problem-behaviors originate from the random areas of the brain (reptilian, limbic or right brain). Respond to problems from the vantage point of the student. Use lectures and left-brain discussions of rules only as a last resort. The message this gives to students is: "I have compassion for your feelings; and I know exactly where you're at."

Six Discipline Models

There are many ways to approach the issue of discipline. The strategies that you use are an extension of your personal beliefs. The following models reflect an evolution of discipline approaches from least effective to most effective. The most effective model will be easy to use, have long-term value to students, and will keep the emphasis on learning rather than intimidation or fear.

1. Behavior Modification

An orderly approach based on the sequence of identify, reward, and punish. This approach keeps track of student behaviors and attempts to control them.

2. Personal Influence

This approach is based on teacher-student relationships. The emphasis is on positive respectful interactions. When behaviors need to be modified, the teacher appeals to the student's natural tendency to want to maintain the positive relationship and on the mutual trust they've developed.

3. Logical Consequences

The teacher, in this approach, helps students to understand the impact of their behavior on others. The student is encouraged to explore positive alternatives. The teacher maintains a high involvement role.

4. Self-Awareness Training

The teacher, using this approach, trains students to observe their own behaviors so they know when they're behaving counter productively. The teacher role is active at first, then students get more involved.

5. Cooperative Discipline

This approach uses the influence of groups and teams and the student-teacher relationship. It emphasizes prevention and group norms.

6. Brain-Based Discipline

This approach emphasizes choice in learning and managing learner states. It is an "Invisible discipline" technique where changing activities, and giving students appropriate emotional and linguistic expression are the norm. The following suggestions reflect a brain-based approach to discipline:

33 Brain-Based Ways to Prevent Discipline Problems

1. Limit the amount of focused, directed learning time; and switch activities frequently. To determine the suggested learning time per activity, use the relative age of the students in minutes to a maximum of 20. For example, with an eight-year-old student, teach in a directed, lecture-driven manner for a maximum of eight minutes. Then, move to a more diffused activity like group work.

2. Use low-level baroque music in the background to soothe and inspire. Good choices include: Handel's Water Music, Vivaldi's Four Seasons and Bach's Brandenburg Concertos.

3. Create more "W-I-I-F-M" for the students: (What's in it for me?). Have them generate reasons to do things. Ask them what they want to get out of the learning.

4. Make sure rules are fair, purposeful, and enforceable. The fewer the rules, the better. Make sure that students know the reasons behind every rule you have.

5. Put students in cooperative groups or teams (with accountability!). Use groups as a source of fun, socialization and positive peer pressure.

6. Make positive contact with each of your students within the first five minutes of each class. Also, connect with parents regularly, if possible. Don't only talk to parents when you have a problem.

7. Boost the ways students can have more input in the classroom. Provide designated question time, seek their input, and install a suggestion box. Respond to suggestions in a timely manner.

8. Provide more outlets for auditory expression: affirmations, group or team time, discussion, cheers, sharing.

9. Let students play the "what if" game to make rules concrete, to find exceptions, role-play or brainstorm.

10. Make the classroom more interesting. Change the bulletin boards and peripherals frequently. The room ought to look busy, colorful, fresh, challenging, and relevant.

11. Anticipate and respond swiftly to student states. Know that frustration often leads to states of apathy, anger or revenge. Make state management a number one priority to prevent problems.

12. Build rapport with students—both verbally and non-verbally. Start with those you relate to least. Know the tendencies of auditory learners who tend to talk a lot and mis-matchers who accidentally disrupt class in an attempt to learn. They're often pointing out what's "off, different, missing or wrong." Use non-verbal signals with them to prevent the disruption of the class.

13. Incorporate movement and physical activity into every hour of class time (i.e., Simon Sez, hands-on, stretching) or switch activities.

14. Reduce your own stress level. Incorporate regular activity that energizes you and balances out the work load.

15. Work towards progress in areas related to your personal goals (i.e., parent communications, improving administrative policies, or staff communications).

16. Give clear mobilizing directions to students. Make them consistent, re-check for understanding, then use same congruent call to action.

17. Give students more control over their learning through choice (i.e., ways to do things, topics, rules, time, partners, scoring, music, etc.).

18. Get parents involved in your discipline program from the very start of the year. Send the plan home and seek agreement.

19. Have lunch with a student to build or maintain a relationship with them.

20. Teach using the multiple intelligences. Make sure that when you plan out your week, you have covered all of the seven intelligences.

21. Provide outlets for students to talk about the things that are important to them. Use discussion time, sharing circles, partner or buddy time.

22. Encourage students to write a monthly letter to you; and write them a response.

23. Role-play discipline problems and positive reactions and responses.

24. Peer management—set up student teams or sets of partners to help learners monitor each other and learn from one another.

25. Be consistent and fair so that students know it's worth following rules.

26. Know when it's time for a whole class break (to go outside or change plans).

27. Let students know you care by attending some kind of outside of class activity that they're in, like a sporting event, a play, a civic event, etc.

28. Manage the group's leaders so they'll set the cultural standards for the group.

29. Develop Sensory Acuity. The periphery of your eye is physiologically built to detect movement far better than the foveal portion of your eye. The way it's constructed, you can gather most of the data you need between a forty-five and a ninety-degree angle. Surprising? You can detect movement, facial responses and changes in breathing on a non-conscious level if you'll just learn to trust that ability. Here are a few other ways:

- While you are talking to one student, break eye contact, politely, so you can scan the room. Listen for unusual sounds and notice any new movements. This keeps students accountable.
- Learn to use up what is called "dead time." All the transition time for collecting papers, starting or stopping activities or in between activities is usually a signal for students to begin disruptive activities. The solution? A stretch break or purposeful discussion.
- If students are restless, give them a break. Have them stand up, inhale, hold their breath for a few seconds, then exhale. Then do some stretching or just a few quick movement exercises to get the circulation going again. Use that time to figure out how you can make the adjustments in your lesson to make learning more valuable, useful, fun or relevant.

30. Include Everyone. Most teachers teach to a minority of the students. Give your presentation three or four very different ways so that it reaches more types of learners. Explain things auditorally, then show visually, then demonstrate kinesthetically. This means that you will be giving directions several different times, different ways, even with a higher or lower voice, to insure that you include everyone.

31. Increase Predictability. Erratic behavior can be caused by anxiety, confusion, and lack of clarity. In earlier chapters, we mentioned the importance of structure, ritual, and predictability. Students like to know that certain things will happen at certain times.

- Build in your own ritual. For example, when you are giving directions, always give them with the same pattern. It might be that you first say, then show visually, then demonstrate, then say again, then post them up. This way, the students will learn quickly to pay extra attention during the style of the explanation they understand the best.
- Post schedules. This reduces classroom confusion. A surprising amount of noise and upsets occur over students not knowing what to do.
- Provide a variety of options within a predictable structure.
- Learn to systematically use your own non-verbals. Read the chapter on presentation skills and the one on interactions. The systematic use of non-verbals is one of the real keys to reducing discipline problems and a minority of teachers use it well.

32. Create Rapport. Webster's defines rapport as "a relation marked by harmony, conformity, accord, or affinity." Do you have this kind of relationship with your students? As reflected in the following strategies, there are many ways to develop rapport:

♦ Match language-style with learners. For example, if they use a visual predicate (i.e., an eyeful), you use a visual predicate in response (i.e., looks like).

Matching Predicates:

Visual	Auditory	Kinesthetic
an eyeful	an earful	a pain in the neck
looks like	sounds like	it feels like
get the picture	pay attention	get the drift of
a dim view	unheard of	underhanded
perspective	an account of	get a handle on

♦ Match the superlatives that they use. For example, words such as "good, great, excellent, super, or fabulous," are all words which form parts of people's language patterns. Use the same words your students use. Particularly, build relationship with the class leaders. Once you have a relationship with them, the rest of the class often follows.

♦ Match body movements. Adjust your body to match stance, posture, and gestures of your students. Match their expressions—eyebrows, mouth, nose, smile, or their angle of leaning. Match the tone, tempo, intensity and/or volume of their voice.

♦ You may also increase rapport by discussing, referring to or simply mentioning things that are a large part of your student's world. It may be an upcoming exposition, a rock concert, a holiday, a symphony, a movie, the weather, clothing styles, movie or TV stars.

♦ You may also do cross-over mirroring. This is when you use one activity to match a different activity with another. For example, pace a student's eye blinks with your finger tapping or foot tapping or pace the tempo of their voice by scratching or nodding.

Once you have established a good rapport with learners, you'll find your learners more willing to follow you. You'll have more influence with them and discipline problems will naturally decline. Of all the tools to reduce discipline problems, the ability to create rapport is certainly one of the most important.

33. Warm the Classroom Climate. Another way to reduce discipline problems is to change the way that you allow yourself to experience others. Avoid seeing students as a problem and start seeing your students as grand possibilities. Refuse to call anyone in your class a "trouble-maker" or "bad kid." Rather, refer to your students as "pending miracles" (ones you haven't reached yet, but will).

Think about it. Anytime you've been in a position in an organization where you felt powerless, didn't you withhold information useful to the hierarchy? Of course. It was your only way to experience power. The way you reduce discipline problems is by understanding this essential "power game" and learning how to meet the needs of your students. The way to "win" the power game is to give away enough power so that others don't want to take it from you. Simple, yet effective. When you empower individuals they don't have to compete with you for power.

In Another World

Before you discipline students, remember they live, virtually, in another world. They are separate from you by age, culture, income, status, and possibly, gender. Their time-reference may be different, too. We are all referenced to a primary time-status: past, present or future. The decisions and behaviors of your students which you may call erratic, negative or undisciplined, may simply reflect a different time frame. For example, if your so-called "problem student" is constantly late, it may be because they are present referenced. This means that decisions are made which indicate a primary concern for "How am I feeling right now?" A present-referenced student might be out in the hallways or lockers talking to friends all the way up until the bell rings, then arrive to class late. While being focused "in the moment" of the present, they forgot to focus on where they were supposed to be in the very near *future* (like in class).

This student is not motivated by *future* rewards (or punishments). They will do their homework if (at the moment they get around to it), they feel like it. Hence, this student is more fun, enjoys spontaneity, lives in the moment and is unpredictable. It would be a mistake to call them "unmotivated or "apathetic." They simply don't relate to the future like some others do.

Using Rules, Guidelines, and Agreements

Studies show that setting limits and consistently enforcing them gives students a sense of stability, structure and self-esteem. Students with clear guidelines seem to behave better. Make a clear distinction, however, between rules, guidelines, and agreements.

Rules

According to Webster's, the definition of rules is: "The exercise of authority or control; prescribed guides for conduct or action." Notice that this definition says nothing about mutually agreed upon standards. Instead, it is the imposition of authority or control. In practice, this definition works best for rules that insure the safety of others or of property. Examples include laws, truancy, profanity, dress codes and health standards. Students don't get to have a lot of input in these areas. The rules are the rules.

Guidelines

Guidelines are: "an indication of policy or conduct." Notice that a guideline itself is not a rule, it merely indicates a rule. This gives a lot of leeway in the interpretation and how it's treated in various situations. Examples might include politeness, noise levels, or ways to get the teacher's attention.

Agreements

Agreements are: "A harmonious accord on a course of action." Notice that the key word in this definition is harmonious. It implies that both parties, of their own free will, agree upon a common code or plan of behavior. With agreements, you and students decide on a behavior code, seating plan, homework policy, evaluation standards, or class procedures.

Make sure you make these distinctions for your students and give them time to discuss the definitions and their implications. Once you have explained the reasoning behind them, most students will not test your boundaries continually (provided you enforce them consistently).

Getting Classroom Agreement: Your students may be ready to help you with the rules. You might say, "Since we want to have our class work well, where everyone is safe and respected and where we can do our best learning, let's all agree on some guidelines. Any suggestions?" Hold a discussion; make it democratic to the degree that it is appropriate. Break down guidelines in the following way:

+ The agreement
+ The reason for the agreement
+ Any exceptions to the agreement
+ The consequences of breaking the agreement

Once you have had a thorough discussion on the agreements, seek consensus. An easy way to do this is to ask for a show of hand of all who are in favor of the agreement, then any who are not. Once agreements are made, post them on the classroom wall for everyone to see.

Suggested Agreements

1. Time
Each student agrees to be seated on time (as determined by the classroom clock) for the start of class or the resumption of class after a break. In other words, each student agrees to arrange their circumstances so that they can be on time.

2. Safety and Respect
Students agree to listen to the person who has the floor. Each student agrees to treat others and all school property safely and respectfully.

3. Support Learning
Every student will have the opportunity to learn; and will allow others to learn without disruption.

4. Classroom Care
Students agree to keep their classroom clean, to pick up after themselves, and to keep their own desk area organized.

5. Speak from Your Own Experience

Students agree to use "I" messages. This means verbal attacks on others is not acceptable. Rather than a student saying, "That guy's a real jerk," the "I" statement would make the speaker accountable. For example, "I don't like him," or "I can't get along with him."

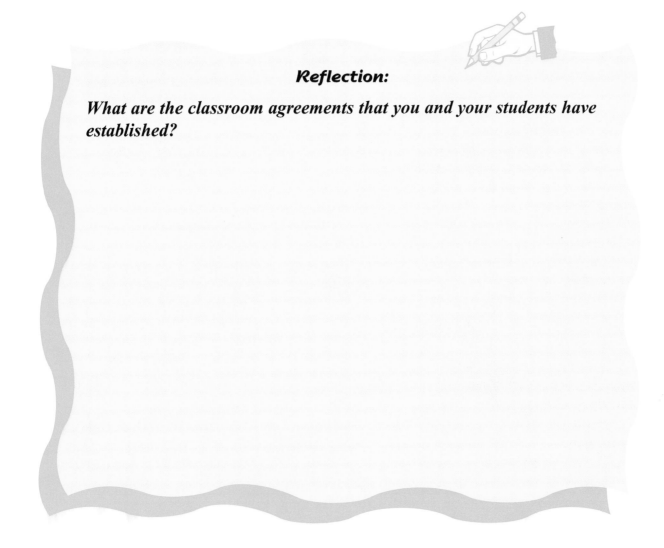

Reflection:

What are the classroom agreements that you and your students have established?

What to Do When Agreements Are Broken

The following suggestions reflect a four-level framework for dealing with problems in the classroom. Hopefully, through prevention, you won't have to resort to using them. However, if problems do occur, handle them immediately. Do not compromise or make liberal concessions. The suggestions below are categorized from level one—how to deal with minor infractions, to level four—how to deal with severe infractions.

Level One: Invisible Action

In dealing with a minor infraction, take invisible action. Handle the behavior by affecting a change in the student without being explicit about it.

Examples of invisible action techniques:

✦ Create novelty; switch activities.
✦ Ask everyone to take in a slow deep breath.
✦ Shift tonality of your voice.
✦ Change of music.
✦ Switch your location in the room.
✦ Do a stretching break or "Simon Sez" game.
✦ Have the class give a "partner-to-partner" affirmation.
✦ Call on the person *next* to the student at issue. This usually brings their attention back to the room.

Level Two: Handling the Problem, Not the Person

In dealing with this level of infraction, the group will probably realize that you're doing something to quiet them down, but no one feels singled out. Continue the class as usual. The following strategies get the job done and still avoid the "bad dog" or "shame" approach:

✦ Name dropping; incorporate three or four students' names in a sentence to personalize the learning.
✦ Use variety of "shhh" like, You ssssshhhould all be listening right now."
✦ Give a gentle touch on the shoulder.
✦ Proximity; stand near the student(s) who are at issue.
✦ Make your facial expression one of curiosity.
✦ Change the pace or activity in the room.
✦ Ask team/group leaders for help.
✦ Use or point to team class charts.
✦ Send the student on an errand to another part of the school (make prior arrangements for this, if necessary).
✦ Give the student special class job that allows them to keep busy and avoid distracting others.
✦ Admonish the object of distraction instead of the student. For example, say, "This is the noisiest pen I've ever heard. Can you keep it under control, otherwise, I'll have to put it in the bad pen box over there?" This way, the pen is the problem, not the student.
✦ Tell or read a story and fluctuate the volume of your voice to maintain student attention. Make eye contact with students, as you tell the story.
✦ Use a quote to release frustration or edginess. For example: "I ran into someone today who was so angry, you know what he said? He said, 'I'm furious! I'm madder than heck and I can't take the noise any more!" Boy, he must have been mad. Can you imagine someone being that mad?"
✦ If you cannot change the state of learners using the above suggestions, you can resort to using the "Hot Spot" approach. With this technique, you go to a particular corner of the room (a change from your normal position). When you move to this corner students will know you mean business. Be firm and to the point. Give eye contact; use same gestures and the same key phrase each time (i.e., "Boys and Girls!" or Exxcuuuse me!"). Then walk back to front of room and continue teaching without sermonizing or lecturing. Do not overuse this approach or it will lose its effectiveness.

Level Three: Student Choice Point

In dealing with this level of infraction, the emphasis is put on individual responsibility, privilege, and consequences. Avoid useless threats you may not want to follow through on. Be straightforward, friendly and matter-of-fact. Use eye contact, ask student to simply choose a behavior and be prepared for the consequences. For example, "Kim, you're a responsible person - hold it down for the next 10 minutes and we'll both be happy." Or, "Kenny, by keeping your hands to yourself, we can finish without interruptions and leave on time." Or, "Can you keep it down for the next few minutes? Otherwise we need a serious talk."

Level Four: Safety Jeopardized

At this level, the infraction is severe or consistent. Some learners are motivated more strongly by negatives. Uncover the underlying cause of the behavior and decide a long-term approach for dealing with the issue(s).

✦ In a private discussion with the student, describe the behaviors and the impact of those behaviors on the class. Describe how you feel about it. Ask the student for possible solutions or input. Propose what you think might be some possible solutions. Offer counseling or a parent meeting. Create agreements that you can both live with; take action to initiate them.

✦ Meet with parents to determine if the student has been experiencing a major loss or change in his/her life. For example, parent's divorce, loss of a friend, or excessive stress or pressure. Create agreements; take action to initiate them.

✦ Take strongest measures for repeated, dangerous, or special circumstances. Insuring a safe and productive learning environment for your class is of utmost priority. Seek help.

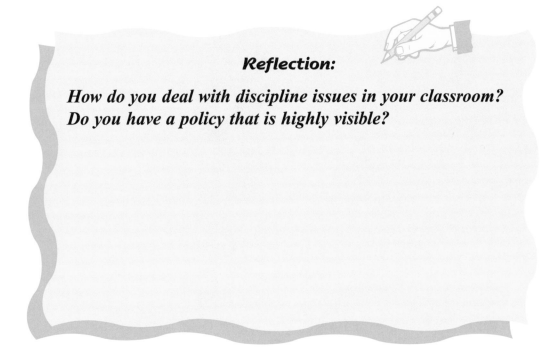

Reflection:

How do you deal with discipline issues in your classroom?
Do you have a policy that is highly visible?

When a Problem Occurs

1. Get centered. Pause, take a breath and relax. Anticipate a positive outcome and visualize a successful resolution for both parties.

2. Do not be confrontational; simply get the job done with minimal fanfare. The bigger the deal you make, the more you lose. This is not a time to win or "nail" someone. It's simply a way to get the class's energy off the distraction and focused back on learning.

3. State the facts regarding the behavior and reserve judgments. Avoid using your feelings to manipulate the student. Comments like: "you make me so mad" are damaging and inappropriate. Nobody else is responsible for your feelings but you. Students might trigger a stimulus-response mechanism within you that allows that emotion to occur, but your internal mechanisms are yours.

Your classroom may not be perfect. Optimal learning, joy and bliss may not be maintained one hundred percent of the time, but then life isn't meant to be perfect. Remember that problems are opportunities for growth. Use your resources to create a well-balanced classroom where students feel safe and trust you. When you develop rapport with your students, they will be willing to abide by the agreements you make together. Having students manage themselves is surely the ultimate sign of teaching success.

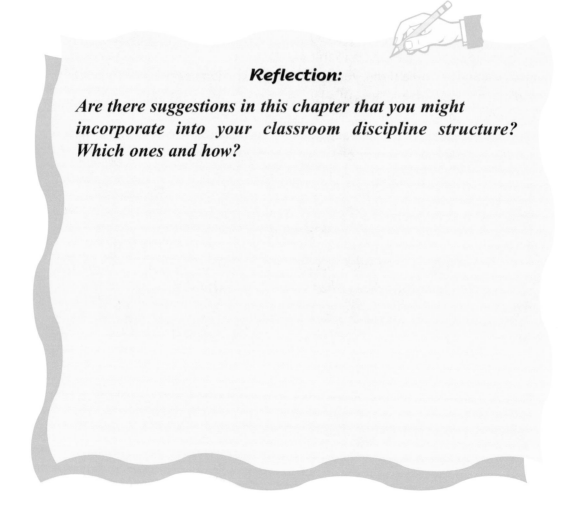

Reflection:

Are there suggestions in this chapter that you might incorporate into your classroom discipline structure? Which ones and how?

Reactions:

What are your feelings about the topics presented in this chapter?

What are some practical applications for what you're learning?

What do you want to remember from this chapter?

He [she] who wishes to teach us a truth should not tell it to us, but simply suggest it with a brief gesture, a gesture which starts an ideal trajectory in the air along which we glide until we find ourselves at the feet of the new truth.

Jose Ortega Y Gasset
Meditations On Quixote

Chapter 22

Relationships

Chapter Preview:

Relationships Make It Happen

The eminent educator, Robert Bills did a survey of 124,000 students in 315 public and private schools. After gathering thousands of pages of research, his first and most critical recommendation was that the quality of relationships at school must be improved. This means primarily the relationships between students and teachers, though others are important, too. Improving the relationships you have is so important that it can make or break your success as a teacher.

At school, students learn based on four primary relationships: 1) the relationship with their teacher; 2) the relationship with the subject matter; 3) their relationships with other students; and 4) their relationship with self. The teacher needs to do whatever it takes to build positive relationships during the first weeks of school; and to maintain them on a daily basis throughout the term.

Of course, it is easier to build relationships at the primary level with students as teachers spend an entire day with them. At the secondary level, it is more challenging because of the departmentalization of subjects. In classes only 50 minutes long, the pressure of teaching content is on; and relationships often suffer. Every move, therefore, must count. Each activity must serve the dual purpose of building strong relationships and content learning.

Building Positive Student-Teacher Relationships

The 10 basic building blocks for developing rapport with students and strong relationships over the long haul include:

1. Love Yourself

In order to take care of others, you must take care of yourself. You cannot give that which is not given to you. Students are very keen observers. Only if you respect yourself, will they feel that you are worthy of respecting.

2. Learn About Your Students

Get to know your individual students. Have them fill out index cards telling about themselves: where they were born, how many siblings, or pets they have, who they love, what they like, dislike, their fears, concerns, or problems. Two of the most important questions you can ask them are: what it's like for them being a student and what's important to them.

3. Appreciate Your Students

Understand the pressures and difficulties of being a student. Know what kind of effort and courage it takes just to get through the day. Discover how much peer pressure your students experience. Learn what kind of academic pressures they feel. To do this, it takes a special effort on your part to listen without judging.

4. Acknowledge Your Students

Thank them for little things. Thank them for big things. Thank them for being in your life. Appreciate every little thing they do. Give verbal praise, write notes, give hugs, smiles and warm gestures. Let them know that they are special to you and that you really like knowing them.

5. Listen to Your Students

Most students feel that no one listens to them—not parents, not teachers and not even their friends. Open up class time to let students share about their lives, joys, or problems. Even the seemingly little things are big things. If you can be a "no-particular-agenda" set of ears for your students, a real open-minded, open-hearted listener, you will be one of the greatest gifts in their lives.

6. Make Small Concessions

Grant some favors. Bring popular music to class. Do things that can make a big difference, even if it is letting class out thirty seconds early or giving no homework over the holidays; everything helps.

7. Include and Empower Your Students

Ask them what they think. Let them participate in decision-making. Give them options in how to do things as long as they are willing to produce the results. Actively solicit their advice. Have a class advisory board. Help students feel important.

8. Respect Students

Never use "put downs." Avoid all sarcasm. Honor student decisions. As soon as it is appropriate, give them more responsibility. Enforce rules, guidelines and agreements consistently. Keep your promises.

9. Treat Students as a "Possibility"

Treat each student as a potential success, not as a past record. Consider the possibility of their greatness even if it is not evident at the moment or currently disguised.

10. Be Open With Students

Share about yourself so students get to know you. Talk about your joys, successes and challenges. You provide a great opportunity for students to learn about adult life.

During the first few days and weeks of school you must establish a foundation for the quality of relationship you seek with your students. Think about how you connect with other adults. Determine commonalties. How are you alike? What brings you together? What do you want and what do they want? Do you share common goals? How do you expect to be treated? These kinds of real issues will be the glue that keeps your classroom family together. Take the time to build a strong foundation.

Maintaining Positive Relationships

Once you have established initial rapport with students, you can start building a relationship with them. The level of responsiveness in the classroom will tell you whether you have been successful. Stay tuned-in to the ever changing needs of your students. Likely, the most important cues you'll get from learners will be non-verbal: posture, breathing, tonality, tempo, gestures, etc. These behaviors are critical to monitor because most people are unaware of them. This means that they are the most accurate indicators of where you stand with another. Learn to make the following distinctions in your audience so that you'll know when you need to make adjustments:

Evidence of Rapport

Auditory

Listen to the questions and responses you are generating. Are students understanding you? Listen to the tonality and tempo. A faster paced, fluctuating or emphatic response could indicate you lack rapport unless that's how *you* speak. Tonality can imply "Gee, I really like what I'm hearing." Or, it can imply, "Why in the world are we even studying this?" When you are in total rapport, you may hear some of your own pet words, phrases and ideas used. Listen for audience chatter. Is the content and timing of it in line with your class purposes? If so, chatter could indicate rapport. Otherwise, it may indicate they're bored.

You can increase rapport with those students who are more auditorally inclined very easily. Vary your tonality. Let your tempo fluctuate, and change your volume often to keep students alert and interested. You may also want to use auditory verbs such as: "Things are *clicking*. How does this *sound*? *Tune* into this. That *rings* a bell. Here's *music* to your *ears*."

Visual

Wear colors which students can relate to while still dressing professionally. Notice what your students wear; many students will unconsciously begin to wear the same colors you wore the previous day. If they do, compliment them. Look for facial expressions that say "I'm confused," or "I want to say something." Move around the class so you can keep students in your field of vision from different angles.

Using visually-related verbs means that you'll gain rapport with those in your audience who are visually dominant. "I *see* what you mean. Take a *look* at this. From my perspective, you'll get a clearer *picture* of this." You can also talk more quickly if your usual pace is slower.

Kinesthetic

Get a sense of learner's postures. Are they leaning towards you? Are they nodding in agreement? Are they yawning or looking away? Are their legs or arms crossed? Is their breathing rate the same as yours? How about eye and mouth movements? Be sure to check out your assumptions.

Those who use the kinesthetic modality as their primary representational system will appreciate two things in your style. First, the pacing of your speech needs to be slower to appeal to the kinesthetic learner. This means... that you may have to... pause a bit... to let things "sit" with your students. The other rapport builder is the use of verbs. Use expressions such as "How do you feel about this? What's your sense of this? Let me give you... a couple of concrete examples... so you can better get a handle on things."

You may be wondering how you can possibly maintain rapport with such varied learners. It might seem impossible to maintain rapport with the visual, auditory and kinesthetic learners. The way to do this is to vary your presentation: speak quickly, use auditory predicates and maintain a kinesthetic posture, for example. Or, you can speak slowly, use kinesthetic verbs, use lots of visuals, and vary the tonality of your voice. Or, you can use one style for two minutes, then another for two minutes, then switch again. Subtly "weave" all of the modalities into your presentation and everyone will relate.

> ## Quotable
>
> *Every once in a while try to truly understand what it must be like to be a student in your own class.*

If your students were randomly selected, approximately forty percent of your audience would process information primarily visually; forty percent would process auditorally; and twenty percent, kinesthetically. This means that regardless of your preferred modality, ("Do you *see* what I mean," or "How does this *sound* to you?" or "How do you *feel* about this?"), to reach all of your students you need to sprinkle diversity into your predicates.

You might also gauge the effects and responsiveness of your use of predicates by the audience you have. In a group of so-called "Special-Ed" or learning-impaired students, use predominantly kinesthetic predicates and metaphors. Also use a lot of kinesthetic predicates in courses where the dominant subject or activity is physical (crafts, physical education, home economics, shop, etc.). In more visually-related courses (art, film, library skills, reading, etc.), use predominantly visual words. And in courses like music, drama, speech, radio, business, politics and film, use predominantly auditory predicates.

Be Responsive

If a student raises their hand, try to acknowledge them right away even if you cannot call them at that moment. Look at them and say, "I'll be right with you," or "I'll be ready for your question in just a moment." Answer questions truthfully and briefly. If students are restless, get them up for a stretch break. Be sure to use your full sensory acuity. Noticing student's feelings makes them feel important, heard, and cared for.

Incorporate Stimuli

Incorporating spontaneous things that happen into your presentation can really help to build rapport. It is a common experience shared in the moment. When you include external and internal stimuli in your teachings, they feel closer to you. For example, if a noisy train goes by, use it to your advantage: "We're all on the right *track*, so let's stay with this." Or, if someone drops their book on the floor, say: "A question may have just *dropped* into your mind, does anyone have one they'd like to ask?"

Provide Liberal Acknowledgments

Give credit to students even when it's marginal. Give it to them when they do what you ask. Thank them if they attempt to do what you asked them to do. Appreciate all that they do. Respect that they are doing the best they can, given how they see the world. You can turn any situation into an opportunity to acknowledge learners if you are both flexible in your interpretations and committed to empowering others. For example, when a student responds to a question with an inaccurate answer. Say, "Thanks for having the courage to offer an answer, I like it when you are willing to go for it."

Play Devil's Advocate

When presenting new information, be especially tuned in to the possibility of a negative or puzzled response. When you get one, *use it*! Change your strategies to either repackage what you just said or play the "devil's advocate" role. If you just said that the moon is made of green cheese and your students smirked, you might say, "now I know some of you may be thinking that's a crazy idea. Truthfully I thought it was, too. But when I heard such and such I changed my mind!" In other words, take the freedom to become the reactive mind of your audience, if need be.

Be flexible and be willing to change points of view as long as you can still get the desired outcome. You might say, "Let's have our class presentation next Friday." To which a student might reply, "Gee, I really couldn't get ready by then." To which you can reply, "On second thought, Friday isn't quite the right day of the week. Which other day did you have in mind?"

Use Names

Do not use student's names to pinpoint culprits or to draw attention to unresourceful behavior. This is a sure way to destroy rapport. Instead, use student's names as a way to appreciate them and to personalize your comments to them. For example, "I like that idea, Kevin. We can implement that in our next project."

Be sure to reference comments students made previously. A great way to build rapport is to use the comments and ideas of your students consistently in your material. For example, "As John mentioned earlier, our balance of trade deficit is getting worse." Or, refer to what the whole class said by taking a poll and using the results. "How many of you think memorizing answers is a key to school success?" Then, later on, "As you all agreed earlier, memory is important to school success, so let's learn how it works."

Use Agreement Frames

Focusing on differences reduces rapport; focusing on similarities increases rapport. What happens if a student is responding to you in a way you disagree with? Use agreement frames to maintain rapport. The three magic phrases of this technique are: 1) I agree; 2) I respect; and 3) I appreciate. If you don't agree with someone, you can at least respect the opinion and the right of that person to express it. If you don't respect someone, at least find a way to agree with the outcome. The following scenarios exemplify this technique:

Student: I hate this class. I can't learn anything.
Teacher: I certainly appreciate you telling me. What can I do to make it more interesting even if you don't (change your tone) *like this class*?

Student: I don't care whether I do well or not.
Teacher: Well, I respect your decision because you usually make good ones. I'm wondering what things are important to you?

Student: Nothing's important to me except motorcycles.
Teacher: I agree motorcycles are well worth your time. If I could help you get a handle on your homework so you'd have more time for your motorcycle, would you be interested?
Student: Yeah, I guess so....

Be Honest

One of the simplest and most effective ways to maintain rapport is simply to be honest with your students. Tell students about yourself, your world and how things are for you. Let your students know when you are happy, sad, frustrated, anxious or excited. Share your dreams, goals and disappointments. Tell the truth about what policies you have to enforce and which ones you don't. Explain why you do what you do and make sure that you include your students in as much decision making as you can. Students who participate in creating and clarifying policies are more likely to carry them out. Last, do not lie. Even if it's a "white lie," it's never worth it. If a student asks you something you don't wish to answer, politely explain that you don't feel comfortable answering that particular question. Your relationship with your students can take months to build and only seconds to destroy, so protect your investment and your integrity by being real and by telling the truth.

Being truthful, of course, does not mean being tactless. It would not be appropriate to tell a student that their paper lacked clarity or correct grammar. Rather, a truthful and more effective response would be "Here's your paper back. To get a higher grade, I suggest you start with ideas we have talked about in class, rough draft it, write with more enthusiasm, then get someone to read it for you, type it, and proof it before turning it into me. By the way, things I liked were your determination to get it in on time and it was the perfect length. Let me know if I can help." Tell the truth, but be compassionate. Have an appreciation for the personal life of your students and especially for their self-esteem.

> **Quotable**
>
> *Your relationship with your students can take months to build and only seconds to destroy, so protect your investment and your integrity by being real and by telling the truth.*

The Student-Subject Relationship

Also critical to student success is a positive attitude or relationship with the subject matter. Here's a summary of some ways to encourage a positive student-subject relationship:

- ✦ Excite your students with a vision of learning possibilities.
- ✦ Ask students to discover what's interesting to them about a particular subject.
- ✦ Have students make a list of benefits.
- ✦ Talk about the subject positively.
- ✦ Role-model your own interest in the subject.
- ✦ Make the subject matter more personal and relevant.
- ✦ Utilize a wider variety of learning styles; implement field trips, guest speakers, hands-on learning.
- ✦ Bring humor, songs and games into the classroom.
- ✦ Have students visualize success with the subject.
- ✦ Have students work in teams.
- ✦ Appeal to and reach more kinds of learners.
- ✦ Create new associations to "re-anchor" the subject.
- ✦ Link up the subject with positive emotions and music.

The Student-Student Relationship

In order to develop powerful student-to-student relationships, the initial groundwork must be laid. Most students at the elementary level are taught to be kind and supportive to their neighbor and help out whenever necessary. Somehow, much of that spirit is often lost however, by the time students reach their teen years. At this stage, typical behavior is put-downs, sarcasm and indifference. There are many ways to alter this negative pattern:

✦ Establish a definition and foundation of integrity.

✦ Ask students to relate to each other in a supportive way.

✦ Set clear class guidelines for behavior.

✦ Role-model teamwork: relate to other teachers, parents, and students in a supportive way.

✦ Express what you have in common with your students.

✦ Have students express what they have in common with each other.

✦ Role-model dependability.

✦ Hold some out-of-class learning activities so students can be in a novel setting.

✦ Choose class projects that students will get excited about; elicit their feedback.

Encouraging Student Friendships

Some students make friends very easily, while others do not. What is the core difference? One important element may be student's self-esteem. Self-esteem or a healthy self-concept means that you "relate" to yourself well; and hence, think highly of others. Chapter 23 focuses on strategies for encouraging positive self-esteem in your students. Some of these strategies are:

✦ You, the teacher, can role-model high self-esteem.

✦ Let the students discover, list, and share their own strengths.

✦ Emphasize integrity.

✦ Build a sense of "family" in the classroom.

✦ Have students work with partners and in teams.

✦ Provide students with a sense of belonging and pride.

✦ Call absent students; send get well cards.

✦ Honor the uniqueness of each student.

✦ Provide a little extra attention on student's birthdays.

✦ Listen to each student with your fullest attention.

✦ Allow students to share about their family, pets, hobbies.

✦ Give students more power and control over their life.

✦ Let them make decisions regarding the class.

✦ Teach them how to deal with criticism more resourcefully.

✦ Share with them options for dealing with problems.

✦ Celebrate the joys and successes of your students.

Do what it takes to build relationships early with your students and preserve them. A poor student-teacher relationship is the cause of many problems. Create an authentic, down-to-earth, honest, and caring rapport based on mutual respect and integrity and you will offset many problems.

The Teacher-Parent Relationship

Another important relationship at school is the one you have with your students parents. Consider the following:

✦ Parents are the number one influence in a child's life.
✦ Ninety percent of teachers say they don't get parent participation.
✦ Parents can provide the individual attention teacher's can't afford.
✦ In 1989 the main teacher complaint was lack of parent participation.
✦ Parents can support at home your efforts with the student in the classroom.
✦ Research demonstrates that students whose parents participate in school performed better than non-participating parent groups.
✦ Failing kids improved dramatically with parent participation.
✦ Research demonstrates only a minority of parents (25percent) are contacted by teachers with direct specific requests for support, but when asked, 85 percent responded positively.

Reflection:

Can you recall a situation where your relationship with a student was damaged temporarily? What did you do to regain your student's trust?

Insuring Open House Success

Develop a Plan for Parental Involvement

Your plan needs to be thorough, flexible and well-thought out. Gather resources on parent involvement:

✦ School materials
✦ Ask other teachers
✦ District materials
✦ Educational magazines
✦ Educational television
✦ Newsletters

Your plan ought to include: 1) your own research, resources, and time available; 2) the type of parents and children you have; 3) what your school has planned; its policies; 4) the school calendar; 5) special situations that come up; and 6) your own educational philosophy.

Assess Before Involving Parents

✦ Gather key information about your student's and parents.
✦ Bounce your ideas off other faculty members.
✦ Learn from colleague's experiences.
✦ Revise the plan accordingly.

Start Off on the Right Foot

✦ Mail a letter home before the Open House or parent meeting.
✦ Develop good public relations.
✦ Send letter introducing yourself to parents at the beginning of the school year. Include in the letter: who you are, your experience, credentials, and specialty; and why you're writing (to say hello, to make contact, to reassure, to excite, and to share your commitments about educating their child).
✦ Provide them with important dates like the Open House.
✦ Talk about the importance of the partnership between you and them.
✦ Get them excited about it.
✦ Add a P.S. to the letter "really looking forward to..."

Make the Open House a Highly Positive Event

This is one of the most important days of the year. This is just as important for secondary grades as it is for elementary. Put a lot of work into this event; it'll pay off all year long! Here are some suggestions for the event:

✦ Send personalized invitations designed nicely on the computer - sign each invitation.
✦ Involve students in your efforts (i.e., recruiting their parents, decorating the room, etc.).
✦ Make it very desirable to be there. Have a contest with no prizes! Or make up a fun event for the night (scavenger hunt, lottery, mystery quest, food, etc.).
✦ Have translators available if needed.
✦ Provide parents with useful written materials that look professional.
✦ Put up posters and student work displays.
✦ Use name tags and have relaxing music playing in the background.
✦ Offer refreshments.
✦ Provide a "baby-sitter" in an area set up for toddlers.
✦ Include *all* children in your slides, video, music, materials, and written pieces; do not leave anyone out.
✦ Make sure the time is well spent; it is limited.
✦ Make it well worth parent's time to attend; and a loss if they don't.
✦ End the Open House on a high note.

Tips for Teacher-Parent Interactions

✦ Greet every parent by name; listen to them thoughtfully and write down their concerns.

✦ Talk about what it takes to make their child a success. Talk about partnerships, and shared responsibility.

✦ Talk about your commitment to their child; establish credibility.

✦ Tell parents specifically what they can do.

✦ Have a theme and parent philosophy and communicate it.

✦ Be respectful of parents and proud of yourself and your work. Avoid self-depreciating jokes and put-downs of either education as a whole, the school or your job. Parents want a professional in the classroom, not a victim of circumstances.

✦ Make sure you have provided a vehicle for receiving feedback from parents; either they leave it at the open house or return in later.

✦ Produce a Parent's Handbook that includes:
  • Greetings, positive affirmations
  • Names of school staff members, important phone numbers, and list of students in class
  • School hours, emergency numbers, school map
  • Nutritional suggestions
  • Rules for both the school and classroom
  • Curriculum and daily class schedule
  • Homework, absentee-make up, and medical policies
  • Calendar, holidays, staff development days
  • Study, learning tips, reading lists, resources

Parent Support for Homework

Talk about homework basics, purpose and types of homework, frequency and amount of it, when and how to complete it, the test schedule, and impact on grades, and what it should look and sound like. Talk about your expectations of the parent's roles in homework and ways to keep kids motivated. Talk about how you reinforce the completion of homework and what you do when it is not done.

Write up your homework policy clearly, simply and professionally. Give it to each of your parents. Have them sign it and return a copy or a lower tear-off slip. If you have decided to give out homework:

✦ Start early in the year with your approach and goals.

✦ Keep parents informed.

✦ Give clear, reasonable expectations.

✦ Follow-up and do what you say you will do.

"On-Site" Parent Participation Program

Send a letter in native language home to parents asking them for help in the classroom. Include: what's in it for them—specific benefits to parents and benefits to their child. List the types of assistance you are seeking from parents and don't forget to make it exciting. Put stakes in the game—tell them what is possible with their help. Match volunteer's skills, time, language parameters, and resources with tasks that need to be accomplished.

Before parents participate, make a list of duties to be done, ways to communicate, classroom guidelines or rules, locations of supplies, what's okay, what's not okay, how to minimize interruptions, on-going to-do list, folders to complete, on-going assessment, cookies, source of "strokes." Provide a variety of ways for parents to help. They can collate papers, write notes to kids, make calls to other parents, cut or paste-up, help with bulletin boards, be a guest speaker, share about cultural background, give library help, do phone calls, help with set-up, put on special events, facilitate an art project assist with projects, locate resources, do individual tutoring, give vocational talks or let them offer ideas. Be sure to always have a list waiting for them, so there's no wasted time.

Additional Ways Parents Can Help:

✦ *Organize school-wide events and fund raisers. Good examples are plays, swap meets, book fairs, bake sales.*
✦ *Recruit volunteers or class speakers.*
✦ *Provide funding ideas.*
✦ *Be a member on the school council or P.T.A.*
✦ *Be a class speaker: dentists, doctors, psychologists, drug experts, self-esteem specialists, celebrities, persons with high profiles, author, artist, discipline specialists, special readers or story tellers, police officers, fire fighters, coast guard or other military branches, etc.*
✦ *Organize a play, newspaper, career day, social services resources, job fair for kids, etc.*

Ideas for Quality Participation

Homework Assistance

Clarify parent's role; let them know exactly what they can and cannot do. Remember to praise, ask questions, coach them, monitor the studies, use a study area. Establish after school homework assistance program if needed.

Communications With Parents

Notes from teachers, report cards, progress reports, phone calls, awards, special projects, newsletter, personal contact, conferences, class participation, survey, make it timely, be friendly, be positive, be complete, give follow-up resources. Keep parents informed as well as report and ask or survey them.

For Student Conferences

✦ Do goal-getting conferences at the start of the year.
✦ Keep a phone log to document the child's progress.
✦ Always include positives or strokes even for the tougher kids.

- ◆ Give a report to each parent on their child's strengths, concerns, goals, questions, and requests.
- ◆ Be sure it's sent in their native language. Using the phone is best and remember to follow-up on paper.
- ◆ Group conferences with key personnel.

For Parent Education
- ◆ Do a major push for parent education.
- ◆ Give parents school policies, homework and playground rules.
- ◆ Provide information about office hours, map, personnel, schedules, and resources.
- ◆ Provide newsletters, bulletins, back-to-school night.
- ◆ Provide information or mini-courses on ESL, nutrition, single parenting, drug awareness, etc.

Acknowledging Parents
Recognizing parent's efforts is very important. The little things mean the most especially when they are sincere and consistent. Remember to have students take home projects, holiday goodies, certificates, newsletters, recognition certificates, newspaper stories, praise notes, etc. Consider giving parent recognition at a year-end assembly where parents share a special moment with their child.

Reactions:

What are your feelings about the topics presented in this chapter?

What are some practical applications for what you're learning?

What do you want to remember from this chapter?

Learning can, of course, take place in the classroom, but most of it doesn't. Today's learners are not just students; learning has suddenly become everybody's business. In fact, learning "how to learn" may now be your most critical survival skill.

Eric Jensen
The Learning Brain

Chapter 23

Better Assessment

Chapter Preview:

Is There a Better Way?

Tests, much like the weather, get plenty of criticism. Are they really different today than they were fifty years ago? Yes, they are. And fortunately they are getting more realistic and practical. Today, in most schools, you can find some variety of assessment for nearly everything. Yet, the experts on the brain and learning see the problem quite differently. They say, most of what we can measure behaviorally, is neurologically immaterial to optimal brain development.

This realization is fueling a massive and urgent movement worldwide in redesigning academic assessment. What we thought was important in the past, may not at all be important. It may have simply been more measurable! In other words, what if the whole testing system was wrong? You can have the most efficient oil rig in the world, but if you're digging in the wrong area, you still won't strike oil.

Objective Versus Subjective

First, there is no such thing as an objective test. All tests are subjective, and all reflect value judgments, priority systems, likes and dislikes. Choice of questions, wording of questions and even the format of the test are formed from the test maker's personal experience. Even a test written by a committee brings to it the previous history, values and individual's subjective backgrounds.

Second, formalized testing is one of the least effective ways to evaluate student performance. It's ineffective because: 1) many students are not good "test-takers"; and 2) by the time you give students a formal test, both you and they should already know how each of you are doing. You should know your weak and strong points well and should have already begun to work on them. Most tests are a perfect example of too little, too late.

Dipsticking is a teaching strategy that provides immediate and accurate feedback as to your student's level of understanding in the teaching moment, rather than days or weeks later at test time. To set up a dipsticking system you develop various non-verbal signals with your learners that represent their needs. For example, you might wish to have a hand sign that means "I need more information"; one that means "okay, I get it"; or one for "I don't understand the usefulness of this information." Learners can use these immediate feedback signals during your presentation so that you know how much is being understood; and they have a means of communicating with you without interrupting to ask a question. When such a system is used, adjustments can be made right on the spot when they're needed for deeper understanding.

Evaluating for Feedback

What you say and how you say it will determine students' test-taking attitudes. An evaluation is a feedback mechanism for the teacher. If the teacher designs it well, it can also serve as a feedback mechanism for the students. Simply tell your students that the tests will measure how well you taught instead of how much they learned. This takes the pressure off the students and reduces the incentive to cheat. Turn evaluations into a game - one that the students want to play. Rename your tests. Call them something fun, like a "loop," as in feedback loop.

Assess often! For feedback to be useful, it must be immediate. Testing (or "looping") during every class is useful. The tests do not have to be written. It's just as easy to create class exercises in which students can respond orally, in unison drills or informal feedback systems. By using creative response-systems, you are constantly updated on how well each student is learning.

Students who are tested infrequently experience anxiety, disassociation, fears, lowered interest and participation levels. Daily testing creates more of a relationship with the subject matter, more interest in it and lowers stress about grades because each test is less significant.

Keep them light! Who says assessing should be painful and traumatic? Find ways to allow the students to devalue the test score, but still learn from the experience. Possibilities include: questions that are silly or giveaways, making the test funny, allowing students to contribute questions, allowing them to take the test with partners, or to develop the scoring system.

Use a variety of testing methods. You may recall from your own experience that some students best express themselves in writing, others talking, others by demonstrating, others on special projects, and others love a basic, standard written test. The greater the variety of testing forms you use, the greater the chances your students will succeed.

Be on the student's side. Allow students to be successful. Tell them ahead of time when you will test, what kinds of test methods you'll use, and the grading system. Help them choose the evaluation methods. Ask them to get involved in the process. Many master teachers test only when they feel students are ready and likely to be high scorers. In the middle of the test, include instructions to stand up and stretch or take a deep breath.

Give immediate feedback. Score the tests as soon as possible. Scoring is what students and teachers need for feedback and course correction. The easiest way is to have students grade their own test as soon as they have completed them. "What if they cheat?", you may ask. Somehow, when you do the things that this book talks about, kids don't cheat. If you make students more resourceful, and give them the learning strategies that they need to succeed, cheating becomes obsolete. Correct tests in class with a light attitude and with humor, then celebrate each right answer with group applause or cheers.

Use the portfolio and processfolio method. This means that you keep a file for each student which does two important things. First, it contains the history of each learner's process. Second, it provides a wide variety of assessment methods. The folder, which reflects an ongoing and up-to-date progress report, is also accessible for learners to review at will.

Many Ways to Assess

Since students use various combinations of learning strategies, they naturally test differently. If some of your students were color-blind and you gave them a test that asked them to distinguish colors, the result would be a high failure rate. Does that mean that your students are "slow?" Of course not. They simply were not given the chance to succeed. It makes more sense to offer assessment in two ways: provide variety in your methods and provide choice in your methods. Why? Your goal is to help provide students with a way to demonstrate what they have learned. It is not to embarrass them or point out what they have missed.

Quick Feedback Methods

Lap Boards
Small notebook-sized cardboards with a vinyl covering on them. They are cheap, easy to use and effective. Basically, they are miniature chalkboards using quick-erase pens instead of chalk. You simply ask a question. Each student writes the answer and holds up the hoard for you to see. With these boards, students can give immediate, personal and private answers to any question you have. Plus, you can quickly scan the classroom to find students whose answer is different and follow up with them.

Non-verbals
Watch for smiles, nods of the head, students who sit back in their chairs with their hands clasped behind their head. Pay attention to changes in breathing patterns, in conversations, and noise level.

Hand and Body Signals

This system is based on the old "thumbs up or thumbs down" signal used to answer questions the teacher asks. Have students use dozens of different hand responses which include using different letters of the alphabet, pointing to different parts of the room, using body parts or partners. It's easy to imagine this working perfectly well in math classes, especially when students can make function signals easily such as add, subtract, multiply or divide. Yet, with some creativity, many other feedbacks can be developed. The desired outcome is to create a quick, easy, workable system to give immediate feedback.

The Role of Homework

Probably the most common form of written evaluation is homework. First, consider the purpose in assigning homework. If it's busywork, don't assign it. If the assignment can be done in class just as well, do it in class. Your classroom is a controlled environment. You can observe, support, give reinforcement and make the learning process more useful and fun for the student. The early steps in a learning process can be compared to baking a cake - you want the corrections made in the batter, not after the cake is in the oven!

Minimize homework; make it shorter and more meaningful. Have it be consistent, fun, and relevant to the learning in class. Encourage creativity. Ask students to read a short synopsis just before going to sleep with a classical music concert as the background. This allows the mind to integrate and store the material for maximum usage. Be sure to follow through during the next class.

Consider a team approach where students support each other instead of competing. Have them work on an assignment together in a group that has been set up to have the greatest academic diversity. Use the group score as the score for each individual. Assign "group homework" which increases student understanding and interest. There are many ways to format group homework. You can give each group the opportunity to plan their respective roles and home assignments; or the group can do a phone tree at home (i.e., one student starts by calling another, who calls another, who calls another, until everyone has been called). Encourage students to share phone numbers and discuss their homework with each other.

A very effective homework format is to have students do a mind-map that depicts what they learned that day. This technique serves as a review; it increases recall, provides reflection time, is fun, and helps learners form questions about the learning. Students should have every possible opportunity to learn. If they turn in something that is of an unacceptable quality, give the project back to them for improvement without grading the original work. Remind them that they can ask for help from class members. Reading homework should only be short passages, not 20 or 50 page chunks to do overnight.

Homework that can easily be translated into real-life learning will be better received and more effective. Consider the following possibilities for home learning:

+ *Parent or Neighbor Interviews:* Obtaining information about their past, opinions, knowledge, etc.
+ *Television Viewing:* Tying in with news, current events, public television programs, movies, science, people, commercials, social studies, history, etc.
+ *Cooking/Gardening/Model Making:* Using measuring devices, identifying, analyzing, and grouping objects.
+ *Journal Writing:* Poetry, diary entries, short stories, etc.
+ *Experiments:* Using common household items.

If you're going to assign homework, make it short, realistic, practical and meaningful. Busywork is out; genuine learning is in. Re-assess what, how and why you assign learning at home. It may be time for a change.

Informal Assessment

Give students a problem to solve which can be solved many different ways and observe them. Do the same thing in small groups and observe. Give students a choice in activities or games and watch. Discover which ones they pick: Pictionary, Monopoly, crossword puzzles, manipulative puzzles, charades, music recognition, etc. Then observe what they do during that game.

Use discussion and reflection after a play, movie, or musical. Ask learners which parts made the most impact on them - was it the music, the action, the relationships, etc.? What type of learning and intelligence is used the most. Students tend to do what they like or are most successful at doing. Find out who are the questioners, the noise and music-makers, the artists, doodlers, the active learners, the talkers, the loners, etc. Give students a chance to design, build and use some kind of a physical representation of the topic learned. Observe what parts of the task they like and excel in most easily. You'll learn a great deal about how each learner learns merely by observing.

When making assessments about learners, consider the following categories of evaluation:

Assessment Categories:

End Result: *What is it that students are creating? What kind of quality is it? The student asks: "What do I know? What do I do with it?"*

Learning Process: *Many educators feel that the journey, the process of how the learner got to the product is as, if not more important, than the product.*

Learner Skills: *This is often referred to as the "improvement gain." The question is: how far has the student come, given the circumstances?*

Keep in mind that much of what's really important cannot be easily measured. However, it is good to know when progress has been made. The basic value of this is not for the schools to be able to compare students, but for learners to have feedback on the milestones in their learning. One way of "grading" learners without judging them is to develop an assessment system that uses non-judgmental phraseology. An example of one such system follows:

NY or "not yet"

This means the student has just started learning in an agreed-upon area or discipline. Progress has not been made yet.

DEV or "Developing"

This means that the student is in process of developing the key skills and information needed for basic competence. There are, however, stages so that progress can be noted.

EX or "Extending"

This means that the learner has already met the criteria for learning in the particular subject or skill and is exploring it further.

In primary and secondary schools, this means that every single unit will need to have each of the above three categories detailed. It is a time-consuming process, but it will provide more stability, fairness and accuracy in the long run. It insures that when a student switches from one school to another, the assessment will help accurately determine where the learner is really at, not solely a subjective opinion.

Is this better than a letter grade? It certainly provides more information. It certainly is less judgmental. It certainly provides a more standard understanding of a learner's progress. Yes, it is better than just a letter grade, as long as it is used properly. Remember, the learner's brains may be as much as three years apart, developmentally, and still be normal. There is no allocation in this assessment for that. As long as it is used for feedback and teacher information, not for comparison, it's acceptable.

Does a Rubric Make Sense?

A rubric is simply a matrix which lists the criteria for measuring what you want. If your criteria is out of date, the use of a rubric won't help, either. A rubric is an attempt to get more objective about the "subjective." The idea of a rubric is simple: Take all the those ideas, intuitions, beliefs and opinions about what is excellent and do your best to objectify them. Many teachers find that the use of rubrics makes assessment easier. A rubric is simply a criteria-based grid which uses specific and defined guidelines to assess learning evidence.

Everything your students submit for assessment ought to have clearly defined success parameters. Grading by the "teacher's intuition" or a vaguely defined opinion about what is or is not quality is out. It's time to invite student input on what they think constitutes quality. Your first rubric for assessment may be rough, but it will evolve over time into a valuable instrument to discover what learners know, feel and can do. To create your own assessment rubric, consider the following seven steps:

1. Explore and gather ideas from other rubrics.
2. Find work samples and explore the range of quality.
3. Discuss the qualities and characteristics of excellent work.
4. Prioritize the list of qualities.
5. Make a sample rubric.
6. Test it with a sample of student work.
7. Revise as needed.

With each of these, you can set a standard, from one (lowest quality) to five (highest) quality. By making your criteria for quality specific, your students will be able to measure their own efforts. You can create a fairly objective set of standards for what is seemingly a subjective student effort. Remember though; if the criteria used for assessment include old fashioned lists of facts, a rubric won't make your system any better.

Criteria for assessment include the following:

◆ Patterns of meaning
◆ Strategies and how-to skills
◆ Personal biases; what and why
◆ Working models of systems
◆ Personal meaning

Granted, the above criteria are a bit tougher to quantify than whether or not a student knows when the Boston Massacre took place. But it sure beats the old style of testing that simply became a game for the students to play and try to beat. There's got to be more to school than playing adversarial games that are a lose-lose.

Personal Meaning

One part of your evaluation criteria ought to be that the learner must demonstrate how the learning is related to their life. In other words, the subject must be understood beyond the level of mere information. The question then becomes, what personal meaning does the learning hold for you. Only when the learning becomes woven into the fabric of one's own life does it become genuinely, internally, meaningfully learned. The following are some of the criteria related to personal meaning:

◆ Evidence of progress towards multiple learning goals - a timeline.
◆ An ability to transfer the knowledge of one subject to another.
◆ An indication of transfer of learning from school to life.
◆ Evidence of self-reflection and self-awareness on a topic.
◆ Items that convey understanding of the basics of that topic as well as details or related tangents.
◆ Something that conveys the relevance and meaning of that topic in a local or global context.
◆ Physical demonstration of the knowledge, skills, or abilities.

Personal meaning must never be graded on a curve or compared to other students. The grading ought to be done both by the teacher and the students, using criteria for mastery that has been agreed upon by both. This insures that the following will occur:

◆ Students will have a way to express what they know, in the way that they know it best.
◆ Students will be measured by consistent standards, ones on which they had some input.
◆ All learners will have equal chance to succeed.
◆ Learners will be encouraged to learn in a meaningful way.

The following reflect some ways that your students can make personal meaning out of content or subject matter:

Mock Newspaper: Let students create their own front page of the paper conveying the learning topic. They can take various points of view and relate the articles to real life.

Commercials: Students take their subject matter and turn it into a commercial. It could be an advertisement for print media, a tape to be played on the radio, or a video production.

Quotable

Personal meaning virtually guarantees that the learning will come alive for the learner and that it will be a part of his or her life for the long-term.

Student Teaching: Allow students time to think and make mind-maps or notes on the topic. Then have them pair up and teach each other; or identify small learning groups. The more props, music and visual aids used, the more meaning the presentation will likely have. Then give individuals or group leaders an opportunity to present to the whole class.

Model-Making: In some cases, students can build a scaled-down or working-size model of the material. This can be particularly useful in demonstrating their understanding of the material when it is physical and involves steps or processes.

Performance: Let students do drama or theatrical performances based on the material. Some material, especially literature, lends itself to being performed. Allow students time to do a quality job, then help them build a fun "stage" to perform on.

Music: Most material can be set to music, written about in music, performed as rap or opera. Or students can re-write an already familiar song using key words or concepts from the learning.

Discussion: Students simply need time to talk freely about the learning. Casual, unstressed discussion-interview time is rarely used and can be of great benefit. The ability to formulate questions and to extrapolate hypothetical answers is a life-long learning skill.

Artwork/Drawing: Let students have a chance to express themselves with art. Experiment with many types of materials. Ask students to depict or demonstrate learning from the topic area. You may be surprised at some of the great examples you get.

Journals/Learning Logs: These reflective mediums offer a good way to discover what students who are more private (or intrapersonal) may know about a subject. Assign specific content or questions about the learning process; encourage learners to add their own feelings and possible applications.

Debates: Much of the value of debates as a personal meaning concept is in the preparation of them. Be sure to make your criteria for assessment very specific, so that students know how they'll be evaluated.

Mind-Mapping: Let students create poster-sized maps of what they know. These webbed, thematic graphic organizers offer colorful peripheral thoughts organized around a key idea. Mind-Maps provide an excellent vehicle for understanding relationships, themes and associations of ideas.

Incorporate some of the suggestions above offering variety and choice in the process and you will have a model which honors and respects all of your learner's gifts. The concept of personal meaning allows you to focus less on *how smart* a student is and more on *how* the learner is smart? Hence, your learners will feel fairly assessed and successful. They will become more confident in their learning and will be willing to take greater risks.

Towards Mastery

The mastery concept means that every student works towards successful completion of the unit of learning. Once mastered, they earn an "A." Either a student has an incomplete or an "A," then they move on. This simple method of evaluation avoids the entire issue of grouping and prescriptive labeling. It also allows students to learn at their own rate which is important for self-esteem and competency. It is a superb evaluation method for these reasons.

Mastery, though brilliant in concept, takes a committed teacher to implement successfully. Fortunately you qualify! The mastery concept states that clear specific criteria be set for student competency in a subject area, and that each student is responsible for achieving mastery, at their own pace. To be fully effective, students need a full toolbag of resources for mastering the material, PLUS the commitment and drive to carry it out.

The following tips need to be considered when evaluating mastery learning: 1) use multiple criteria: attendance, class participation, daily sub-quizzes, portfolios, weekly quizzes, demonstrations, debates, monthly exams, models, projects or papers; 2) provide ways for students to make up absences or increase scores; 3) provide students with the specifics of your grading/evaluation criteria. They need to know exactly how to get a top score in your class; 4) remove any threat of failure - it's counter-productive to learning; 5) provide students with immediate and consistent feedback; and 6) treat the whole grading system lightly, and still respect its meaning to the students.

Testing Environment

Everard Blanchard of Villa Educational Research Associates has done some excellent work in the area of the actual testing environment. To put it briefly, environment matters. The tone of your voice, the tempo, the content, the expectations, all matter. Think carefully in terms of your purpose and intended result. In addition, Blanchard confirmed that students who take exams with a light classical music background scored higher than those who took the exam in silence. The lesson? Improve the aesthetic and emotional atmosphere in your testing situations.

Cheating Solutions

For many students, cheating is their best success strategy. Students who cheat may well be very smart. As Wayne Dyer, teacher and author of the well-known book, *The Sky's the Limit*, (1980) put it:

> I saw a study which tested chickens to see which ones were dumb and which ones were smart.
> A length of chicken wire was set up in front of their feed and the ones that were eventually
> labeled dumb just sat and died of starvation. The chickens labeled smart walked around the
> barrier and got to their food. Now when chickens go around barriers for rewards, they're
> labeled smart, but when students do the same thing, we label it cheating.

Does this make sense? It's so curious in our culture that if a student gets answers from a teacher or a textbook, it's okay. But when students get an answer from another student, we call it cheating! This is not to justify cheating. Cheating is wrong. It's just that we have somehow set up a system that makes cheating necessary. It is better to:

✦ Provide clearly stated objectives; be sure that students know what you want and expect.
✦ Increase feedback; more consistent and better quality feedback every day at least once per student, per one hour of learning time.
✦ Provide learn-to-learn skills; teach your students how to find information, how to learn better and give them class time for specific practice.
✦ Provide tutoring or some kind of extra help; maybe it comes from students at a higher grade level.

- Give students more opportunities to work in groups; the more they work in groups the more they will want to be tested by themselves. Most students want to know how they truly are doing in your class.
- Give each student a "study-buddy"; either formal or informal, everyone needs some support.
- Offer help during "down" times so that gaps in learning are discovered before test time reducing the need to cheat.
- Give better directions at test time so students don't have to ask others for them.
- Have a clear policy about what is cheating and what is not.
- Be consistent, fair and firm in dealing with cheaters.
- Provide plenty of space around each student at test time.
- State your own personal views, rules and class policy related to cheating.

Follow-Up

One of the most difficult moments for a student is when a test result is below expectations. It is possible and advisable at such a time to reframe the student's experience. Find a different way of integrating the test experience so that each and every test causes the student to feel resourceful rather than beaten down. What if the following assertions were reinforced with your students:

- A low score indicates a gap in teaching effectiveness.
- There's no such thing as a mistake
- What is called a failure is an outcome that we've prejudged as bad.
- Every outcome gives the information you need to succeed next time.
- Each experience is part of a larger success.
- With every adversity comes the seed of an equal or greater benefit.

Reflection:

What combination of assessment strategies do you currently use in your class? Are there others here you wish to incorporate?

These beliefs may or may not be true, but you'll produce more confident students by applying them. These new beliefs create the willingness to gain something from each setback. Imagine the change in feelings in your students when they call a test a result or a grade simply an outcome! Or, if each time you give test scores, your students were asked to come up with a decision about their results that would allow them to be even better learners. After all, one of the major differences between kinds of learners is the strategy used. Successful learners include, as part of their strategy, a decision about the learning event that makes them: 1) Have more choices for next time; 2) Feel stronger and better; it elicits positive emotions; 3) Appreciate the valuable feedback; and 4) Re-evaluate ineffective strategies for next time.

Another important role for teachers is to teach the necessary study skills. It's easy to assume that someone else has prepared your students for studying successfully, but this is usually not the case. Unless you are well-versed in the latest study strategies and have the time to teach them to your students, have your students get a copy of *Student Success Secrets* (1989). It's listed in the bibliography and provides the fundamentals as well as the specifics for learning how to learn.

As you continue to increase your ability to communicate effectively and bring out the best in your students (who are all of approximate equal ability), the results will be that their best is an "A" and since they are all equal in ability, all of them will deserve one. If you are mandated to give out a certain number of "Bs" and "Ds," or if you have been grading on the curve, you might want to re-examine that procedure and ask yourself why would you want to guarantee that a certain number of students do poorly?

Affirm the Positive

A little girl came up to me one day and said, "Mr. Jensen, Mr. Jensen, look at my paper." She showed me her paper, and every single word on it was misspelled. I looked at her and said, "Maureen, I really like your paper—the margins are nice and neat, and your printing is clean and readable." And she said, "Thank you, Mr. Jensen - I've really been working hard on it. Next, I'm going to work on my spelling."

The ultimate success as a teacher in the classroom is to have *all* of your students succeed. If half of them do well, you didn't reach the other half and that could be your goal next time. It should be the dream of every teacher to have every student in your class succeed. If any of them don't, adjust the variables: your teaching, the tests, the grading system, etc. Behavioral flexibility, teaching skills, rapport, presentation methods all can bring you closer to the 100 percent goal.

Reactions:

What are your feelings about the topics presented in this chapter?

What are some practical applications for what you're learning?

What do you want to remember from this chapter?

Human nature is not a machine to be built after a model, and set to do exactly the work prescribed for it, but a tree, which requires to grow and develop itself on all sides, according to the tendency of the inward forces which make it a living thing.

John Stuart Mill
On Liberty

Chapter 24 —————————————————

From Surviving to Thriving

Chapter Preview:

- ◆ **A New Way of Thinking**
- ◆ **Motivating Yourself**
- ◆ **Dealing With Unlikable Colleagues**
- ◆ **The High-Energy Teaching Diet**
- ◆ **Maximum Alertness**
- ◆ **Energy Management**
- ◆ **Knowledge and Skill Base**
- ◆ **Sweetening the Pot**
- ◆ **How to Make More Money in Education**

A New Way of Thinking

Almost anyone can survive a day. But what a waste! There's more to life than just surviving. We all want life to be rich, meaningful and fun. We want to thrive! This chapter presents the tools, tricks and strategies that will take you beyond surviving to thriving in the classroom. Whether it's dealing with waning energy levels (your own or other's), hassles from students or parents, reports cards or personal satisfaction in your job, you'll find ideas that you can implement immediately.

If you find yourself having a tough time motivating yourself to go to work, use it as a wake up call! Try to get clarity on what the problem is so that you can begin to effectively deal with it. Is it an irritating colleague, a frustrating student, or unresponsive administrator? Is it a particular parent or is it everything? If after isolating the problem(s), you still have a tough time getting motivated to go to work, you may need a leave of absence, or even a new career! But most of the time, the following suggestions will work for you.

Motivating Yourself

- ◆ Plan a special personal highlight for yourself each day—a fun, interesting activity or appointment.
- ◆ Think of the difference you make in the lives of others. If you can't come up with the difference, start doing something different.
- ◆ Start each day with a simple, short task that you can achieve success with.
- ◆ Set goals for yourself every day. Poorly sized goals may be too big, others too small. Vary the size of them until you find the size that is most motivating.
- ◆ Meet with another person who is an expert in a field you want to learn more about; learning can be very motivating and inspiring.

- Improve your work environment. Add plants, an ionizer, pictures, fresh air, an aquarium, music.
- Demonstrate an attitude of gratitude. Think about how fortunate you are to have your work or any kind of work at all.
- Think about what gets you motivated in other areas of your life and use those strategies.
- Predict how much time a task will take; then try to beat your own predicted goal. Make it fun and challenging.
- Teach another person something that you are learning - something that you'd like to be better at doing.
- Call a local newspaper and tell them about something positive at your school that has just enough of a twist to it that it warrants media attention.
- Hang around more excited and enthusiastic friends.
- Give a compliment to three people each day; especially people who seem "down."
- Rearrange your time so that your are doing fun things to start and end the day.
- Go for a passion walk. Use the time to work yourself up into a bubbling passion about something.
- Celebrate your successes every day—even the little ones.
- Chunk your tasks into smaller more manageable, motivating ones.
- Make a list of everyone you support and those who support you. Have a talk about your job with those who support you.
- Read inspiring biographies or listen to inspiring people speak.

Dealing With Unlikable Colleagues

- Start with what you have in common. Seek first to understand; then to be understood. Start talking at any chance you get. In conversations, be interested in and curious about their world. Begin conversations about what you both share: work, supervisor, stress, weather, etc.
- Get-to-know each other beyond the professional level. Find the softer side: ask about children, hobbies, hopes, dreams, retirement, etc.
- Discover who influences them - their mentors, favorite people, etc. Can you influence this person through their friends?
- While in conversation change your conversational "buts" to "ands," match verbals, non-verbals, superlatives, and visual-auditory-kinesthetic modalities.
- When you very much disagree, use the three magic disagreement words: respect, appreciate, and agree. Regardless of the issue, there is something you can agree with, respect or appreciate.
- While having discussions, change your use of words like "I" and "you," to "we" and "us." This keeps the conversation friendly.
- Stay low key. Do your best to have conversations in casual, non-confrontational postures or locations. Match physical height in conversation if there's a big difference (i.e., sit on the table, bend down, etc.).
- Refer to their ideas (positively) in conversation and let them know you listen to them. In general, keep asking for their opinion. Asking doesn't mean you have to agree with it or use it.
- Provide a venue change - a school picnic, a game, a barbecue.
- When all else fails, ignore the problem for awhile. It may cease to be an issue over time. Otherwise, you might apply for a transfer to another school (it might even pay more).

The High-Energy Teaching Diet

Teaching requires a great deal of energy. Your body cannot run on inadequate or poor nutrition without you paying the price. When you abuse your health, you can feel run-down, irritable, depressed, or get sick. When you take care of your health, you have more energy and feel good about your life. A good deal of research has been done on the effects of food on your mind and mood. this chapter presents a few of the highlights of years of scientific research on maintaining alert, low stress, high-energy diets.

Drink pure fresh water. Brain specialists recommend between eight and twelve glasses per day. Cut the bad fat. Good fat is the omega-3 fatty molecules. These are the unsaturated ones found in fish oil, cottonseed oil, even butter is better than margarine. Subjects on a diet of polyunsaturated fats learned 20 percent faster than those on a saturated fat diet. They also retained the information longer. The brain runs best on a "nibbling diet." Studies showed increased learning and performance when subjects ate from five to nine small snacks or meals per day. Bring snacks to your classroom. Eat often through the day, even if it's just a piece of fruit. Buy foods in bulk like small juice containers with built-in straws, fruit, seeds or nuts.

Maximum Alertness

To boost your alertness and mental performance, include a natural source of tyrosine in your diet: eggs, fish, turkey, tofu, pork, chicken, and yogurt. It's also available in capsule form. Ginkgo biloba extract is known for increasing the flow of nutrients and oxygen to the brain and is available at fitness and natural health food stores. Many now carry a whole product line of neural or neuro-supplements. Many have strong advocates. Experiment with them.

A good rule of thumb is to eat proteins early in the day, and carbos later in the day. Eating foods low in refined carbohydrates promotes relaxation. Avoid a high sugar and carbohydrates combination as sugar is utilized differently by the brain when "carried in" with protein. Eat carbohydrates with protein for a better nutrient balance to the brain. Take multivitamin supplements, especially the B vitamins. Thiamin may be able to increase visual acuity, reaction time, and fine motor control.

Lecithin, found in egg yolks and wheat germ can boost memory. Folic acid was discovered to reduce depression and boost learning performance. Folic acid is found in leafy green vegetables, beef liver and beans. Selenium improves memory and concentration. It is a mineral found most concentrated in seafood, whole grain breads, Brazil nuts and white meat tuna. Boron supplements improve mental activity. The trace mineral boron is found in broccoli, apples, pears, peaches, grapes, nuts and dried beans. Use zinc supplements for short term memory and attention span. Better yet, zinc can be found in fish, beans, whole grains and dark meat turkey. Eat iron-rich foods like dark-green vegetables, meat, beans, and fish for improved attention, memory, perception, and visual-motor coordination.

Energy Management

We've all had the experience of coming home from work so utterly drained, you wonder if you can make it back the next day. But did you know you can have positive, uplifting, high-energy days, every day? Here are some tips to managing your health and energy levels:

✦ Start your day with a positive image. Visualize yourself reaching your goals for the day.

- Learn to enjoy the little things in life - a smile, a puffy cloud, a favorite food, a short line at the store.
- Identify and use personal revitalizers. Listen to a favorite song. Have a cup of your favorite tea. Visualize yourself playing a sport successfully. Get a cold drink. Read the comics. Browse through a catalog. Play a desktop toy such as a yo-yo or use a dart board. Walk around the block. Go outside and watch the weather. Write in a journal. Look at old photographs that mean a lot to you. Call your parents. Plan your next vacation.
- Learn to say no. Say no to a committee you don't really want to join. Say no to an extra luncheon you might dislike. Say no to a favor that you can't do without tremendous resentment.
- Understand how you relate to others. We all need to have a person in our lives who is a real "upper." This the high energy positive person who inspires us. We also need to have someone with whom we can dispose our "emotional refuse" - the disappointments, upsets and complaints that are inevitable. Learn what people combination recharges your batteries. Most people get recharged by either being by themselves or being with others. Once you know which is your mode, apply that learning to your life to maximize personal energy.
- Take "power naps." These are short (10- to 30- minute) naps during the day. Block out distractions, close the door, turn down the lights, prop your feet up and put on a meditative tape. Or, simply enjoy the quiet. Learn to put yourself into a brief sleep (take a self-hypnosis course) and you'll be able to refresh yourself throughout the day.

Knowledge and Skill Base

The whole concept of thriving means that you are not staying the same; you're stretching and growing. Your greatest asset is your ability to learn and communicate what you have learned. If you are in education, chances are good that you highly value education. If so, what have you done lately to boost your own knowledge and skill base? The average teacher reads three books a year, two fiction and one non-fiction. Less than 30 percent of all teachers read professional journals. Fewer than 15 percent of all teachers attend a professional development seminar outside of what is offered by their school or district. If you were having surgery, would you want to be operated on by a physician who had not kept up with the latest knowledge in the industry? It's doubtful. Are your students any less important?

Make a commitment to yourself to continue your education. Read a book a month; and if you are strictly a fiction reader, at least, alternate with some nonfiction. Attend seminars, workshops and summer institutes. Find out what is in your school or district's staff development library. If there isn't one, this would be a good project to get started! Organize a monthly meeting at your school of the movers and shakers to discuss what's new. At one school, there's a Friday afternoon Happy Hour group that meets at a local restaurant for drinks and success stories from the week. This is one way to keep up the collegial sharing. The knowledge about the brain and learning is exploding at dramatic rate. If you're not keeping up, you're falling behind. And if you're not building your knowledge and skill base, your market value may be dropping. Learning keeps you excited, motivated and thriving.

Sweetening the Pot

There are hundreds of ways to do what you love to do and earn an extra $500 to $50,000 a year. Each carries its own risks and rewards. The key is to identify: 1) what your best gifts and talents are; 2) what the marketplace needs more of; 3) what would be compatible with your family and lifestyle; and 4) how much or little time and money you are willing to invest. If you're ready to get serious, here's how others have done it:

How to Make More Money in Education

✦ Teach evenings or weekends at a local junior college or university.

✦ Create a simple product (like this one!) and sell it at conventions or by mail in magazines. The easiest idea is to create a great picture, drawing or slogan and put it on a sweatshirt or T-shirt. They sell like crazy at educational conferences!

✦ Write yourself into a grant proposal.

✦ Become a weekend or evening salesperson for educational products.

✦ Design educational software and sell the rights to a company.

✦ Organize weekend study skills programs that parents pay for to get extra help for their kids.

✦ Research nearby districts who have a higher pay scale. It may be well worth a transfer.

✦ Get summer work teaching overseas.

✦ Your employer may have a higher grade pay scale if you upgrade your educational credentials.

✦ Start up a home education business: writing, teaching, consulting.

✦ Become a coach or assistant coach of an athletic team.

✦ Write a book, sell it and collect royalties. If it won't sell, then either edit it to make it better or self-publish (sounds like *SuperTeaching*, doesn't it?)

✦ Be a consultant and do work in other counties, districts, and states.

✦ Tutor students after school, 4 at a time @ $15/hr = $60 hour.

✦ Contribute to magazines or journals that pay for articles.

✦ Do a video on a subject of interest.

Reactions:

What are your feelings about the topics presented in this chapter?

What are some practical applications for what you're learning?

What do you want to remember from this chapter?

Whatever you can do or dream you can, begin. Boldness has genius, power, and magic in it. Begin it now.

Johann Wolfgang von Goethe

Chapter 25

What's Next?

Chapter Preview:

- ✦ **Being Part of the Solution**
- ✦ **Starting With Your Passion**
- ✦ **Modeling Leadership**
- ✦ **Communicating Vision**
- ✦ **Committing to Reform**
- ✦ **Building Partnerships**
- ✦ **Creating Successful Transformations**

Being Part of the Solution

What will it take to make education work in the way we all know it can? Let's not kid ourselves. It will take plenty. As a profession we are redefining the way we teach, educate, run systems and administrate. It will take one of the most purposeful, courageous and sustained commitments ever made. It will take an unrivaled ability to bring forth your vision on a daily basis. It will require a relentless insistence on seeing beyond the problems, circumstances and complaints that make up much of the current conversation about education.

It will take stronger, new partnerships and relationships in every area of our professional and personal lives. It will take more focused planning and insightful thinking. It will necessitate knowledge of new paradigms about the brain and how we learn. It will require a rediscovery and realigning of values and a certain ruthlessness to tell the truth. Finally, it will require that each individual teacher bring forth every last bit of integrity, personal power and ability to manage than ever before. It means being willing to live and teach holding the best and brightest vision of our world. The words of the great philosopher Robert S. De Ropp (1979) provide a worthy goal:

> Seek, above all, a game worth playing. Having found the game, play it with intensity - play it as if your life and sanity depended upon it. Though nothing means anything and all roads are marked "No Exit", move as if your movements had some purpose. For it must be clear, even to the most clouded intelligence, that any game is better than no game. But although it is safe to play the Master Game, this has not served to make it popular. It remains the most demanding and difficult of games, and in our society, there are few who play. Once a person has decided to play, he [she]are no longer able to sleep comfortably. A new appetite develops within him [her], the hunger for a real awakening.

Choosing to make a difference is a commitment on par with the most difficult on earth. No awards are likely to be given. Expect no hero's welcome for playing the game or even winning the game. Expect criticism, difficulty, and unthinkable challenges. Your prize, your reward, your monument for all your efforts is likely to be quite simple. Education will work. Our children will be empowered, enriched, and opened to the grand possibilities of who they truly are.

Starting With Your Passion

A good place to start is by choosing an area of instructional reform or a teaching and learning priority that you care deeply about. It may be instructional strategies, positive classroom environments, relevant assessment, brain-compatible curriculum, or systems thinking. Whichever area you feel most passionate about, is the place to start. This way, you'll have the energy to stay committed when you're tired, when you're getting criticized, and when you're running into stumbling blocks along the way.

In what ways can you be a leader in the area you choose? There are many. There are some recommended resources in the appendix. You can attend workshops and seminars. You can also get started, just by reading the next few pages.

Modeling Leadership

To make this work, no matter what your role, you'll need to be a leader. A leader in any organization is someone you feel good being around. There's a sense of vitality and hope in them. A good leader does not bully or boss people around. Instead, a leader inspires you to be your best self. Here's some important distinctions:

What's Changed?

Old:
The old leader led by dominating and controlling circumstances and people, by wielding power, by manipulating.

New:
The new leader leads by empowering others to be their best selves, by modeling desirable traits and behaviors, by holding a vision that inspires others to action.

The most visible and simplest form of leadership is role-modeling professionalism. Do you speak highly of the teaching profession or do you make jokes about it, put it down, demean it and complain about it? Are you a teacher who keeps track of the number of days until vacation - like a convict, counting days in prison? No doubt you have seen teachers sporting T-Shirts or mugs with belittling comments like: "school is what we sandwich in between weekends"; or "wake me up when it's Friday."

Of course, sayings like this are intended to be humorous and we all need to laugh, but what's left after the joke? The residue is a sarcastic comment that degrades the profession, implies the job is distasteful, and conveys negative suggestions and attitudes to the students and other faculty. Get rid of them! Leaders recognize that schools are about learning. To create a school of successful learners and a staff committed to being learning leaders, everyone must understand the value of a learning organization. How do you know whether you're in a learning organization? Do you hear any of these comments?

Words from a Learning Organization:

+ *I am a catalyst.*
+ *We are all part of the solution.*
+ *We ask what's working.*
+ *Learning means creative skills in achieving both process and results.*
+ *The greater the rate at which we learn the more fun we'll have while solving life's infinite problems*

Words from a Traditional Bureaucracy:

+ *I teach; they better learn.*
+ *The solution is out there.*
+ *We assume we're going in the right direction.*
+ *Tests tell the final story.*
+ *If we could just solve this problem...*

As an instructional or staff leader, it makes much more sense to be a source of inspiration and positive energy. Turn your faculty lounge into a "staff revitalization center" with fun and relaxing ways for teachers to unwind and stay positive. Put positive signs up in your staff lounge like these.

Communicating Vision

If you haven't already done so, develop your vision. You will only be as powerful in life as that which you are willing to envision. A vision is two things: 1) what you would like to have happen; and 2) your commitment to that happening. You must be willing to take a stand and communicate your ideas to as many people as possible. Once you have a vision, you'll need a mission. A mission is the "work" necessary to accomplish the goals. Speak to individuals, groups, young and old. Excite people. Get them thinking about the possibilities, rather than the obstacles. Act as if you are the secretary of education and your actions alone determine the fate of education in this country. If you bring that quality of presence to your work, things will change. They have to change with that kind of momentum. Once you've created a vision and a mission, the wheels are set in motion for the next step. With your commitment firmly in place, your value now as a contributor increases dramatically. Bring your vision to every group you join. Inspire others to share in it. Assist in the planning for tomorrow's schools in any way you can.

Quotable

A leader speaks mostly about possibilities and vision - they keep the dream alive - while a non-leader speaks mostly about circumstances and obstacles - they keep the problems alive.

Positive Suggestions for Teachers:

- ✦ *Never give up on anybody; miracles happen everyday.*
- ✦ *Expect others to follow your example and ignore your advice.*
- ✦ *Give yourself time to cool before responding.*
- ✦ *Never deprive someone of hope —it might be all they have.*
- ✦ *The true joy in life is lighting a spark and feeding the flames of learning.*
- ✦ *Every student has a right to succeed.*
- ✦ *The relentless pursuit of excellence is worth the effort.*
- ✦ *Teaching—you gotta love it!*
- ✦ *I teach; I touch the future.*

Taking part in the planning process means that you are accepting responsibility. No one can assign or "fix" responsibility to another. Responsibility is something that an individual "takes on" for him or herself. It always comes from within. It's a gift or a privilege, not a weight. There's no guilt or burden in responsibility, only an opportunity to step out and be courageous. It allows you to be at the cause of things, not the effect. And best of all, it empowers you to be your best. You are only as "big" in life as the responsibilities you are willing to accept.

Quotable

<u>My vision</u> is a world of confident and capable learners who love to learn and who have fair, unlimited, and enriched access to learning.

<u>My mission</u> is to make a significant, positive and lasting impact on the way the world learns.

Committing to Reform

One thing for certain that does *not* work in education is the empty opinions about how to fix things. Opinions are relatively useless in the face of what's required to make education work. Opinions come across like a cabby's babble or the guy in a diner who has an opinion about everything. The problem with opinions is that they're often just that - lacking the commitment required to improve things.

Let's quit *talking about* what needs to be done and start committing to *doing* what needs to be done. Your commitment is the stand, the position you take, and the place from which you operate. You need that stand, that backdrop of grounding, from which to express yourself. So the next time someone has a great idea about how to fix something in education, ask them what they personally are committing to so that change has a chance to happen.

Teachers are becoming co-explorers with students because no one person can know it all. We are moving into a high-tech and high-touch partnership with interchanging roles. Because so much learning will occur at home, it will become a new center of learning. In a curious reversal, preschoolers will come to school to play more than learn. Elementary students who will have already learned reading, writing and math on television or home computers, will also be gaining from school the important opportunity to interact with other students and adults. School will become the place for social skills, field trips, experiments, plays, dance, music; and the underlying issues that, if left unattended, will result in behavior problems like low test scores or drug abuse.

Unless we prepare our educators to deal with social change at its root, the money spent on symptomatic relief will continue to be wasted. These causal changes or trends must be addressed for they are at the core of education's current difficulties. To be effective, to be pro-active (as opposed to reactive), we must have some awareness of what's going on so we can begin to predict what's needed. If you want to make a real difference in education, what are some of the key areas you can impact? Consider the following project areas:

Staff Development: Prepare to deal with more areas relative to students' lives. Boost training in counseling, listening, conflict resolution and facilitation skills.

New Skills: Prepare students with more lifelong learning strategies and tools. Teach more *process* and less *content*. Teach to a greater variety of learning styles. Teach students how they learn and how to become more accountable for their own learning process.

Role Changes: Ask teachers to relinquish the role as the only source of information. Have students take on additional roles, becoming more responsible for their learning. Use textbooks as reference books, not as standard issue for every student. Rely more on magazines, computers, video, and television.

Time Management: Creatively, find ways to allow teachers more planning time, more collegial discussion time, and more staff development time. Do this with doubling up on classes once a week, better use of support staff and other innovative systems.

Brain-Based Approach: Learn more about the brain. Attend courses, watch videos, and read books. Begin to design learning around the way the brain is best designed to learn. You'll find that your learners become more motivated, learn more, and recall information longer. They will apply their learning better and will be more capable citizens in the community.

Resource Sharing: Find a way to inventory school resources, including supplies, rooms, machinery, talent, creativity, parents, hobbies, contacts, speakers, curriculum and teaching strategies. Next, find a way to share all this so that it is available to all staff members. You have an amazing amount of resources, but you've got to discover them and share them.

Scheduling: Modify school schedules at the secondary-level to reflect more of the single-teacher-all-day model used in elementary schools. Do this by rotating schedules so that students have one class, such as history, with one teacher all day one day of the week. Having one teacher all day would provide the opportunity to build relationships beyond the what a 50-minute class period enables. Such a change would be a significant step towards reducing absenteeism, discipline problems, improperly diagnosed learning problems, vandalism, alienation and dropouts.

Communications: Re-structure the school's lines of communications, support and accountability for teachers. Create new positions for the coaching and support of teachers (This role would be separate from a principal's role). Teachers need constant, direct, qualified coaching on what they are doing and what can be improved. They also need daily, weekly and monthly systems set up to acknowledge and support that growth. Greater measurable accountability on the part of teachers for the progress of their students is essential. Not solely in the form of test scores, but also in the form of self-esteem, participation, personal breakthroughs, and achievement.

Respect: Set up specific channels where teachers can have their concerns heard, acted upon, and acknowledged. Create ways for teachers to fully participate in the processes affecting them the most, such as teacher-student ratio, class hours, curriculum and classroom design. Increase the salary incentives for mastery-level teaching.

Parent Relationships: Find a way to open communication lines with parents. Use telephone hot lines, newsletters, students, events and the media.

Cultural Awareness: Have qualified organizations train teachers on how to incorporate self-esteem, diversity, and team building skills into their curriculum.

Community Ties: Look for unexpected sources of funding. Create better partnerships with the military or national service organizations for students who want to quit school. Create new, more effective partnerships with businesses in the community.

Educational Activism: Your state legislators need to know what kinds of curriculum should be included or deleted to make things work. Your schools need to know the specific kinds of teacher training you need to make your school a total success. Parents must be included in more ways. Your community needs to know that you would like to make a shift in the quality of education and you must invite citizens to give input. Your school board needs to re-prioritize teacher needs so that you can get the job done. This means less red-tape, more administrative support, less mandated curriculum, more acknowledgment for work well done, and more "say-so" in how the system is set up. School moneys invested in teachers are better spent because the effect is multiplied: one teacher affects many students. Whereas moneys spent on students are dead-end funds; the effect stops with the students.

You'll discover that people are either adapters or innovators. The adapter is right at home in a bureaucracy. This person tends to make the existing system do. The innovator, on the other hand, sees dogmatic and inflexible rules and regulations as a stumbling block to progress. This person wants to do things differently. The adapter accepts traditional frameworks, while the innovator breaks accepted patterns. It will take both to make education work. As you find out who wants to join you, keep in mind that your game is not the only game in town. This means that when it's not right for others, don't waste valuable energy being righteous about your game; just keep playing.

Building Partnerships

We may think of ourselves as just one, but our effects move like the ripples on a pond. So what would happen if we began to share ourselves and our mastery with other teachers and administrators? If we teachers are going to continue to grow, we have to do it together. There is little growth in isolation and the gifts you have must be distributed in order to have impact. All you have to do is make a commitment. Tell the teachers around you what you intend to have happen. "I'm committed to helping make this school work for the students and me." Just by saying it, your words begin to make it happen. Fortunately, there will be those teachers who immediately want to jump on the bandwagon and join you. Others may not be interested at all. Include those interested and allow the others to go their own way. Eventually, they may discover that what you've got provides joy and satisfaction.

The next step, once you have networked and gained supporters, is to create leadership groups, agendas, and action items. Choose one grand goal as a beacon or mission, roll up your sleeves and begin building on little successes. Many small successes lead to the grand goal. Leadership groups can build credibility, momentum, and support for the vision. They can be in the form of support meetings, acknowledgment ceremonies, a gala teacher barbecue or fund raisers for classroom supplies.

Include other teachers who want to get involved. The better you make the "game" of transforming education, the more others will want to join in. Make it light, fun, and accomplish things at the same time! One of the things Walt Disney credited to his success was the notion that one must "do what you do so well that when people come to see you, they'll get excited and want to bring back their friends; and those people will get excited and bring back their friends." This is exactly what many schools are doing. This is how well your game of transformation in education can be played.

The key to creating transformation is rapport. You will get nowhere if you start by making other teachers wrong or blaming them for not supporting you. Include parents, students, administrators, and anyone else who will listen in your group because you need their support. Include their ideas and find out how you can make the system work for everyone. A fundamental law of humanity is when you help others get what they need, they can better help you get what you need.

Creating Successful Transformations

There are many "right" ways to get started with better schools. Nobody has the answer for you because the answer needs be a local solution. However, in a year-long study of successful schools, it was found that all successful transformations had the following five characteristics:

1. Search

What else is out there? The staff searched near and far for successes and solutions. Read, network, call other schools, attend conferences, check out books, buy newsletters, and hold discussion groups.

2. Consolidate

What do we have so far? Analyze and modify the solutions for your own needs and culture. Commit to building on existing strengths.

3. Unify

Can we all agree on what we want? Get complete input and "buy-in" on the vision and steps to take. Develop a complete staff unity of purpose.

4. Solidify

If this is good, then let's make it a policy. Transform good ideas into policies. Willingly assume responsibility with corresponding amounts of authority to act on what is needed at any given time.

5. Commit

If we believe in it, let's stick with it! Commit to staying with a new program or strategy until it works. No excuses. Emphasize the positives and celebrate the successes. Learn to communicate what isn't working and fix it. Take on reform as a permanent on-going process, not a one- or two-year gimmick to quiet critics. Quality is an endless process.

If you were to get a closing "homework assignment" from this book, it would be this: Do what you do so well, set such a good example, that the enthusiasm, the shouts of aliveness and joy from your work area reaches out to others and wakes them up. Be so committed and so purposeful and so excited about what you do that others either want to join you or are embarrassed by the high standard you set and want to leave the profession for some other job more suited to their commitment level.

Go out and teach so well that you literally reinvent the profession. Redefine teaching the way that Picasso redefined painting or the way Julius Erving and Michael Jordan reinvented the game of basketball, or the way Casio reinvented the wristwatch, and Apple reinvented the computer. Be creative. Be outrageous. Somehow, get the message out about your commitment to make education work and most importantly, *live it*. Futurist Marilyn Ferguson in her landmark book *The Aquarian Conspiracy* (1980) says:

> Our past is not our potential. In any hour, with all the stubborn teachers and healers
> of history who called us to our best selves, we can liberate the future. You are not just you.
> You are a seed, a silent promise. You are the conspiracy.

The end of *SuperTeaching* is just the beginning for you. There is a new you who has just turned the last few pages of this book. May you grow and reach into a realm you never thought possible before. You have been an inspiration for me and you are the person from whom this book was written.

You knew there was more to education than showing up and waiting for the last bell. Teaching is so much more than that. It is discovery, sharing, growing, excitement and love. It's not a burden, it's a joy. And it's like a consuming, fulfilling bonfire that provides you with a glow of warmth and a blaze of passion. You've already demonstrated a commitment to education by reading this book. The intention to grow and willingness to improve sets you well above and beyond the average. Keep growing! There's no such thing as standing still; we are either expanding or contracting.

Commit yourselves not only to your cause, crusade or mission, but to your own aliveness and self-expression. If you have a commitment to education with anything less than your life, it will be insufficient to the task at hand. Keep taking on more responsibility and more challenges. I know you might be tired. I know you have given a lot already. It's been great, but the results say that it's not enough. We must all recommit to a vision that works and the work that must be done.

It is you, and the choices you make in the classroom that will make a difference in this world. Each move you make, each class you give, and thought you think is shaping our tomorrow's. So don't worry about how or why or when, begin now. Begin with your commitment. The possibilities are more grand than we may have yet imagined. There is a lot riding on our jobs as educators. If you stumble or fall, there are plenty of us who will reach to pull you up on your feet again. We know what kind of journey we are beginning and we are already taking the first and most important step. The following closing parable illustrates the perch upon which we stand right now and the choice awaiting our decision.

There once was a wise old man who always knew the answer to every question posed to him. People came from far and away to ask the elder for advice. An envious village smart-aleck decided one day to devise a plan to outsmart the wise man. He would hold a live butterfly in his hands behind his back and ask the elder what was in his hands. When answered correctly, the smart-aleck would ask if the butterfly was alive or dead. If the wise man said dead, he would show the living butterfly; and if he said alive, he would kill the butterfly. The smart-aleck went before the wise man with his plan. Holding the butterfly behind his back, he asked what he was holding and the wise man answered, "a butterfly." When the smart-aleck asked if it was alive or dead, the wise man gave an answer which I believe sums up our potential in the teaching profession right now: "That remains in your hands."

Reactions:

What are your feelings about the topics presented in this chapter?

What are some practical applications for what you're learning?

What do you want to remember from this chapter?

Appendix
Bibliography

Bandler, Richard (1988) *Learning Strategies: Acquisition and Conviction*. (Videotape) NLP Comprehensive: Boulder, CO.

Barkley, Russell (1988) *Taking Charge of ADHD*. The Guilford Press: NY.

Black, Ira (1991) *Information in the Brain: A Molecular Perspective*. MIT Press: Cambridge, MA.

Caine, G., & R.N. Caine (1990) "Downshifting: A Hidden Condition That Frustrates Learning & Change", *Instructional Leader*, Vol. I3, 1-3, 12.

Caine, Geoffrey, Renate Nummela Caine, & Sam Crowell (1994) *Mindshifts*. Zephyr Press: Tucson, AZ.

Campbell, Don (1983) *Introduction to The Musical Brain*. Magnamusic: St. Louis, MO

_____ (1992) *100 Ways to Improve Your Teaching Using Your Voice and Music*. Zephyr Press: Tucson, AZ.

Campbell, D. Ed. (1992) *Music and Miracles*. Wheaton, IL: Quest Books.

Carbo, Marie, Rita Dunn, & Kenneth Dunn (1986) *Teaching Students to Read Through Their Individual Learning Styles*. Prentice-Hall: Englewood Cliffs, NJ.

Cavalli-Sforza, Luigi Luca, & Paolo Menozzi, & Alberto Piazza (1994) *History and Geography of Human Genes*. Princeton University Press: Princeton, NJ.

Churchland, Paul (1995) *Engine of Reason: Seat of the Soul*. MIT Press: Boston, MA.

Damasio, Antonio (1994) *Descartes' Error*. Putnam & Sons: New York, NY.

De Ropp, Robert S. (1979) *Warrior's Way: The Challenging Life Games*. Delta/S. Lawrence: New York, NY.

Diamond, Marian (1988) *Enriching Heredity: The Impact of the Environment on the Brain*. Free Press: New York, NY.

Drucker, Peter (1994, November) "The Age of Social Transformation." *Atlantic Monthly*, 274, (5) pp. 53-80.

Dunn, Rita, & Kenneth Dunn (1987) "Dispelling Outmoded Beliefs About Student Learning." *Educational Leadership* 44.6, pp. 55-61.

_____ (1992) *Bringing Out The Giftedness In Your Child*, John Wiley: New York, NY.

Dyer, Wayne (1980) *The Sky's the Limit*. Simon & Schuster: New York, NY.

Ferguson, Marilyn (1980) *The Aquarian Conspiracy*. J. Tarcher: Los Angeles, CA.

Ford, Martin (1992) *Motivating Humans*. Sage Publications: Newbury Park, CA.

Gardner, Howard (1993) *Multiple Intelligences: The Theory in Practice*. Basic Books: New York, NY.

Gazzaniga, Michael (1992) *Nature's Mind*. Basic Books: New York, NY.

Glasser, William. (1985). *Control Theory*. New York, NY: Harper Collins.

Gray, John (1992) *Men are from Mars and Women are From Venus*. HarperCollins: New York, NY.

Greenough, William, & B.J. Anderson (1991) "Cerebellar Synaptic Plasticity: Relation to Learning Versus Neural Activity." *Annuals of the New York Academy of Science* 627, pp. 231-47.

Grinder, Michael. (1989). *Righting the Educational Conveyor Belt*. Portland, OR: Metamorphous Press.

Halpern, Steven (1985). *Sound Health*. Harper & Row: New York, NY.

Hart, Leslie (1975) How the Brain Works: A New Understanding of Human Learning. Basic Books: New York, NY.

____ (1983) *Human Brain and Human Learning.* Books for Educators: Kent, WA.

Heider, John (1985) *The Tao of Leadership.* Humanics New Age: Atlanta, GA.

Howard, Robert, ed. (1993) *The Learning Imperative: Managing People for Continuous Innovation.* Harvard Business Press: Boston, MA.

Hynd, G.W., et al. (1991) "Attention-Deficit Disorder Without Hyperactivity: A Distinct Behavioral and Cognitive Syndrome." *Journal of Child Neurology* 6, pp. 37-43.

Hynd, G.W., et al. (1991) "Corpus Callosum Morphology in Attention Deficit- Hyperactivity Disorder: Morphometric Analysis of MRI." *Journal of Learning Disabilities* 24.3, pp.141-6.

Jensen, Eric (1989) *Student Success Secrets.* Barron's Educational Series: New York, NY.

Kandel, M. & Eric Kandel (1994, May). "Flights of Memory." *Discover Magazine*, pp. 32-38.

Kandel, Eric & R. Hawkins (1992, September) "The Biological Basis of Learning and Individuality." *Scientific American* pp. 79-86.

Kazdin, Alan (1977) T*he Token Economy: A Review and Evaluation.* Plenum Press: New York, NY

Kimura, Doreen (1992, September) "Sex Differences in the Brain." *Scientific American* pp. 119-25.

Kohn, Alfie (1993) *Punished by Rewards.* Houghton Mifflin: New York, NY.

Lazear, David (1994) *The Seven Pathways of Learning.* Zephyr Press: Tucson, AZ.

Livingstone, M., et al. (1991, September). Physiological and Anatomical Evidence for a Magnocellular Defect in Developmental Dyslexia. Proceedings of the *National Academy of Science* 88, 9743-7947.

Lozanov, Georgi (1979) *Suggestology and Outlines of Suggestopedia.* Gordon & Breach: New York, NY.

Malloy, John (1975) *Dress for Success.* P.H. Wyden: New York, NY.

Orlock, Carol (1993) *Inner Time.* Birch Lane Press: New York, NY.

Pearce, Joseph Chilton (1992) *Evolution's End.* HarperCollins: San Francisco, CA.

Pert, Candace (1997) *Molecules Of Emotion*, Simon & Schuster: New York, NY.

Reichenberg-Ullman, Judyth, & Robert Ullman (1996) *Ritalin Free Kids.* Prima Publishing: Rocklin, CA.

Rosenthal, Robert, & Lenore Jacobsen (1968) *Pygmalion in the Classroom.* Rinehart & Winston: New York, NY.

Samples, Bob. (1987). *Open Mind/Whole Mind.* Jalmar Press: Rolling Hills, CA.

Sternberg, Robert (1985) *Beyond IQ: A Triarchical Theory of Human Intelligence.* Cambridge University Press: Cambridge, NY.

Sternberg, Robert & Richard Wagner (1994) *Mind in Context.* Cambridge University Press: Cambridge, NY.

Tannen, Deborah (1991) *You Just Don't Understand.* Ballantine Books: New York, NY.

Additional Resources

Books on Learning, Teaching, and the Brain

The Brain Store® features countless books, posters, CDs, and brain-related products. This innovative education resource company is all about the science of learning. You'll find resources for:

- **Teaching and Training**
- **Enrichment**
- **Staff Development**
- **Music and Dance**
- **Organizational Change**
- **Early Childhood**

To view all of our products, log on at: **www.thebrainstore.com**, or call (800) 325-4769 or (858) 546-7555 for a FREE color resource catalog.

Conference: The Learning Brain Expo

A world-class gathering featuring more than fifty renowned speakers on the brain and learning. Session topics include music, movement, early childhood, emotions, memory, the fragile brain, and brain imaging. Get dozens of practical ideas and network with like-minded professionals. This enriching event is held twice a year. For more information, log on at: **www.brainexpo.com**, or call (800) 325-4769 or (858) 546-7555.

Free Samples

Go to **www.thebrainstore.com** to get free tips, tools, and strategies. You'll also find selected products at 40 percent savings. In addition, many books offer you a sneak online preview of the table of contents and sample pages so you'll know before you order if it's for you. At The Brain Store®, online shopping is safe, quick, and easy!

About the Author

Eric Jensen is a visionary educator who is committed to making a positive, significant, and lasting difference in the way we learn. He's a member of the prestigious Society for Neuroscience and New York Academy of Sciences. A former middle-school teacher and college instructor, Jensen is the author of more than a dozen books on learning and teaching. He co-founded the world's first experimental brain-compatible academic enrichment program in 1982 that now has more than 30,000 graduates. Currently, he's a staff developer and consultant living in San Diego, California.

Other Books by Eric Jensen

Super Teaching, Student Success Secrets, The Learning Brain, Brain-Based Learning, Trainer's Bonanza, Teaching with the Brain in Mind, Joyful Fluency (with Lynn Freeman Dhority), *The Great Memory Book* (with Karen Markowitz), *Learning with the Body in Mind,* and *Different Brains, Different Learners.* Available through The Brain Store®. Log on at: **www.thebrainstore.com**, or call (800) 325-4769 or (858) 546-7555.

Trainings Facilitated by Eric Jensen

"Teaching with the Brain in Mind" is a 6-day workshop for teachers, trainers, and other change agents with a focus on the brain, how we learn, and how to boost achievement.

"The Fragile Brain" is a 3-day program for teachers, special educators, counselors, and other change agents with a focus on what can go wrong with the learner's brain and how to treat it.

For registration information, dates, and costs call (888) 638-7246 or fax (858) 642-0404.

Author Contact

Fax (858) 642-0404 or e-mail at eric@jlcbrain.com